CHRISTIAN LIFE AND CHRISTIAN HOPE

CHRISTIAN LIFE
AND
CHRISTIAN HOPE

Raids on the Inarticulate

ROWAN A. GREER

Forsan et haec olim
ze operall jivabit
Rowan A. Greer

A Herder and Herder Book
The Crossroad Publishing Company
New York

Herder ^{SM}

The Crossroad Publishing Company
481 Eighth Avenue, New York, NY 10001

Copyright © 2001 by Rowan A. Greer

Herder ^{SM} is a service mark of The Crossroad Publishing Company.

Printed in the United States of America

Library of Congress Cataloging-in-Publication Data

Greer, Rowan A.
    Christian life and Christian hope : raids on the inarticulate /
Rowan Greer.
       p.   cm.
    Includes bibliographical references and index.
    ISBN 0-8245-1916-7 (alk. paper)
    1. Salvation—History of doctrines. 2. Future
life—Christianity—History of doctrines.   I. Title.
BT751.3 .G74 2001
234—dc21

                                    2001001801

1 2 3 4 5 6 7 8 9 10 05 04 03 02 01

Contents

Introduction

IN THE MEDITATION with which he begins *Theology of Hope,* Jürgen Moltmann laments "the fact that Christian faith banished from its life the future hope by which it is upheld, and relegated the future to a beyond, or to eternity . . . owing to that, hope emigrated as it were from the Church and turned in one distorted form or another against the Church."[1] He locates this emigration of hope at the time when Christianity increasingly "became an organization for discipleship under the auspices of the Roman state religion." There may well be truth in the claim that as Christianity developed after the Constantinian Revolution it became more at home in this world. But as I hope to show in the essays that follow, understandings of the Christian hope by no means disappear. Indeed, it seems more likely to me that the emigration of hope has far more to do with the sea changes undergone by Christianity in the Western modern and postmodern world. Moltmann cites with approval Feuerbach's judgment that the soul must put "in place of the beyond that lies above our grave in heaven the beyond that lies above our grave on earth, the historic *future,* the future of mankind."[2] But it would seem obvious that Feuerbach has abolished any object of hope that lies outside the world of our experience. Hope seems to have become a naturalized citizen in Christian experience.

In his *Philosophy of Religion* Hegel makes the following claim: "Religion possesses its object within itself—and that object is God, for religion is the relation of human consciousness to God."[3] Hegel may well be attempting to overcome the dualism of subject and object implied by Descartes' philosophy. Nevertheless, it is difficult to avoid Hannah Arendt's conclusion:[4]

> in this internalizing way [Hegel] achieves the *"reconciliation"* of Mind and World. Was there ever a greater triumph of the thinking ego than is represented in this scenario? In its withdrawal from the world of appearances, the thinking ego no longer has to pay the price of "absent-mindedness" and alienation from the world. According to Hegel, the mind, by sheer force of reflection, can assimilate to itself— suck into itself, as it were—not, to be sure, all the appearances but whatever has been meaningful in them. . . .

1

German idealism, then, tends to obliterate the object of Christian hope by assimilating it to the religious consciousness of the believer. Part of the motive for this move must have been a loss of confidence in the reality of traditional Christian ideas of an age to come, of the resurrection and a heaven beyond the grave. We can wonder, however, whether the pie in the sky has not become a figment of the imagination on earth.

Much modern theology is informed by this sort of idealism. Nietzsche once assessed post-Kantian German philosophy as[5]

> the most fundamental form of . . . homesickness there has ever been: the longing for the best that has ever existed. One is no longer at home anywhere; at last one longs back for that place in which alone one can be at home: the *Greek* world! But it is in precisely that direction that all bridges are broken—except the rainbow-bridges of concepts. . . . To be sure, one must be very light, very subtle, very thin to step across these bridges! But what happiness there is already in this will to spirituality, to ghostliness [*Geisterhaftigkeit*] almost! . . . One wants to go *back,* through the Church Fathers to the Greeks. . . .

The Christian hope, then, becomes "rainbow-bridges of concepts" and, in some sense a construct of religious experience and consciousness. According to Moltmann, both Barth and Bultmann follow in this tradition, at least to the degree that they both appear to omit a "cosmic eschatology."[6] As we have seen, Moltmann appears to respect these developments when they are understood as ways of seeking to make the Christian hope relevant to our present life. But he clearly wishes to part company with German idealism.

Moltmann's concern is a double one. We should not relegate eschatology to a meaningless above or beyond, but neither should we merely assimilate it to the present as some kind of transcendental reality that represents the ultimate meaning of the present:[7]

> The real language of Christian eschatology, however, is not the Greek *logos*, but the *promise* which has stamped the language, the hope and the experience of Israel. It was not in the *logos* of the epiphany of the eternal present, but in the hope-giving word of promise that Israel found God's truth. . . . These differences between Greek thought and that of Israel and Christianity, between *logos* and promise, between epiphany and *apokalypsis* of the truth have today been made clear in many fields and by various methods.

To speak of Christ and his future is to speak "the language of promises." In turn, this language recognizes the "as yet unrealized future of the promise." The discontinuity of the promise with the present in this sense means that it "stands in contradiction to given reality." But understood as the revelation of God in the cross and resurrection, the *promissio* becomes "the universal *missio* of the Church to all nations."[8]

Needless to say, Moltmann's theology of hope is far more complicated and wide reaching than I have suggested. Nevertheless, what seems to me intriguing about it is its insistence on hope's simultaneous continuity and discontinuity with our present existence. It might be possible to argue that similar or at least related stances inform the work of Thielicke, Pannenberg, Rahner, and others.[9] The danger many people saw in the late seventeenth and eighteenth centuries was that traditional Christian eschatology was not only no longer credible but often functioned as an escape from life in this world. Moltmann sees this danger but also the risk that the last things have often become no more than a way of talking about the meaning of the here and now. My concern in what follows is clearly related to the theological issues raised by Moltmann and others. At the same time, it is more specifically a religious concern. It has seemed to me that in our culture a this-worldly understanding of Christianity has come to prevail. The here and now has eclipsed the there and then. By no means should I wish to lose this perspective, but I do wish to argue that it takes on its real significance only in relation to the there and then. Christian hope in its fullest sense cannot exist apart from its object, which is outside or beyond the world of our experience and, consequently, is really beyond adequate articulation. Equally, Christian hope cannot be hope unless it informs our understanding of life as we experience it.

The point I am trying to make is that a "here-and-now" Christianity, at least in my view, runs two risks—reducing the Christian life to a moralism of some kind and making the world of our experience ultimate and the only possible frame of reference. Let me say something more about the first risk. It has seemed to me that Christianity has always appeared historically as both a message of salvation and a way of life. It may well be that these two dimensions can never be perfectly balanced. In earliest Christianity, I should argue, the message of salvation often dominated the way of life. Yet, in our time the opposite would seem to me the case. We have all heard the argument that such and such a person, who never goes to church and has no obvious use for Christianity, is a "better Christian" than most of the regular church-goers. The implication is quite clear; it is moral character that defines a Christian. Even our contemporary preoccupation with spirituality drives in the same direction. Meditative techniques can sometimes appear as ways of managing stress and helping people live better. It is difficult to understand where the tendency to reduce Christianity to the moral life comes from. To be sure, the central place of the Atonement in Western Christianity places an emphasis on sin and forgiveness that can easily be understood largely in terms of this life. Moreover, late medieval piety, especially the *devotio moderna*, turned away from the purely contemplative life to the active life of virtue. Perhaps more important is the shift in religious thinking to be located at the end of the seventeenth century. The religious wars after the Reformation apparently taught many that ultimate questions were insoluble and that it made more sense to attend to our duties in this life, even our duties as taught us by nature and reason. The emergence of a secular society, the empirical worldview espoused by modernism, and a post-Cartesian emphasis on religious experience may all be involved. Explaining the tendency to reduce Christianity to the moral life lies beyond my competence and my interest here. My only wish is to claim that in many ways the "here and now" of the Christian life has supplanted the Christian message of salvation. The issues that now divide Christians from one another tend to be moral ones.

The first risk attaching to the "here and now" is compounded, I think, by the simple fact that we are living in a time of moral relativism. Schools are increasingly obliged to teach "values." But it is not entirely clear what these values are or why we should honor them. Alasdair MacIntyre makes the point in *After Virtue*.[10] His argument begins by pointing out that we no longer have any accepted framework within which to discuss moral issues. He uses the analogy of the aftermath of a nuclear disaster. There is a widespread revulsion against science, and the mob destroys scientific books and apparatus. Later when people seek to reconstruct science, they have no framework by which to do so. Only fragments remain. Similarly, in our time fragments of morality remain in our possession; but we have lost any real sense of the framework in which these fragments originally made sense. We are left with a set of taboos, whether they are ones we have inherited from the past or ones that we have newly invented. As a result, it becomes impossible to engage in any true discussion of the issues that confront us. Our differing points of view become collective solipsisms that people must either accept or deny. Thus, while I argue for a tendency in our time to reduce Christianity to morality, I want to add that this happens in several different ways, leading to competing moralities without any framework capable of bringing the different voices into dialogue with one another. Not only must the good news be a promise before it can become a moral demand, we also need to find some common perspective from which to engage in the difficult enterprise of discerning the ways we can respond to the demand of the gospel.

The second risk I can see in the "here and now" is a tendency to regard the world of our experience as ultimate. This tendency can betray itself as a millennial optimism. We suppose that we can bring in the Kingdom of God, perfecting ourselves and society and eliminating evil and the social and economic injustices that now beset us. Perhaps no one really believes this, but we speak as though we did. "Salvation" tends to be located in this age to the exclusion of any notion of an age to come. In Tillichian terms alienation must yield to ultimate concern, and at a less sophisticated level what Sydney Ahlstrom has called "harmonial religion" often prevails. The gospel of prosperity espoused by the likes of Jimmy and Tammy Fay Bakker appears to have transformed a religion of rewards and punishments to one that has retained the first but eliminated the second. At an individual level the "good" receive their rewards materially as well as spiritually. Lazarus will no longer be obliged to wait until he dies and is taken to Abraham's bosom to have his reward. Moreover, at a social level there remains the dream of a just society and of world peace despite all the evidence that would make such a dream a delusion. By no means should I wish to deny the value of the aspirations that underlie these hopes at both the individual and the social level, but I should want to say that there is very little to persuade us that the hopes can ever be fully realized in the "here and now."

Another obvious dimension of the risk I am describing is the notion that we can ourselves bring about salvation. Of course, we give lip service to God's work, however that might be understood and described. But the emphasis appears to be very much upon our own efforts. As Ahlstrom has argued, American religion is for the most part not only evangelical but also "Arminian." The warmed heart carries with it a strong sense of mission, and the mission depends at least in part on our efforts. Sometimes one has the impression that intercessory prayer is designed to compel God to effect our desires. If we simply pray hard enough, God will grant our requests. But, we might ask, do we always know what we are asking and what is best for us? Do we always understand God's providence? Is God a cause, or an agent; or are these ways of speaking of God at best anthropomorphisms that say more about us than about God? If we sometimes think we can straighten human life out for individuals, we also often suppose that we are the ones destined to bring in the just society. It occurs to me that what may lie behind these attitudes, if I am correct in discerning them, is a Cartesian dualism that still infects our thinking. The distinction between subject and object can easily become a dualism, and that dualism can imply that the objective world is fundamentally meaningless. We are thrown into that meaningless world and obliged as subjects to carve out meaning for ourselves. The idea that we can do this is titanic. We are not only the measure of our world, but the makers of it. To suppose that we can create meaning for ourselves and for our world places what seems to me an impossible burden upon the individual. We begin by supposing the world of our experience to be ultimate, continue by relegating God to the sidelines, and end by making ourselves ultimate.

It may be that I am overstating my case, but to the degree that a this-worldly religion prevails in our culture, to that degree I think we find a view that tends to neglect the tragic dimension of human life. If salvation can be located solely in this age, then we must suppose that the tragic will finally disappear. And if we are the ones destined to usher in salvation, then we need no longer see the tragic as anything more than a temporary obstacle to perfection. In fact, however, we are beset with tragedy in many different ways; and there would be many approaches I could take to make my point. Indeed, one could simply take the daily newspaper as a point of departure, since bad news tends to take precedence over good news. But I think, for example, of Samuel Johnson's poem *The Vanity of Human Wishes*, published in 1748. Jackson Bate, one of Johnson's biographers, describes the argument of the poem. Much of it simply repeats themes that can be found in Ecclesiastes and in Juvenal's *Satires*.

> In the first place [Johnson] dwells on the helpless vulnerability of the individual before the social context—the tangled, teeming jungle of plots, follies, vanities, and egoistic passions in which anyone—the innocent and the virtuous no less than the vicious—is likely to be ambushed. . . . In the second place Johnson traces the inevitable doom of man to inward and psychological causes. The medley processes of hope and fear, desire and hate intercept each other and make it impossible for the heart to be satisfied if only because its own basic impulses are in conflict. More than this Johnson makes clear the inevitable self-deception by which human beings are led astray. Because the betrayal is from within, the human being seems peculiarly defenseless before it."[11]

In our time the tragedy of the social world finds expression in the ethnic conflicts that have followed the end of the Cold War. We can see the tragedy of our environment in the various causes we are asked to support and in the various ingenious ways in which the prophets of doom suggest the end of our world—the atomic bomb, global warming and the greenhouse effect, the melting of the polar ice caps, meteoric bombardment, a solar explosion. But more to the point we can no longer see science as a panacea. Brecht's play *Galileo* sought to avoid an Aristotelian structure and to underline the ambiguity of the successful smuggling of the *Discorsi* out of Rome to Holland. Are we to think of truth prevailing over benighted human attempts to suppress it? Or are we to think, as Brecht himself suggested, of the "original sin" of science, which inevitably led to the creation of atomic warfare? Finally, in a post-Freudian age we can no longer place full trust in human motives. The tragedy is within as well as outside us. We are on thin ice not merely because of our environment and our society but also because of ourselves. And it would seem delusory to suppose that within this world order the tragic can ever be eliminated. Locating salvation within this tragic "here and now" may be possible in an incomplete and distorted fashion. But it is surely impossible to speak in this way of full salvation. Can we really suppose after the Holocaust that evil can be removed from our world? And in another dimension, if salvation is to be understood as moral and spiritual growth or as the ushering in of the just society, what can we say to the old woman dying in a nursing home?

In the essays that follow I wish to study the interaction between views of Christian destiny that locate that destiny outside our world and understandings of the Christian life in the present. In broad terms the presence of this interaction in the New Testament, in the ancient church, and in two seventeenth-century Protestant writers correlates with Moltmann's basic plea and with the theological developments to which I have alluded. My interest, however, is not in the philosophical and logical dimensions of the interaction. Rather, it is to examine how these "raids on the inarticulate" inform understandings of the Christian life. The various versions of the Christian hope we shall encounter are more rhetorical than logical. In a sense, they are poetry in prose. I have chosen to study precritical writers not only because I am more familiar with them but also because their thought remains uncluttered by critical preoccupations with historicity and with how to affirm religious claims in the context of purely empirical worldviews. I recognize the impossibility in our time of simply returning to these earlier views; but I wish to argue that as we move into what appears to be a postcritical phase of Christian theology, our thinking can be informed by traditional approaches.[12] These approaches, of course, root themselves in the New Testament. But they move in various directions. There are, I think, two fundamental sensibilities that appear not only in the ancient church but also in the seventeenth-century writers I shall examine. For Gregory of Nyssa and Jeremy Taylor the Christian hope, while its object is firmly located in the age to come, is nonetheless a heavenly and eternal reality in which it is possible to participate here and now. For Augustine and John Donne the spatial perspective yields to a temporal one. They locate the object of the Christian hope in a future beyond all futures and understand the Christian life as an anticipatory movement toward that goal.

Despite these fundamental differences and despite great diversity in the details of these raids on the inarticulate, I wish to conclude that both the New Testament and the four figures whose ideas I shall explore support the conviction that, paradoxically, it is only the appeal to the "there and then" that can make sense of the "here and now." The moral demands of the gospel both at a social and an individual level will prove bearable only to the degree that they are rooted in the hope of the gospel. And only a hope firmly located outside the world of our experience can give that world meaning and value. Some years ago a student asked me to supervise a reading course in which he wanted to come to terms with two writers in the ancient church—Origen and Augustine. Augustine appealed to him because he appeared to focus attention on the human scene, whereas Origen offended him because his speculations were concerned with ideas such as preexistent souls, their precosmic fall, and their postcosmic salvation. By the end of the course the student had changed his mind and had concluded that Origen's theology by appealing to structures outside this world order actually gave it a meaning it could not otherwise have. Origen speaks a great deal of human freedom, and whenever people talk a lot about something, it is often something they feel they do not have. Origen's world did not leave much room for freedom, and most people appear to have felt trapped in a deterministic world where choices were few and far between. But Origen's appeal to a wider context was meant to reassure his readers that despite appearances, the small choices we make add up and count for something. Slowly and almost imperceptibly they move us toward a destiny beyond anything we can really understand or imagine here and now. And so in this way the here and now becomes meaningful because it points beyond itself to the there and then.

Alfred North Whitehead, in *Science and the Modern World*, puts the point in a broader fashion by speaking of religion in general rather than of Christianity in particular:[13]

> Religion is the vision of something which stands beyond, behind, and within, the passing flux of immediate things; something which is real, and yet waiting to be realised; something which is a remote possibility, and yet the greatest of present facts; something that gives meaning to all that passes, and yet eludes apprehension; something whose possession is the final good, and yet is beyond all reach; something which is the ultimate ideal, and the hopeless quest.

We might even say some such thing of God. During the 1960s I knew someone who was asked to speak at a college during "Religious Emphasis Week" and was assigned as his topic the relevance of God. His response to the invitation was to say he would address that topic provided he could argue that the only relevance of God is his total irrelevance. What he meant was that a God relevant to 1965 might well be a God irrelevant to 1966. Only a God transcending all time can be relevant to all times. The paradox is the same one that Whitehead describes and the one that informs my basic thesis.

What, then, is the function of a "there-and-then" hope? In some ways the function seems to be negative in character. We are speaking of hope and not of sight. And so the hope is only partially and imperfectly perceived. That is why different people have attempted to describe it in such differing ways. Hope sometimes attaches to a future beyond all futures we know, sometimes to an eternity that transcends our temporal world. And in each of these dimensions hope can take on different forms. In a Christian context it can be the final victory over death, or the perfect vision of God, or the final completion of a universal and spiritual humanity, or the City of God's elect. We could go on. But differing understandings of hope suggest that it is a will-o'-the-wisp, luring us forward on our journey. Hope entices us to ask questions, and in this way it takes on a fundamentally negative function. Hope in the "there and then" often defines itself in contrast to the hopeless aspects of our lives and our world. It supplies a perspective that calls our world into question and displays its ambiguity, its fragility, its flux, its unpredictability. It shows us where there are forces for good and creative energies. And it also shows us where tragedy lies. But in the long run hope is not negative but positive. After Pandora had released from her jar all the evils that plague human life, the last thing left was hope, the hope that alone could make the evils bearable. Think of Emily Dickinson's poem:

> Hope is the thing with feathers—
> That perches in the soul—
> And sings the tune without the words.
> And never stops—at all—
> And sweetest in the Gale is heard.
> And sore must be the storm
> That could abash the little Bird
> That kept so many warm.
> I've heard it in the chillest land
> And on the strangest Sea
> Yet never in Extremity
> It asked a crumb of me.

Notes

1. Jürgen Moltmann, *Theology of Hope: On the Ground and the Implications of a Christian Eschatology* (New York and Evanston: Harper & Row, 1967), 15–16.

2. Ibid., 21.

3. *The Hegel Reader,* ed. Stephen Houlgate (Oxford: Blackwell Publishers, 1998), 483.

4. Hannah Arendt, *The Life of the Mind: Volume Two, Willing* (New York & London: Harcourt Brace Jovanovich, 1978), 40. Cf. *Volume One, Thinking*, 63: "But the new brand of philosophers—Fichte, Schelling, Hegel—would scarcely have pleased Kant. Liberated by Kant from the old school dogmatism and its sterile exercises, encouraged by him to indulge in speculative thinking, they actually took their cue from Descartes, went hunting for certainty. . . . "

5. Cited by Arendt, *The Life of the Mind*, 2:157.

6. *Theology of Hope*, 39-40, 50-69.

7. Ibid., 40-41.

8. Ibid., 224-25.

9. See, e.g., James T. Bridges, *Human Destiny and Resurrection in Pannenberg and Rahner* (New York: Peter Lang, 1987) and the discussion in the second edition of Alister E. McGrath, *Christian Theology: An Introduction* (Oxford: Blackwell, 1997), 545-52.

10. Alasdair C. MacIntyre, *After Virtue* (Notre Dame, IN: Notre Dame Press, 1981), 1ff.

11. W. Jackson Bate, *Samuel Johnson* (New York and London: Harcourt Brace Jovanovich, 1975; First Harvest/HBJ edition, 1979), 281-82.

12. At one point in his argument Moltmann recognizes that the paths of theology and modern science divided from one another in the modern world. He attributes this "modern break with tradition" to "the basing of assured knowledge upon the method of doubt since Descartes." He goes on to cite Pascal's opinion that "we shall lament the blindness of those who in physics allow the validity of tradition alone, instead of reason and experiment; we shall be horrified at the error of those who in theology put the arguments of reason in place of the tradition of scripture and the fathers" (*Theology of Hope*, 292).

13. Alfred North Whitehead, *Science and the Modern World* (Mentor Book: The New American Library; New York: Macmillan, 1925), 191.

1

The New Testament–God's Reign and the New Humanity

PEOPLE HAVE APPROACHED Christianity in a number of different ways, but what lies behind these various understandings is a response to the Jesus of the New Testament. Indeed, if we make guesses as historians and try to imagine the earliest responses to Jesus, it is possible to argue that there were to begin with not only different but also competing understandings of Jesus' significance. Paul the Apostle in his second letter to the Corinthians must defend his authority against that of his rivals, the "super apostles." It is by no means clear who these rivals are or what they are teaching. Are they connected with the people who say "I belong to Cephas" and so are in all likelihood concerned to emphasize the earthly Jesus, his teaching and his working of wonders? Is this why they reject Paul's authority as one who has not known Jesus before the resurrection? What are we to make of the people in Corinth who say "I belong to Apollos"? To what degree are the errors of the Corinthians tied to these other Christian apostles? Or can their misunderstandings of the gospel spring from a failure to grasp Paul's version of that gospel? These questions cannot probably be answered with any certainty, and we need not attempt any answers in order to conclude that we are in the presence of differing and competing understandings of Jesus.

In a general way we can say that there were some who saw Jesus primarily as a teacher, some who saw him primarily as a healer, some who saw his death and resurrection as central, some who saw his resurrection as designating him the Messiah. Some of the later writings that survive from the earliest period may reflect these various options. On the one hand, the *Preachings of Peter* imply a Christianity not radically different from rabbinic Judaism as it develops in the first two centuries of this era after the destruction of Jerusalem in 70 C.E. The focus is on Jesus' teaching. On the other hand, the apocryphal correspondence between Jesus and Abgar, King of Edessa, places Jesus' power to heal at center stage. We could easily complicate and elaborate this picture. But it seems clear enough that the response that dominates the New Testament itself is one that gives pride of place to Jesus' fate, to his death and resurrection. Paul himself, whose letters are older than any of the other writings in the New Testament, so emphasizes the dead and risen Lord that he appears to exclude anything related to the earthly Jesus. Jesus' teaching and his miracles have no real significance for Paul. The Gospels, I think, agree with Paul's emphasis, but seek to correct it by including the traditions that are tied to the earthly Jesus.[1]

Mark most clearly illustrates this last point. His basic literary device is dramatic irony; his readers know Jesus' identity, but in the story he tells only the demons know the secret. Jesus' parabolic teaching is mysterious not only to the crowds but also to his obtuse disciples, who must have the parables explained privately. In a similar fashion the disciples are gradually drawn into Jesus' ministry of wonder-working and healing. We may even suppose that they participate in Jesus' mission to the Gentiles. Presumably the disciples learn to understand Jesus as a teacher and a healer, perhaps also as sent to Gentiles as well as Jews, but they remain ignorant of his identity (Mark 8:17-21):[2]

> Jesus said to them, "Why are you talking about having no bread? Do you still not perceive or understand? Are your hearts hardened? Do you have eyes, and fail to see? Do you have ears, and fail to hear? And do you not remember? When I broke the five loaves for the five thousand, how many baskets full of broken pieces did you collect?" They said to him, "Twelve." And the seven for the four thousand, how many baskets full of broken pieces did you collect?" And they said to him, "Seven." Then he said to them, "Do you not yet understand?"

Even when Jesus tells them he must die and be raised, they fail to understand, "questioning what this rising from the dead could mean" (Mark 9:10). And at the least the disciples remain quite unable to see that Jesus' fate must be paradigmatic of theirs. Jesus' third prediction of his passion and resurrection leads directly to the story of how James and John ask to be seated on either side of Jesus in his glory. They cannot grasp the necessity of drinking his cup and receiving his baptism, his passion (Mark 10:35ff.).

The dramatic irony that conceals Jesus' identity for most of Mark's Gospel finally reveals it at the moment of his death upon the cross (Mark 15:37-39):

> Then Jesus gave a loud cry and breathed his last. And the curtain of the temple was torn in two, from top to bottom. Now when the centurion, who stood facing him, saw that in this way he breathed his last, he said, "Truly this man was God's Son!"

The curtain of the temple divided the sanctuary from the Holy of Holies, where God's presence was located. Mark would have us understand that Jesus' death removes the barrier between God's presence and his people. The curtain is torn in two not from the bottom up, as though human beings in their idle curiosity had sought to discover what lay behind the curtain, but from top to bottom, as though God in his heart of love had chosen himself to remove what prevented access to his presence. The Gentile centurion perceives what the disciples had not understood, and he correctly pronounces Jesus' identity. But the story is not yet quite complete. The women find the tomb empty on Easter morning, and the angel commands them to tell the disciples and Peter and to expect to see Jesus in Galilee. On this puzzling note the Gospel ends (Mark 16:1-8). The women do not obey the angel's command and say "nothing to anyone." And Mark gives us no story of the appearance of the risen Lord. It is the readers, I think, who are meant to complete the story. It is their vision of the risen Lord that will fulfill the angel's command and promise.

Mark, therefore, agrees with Paul that it is Jesus' death and resurrection that represents the center of the good news. But unlike Paul he regards Jesus the teacher and Jesus the healer as significant. Mark's Jesus is multifaceted; but his different facets, however necessary, are not sufficient to explain his identity as the dead and risen Lord. As I shall argue toward the end of this chapter, the same sort of conclusion must be made regarding John's Gospel. The point may be somewhat more difficult to make of Matthew and Luke. Matthew's Jesus does seem to be primarily the teacher, while Luke's Jesus is the "prophet mighty in deed and word" (Luke 24:19), whose work appears chiefly expressed in his compassionate healing. Nevertheless, I should argue that Matthew's teacher *is* the dead and risen Lord. The final scene of the Gospel takes place in Galilee, on "the mountain to which Jesus had directed" the disciples. (Matt 28:16) The phrase could also mean "the mountain where Jesus had instructed them," and on that reading we have the Sermon on the Mount tied to the commissioning of the disciples by the risen Lord. They are, at any rate, not only to make disciples of all nations and to baptize them in the name of the Trinity, but also to teach them to obey everything that Jesus has commanded. Matthew also seems to imply that Jesus is to be identified with God's Wisdom. We can remember that the rabbis, following the Wisdom of Sirach, identified Wisdom with the Law. And so we might argue that Matthew sees Jesus not only as the giver of the Messianic Torah but also as that Torah itself, the Torah through which God effects creation and redemption.[3] Similarly, Luke places much of Jesus' teaching in the context of his "travel narrative"

(Luke 9:51–19:27). We are meant to understand that this teaching needs to be understood as the way of the cross, tied to Jesus' fate in Jerusalem. Moreover, we may understand Luke to have given a summary of his preaching in the risen Lord's words to the two disciples on the road to Emmaus. Like Elijah and Elisha Jesus was a prophet mighty, first, in deed, and then in word. He was put to death and raised, fulfilling what the prophets declared, that it was "necessary that the Messiah should suffer these things and then enter into his glory" (Luke 24:13-35).

My argument is really a double one. First, it is the preaching of Jesus' death and resurrection that acts as a unifying principle for the judgments of the New Testament writers concerning the significance of Jesus. But second, this basic rubric includes a wide variety of subordinate themes—teaching, healing, Messianic claims and categories. It is, however, the first of these points that is crucial for my basic thesis. While Jesus' death is surely quite within the context of this world, his resurrection breaks those boundaries and introduces a perspective quite beyond history, this world, and the "here and now." We can no more sever his death from his resurrection than we can divide the labor pangs of a woman in childbirth from the birth of the child.[4] Jesus' death and resurrection, then, represent a passage from this world to the age to come, from the "here and now" to the "there and then." The disciples who saw the risen Lord did not see Jesus resuscitated and brought back to this life, nor did they suppose they had seen a ghost. There are, of course, mysteries and puzzles. Why did the risen Lord appear only to those who had already been his disciples? He did not appear to the Jewish leaders or to Pontius Pilate. Why did many of those who had been disciples refuse to believe?[5] The Gospels face these questions, but cannot answer them save by an appeal to faith. I like to think that the disciples who did believe experienced something quite overwhelming and incapable of full articulation. And they tried to explain what had happened by appealing to an idea familiar to them as Jews, the resurrection of the dead. But, of course, that idea had to do with what would happen at the end of the world and with a general resurrection of the dead. And so the problem for the earliest Christians, who were, of course, Jews, was not the claim that God had raised Jesus from the dead to the life of the new age, but the question why Jesus should have been raised, so to speak, ahead of time. There can be no real doubt that the self-styled eyewitnesses of the risen Lord made the claim. What remains in doubt is the question whether that claim is a lie, a delusion, or the truth. And as John in his Gospel suggests, it is only faith that can enable anyone to accept the claim.[6]

Jesus' resurrection, then, becomes the "there and then," a basic perspective from which to examine not only the meaning of what Jesus said and did but also the character of the Christian life in the "here and now." One can, obviously, argue that this perspective was not the only possible one. Historically, there is something to be said for describing Jesus as a Jewish peasant Cynic preacher. But if this is the conclusion implied by the Jesus seminar and if that historical conclusion is meant to be normative for Christian belief, then much of the New Testament must be discarded.[7] Paul's letters, in particular, will not do. Nor can we suppose that Jesus' teaching revolved around preaching the immanence of God's reign, the end of the world, and the vindication of his people. To be sure, there was no such thing as a New Testament until the end of the second century, even though the writings included in the canon are earlier. And the historian might be able to argue that the New Testament and the development of mainline Christianity represent misunderstandings of the historical Jesus. But underlying this sort of conclusion is, I think, the presupposition that the history of Christianity is a series of gaps rather than continuities. Paul misunderstood Jesus; the early church misunderstood Paul. And to see the development of Christianity this way may well reflect, whether consciously or unconsciously, the judgment of the Reformation that we must get behind the unfortunate institutional and Hellenized aspects of the church to the pure, original gospel. Moreover, it seems fair to conclude that views of the historical Jesus almost always tend to say more about those espousing them than they do about Jesus himself.

Needless to say, my discussion may well have raised more questions than are necessary for my purpose. I want to assume that we can start with the New Testament as it has been handed down to us. And I wish to argue that at every level the New Testament espouses a "there and then" perspective in order to say something about the "here and now." But this happens in differing ways. For the Jesus of the Synoptic Gospels the "there and then" has to do primarily with the Kingdom of God. Here I am obviously following what till recently has been a dominant tendency of New Testament scholars—to see the heart of Jesus' message in his preaching of the kingdom. For Paul it is, I think, the theme of death and resurrection that supplies the other-worldly perspective that undergirds his view of the Christian life. And this perspective emphasizes the "then" rather than the "there." That is to say, Paul tends to see salvation and the Christian life in terms of a temporal framework concerned with the relationships of past, present, and future. Finally, John thinks primarily of the "hour" and the "glory," which are simultaneously Jesus' death and his resurrection. And he focuses on the "there" rather than the "then." That is, the "hour" becomes a heavenly and timeless reality, and its relationship to Christians in this life is understood from a spatial perspective designed to relate heavenly to earthly realities.

Jesus' Message of the Kingdom

Matthew's Gospel begins with the five stories that comprise his infancy narrative and goes on to describe John the Baptist's ministry and the baptism and temptation of Jesus. He then turns to his account of Jesus' public ministry in Galilee, the fulfillment of Isaiah's prophecy (Matt 4:12-17, citing Isa 9:1-2): "From that time Jesus began to proclaim, 'Repent, for the kingdom of heaven has come near.'" Matthew's Jesus, then, repeats John the Baptist's message (Matt 3:2) in precisely the same words, and we may note that "heaven" is almost certainly a name for God rather than the designation of a place. But the message appears to be not merely more authoritative but also somewhat different from John's understanding of the imminence of God's reign.[8] John designates his follower, the one "coming after me," as the one who will baptize "with the Holy Spirit and with fire. His winnowing fork is in his hand, and he will clear his threshing floor and will gather his wheat into the granary; but the chaff he will burn with unquenchable fire." John sees Jesus as Elijah, bringing a fiery judgment on God's people and so fulfilling Malachi's prophecy.[9]

Jesus, however, proves to be a disappointment to John. He does not behave like Elijah but instead consorts with the poor and sinners and brings healing. John, arrested and in prison, sends his disciples to Jesus to ask whether he is the one to come, "or are we to wait for another?" Jesus answers (Matt 11:2ff.):

> "Go and tell John what you hear and see: the blind receive their sight, the lame walk, the lepers are cleansed, the deaf hear, the dead are raised, and the poor have good news brought to them. And blessed is anyone who takes no offense at me."

Jesus goes on to say that if anyone is Elijah, it is John the Baptist, "if you are willing to accept it." What Jesus seems to mean is that he *is* the one to come, but that his role is not to be the one envisaged by John the Baptist but instead is to be understood by the passages from Isaiah 35 and 61 to which Jesus alludes. His ministry is one of healing and of good news rather than one of judgment. He is not only the messenger of God's reign but also its agent. The Kingdom, to be sure, is located beyond this world order; and Jesus' proclamation in the first instance announces the nearness of the end of the world and of the new age when God will reign over all his enemies, removing all evil and vindicating his own. But Jesus makes two further claims. First, the immanence of the Kingdom is a promise rather than a threat. Second, it is already breaking into the present through his ministry.

Mark and Luke do not tell the story quite the same way. Mark, of course, begins his Gospel with John the Baptist and with Jesus' baptism and temptation. Like Matthew he then turns immediately to Jesus' message, but he recasts it (Mark 1:14-15):

> Jesus came to Galilee, proclaiming the good news of God, and saying, "The time is fulfilled, and the kingdom of God has come near; repent, and believe in the good news."

The peculiarity of this version of Jesus' message is the mention of the "good news" or the "gospel." The good news is Paul's regular way of referring to the proclamation of Jesus' death and resurrection, and there is much to be said for the view that Mark's Jesus ties the good news to his own death and resurrection. Paradoxically, it is the risen Lord who goes to the cross.[10] Mark, then, elaborates Matthew's version of the story but does not necessarily contradict it. Luke, as well, has a different way of beginning the story. After Jesus' temptation, he returns "filled with the power of the Spirit" to Galilee, where he teaches in the synagogue at Nazareth. Luke's elaboration of the rejection at Nazareth revolves around Jesus' claim to be anointed by the Spirit of the Lord "to bring good news to the poor . . . to proclaim release to the captives and recovery of sight to the blind, to let the oppressed go free, to proclaim the year of the Lord's favor" (Luke 4:18f., citing Isa 61:1-2; 58:6). Since he interprets that claim as one that includes a mission to the Gentiles, his own people reject him. It is not until Jesus has performed the miracles in Capernaum that he prophesied in Nazareth that Luke's Jesus refers to the Kingdom. When the crowds find him in a desert place and try to keep him in Capernaum, Jesus says, "I must proclaim the good news of the kingdom of God to the other cities also; for I was sent for this purpose" (Luke 4:43).

The first conclusion we can draw, I think, is that at least according to the Synoptic Gospels Jesus' message focuses on the proclamation of the Kingdom of God. Luke in Acts, his second volume, continues to refer to the Kingdom of God. The risen Lord during the forty days before the Ascension speaks to the apostles "about the kingdom of God" (Acts 1:3). And the apostles want to know whether this is "the time when you will restore the kingdom to Israel" (Acts 1:6). In the rest of the narrative there are several references to the church's preaching of the kingdom of God.[11] Paul's letters refer to the theme a number of times.[12] Outside the New Testament the Gospel of Thomas includes references to the Kingdom, the Kingdom of heaven, and the Kingdom of the Father.[13] What seems a little surprising is the eclipse of the theme in the Johannine literature. The Kingdom of God appears in only one context in the Gospel, Jesus' conversation with Nicodemus (John 3:3, 6). And we find only one possible allusion in Revelation 12:10: "Now have come the salvation and the power and the kingdom of our God and the authority of his Messiah." One possible explanation is that once the proclaimer became the proclaimed, attention shifted from Jesus' message of the Kingdom to Jesus himself. He now becomes the King, and he is himself the message.[14] There are obvious complications when we examine the evidence, but it does seem to be a perfectly reasonable conclusion to argue that the heart of Jesus' message lies in his proclamation of the Kingdom of God.

As I have noted or at least implied, part of what Jesus means by announcing the nearness of the Kingdom has to do with the common expectation of his time that the world would come to an end and that this time of great tribulation would be succeeded by a new age in which God would reign, overcoming all evils. Modern scholars have tended to locate this "apocalyptic" worldview in the failure of Hebrew prophecy to give people hope. If I may be allowed greatly to simplify the view I take to be widely held, I can tell the story this way. Hebrew prophecy, as we think of it by reading Isaiah, Jeremiah, Ezekiel, and the Book of the Twelve, probably emerged from ancient soothsayers and professional "prophets." Amos, for example, denies that he is a prophet and sees himself as someone called by God to denounce Israel for its sins and to proclaim God's judgment. He and others like him pronounced doom upon Israel and Judah. And the doom came within the ordinary circumstances of Near Eastern history. First the Assyrian Empire crushed the kingdom of Israel, and finally Judah went into Babylonian captivity. But once the punishment had come in this way, prophets of hope succeeded the prophets of doom. We can speak most obviously of the prophet or prophets in the school of Isaiah who wrote chapters 40–66 of the present book of Isaiah. The hope was that Israel would be restored and that this restoration would enable Israel to bring right religion to the ends of the earth. The restoration, of course, took place. Cyrus the Persian allowed the captives to return to Jerusalem; and, though we do not fully understand what happened, Nehemiah and Ezra were instrumental in rebuilding Jerusalem and Judah.

Nevertheless, the restoration proved disappointing; hopes were deceived. And so there gradually emerged the conviction that what people longed for could never come to pass within the framework of this world order. Consequently, what is called apocalyptic developed out of prophecy; and the touchstone that marks the difference is the idea that hope will be fulfilled not in this world but in the age to come. The book of Daniel, which can be securely dated by its references to events in the second century before this era, represents the watershed between prophecy and apocalyptic. At the end of days (Dan 12:1ff.),

> Michael, the great prince, the protector of your people, shall arise. There shall be a time of anguish, such as has never occurred since nations first came into existence. But at that time your people shall be delivered, everyone who is found written in the book. Many of those who sleep in the dust of the earth shall awake, some to everlasting life, and some to shame and everlasting contempt. Those who are wise shall shine like the brightness of the sky, and those who lead many to righteousness, like the stars forever and ever.

The idea of a new age and of the resurrection of the dead is, of course, foreign to most of the Old Testament. Only here in Daniel and in a few other late passages do we encounter the view that the Pharisees held and that was central in classical, rabbinic Judaism as well as in Christianity. The New Testament rightly perceives that Jesus and his followers are in fundamental agreement with the Pharisees and like them opposed the Sadducees, the conservatives who resisted accepting novel ideas into their religion.[15]

There can be little surprise, then, in understanding Jesus to have predicted the end of the world and the ushering in of God's reign and the time of the resurrection. To be sure, there may be details that are peculiar to his way of couching that message. We might even conclude that to ally it with the theme of God's reign is Jesus' own contribution. And, of course, he seems to have supposed that the end of the world would come within the lifetime of his own followers. "Truly I tell you, there are some standing here who will not taste death until they see that the kingdom of God has come with power" (Mark 9:1).[16] At any rate, Mark's Jesus predicts the end of the world in conventional apocalyptic terms in chapter 13 of his Gospel. To be sure, Jesus nowhere in his speech mentions the Kingdom of God, but both Matthew and Luke in their reworking of the speech connect it with the Kingdom. Matthew adds the words: "this good news of the kingdom will be proclaimed throughout the world, as a testimony to all the nations; and then the end will come" (Matt 24:14). And Luke completes the parable of the fig tree by saying: "So also, when you see these things taking place, you know that the kingdom of God is near" (Luke 21:31). Consequently, it does not seem entirely unfair to associate Jesus' speech in Mark 13 with his proclamation that the Kingdom of God is near.

Jesus begins by predicting the destruction of the Temple. But before that happens there will be false Christs, wars, earthquakes, and famines.

"This is but the beginning of the birth pangs," the woes associated with the end of this age and the birth of the next. Persecution will accompany the preaching of the gospel; families will be divided. When the mysterious desolating sacrilege is set up, the true sufferings will begin (Mark 13:14-19):

> then those in Judea must flee to the mountains; the one on the house-top must not go down or enter the house to take anything away; the one in the field must not turn back to get a coat. Woe to those who are pregnant and to those who are nursing infants in those days! Pray that it may not be in winter. For in those days there will be suffering, such as has not been from the beginning of the creation that God created until now, no, and never will be.

The sun and the moon will no longer shine, and the stars will fall from heaven. Finally, the Son of Man will come "in clouds with great power and glory." The angels will gather his elect "from the four winds, from the ends of the earth to the ends of heaven." The changes that Luke makes in this speech are more significant than Matthew's. Luke omits the reference to the "birth pangs," and places the persecution of Jesus' followers *before* the beginning of the end and so makes it an ordinary mark of discipleship. He also includes what we should almost certainly read as a description of the destruction of Jerusalem in 70 C.E. (Luke 21:12, 20). Nevertheless, all three Synoptic Gospels place on Jesus' lips an account of the end of the world that is saturated with allusions to prophetic verses from the Old Testament and that reflects commonplace ideas about the end of the world and the terrors that will accompany it.

While we cannot be sure that Jesus himself predicted doom in quite this fashion, it is not impossible that these stock ideas were a part of his message. The Lord's Prayer includes petitions that should probably be translated "save us from the time of trial, and deliver us from the Evil One." That is, we pray not to be overwhelmed by the doom attached to the end of the world and to be delivered from Satan's power. At the same time, it seems possible to argue that Jesus' emphasis was not so much on the horrors of the end of the world and the coming of the Kingdom, but rather on the more hopeful aspect of the arrival of the new age. Jesus reveals the mystery of the Kingdom of God to his disciples (Mark 4:11).[17] They are the chosen ones, and the least of those in the Kingdom of God are greater than John the Baptist (Matt 11:11-12).[18] The message is one of reassurance. Luke adds to Jesus' command to avoid worrying about food and clothing and to "strive for God's kingdom," the words: "Do not be afraid, little flock, for it is your Father's good pleasure to give you the kingdom" (Luke 12:31-32).[19] Those who gain entrance into the Kingdom are not its obvious heirs, but rather the poor and the outcast, even the harlots and the tax collectors (Matt 8:11-12).[20] Those who have renounced home and kindred "for the sake of the Kingdom of God" will be rewarded in this age and will receive eternal life in the age to come (Luke 18:29).[21]

Jesus' preaching of the Kingdom of God as something in the future, in the "there and then," in this way treats the Kingdom as a hope that can be grasped in the present. But he goes one step further by saying that it has already broken into this present age. Here Jesus clearly parts company with the conventions of his time. The age to come is not merely future but is already present in Jesus and his mission. The Pharisees accuse Jesus of casting out demons by Beelzebul, the prince of the demons. But Jesus repudiates the accusation on the grounds that a house divided cannot stand, and he claims that the true significance of his exorcism is that "the kingdom of God has come to you" (Matt 12:28).[22] The Greek verb can mean to anticipate or to come ahead of time. We can remember the demons' question in Matthew's version of the healing of the Gadarene demoniacs: "What have you to do with us, Son of God? Have you come here to torment us before the time?" (Matt 8:28). That is, God's victory over Satan and his angels ought to be located at the end time; but it has now already begun to take place. Moreover, in a passage peculiar to Luke Jesus denies that one can calculate the coming of the Kingdom of God. No one knows when it will come. Indeed, "the kingdom of God is among you" (Luke 17:20-21). Jesus' words are somewhat ambiguous. But it seems possible that his answer to the Pharisees is to tell them that the Kingdom of God has already come and is present in himself and in his little band of followers, if only they had eyes to see.

The Kingdom, therefore, is present as well as future. The "there and then" is also a "here and now." But we can raise the question how the presence of the Kingdom betrays itself. To be sure, we have already learned that Jesus' exorcisms are signs of that presence. His healing and his wonder-working represent the in-breaking of God's reign and are, as it were, sacraments of the life-giving healing that will be completed and perfected in the age to come. But it is possible to argue that there is another dimension of the presence of the Kingdom, a dimension located in Jesus' followers. They are not the powerful and rich, but the poor, the sick, the sinful, and the outcasts. This is where we find the Kingdom. I like to think that the idea is one implied by the Beatitudes (Matt 5:3-12). Most of the blessings are couched in the future tense—mourners *will* be comforted, the meek *will* inherit the earth, those who long for righteousness *will* be filled, the merciful *will* receive mercy, the pure in heart *will* see God, the peacemakers *will* be called children of God. Only the first and the last of the blessings are in the present tense, and only they tie the blessing to the possession of the Kingdom of heaven. This Kingdom belongs to the poor in spirit and to the persecuted. Whether "poor in spirit" means the meek or those who have become literally poor by the Spirit, they are not those noticed and honored by the world. And persecution appears to be a hallmark of Jesus' followers. Perhaps we can say that the presence of the Kingdom of God is hidden in the disciples and partly revealed in Jesus' healing miracles.

I am suggesting that the presence of the Kingdom of God can be understood as paradoxical. The poor are really those who are rich; and the persecuted, far from being the victims, are in reality the victors. For the most part the presence of the Kingdom remains hidden to the eyes of the world. And yet Jesus' miracles give an occasional and scattered revelation of what is hidden. We catch glimpses of what will be when the future Kingdom comes with power and glory. Nevertheless, the New Testament has, I think, a rather ambiguous attitude toward these glimpses. Sometimes the healing miracles appear to depend upon the faith of those healed.[23] Mark actually says that Jesus was *unable* to perform miracles in Nazareth because of their unbelief. Matthew, however, takes the view that Jesus was *unwilling* to exercise his powers. Are the healings the products of Jesus' divine or prophetic power, or are they contingent on the faith of those healed? Sometimes the miracles are celebrated and help to proclaim Jesus.[24] On the other hand, Jesus often seeks to keep the healings secret, particularly in Mark. Even Luke, who emphasizes the prophetic deeds and miracles of Jesus, betrays a degree of ambiguity (Luke 10:17-20):

> The seventy returned with joy, saying, "Lord, in your name even the demons submit to us!" He said to them, "I watched Satan fall from heaven like a flash of lightning. See, I have given you authority to tread on snakes and scorpions, and over all the power of the enemy; and nothing will hurt you. Nevertheless, do not rejoice at this, that the spirits submit to you, but rejoice that your names are written in heaven."

Miracles are not quite at center stage. And even though, particularly for Matthew and Luke, they function to proclaim the presence of the Kingdom of God in Jesus and his ministry, they do not succeed in persuading Jesus' enemies, who continue to seek a sign and regard his miracles as demonic.

Let me suggest one other point regarding Jesus' healings. As John 9 implies, the Judaism of Jesus' time usually supposed that sickness was a punishment for sin. This is why the man *born* blind poses so difficult a problem. Could he have sinned in his mother's womb? Or if his blindness is a punishment for his parents' sin, what becomes of the idea of individual responsibility? John's Jesus refuses to answer the question why the man was born blind and implies that sickness and infirmity are not necessarily punishments for sin. Luke's Jesus denies that "the Galileans whose blood Pilate had mingled with their sacrifices" were worse sinners than other Galileans and that the "eighteen who were killed when the tower of Siloam fell on them" were worse offenders than the other people in Jerusalem (Luke 13:1-5). The fate of these people was not a punishment for their sin, even though one cannot use this judgment as an excuse for failing to repent. Finally, the story of the paralyzed man in all three Synoptic Gospels also suggests that Jesus repudiates the doctrine that misfortunes are always a retribution for sin (Mark 2:1-12).[25] In the story Jesus turns to the paralyzed man and says, "Son, your sins are forgiven." He does not heal him. But the scribes silently suppose that Jesus is blaspheming. Jesus then turns to them and says, "Which is easier, to say to the paralytic, 'Your sins are forgiven,' or to say, 'Stand up and take your mat and walk'? But so that *you* may know that the Son of Man has authority on earth to forgive sins"—he said to the paralytic—"I say to you, stand up, take up your mat and go to your home." Jesus apparently sees no connection between the paralysis and sin, but his enemies do. And so Jesus proves his claim on their terms.

The ambiguities I have noted with respect to the miraculous suggest to me that the presence of the Kingdom of God is not to be primarily located in Jesus' miracles. They are, indeed, ahead of time and can be regarded as inklings of the future Kingdom. But they are not normative here and now. The present Kingdom, then, is not triumphalist but is hidden and often found in poverty and suffering. Jesus' parables draw this contrast between the humble, hidden present and the glorious, open future. The Kingdom is a seed growing secretly, a mustard seed that one can scarcely believe will produce a great tree (Mark 4:26).[26] Like wheat growing together with weeds before the harvest of the end of the world, those who belong in the Kingdom do not yet possess the triumph of being placed in God's granary (Matt 13:24ff.). The Kingdom of God in this present age is a leaven at work before the baking of the bread (Matt 13:33).[27] We can argue that these parables are meant to be reassuring. The small, hidden beginnings in the here and now will have a glorious conclusion in the age to come. Something like this may even be the original meaning of the parable of the sower. One could scarcely imagine that broadcast sowing would result in a bounteous harvest. The seeds are scattered in a random way over rocks and thorns, but everyone knows that the result will be a good crop. In the same way the humility of the presence of the Kingdom will grow into the triumph of its future.

Jesus' parables often treat the presence of the Kingdom as the greatest of promises. It is a treasure hidden in a field, the pearl of great price that exceeds all other valuable things (Matt 13:44-45). The idea is that one will do almost anything to gain this promise. But in another way the promise is not so much something for us to gain as it is something given us as a gift. The master of the vineyard gives to all who come the promise of fair wages. They are fair not because they are tied to what we have done or how we have performed our labor. They are fair because they express the goodness of the master. Indeed, the wages have nothing to do with how long we have worked; all receive the same. Our hope of the Kingdom is one we receive quite gratuitously. It is a promise we do not necessarily deserve (Matt 20:1). We all receive invitations to the great banquet prepared for us, and those invitations are extended to the poor and outcast (Matt 22:2).[28] I am reminded of an examination question I once heard of: Explain the doctrine of justification by faith to someone who has read the Gospels but not the Epistles. In other words, just as Paul insists that God's justification, his forgiveness, comes to us without our deserving and before we have done anything, even before we have repented, so these parables treat the gift of the Kingdom as one beyond earning and deserving.

Nonetheless, the parables also treat the presence of the Kingdom as a demand. Indeed, the promise, while it must come first, carries with it a demand. Rightly received, the promise compels us to respond in the right way. The idea helps explain what at first seems confusing about Matthew's version of the parable of the Great Supper. Those invited refuse to come, and the king not only repudiates them but he also slaughters them and burns up their city. He then commands his servants to invite everyone else, "good and bad." But when the guests arrive, the king spots one of them without a wedding robe and expels him into "the outer darkness, where there will be weeping and gnashing of teeth" (Matt 22:1-14). The idea is that receiving the promise involves a true response to it. And there is much to be said for the interpretation that equates the wedding robe with repentance. If the promise, which we cannot deserve or earn, grasps us, it leads us to repentance. It is not so much that we repent and are then forgiven, as that, forgiven, we learn to repent. The parable of the unforgiving servant teaches the same lesson (Matt 18:23-35). The king forgives the servant his debt, but the servant turns around and tries to exact what is owing him from his fellow servants. It is a cautionary tale. We must not follow the bad example of the wicked servant, but forgiven ourselves, we must forgive.

Perhaps even the petition in the Lord's Prayer should be understood to mean "forgive us our sins that we may forgive those who sin against us."

The demand of the Kingdom, of course, can be elaborated. Like the wise virgins of the parable we must be prepared for God's judgment (Matt 25:1ff.). And while the parable of the sheep and the goats refers to judgment based on how the nations of the world have treated the followers of Christ, we might still affirm the common interpretation of that parable that sees the demand of the Kingdom as requiring us to feed the hungry, clothe the naked, and visit the sick and the prisoners (Matt 25:31ff.). Following Jesus also requires us to renounce our ordinary human loyalties. Luke's Jesus forbids his would-be followers from burying their dead and from saying farewell to their family. He says, "No one who puts a hand to the plow and looks back is fit for the kingdom of God" (Luke 9:57-62). Later in the Gospel Luke's Jesus understands how hard it is for the rich young ruler to renounce his riches. Getting the rich into the Kingdom of God is an affair of the camel and the eye of the needle. Peter then appeals to the disciples' renunciation (Luke 18:24-30):[29]

> Then Peter said, "Look, we have left our homes and followed you."
> And he said to them, "Truly I tell you, there is no one who has left
> house or wife or brothers or parents or children, for the sake of the
> kingdom of God, who will not get back very much more in this age,
> and in the age to come eternal life."

Mark's version of this passage is instructive (Mark 10:23-31). In this age those who have renounced home and kindred will receive "a hundredfold" but "with persecutions." Mark ties the demand to renounce all for the treasure and precious pearl of the Kingdom to the likelihood of persecution and martyrdom; and perhaps he thinks of the hundredfold restoration as incorporation into the new family of Christ's followers.

The renunciation required to meet the demand of the Kingdom basically involves shifting our trust from ourselves to God. We are to cut ourselves off from whatever causes us to stumble, and we are to become like children totally dependent on God our Father (Mark 10:42-48).[30] Mark's Jesus commends the scribe who summarizes the Law as the love of God and the love of neighbor by commenting, "You are not far from the kingdom of God" (Mark 12:34).[31] Thus we might say that one way of expressing the demand of the Kingdom is to equate it with the summary of the Law. But, of course, as Matthew argues, the obedience required goes beyond that taught by the scribes and the Pharisees. The Law remains (Matt 5:19-20):

"Therefore, whoever breaks one of the least of these commandments,
and teaches others to do the same, will be called least in the kingdom
of heaven; but whoever does them and teaches them will be called
great in the kingdom of heaven. For I tell you, unless your righteousness exceeds that of the scribes and Pharisees, you will never enter the
kingdom of heaven."

The demand of the Kingdom requires people to practice what they
preach, but it also deepens and completes the old Law. Matthew's Sermon on the Mount is his way of explaining the new Law and the new
righteousness and of articulating the demand of the Kingdom.

The Kingdom of God, then, in Jesus' proclamation and teaching, at
least as they are represented in the Synoptic Gospels, is both "then" and
"now." It lies in the future beyond the confines of this world order. And
in this mode it represents a vision of what will be. All evils will disappear. There will no longer be war or violence, hunger and thirst, cold
and nakedness. Weeping and sorrow will be no more. Death's reign will
end. Moreover, the Kingdom yet to come will see a transformation of all
the values held dear in this world. Power and wealth will count for nothing. Even the wisdom we think we have now will be transformed to the
true wisdom of God. Jesus seems to have preached this vision primarily
as a promise. To be sure, the threat of exclusion from the vision may still
be part of the picture; but that is not where the emphasis lies. And we
can also recognize that entering into this vision will mean hardship,
anguish, and suffering. The end of the world will not be easy or pleasant. And waiting in this world for the vision to come will be attended by
difficulty and persecution. The missionaries of Acts "strengthened the
souls of the disciples and encouraged them to continue in the faith, saying, 'It is through many persecutions that we must enter the kingdom of
God'" (Acts 14:22). But the waiting and the hardship will find their
reward in the fulfillment of the vision in the age to come.

If, however, this were all that could be said, it would be difficult to
attach any real value to the "now" and to the "already" dimension of
the Kingdom of God. The lesson would be simply that we must hold our
noses for the time being, confident that there will be an end of waiting.
Jesus' message of the Kingdom takes us further than this. In his healing
and his other miracles we catch glimpses of the future in the present.
More importantly, we find the presence of the Kingdom in Jesus and his
band of followers. In other words it is in community that we find the
Kingdom present. Those incorporated into this new community find a
deliverance from their alienation in this world. This seems to me why
there is such an emphasis in the New Testament on the poor, the sinful,
and the outcast. People who had no real place to belong in their world

for one reason or another find in the community of the Kingdom a belonging they had never known. The promise of the Kingdom, therefore, is a present reality as well as a hope oriented toward the future. Finally, that present promise carries with it a demand. Old ties are broken in order that new ties may be established. And much of the demand of the Kingdom in the present revolves around the love of one's brothers and sisters. We can agree with Saint Augustine's equation of this love with the love of God, since to love God surely draws us into his love for humanity and for his creation. In the first instance, the demand of the Kingdom expresses itself in the community solidarity that seems to be characteristic of earliest Christianity. But the early Christians were missionaries, and the community was in principle meant to be welcoming to the stranger.

The picture I have tried to draw of the paradoxical "then" and "now," the "not yet" and the "already" of the Kingdom of God, is one that is informed by my general understanding of the character of Christianity in its formative period. Two pieces of evidence will suffice. The rhetorician Lucian of Samosata wrote a satirical attack on a man he regarded as a religious charlatan and whom he calls Peregrinus.[32] Peregrinus died by setting himself on fire at the Olympic Games in 165 C.E., but earlier in his career he was for a time a Christian. Lucian's description of the Christians aims at showing how Peregrinus took advantage of these simple people, gaining himself a small fortune particularly by being arrested as a Christian—something that enabled him to be hailed as a latter-day Socrates. In any case, Lucian notices two characteristics of the Christians, both of which he regards as marks of their folly. First, they believe that they are going to live forever. Second, once they join the Christian community they call one another brother and sister and spare nothing in caring for one another. The evidence seems to me important because it comes from a point of view that if not hostile is condescending. Lucian ridicules the Christians. But what he notices coheres very well with ways in which early Christian writers characterize their religion. The hope of immortality and resurrection and a strong sense of community solidarity are the two chief features. The first, of course, has to do with a hope directed toward a future beyond this life. The second describes the present reality of the Christian community. And, I should want to argue, it is the hope that creates and forms the community.

The frescoes in the Christian catacombs of Rome suggest a similar conclusion. The catacombs were, of course, located outside the official boundary of the city of Rome and were underground passages where Christians were buried. While there were certainly rituals and services connected with the catacombs, they were not places of refuge for Christians in times of persecution. The church assemblies took place in house churches in the city. Thus, the frescoes that ornament the catacombs are funerary art. The major theme to be found in this art revolves around the idea of deliverance—Noah from the flood, Jonah from the whale, Daniel from the lions' den, the Three Children from the burning fiery furnace, the children of Israel from Egypt. The Good Shepherd gathers and teaches his flock. There are banquet scenes that may be related to the miraculous feedings in the Gospel as well as to the heavenly banquet prepared for the dead. The frescoes are more than decoration. They establish the hope that attaches to the Christian dead, and the deliverance they often express must surely be related to the Christian belief that the dead will be raised in the general resurrection of the last day. At the same time, at least some of the scenes we find can be related to Christian baptism. The stories of Noah, Jonah, and Israel crossing the Red Sea are obvious examples. But we might also add the Good Shepherd gathering his flock and might even correlate the banquet scenes with the church's eucharist. Deliverance, then, appears to have a double reference, to the resurrection of the dead in the future and to deliverance from alienation by incorporation into the Christian community in the present.

The pattern I have sought to discern in Jesus' proclamation of the Kingdom is one that can be found in other contexts. Indeed, Jesus' mysterious self-designation as the Son of Man fits the pattern almost exactly. We can divide the Son of Man sayings into three categories—the present suffering but authoritative Son of Man, the dying and rising Son of Man of the passion predictions, and the future glorious Son of Man who will return at the end of the world. It is not entirely clear where these themes come from save that they appear to have some connection with Daniel 7 and with the Aramaic idiom that employs son of man (*bar nasha*) as an oblique way of referring to oneself. But as we have the pattern in the Synoptic Gospels, it tells a story and equates that story with Jesus'. On earth Jesus is the Son of Man who has nowhere to lay his head and yet is Lord of the Sabbath and capable of forgiving sins. This same Son of Man is rejected, put to death, and then raised from the dead. Finally, at the end of the world he will return in majesty to pronounce judgment. Like the Kingdom in the present the earthly Son of Man is lowly and hidden, and like the Kingdom in the future the heavenly Son of Man is glorious and powerful. Already we can see the basic pattern shifting from Jesus' message to his person. And when we turn to St. Paul we can argue that it is Jesus' fate, his death and resurrection, that becomes the central meaning of the pattern by which the hope associated with the age to come gives form and substance to the Christian life in the present.

Saint Paul: Dying and Rising
with Christ—the New Humanity

Paul tells the story of his conversion in his letter to the Galatians. A zealous Jew, he "was violently persecuting the church of God and was trying to destroy it." Unexpectedly he received his gospel "through a revelation of Jesus Christ." The decisive event was his encounter with the risen Lord.[33] Alluding to Isaiah 49:1 and Jeremiah 1:5, Paul describes his conversion as a prophetic call (Gal 1:15-16):

> But when God who had set me apart before I was born and called me through his grace, was pleased to reveal his Son to me, so that I might proclaim him among the Gentiles, I did not confer with any human being. . . .

Paul's emphasis here is on the immediate and revealed character of his call to be the apostle of the Gentiles. His authority does not derive from the Jerusalem church or from any human source. It may well be that he exaggerates. Certainly Luke's three accounts in Acts of Paul's conversion associate it with the Christian community in Antioch. In Galatians Paul is arguing for his independence of the Jerusalem church but also for that church's recognition of his Gentile ministry. There is much to say about the difficulties of the evidence on this point and about the origins of the Gentile mission. But I am more interested in how Paul understands the gospel revealed to him by the risen Lord than in how he justifies preaching that gospel to the Gentiles.

I wish to argue that Paul's theology, if we may call his ideas that, originates in his conversion experience and that he articulates the meaning of that experience in the opening chapters of Romans. In the gospel "the righteousness of God is revealed through faith for faith." This revelation finds its proof text in Paul's reading of Habakkuk 2:4: "The one who is righteous [or just] by faith will live." Habakkuk meant that in a time of extraordinary evil and calamity the righteous person will survive because of his faithfulness to God. But Paul draws a very different meaning. The one whom God justifies by faith will live in the age to come. Instead of "the just, by [his] faith will live," we should read "the [one] just by faith, will live." We simply have to move the comma to understand Paul's reading of the prophetic text.[34] If I am correct in suggesting that Paul's gospel is at its heart justification by faith, we need to go on to explain what he means by this rather obscure expression. We must remember that "just" and "righteous" are two English translations of the same Greek word, and that "justify" can mean both "account righteous" and "make righteous." And with this in mind we can point to the basic structure of Paul's opening argument in Romans. In the gospel we find the revelation of God's righteousness (1:17), first as his "wrath . . . against all ungodliness and wickedness" (1:18), and then as his saving righteousness (3:21).

The gospel appears first as the bad news of God's wrath against sinners. Paul follows the common Jewish understanding of three categories of sin—idolatry, sexual immorality, and bloodshed (a catch-all category). God condemns idolaters, the sexually immoral, and the list of sinners found in Romans 1:29ff. The root sin is idolatry, worshipping and serving the creature rather than the Creator. The other sins represent both the consequences of idolatry and God's punishment of it. "God gave them up" to these other sins (1:24, 26, 28). We can imagine those receiving the letter nodding knowingly. It is obvious that God condemns the people Paul speaks of in chapter one. Surely the Roman Christians have not sinned in any of these ways, and surely they will align their judgments with God's. Thus, the first verse of Romans 2 comes as a shock:

> Therefore you have no excuse, whoever you are, when you judge others; for in passing judgment on another you condemn yourself, because you, the judge, are doing the very same things.

I suppose the verse might mean no more than that everyone is sinful in one way or another. But a deeper reading seems to me required. If we argue that only God can make absolute judgments, then for human beings to indulge in this kind of judging means that they are placing themselves in the position of God and committing a far more subtle and dangerous kind of idolatry than the obvious sinners. In any case, Paul's conclusion is that "all have sinned and fall short of the glory of God" (3:23). The wrath of God is universal; all stand condemned.

The other side of the coin is God's saving righteousness. The "all" who have sinned (Rom 3:24-26)

> are now justified by his grace as a gift through the redemption that is in Christ Jesus, whom God put forward as a place of atonement by his blood, effective through faith. He did this to show his righteousness, because in his divine forebearance he had passed over the sins previously committed; it was to prove at the present time that he himself is righteous and that he justifies the one who has faith in Jesus.

As Luther rightly saw, God's righteousness is not a moral quality he possesses but is the righteousness he gives to those whom he justifies. Paul's reference to Christ as a place of atonement helps clarify his meaning. The mercy-seat in the Temple was the place where sacrifices were made in order to effect reconciliation between God and his people. Christ functions in the same way by his death and resurrection. If sin can be understood as the breach of a relationship and, specifically, as a breach in the relationship between God and his people, then atonement must be a healing of that breach, a "right-wising" of the bond between God and humans.

Paul's emphasis is on God as the one who has effected reconciliation. Since all humans stand condemned before God, they have no possibility of reconciling God. Rather, "God was in Christ reconciling the world to himself" (2 Cor 5:19). One might suppose, of course, that the Law was designed to effect reconciliation. But Paul treats the moral dimension of the Law as inadequate for this purpose. To be sure, "the law is holy, and the commandment is holy and just and good" (Rom 7:12). Moreover, it is possible to be righteous according to the Law. Paul can call himself "blameless" from the point of view of "righteousness under the law" (Phil 3:6). Nevertheless, this kind of righteousness is that of children who obey their parents, but whose obedience does not spring from a mature and inner relationship with them as friends. The reconciliation Paul has in mind implies more than an outward obedience, and it requires a full and immediate relationship with God. From this perspective the Law can do no more than act as a criterion for sin. Indeed, the Law has the negative effect of actually driving those who receive it into sin (Rom 7:7ff.). Paul does not, I think, wish to characterize life under the Law as a legalistic existence. Rather, his point is that the Law is not God's final dispensation, and to treat it as such is to fail to understand that true righteousness stems from a right relationship with God that only God can effect.

Paul's arguments are complicated and sometimes obscure because he is obliged to deal with the problem of the Law's relationship to his gospel and to the final revelation of God in Christ. But setting aside this problem, we can conclude that what he means by justification by faith is really no more or less than the reconciliation effected by God's forgiveness of sins. "Therefore, since we are justified by faith, we have peace with God through our Lord Jesus Christ" (Rom 5:1). If justification by faith means peace with God, forgiveness, and reconciliation, why does Paul fail to use simpler language? In particular, if as John Wesley said the simple, biblical meaning of justification is forgiveness, why does Paul avoid the term?[35] The answer may well be that to speak of forgiveness might imply that one must first repent and only then be forgiven. And that, I think, is precisely what Paul does not want to say. If anything, the terms should be reversed. First comes forgiveness, and repentance becomes the fruit of forgiveness. Paul's understanding emphasizes the double fact that while we have no power whatsoever to help ourselves, God in Christ has helped us. Even the faith by which we appropriate God's righteousness is God's gift.

Are we, then, helpless? Is there nothing we can do? St. Augustine, whose doctrines of original sin and prevenient grace find their basis in Paul's letters, would answer these questions in the affirmative. And he would also restrict justification to the vessels of mercy whom God elects. I am not so sure, however, that we need to read Paul the way Augustine, Luther, and Calvin read him. Indeed, it seems clear to me that the logic of Paul's idea is universal. After all, if everyone stands condemned under God's wrath, would it not follow that all are equally the beneficiaries of God's mercy? We could even understand justification as a kind of realized version of the Last Judgment. Terms like "wrath" and "justify" find an easy place in widespread ideas about the Last Judgment. Paul even alludes to these ideas in Romans 2:3ff. At the End God will condemn some and vindicate others. But, let me suggest, in Christ the Last Judgment has been made present in such a way that God condemns all in order to vindicate all. "God has imprisoned all in disobedience so that he may be merciful to all" (Rom 11:32). Not only is justification, at least in its logical implication, universal, it also need not cancel out our part in conversion. Paul never addresses the difficult question of the relation between grace and freedom, but it seems more reasonable to assume that he does not find them incompatible. Take the analogy of falling in love. We understand the experience as one that happens to us, that is quite beyond our control. We cannot make ourselves fall in love. But this perception by no means robs us of our freedom. Indeed, falling in love frees us to act upon the relationship given us. Similarly, faith happens to us in a mysterious way. But it does not rob us of our freedom, and once received it becomes an obedience expressing itself in love.

In some such way, I think, Paul understood his conversion. The risen Lord interrupted him on his journey and gave him a deep sense of reconciliation with God, as well as a call to preach that message of reconciliation to the Gentiles. The "here and now" of this experience was the product of the "there and then" of Christ's death and resurrection and pointed toward the "there and then" of the age to come. And so we must now turn to ways in which Paul seeks to bind his present experience to the fulfillment of God's purposes in the dead and risen Lord and to the consummation of those purposes at the time of the general resurrection. Once again we can take his letter to the Romans as a point of departure. Notice the tenses in the following selection from Romans 5:1-11:

> Therefore, since we *have been justified* by faith, we *have* peace with
> God through our Lord Jesus Christ, through whom we *have obtained*

access to this grace in which we *stand*. . . . For while we *were* still weak, at the right time Christ *died* for the ungodly. . . . God *proves* his love for us in that while we *were* sinners Christ *died* for us. Much more surely, then, now that we *have been justified* by his blood, *will we be saved* through him from the wrath of God. For if while we *were* enemies, we *were reconciled* to God through the death of his Son, much more surely, *having been reconciled, will we be saved* by his life. . . .

Our present peace with God is the consequence of what has already happened, Christ's death in the past and the reconciliation and justification effected for us. But that present peace with God is an assurance of what has not yet taken place, our final deliverance from God's wrath and our participation in the life of the resurrection.

What I am suggesting is that Paul locates his experience of forgiveness and reconciliation, mediated by the risen Lord, in the context of the story of salvation. In Romans 5:12ff. he portrays Christ as the second Adam. His argument is complicated and, to some extent, obscured by his concern to say that the Law does not affect his conclusions and by the fact that v. 12 is an anacoluthon, that is, an incomplete sentence. But it is clear enough that he begins with an analogy between Christ and Adam. His readers may well wonder what Christ's fate in the past has to do with them, but Paul appeals to their assumption that Adam's fate has somehow determined theirs. Adam sinned and received death as his punishment, and this pattern of sin followed by death characterizes all Adam's progeny. All die because all sin. One problem raised at this point in the argument is that the logic of what Paul is saying implies that somehow Adam's sin and death determine the sin and death of all humanity, while the simple word "because" implies that humanity after Adam sins freely.

It may well be that a very difficult theological question emerges. But there is a passage in the rabbinic midrash *Sifra* that supplies a common-sense solution to the problem.[36] Leviticus 26:39 specifies as a punishment for disobedience that "those of you who survive shall pine away for their sins . . . and for the sins of their fathers." The rabbinic comment points out that the text appears to contradict Deuteronomy 24:16, which is the promise of the Holy One Blessed Be He that children will *not* die for the sins of their fathers. In other words, we find an apparent contradiction in scripture between passages that imply that guilt and punishment are passed down from one generation to another and passages that insist that penalties for sin are a matter of individual responsibility. The midrash resolves the contradiction by saying that "generation after generation, when the children see the sins of their fathers and embrace them, they are punished on their own account." The resolution depends on distinguishing the explanation for sin from the issue of moral responsibility. Similarly, Paul can argue that sin, introduced into the world by Adam, is passed down through all the following generations, but that this fact does not eliminate the moral responsibility that stems from embracing sin.

At any rate, Paul defines the Adam pattern as sin followed by death, one that has become universal. He then implies that in a similar way the pattern that attaches to Christ's fate is one also meant to be universalized. In 1 Corinthians 15:22 he puts the point succinctly by saying "as all die in Adam, so all will be made alive in Christ." In other words the pattern of death followed by resurrection replaces the pattern of sin followed by death. And yet it is not the case that the new Adam simply abolishes and replaces the old Adam. To return to Romans 5:12ff., there are differences between the act of Christ ("the free gift") and the act of Adam ("the trespass"). First, Adam's act is "one man's trespass," while Christ's act is that of "the grace of God and the free gift in the grace of the one man." That is, Adam's act was purely human, but Christ's act is somehow the act of God's grace. And we may remember that for Paul Christ is the redeemer, who was "in the form of God and did not think equality with God something to be grasped" (Phil 2:6). Second, Adam's sin starts from square one; there is no previous context of sin. But Christ's free gift bringing justification is one "following many trespasses." In other words Christ introduces the pattern of the new humanity into the context of humanity as defined by Adam.[37] Finally, the effect of Adam's act was to allow death to reign over all, while the effect of Christ's act is to enable all to reign with him.

These differences help explain how Paul understands the relation of the two patterns, and his understanding also finds expression in the simple fact that the two patterns overlap. Death is common to both. In the Adam pattern, however, death is the penalty for sin and the completion of the pattern. But in the Christ pattern death becomes the gateway to life and resurrection. Paul's argument is that Christ, by identifying himself with our death, inherited from Adam, changes its meaning and makes it the gate whereby we pass through death to the resurrection and the age to come. God does not simply discard the old humanity. Instead, he transforms it. God sent his Son "in the likeness of sinful flesh" and so made him "a curse for us" that we might be "redeemed . . . from the curse of the law" (Rom 8:3; Gal 3:13). God "made him to be sin who knew no sin" (2 Cor 5:21). There are, of course, many places where Paul speaks of the future dimension of salvation. It is, however, in 1 Corinthians 15 that he defends and explains the resurrection of the dead. In all likelihood the Corinthians' error is to suppose that the resurrection must be understood only as a present, spiritual reality and to deny that there can be a future, bodily resurrection. Paul's response is to say that if we place our hope in this life and in this life alone, "we are of all people most to be pitied." Christ's resurrection was "from the dead" and must be understood as a bodily one. More importantly, his death and resurrection are paradigmatic of ours. He is "the first fruits of those who have died." He has been raised, and when he comes at the end of this age, he will usher in the general resurrection. The bodily character of the resurrection involves discontinuity as well as continuity with our present bodies. What is now perishable, corruptible, and physical will be raised a spiritual body, incorruptible and glorious. But just as there is continuity between the grain of wheat we sow and the wheat we harvest, so there will be continuity between our present condition and what we shall be in the resurrection.

Paul can think of the general resurrection in terms of the conventions of his tradition as a Pharisee. God's trumpet will sound, summoning the dead to life. The archangel will call. Those left alive at that last great day will not die but be changed into their resurrection bodies and will be caught up to meet the Lord in the air (1 Thess 4:15-17). This future drama is one that Paul takes pains to defend (2 Thess 2:1ff.):

> As to the coming of our Lord Jesus Christ and our being gathered together to him, we beg you, brothers and sisters, not to be quickly shaken in mind or alarmed, either by spirit or by word or by letter, as though from us, to the effect that the day of the Lord is already here . . . for that day will not come unless the rebellion comes first and the lawless one is revealed, the one destined for destruction. He opposes and exalts himself above every so-called god or object of worship, so that he takes his seat in the temple of God, declaring himself to be God.

Though not all would grant that Paul wrote these words, their general insistence on the future apocalyptic scenario accords with what we find in the letters all agree he wrote. The details of the picture drawn here are remarkably like those we find in the Synoptic apocalypse. Is the lawless one associated with the abomination of desolation? the anti-Christ? The passage goes on to speak of the one who restrains and of the restraining power. They will delay the end but not prevent it.

Paul, then, firmly locates the consummation of salvation in the age to come and thinks of it as the resurrection of the dead. But, as I have argued, he also understands salvation to be something located in the here and now. The question we must ask is how does he relate these two perspectives. How can the "not yet" be the "already"? How can "then" be "now"? I should want to answer by appealing to the way he employs the theme of "dying and rising with Christ." It is reasonably certain that the theme existed before Paul's conversion as a way of explaining the meaning of Christian baptism.[38] Those plunged beneath the waters of baptism and brought forth from them enacted ritually the drama that awaited them in the future. The ritual assurance of baptism guaranteed their hope. We find the theme not only in Paul's writings but elsewhere in early Christian literature. For example, the letters of Ignatius of Antioch play on the theme and use it as a way of articulating the meaning of Ignatius's expected martyrdom. He is on his way to Rome to be condemned and executed. In this way he will die with Christ in order to rise with him. His journey is from the rising of the sun to its setting, and so to death. But this death will be his rising with Christ. Ignatius repeatedly says that he is now beginning to be a disciple. What he seems to mean is that the promise of his baptism is about to be fulfilled. His professed death and resurrection with Christ will soon be a reality, and the theme of dying and rising with Christ is firmly oriented toward the future dimension of salvation.[39]

Paul, I think, would not disagree with the meaning Ignatius gives the theme, but he would seriously qualify it and would seek to give it a present as well as a future meaning. In Romans 6 Paul appeals to the baptismal tradition:

> Do you not know [or, surely you are aware of the fact that] all of us who have been baptized into Christ Jesus were baptized into his death? Therefore we have been buried with him by baptism into death, so that, just as Christ was raised from the dead by the glory of the Father, so we too might walk in newness of life.

It is clear enough that Paul sees one reference of baptism pointing toward the future, but his emphasis is on a present and spiritual dying and rising with Christ. We should expect him to say "just as Christ was raised from the dead, so we too shall be raised." But he breaks the logic of his statement and concludes it by saying "so we too might walk in newness of life." Death and resurrection have a metaphorical meaning that allows the theme to describe the Christian life in the present. That life is, in the first instance, death to an old vision of life and resurrection to a new one. "So you also must consider yourselves dead to sin and alive to God in Christ Jesus." The reconciliation Paul describes as justification by faith is a transformation of the believer's fundamental attitudes. But the spiritual and metaphorical dying and rising is also a transition from an old way of behavior to the new imperative of the Christian life. "For just as you once presented your members as slaves to impurity and to greater and greater iniquity, so now present your members as slaves to righteousness for sanctification."

My argument is that Paul sees dying and rising with Christ in its present mode—here and now—in a double way. It is the birth of a new vision springing from the believer's reconciliation to God, and at the same time it is the new way of life, the new virtue that springs from that vision. The indicative of the believer's union with God in Christ immediately becomes the imperative of the new way of walking. In Romans 12 Paul turns from his account of the gospel and from his wrestling with the question of the place of Israel in God's plan to moral exhortation:

> I appeal to you therefore, brothers and sisters, by the mercies of God, to present your bodies as a living sacrifice, holy and acceptable to God, which is your spiritual worship. Do not be conformed to this world, but be transformed by the renewing of your minds, so that you may discern what is the will of God—what is good and acceptable and perfect.

The new vision is the transformation effected by the renewing of the mind, and we cannot go far astray if we equate this transformation with justification by faith and reconciliation with God in Christ. Moreover, it springs from the "mercies of God," which we can discern not only in God's mysterious plan to save Israel but also in Christ crucified and raised from the dead. The transforming vision should persuade believers to offer themselves fully to God and from that stance to seek God's will in all the particularities of their lives.

Paul binds this transition from vision to virtue with life in the Christian community. The one body of the church has many members, and the argument is not so much that Christians are obliged to maintain the solidarity of the community as that the community ought to enable its diverse members to function in diverse ways. Each one has a gift and must use that gift to upbuild the body in love. Each one also has the obligation to care for fellow Christians. Still more, to the degree possible, the mutual love that ought to characterize the Christian community should extend to outsiders. "If it is possible, so far as it depends on you, live peaceably with all" (Rom 12:18). Paul clearly has in mind the hostility of the Gentile world toward the Christians, perhaps also the hostility of the Jewish synagogues. Christians cannot always escape persecution, but so far as possible they must seek peace with outsiders, must obey the government. In Romans 14–15 Paul turns to what may well be the specific aim of his letter by urging the "strong" and the "weak" Christians to live in harmony with one another.

While any reconstruction of the setting of Romans must inevitably be hypothetical, an informed guess, there is one such guess that seems persuasive to me. We must remember that Paul did not found the church in Rome, indeed had never even been there. And we can also remember that not so very long before Paul wrote his letter the Emperor Claudius had expelled the Jews from Rome because they had rioted, as Suetonius tells us, "at the instigation of Chrestus." Suetonius has probably misunderstood his information, and it seems likely that the riots in the Jewish quarters of Rome were caused by the claims of the new Jewish sect that called itself "Christian." We learn from Acts that Aquila and Priscilla, Christians expelled with the Jews from Rome, joined Paul and his mission in Corinth (Acts 18:1-4). But in Romans 16 Aquila and Priscilla (or Prisca) are back in Rome, together with a number of Paul's other acquaintances. The guess is that Aquila and Priscilla had become Christians in Rome, Christians who observed dietary rules and treated certain days as special. That is, they began as "weak" Christians; but once they joined Paul's mission, they adopted the "strong" Christianity of Paul. Though it may be putting the point a little too broadly, they left behind a Jewish Christianity and adopted a Gentile one. Then when they returned to Rome, they introduced this "strong" Christianity and by doing so threw an apple of discord into the midst of the Christian communities in Rome. Paul, then, knowing this but having no authority over the church in Rome, makes a gentle argument rooted in his understanding of the gospel and his vision of Israel's destiny. The "weak" Jewish Christians must not judge the "strong," nor must the "strong" Gentile Christians despise the "weak." The two groups must learn to agree to disagree and to regard their common bond in the body of Christ as one that transcends their differences.

Whether this reconstruction is accurate or not, Paul surely attempts to move from his understanding of salvation to the implications it has for the moral life of Christians. And, it seems to me, this move needs to be understood not in individualistic terms but as one that primarily addresses life in community. In Romans 7–8 Paul moves from his despairing cry, "Wretched man that *I* am! Who will rescue *me* from this body of death?" to the triumphant conclusion that absolutely nothing "will be able to separate *us* from the love of God in Christ Jesus." It does not matter whether Romans 7 refers to Paul's condition before his conversion or to the "not yet" dimension of his life as a Christian. On either reading the transition from what is unredeemed to what is being redeemed correlates with the transition from the first person singular to the first person plural. The "I" is without hope until the individual finds a place to belong in the "we" of the community. The analogy of the body we have found used in Romans 12 also appears in 1 Corinthians 12. In both cases Paul's emphasis is on the diversity of functions within the one body. But in 1 Corinthians he also wishes to make the point that equal status attaches to all the members of the body. "For in the one Spirit we were all baptized into one body—Jews or Greeks, slaves or free—and we were all made to drink of one Spirit" (1 Cor 12:13).

Paul's letters are primarily designed to deal with obstacles to this ideal of equal status and diverse functions. Even Romans fits this picture, provided the sort of interpretation I have given of its purpose be accepted. The best illustration of my point, however, is 1 Corinthians. Reading the letter is a little like hearing only half of a telephone conversation. Paul is responding to a series of questions the Corinthians have sent him by letter and to the information brought him by "Chloe's people" (1 Cor 7:1; 1:11). The general problem in the Corinthian church revolves around factions at enmity with one another. This seems to have something to do with competing authorities—Paul, Apollos, Cephas, Christ. We cannot be sure exactly what is involved, but the breakdown of community expresses itself in the community meal and eucharist. "For when the time comes to eat, each of you goes ahead with your own supper, and one goes hungry and another becomes drunk."[40] The specific problems with which Paul must deal include cases of sexual immorality, lawsuits among believers, Christians who eat meat sacrificed to idols, the veiling of women, Christians who speak with tongues, and some who deny the future bodily resurrection. He deals with these problems in turn but also sees them in relation to a larger pattern which I should want to describe as the boast of a self-styled spiritual elite in the Corinthian community that results in the repression of the "weak" by the "strong."

We must not think here of Jewish and Gentile Christians. Instead, we can characterize the "strong" partly by their slogans as reported by Paul. "All of us possess knowledge." "No idol in the world really exists; there is no God but one" (1 Cor 8:1-6). These slogans imply that the "strong" Christians think that they have been so delivered from idolatry as to be able to eat meat sacrificed to idols with impunity. They apparently think of themselves as "spiritual" Christians and regard their ability to speak in tongues as proof of their claim. In the opening chapters of the letter Paul plays upon these themes. The knowledge and wisdom Christians ought to profess is foolishness to the world, and their power ought to lie in their weakness (1 Cor 1:23-29):

> but we proclaim Christ crucified, . . . Christ the power of God and the wisdom of God. For God's foolishness is wiser than human wisdom, and God's weakness is stronger than human strength. Consider your own call, brothers and sisters: not many of you were wise by human standards, not many were powerful, not many were of noble birth.

> But God chose what is foolish in the world to shame the wise; God
> chose what is weak in the world to shame the strong; God chose what
> is low and despised in the world, things that are not, to reduce to
> nothing things that are, so that no one might boast in the presence of
> God.

Paul does not deny the principles to which the trouble-makers appeal. In
principle, it is no sin to eat idol meat. But upbuilding the community in
love is a higher principle, and the strong must beware lest their behavior offend their weaker brothers and sisters. And they must also be cautious lest thinking they stand, they fall. Speaking with tongues, in Paul's
view, is a genuine gift of the Spirit. But it by no means conveys special
status, and the proper use of the gift ensures that it will upbuild the community in love.

Paul, then, sees the elitist claims of the "strong" Christians as what
must be repudiated. But there may well be another dimension of the
view he is opposing. We have already seen that the Corinthians suppose
the resurrection to be a present, spiritual reality and that they reject a
future, bodily resurrection. It seems likely that they think they are
already living in the new age. Such a view would help explain one puzzle in the letter. The Corinthians apparently want to insist on celibacy;
the conditions of the age to come when there will be no marriage or sexuality and when in Christ there will be neither male nor female have, in
their view, already been realized. And some of them are apparently living together as spiritual brothers and sisters. What is hard to reconcile
with these views is the charge of sexual immorality. Yet it is easy enough
to understand the danger of a delusory view that becoming a Christian
delivers people from the conditions of the old world order. To be sure,
the death and resurrection of Christ represent for Paul the inauguration
of the age to come, and dying and rising with Christ enables believers to
participate in the new age. But that participation is not the consummation of salvation and is a participation by hope rather than by the facts
of the matter. To ignore the tension between the old and the new humanity is to forget that the old humanity still has power to deceive and to
cause people to fall. Pretending that the old Adam is dead and gone gives
him a power he would not otherwise have.

While it seems to me true that Paul thinks of the present dimension
of salvation as one that expresses itself in the community, the very fact
that he is realistic about the problems that beset his churches clearly
implies that the present points toward but cannot be equated with the
consummation of the age to come. The community is always in the
process of becoming more and more in fact what it already is by hope
and promise. A kind of dialectic is established. The future informs the

present, and the present grows toward the future. From this perspective the moral norms we find in Paul's writings are norms that belong in the age to come and are not capable of full realization in this age. Let me try to explain what I mean by reflecting on the baptismal tradition to which Paul appeals in Galatians 3:28—"There is no longer Jew or Greek, there is no longer slave or free, there is no longer male and female; for all of you are one in Christ Jesus." It would seem obvious that Paul is not appealing to what is outwardly the case. The Christian communities clearly include Jews and Greeks, slaves and free people, men and women. It is only in Christ Jesus that these divisions no longer exist or at least no longer count for anything. And, I wish to argue, this will be true in a complete fashion only in the age to come. Therefore, the moral imperative becomes the task of finding ways of anticipating the norms of the age to come in the context of this age.

Paul's fullest discussion of the division between Jews and Gentiles is in Romans 9–11. There he is concerned with the apparent apostasy of the Jews; they have rejected Christ, their own Messiah. Is this because God has withdrawn his election of Israel and in an arbitrary and tyrannical way chosen the Gentiles instead? Or is it because Israel has refused to hear and to accept the message of salvation, rejecting God and thereby provoking their own rejection by him? This is how it seems, but beneath the surface Paul discerns the mystery of God's merciful plan. The apostasy of Israel is both partial and temporary. A remnant remains as the heart of the new Israel. The apostasy of the majority of Israel is what enables the gospel to be preached to the Gentiles. And when the Jews see the ingathering of the Gentiles, they will be provoked to jealousy and will return. Thus, God's mysterious plan included all under disobedience that his mercy might be extended universally. Election will have exploded to include all in the new Israel, and this will have been accomplished fully in the age to come. The question then becomes: if in the long run the division between Jew and Gentile will disappear, how are we to move toward that goal in the present time. Paul's policy, I think, is one that preserves the distinction between Jewish and Gentile Christians. The Galatian churches, which are presumably Gentile, must not return to the Law by observing its requirements. And so the Gentile churches must not be law-observant. But the Jewish churches may be law-observant. Perhaps in Rome the different house churches were one or the other. Nevertheless, even though at a practical level the Jew– Gentile division remains, Paul wishes to insist that they must be in fellowship with one another. Presumably, his policy reflects all that the traffic will bear. And his agreement with the Jerusalem church treats the collection he gathers from his churches to take to the poor in Jerusalem as an outward symbol of the solidarity of the Jewish and Gentile churches, a sign that the division that still exists is destined to pass away. What has changed is not the outward division between Jew and Gentile, but the inner attitude toward that division.

We must draw the same conclusion regarding the division between slave and free. However much "in Christ there is neither slave nor free," from an outward point of view Paul does not argue for any change in the structures of society.[41] Indeed, his conviction that the world is swiftly drawing to an end leads him to deny the value of any change, even at an individual level (1 Cor 7:21-24):

> Were you a slave when called? Do not be concerned about it. Even if you can gain your freedom, make use of your present condition now more than ever. For whoever was called in the Lord as a slave is a freed person belonging to the Lord, just as whoever was free when called is a slave of Christ. You were bought with a price; do not become slaves of human masters. In whatever condition you were called, brothers and sisters, there remain with God.

Paul's emphasis is on his conviction that what matters is not the conventions of the old humanity which divide people from one another in various ways, but rather the new humanity in which all have the same status with various gifts that function to upbuild the body of Christ in love.

There may, however, be another implication of his view. It is obvious that Christianity was widely perceived as a movement that disrupted social ties. The Roman historian Tacitus says that the Christians were blamed for the great fire of Rome in 64 C.E. and were put to death as arsonists not because anyone really supposed they had started the fire, but because of their "hatred of the human race." The Christians were in his view and in that of many others enemies of family values, setting children against their parents, students against their teachers, and slaves against their masters. Christians often sought to counter this view by insisting on moral rules that were designed to protect all social structures, and we find in the New Testament several examples of these "rules for households." For example, in Colossians Paul (if we can assume he is the author) gives instructions to husbands and wives, children and parents, and then turns to slaves (Col 3:22-4:1):[42]

> Slaves, obey your earthly masters in everything, not only while being watched and in order to please them, but wholeheartedly, fearing the Lord. Whatever your task, put yourselves into it, as done for the Lord and not for your masters. . . . Masters, treat your slaves justly and fairly, for you know that you also have a Master in heaven.

In all likelihood we should understand Paul's letter to Philemon in the light of these views. Paul is writing Philemon to ask him to receive his runaway slave, Onesimus. Philemon is to receive Onesimus "so that you might have him back forever, no longer as a slave but more than a slave, a beloved brother" (Phlm 15-16). Philemon and Onesimus will still be master and slave, but what really matters is that they are brothers in Christ. Paul has no wish to undermine the social order, but it would seem obvious that by subordinating the societal norms of his day to the norms of the new humanity he introduces a perspective that will begin to transform the old conventions.

The third social division found in the formula of Galatians 3:28 is that of male and female, a division overcome in Christ. Paul takes this conclusion quite seriously and is not, I think, the misogynist some have made him out to be. As a norm for the age to come the abolition of the distinction between male and female is also an abolition of sexuality. This is why the Jesus of the Synoptic Gospels refutes the Sadducees the way he does. The Sadducees, who denied the resurrection, pose Jesus the problem of a woman whom seven brothers married, obeying the Levirite law. Whose wife will she be in the resurrection? Jesus' answer is "when they rise from the dead, they neither marry nor are given in marriage, but are like angels in heaven" (Mark 12:25). Presumably human sexuality is tied to procreation; and since in the age to come there will no longer be a need for procreation, sexuality will disappear altogether. As we have seen, some of the Corinthians appear to have applied this norm to their present life and to have insisted on celibacy as the only Christian norm. We find Paul's response in 1 Corinthians 7, where he does not deny the validity of the Corinthian view. Indeed, he wishes that "all were as I myself am," that is, "unmarried." Celibacy, then, is one way of anticipating the norm of the age to come. But it has its risks. If the unmarried and the widows "are not practicing self-control, they should marry. For it is better to marry than to be aflame with passion."

Marriage, then, becomes another way of anticipating the age to come and of seeking to apply "in Christ neither male nor female" to our present conditions. But Paul qualifies this understanding in two ways. First, he recognizes the possibility that a man and his wife may "by agreement for a set time" refrain from sexual relations in order to pray. But he argues that this should not be made permanent and that the sexual relationship should be resumed after the set time. Second, and more important, he alters the usual ancient understanding of marriage that subordinated the wife to the husband. The wife and husband should give one another their conjugal rights because "the wife does not have authority over her own body, but the husband does; *likewise the hus-*

band does not have authority over his own body, but the wife does."
What I have italicized does not seem to us very surprising, but in the
context of late antiquity Paul is advocating an extremely radical view.
Neither Romans nor Jews would have understood at all the idea that the
partners in a marriage are equal with one another. Thus, it is not just
celibacy but also a radically redefined kind of marriage that anticipates
the norm of the age to come.

Two passages in 1 Corinthians appear to contradict Paul's insistence on the equality of men and women, or at least they seem to exclude
that equality from the way women are permitted to participate in the
worship of the community. In chapter 11 Paul insists that women be
veiled, and he gives reasons that are somewhat obscure (1 Cor 11:7-12):

> For a man ought not to have his head veiled, since he is the image and
> glory of God; but woman is the glory of man. Indeed, man was not
> made from woman, but woman from man. Neither was man created
> for the sake of woman, but woman for the sake of man. For this rea-
> son a woman ought to have a symbol of authority on her head,
> because of the angels. Nevertheless, in the Lord woman is not inde-
> pendent of man or man independent of woman. For just as woman
> came from man, so man comes through woman; but all things come
> from God.

Interpreting this passage is by no means easy, but it is possible to argue
that Paul is making a contrast. In the old creation Eve was taken from
Adam's rib, and this is a sign that women are inferior to men. But in the
new creation, "in the Lord," the old convention disappears, and women
have perfect equality with men. The angels, I should argue, are the evil
world rulers of the old order of things. They are a threat to the women,
who in the old creation are inferior and vulnerable. Consequently, the
women are to wear a veil as "a symbol of authority," warning off the
evil angels. In 1 Corinthians 12:23 Paul treats veiling as a symbol of
honor. The less honorable parts of the body are veiled to give them an
honor they do not seem to have. So here, I think, the veil confers on the
woman the honor and authority of her new status in Christ, a status that
gives her full equality with the man but a status that could not be discerned in any outward way. This interpretation, or one along the same
lines, convinces me for the simple reason that it enables us to avoid arguing that Paul contradicts himself.

The other passage that appears to show that Paul fails to take "in
Christ neither male nor female" seriously is more difficult to dispose of.
1 Corinthians 14:34-35 forbids women from speaking in the church
assembly, requiring them to be taught by their husbands at home. The
verses not only contradict the view I am seeking to explain but also fly

in the face of Paul's recognition in chapter 11 that women *do* speak and prophesy in the assembly. Moreover, the textual tradition makes these verses suspect. They sometimes appear at the end of chapter 14 and so wander about in the textual tradition. For these reasons there is much to be said for the view that they are not Paul's words, but are a gloss that has crept into the text. One further passage occurs in Ephesians, a letter that not all would agree is Paul's. Here wives are to "be subject" to their husbands, and husbands are to "love" their wives (Eph 5:22-33). At first—and perhaps even at last—these exhortations seem to contradict the view Paul takes of marriage in 1 Corinthians 7. And that conclusion might even be an argument for rejecting the Pauline authorship of Ephesians. Nevertheless, taken as a whole the discussion in Ephesians can without great difficulty be interpreted to teach that love amounts to the same thing as obedience. The analogy suggested in the passage is the love of Christ for the church. Granted that the church must be subject to Christ as to the head of the body, nevertheless Christ's love for the church was so great that he "gave himself up for her."

For Paul, in conclusion, the "then" and the "not yet" of the future break into the present. The future consummation of what was fulfilled in Christ's death and resurrection brings about the possibility of our reconciliation not only with God but also with one another. The "then" becomes the "now" of the community that has been drawn into the pattern of Christ's death and resurrection and that represents the context in which reconciliation is at work. Moreover, the churches are to be agents of reconciliation, leavening the old order of things and widening the scope of the salvation wrought by Christ. From another point of view Christians in the churches must seek to move the "now" of their walking toward the "then" of the resurrection life when they shall attain the perfection toward which they now strive. We find several creative tensions—between the future and the present, between the community and the individual, between the visionary promise revealed in Christ's fate and the imperative that flows from it for us, between God's work in guiding us toward the full attainment of the promise and our own striving for it. Finally, Paul's basic perspective, time-oriented as it is, correlates with that of the Synoptic Gospels. The basic message is one, but its expression is manifold.

John's Gospel: The Glory of the Cross and the New Family of God

John ends his narrative of the savior's ministry in chapter 12 and does not resume his story and its climax until the passion and resurrection narratives that begin in chapter 18. It is as though we hear the clock's mechanism preparing to strike but are obliged to wait for a moment until the chime begins. In chapter 12 Mary of Bethany anoints Jesus for his burial; the chief priests plot to kill Lazarus; Jesus enters Jerusalem in triumph. At this point the Pharisees say to one another, "You see, you can do nothing. Look, the world has gone after him!" On cue some Greeks come to Philip and ask to see Jesus. Jesus then defines the meaning of this by saying, "The hour has come for the Son of Man to be glorified." A few verses later we encounter the Johannine version of the agony in the garden: "Now my soul is troubled. And what should I say—'Father, save me from this hour'? No, it is for this reason that I have come to this hour. Father, glorify your name." A voice comes from heaven, perplexing and dividing the crowd. But Jesus goes on to interpret its meaning: "Now is the judgment of this world; now the ruler of this world will be driven out. And I, when I am lifted up [or: exalted] from the earth, will draw all people to myself." The chapter ends with a description of the unbelief of Jesus' own people as the fulfillment of Isaiah's prophecy and with a kind of summary of Jesus' revelation.

There are two key words in the chapter—hour and glorify. Both point directly to the cross, which is the hour and the glory. Similarly, in chapter 13, which introduces the Supper discourses, John notes that "Jesus knew that his hour had come to depart from this world and go to the Father." Moreover, the moment Judas receives the sop of bread and leaves, "it was night." But Jesus says, "Now the Son of Man has been glorified, and God has been glorified in him." It is as though the death of the savior on the cross has already taken place. Yet at one level John's narrative dominates, and the glory of the hour simply reminds the reader of the climax toward which that narrative moves. Earlier in the story we are reminded that Jesus' hour has not yet come. It is for this reason that he is reluctant to obey his mother and provide wine for the wedding at Cana and for this reason that he is not arrested earlier in the narrative (John 2:4; 7:30; 8:20). The disciples only understand what Jesus says retrospectively; it is the gift of the Spirit, tied as it is to the hour of glory, that enables them to remember and understand.[43] The story takes on its true meaning only later and from the perspective of the cross.

At the same time, John constructs his narrative so that the savior's deeds and words during his ministry point toward the cross. For John, Jesus' miracles are "signs," and the word has a double meaning. Understood only as miracles, signs produce only a very frail and unstable faith. The signs Jesus performs at his first Passover in Jerusalem cause "many" to believe in him, but Jesus is unwilling to "entrust himself to them," presumably because he knows how quickly this kind of faith can vanish.

His implicit rebuke of Nicodemus, who comes to him by night because he is impressed by the signs, suggests that a full faith requires being born of water and the Spirit (John 2:23ff.). Later in the story those who are miraculously fed in the wilderness initially respond to Jesus in faith. But by the next day they are seeking a sign, and Jesus recognizes that they are looking for him "not because you saw signs, but because you ate your fill of the loaves" (John 6:2, 14-15, 26). Nevertheless, "signs" are not merely miracles, but properly understood point beyond themselves to the cross, the hour of glory. John's conclusion about Jesus' first sign at the wedding in Cana of Galilee makes the point clear in a general way. What Jesus did by turning the water into wine "revealed his glory; and his disciples believed in him" (John 2:11). We must guess what John means by this, but there are clues. The miracle takes place "on the third day," and we are probably supposed to see a reference to the resurrection of Jesus and to the Messianic banquet and marriage feast that is its result.[44] Perhaps we are also to understand the sign as pointing toward the way the cross transforms the water of the old dispensation into the wine of the new one.

The signs, of course, need not have a single meaning. They are, in one sense, mysteries with many connotations. Nevertheless, they can all be regarded as pointing toward the life given by the cross. The healings of the official's son, of the man at the pool of Bethzatha, of the man born blind, and the raising of Lazarus all suggest new life. Moreover, the connection with the cross appears explicitly in the last of these stories. When Jesus hears that Lazarus is ill, he says, "This illness does not lead to death; rather it is for God's glory, so that the Son of God may be glorified through it" (John 11:4). As we shall see, the thematic connection is also a dramatic one. The wine of the first sign at Cana and the bread of the miraculous feeding may also refer to the new life given by the savior. And even though it does not appear in the context of a sign, we may also think of the living water promised the Samaritan woman by Jesus. Jesus' walking on the Sea of Galilee, provided we understand the sign in its paschal context, might possibly allude to the crossing of the Red Sea and the new life given by the new Passover. This suggestion implies that the signs can also be understood as giving new meaning to the old observances. Jesus heals the man at the pool of Bethzatha on the sabbath. The miraculous feeding and the walking on water take place at Passover, and the healing of the man born blind reflects the Tabernacles themes of light and water.[45] No matter how we interpret the particularities of the signs, it seems clear that they are meant to be foreshadowings of the cross, the hour of glory.[46]

From another perspective the signs often function in the dramatic structure of the Gospel. The healing at Bethzatha provokes the first confrontation between Jesus and his enemies—the dispute over healing on the sabbath. The two miracles in chapter 6 function in the context of a fundamental shift in the narrative. Until chapter 6, with the one exception of the dispute over the sabbath, Jesus meets little or no opposition. His deeds and words reveal himself to the world. But at the end of chapter 6 we find Jesus rejected not only by the Jews but also by some of his disciples (John 6:66-71):

> Because of this many of his disciples turned back and no longer went about with him. So Jesus asked the twelve, "Do you also wish to go away?" Simon Peter answered him, "Lord, to whom can we go? You have the words of eternal life. We have come to believe and know that you are the Holy One of God." Jesus answered them, "Did I not choose you, the twelve? Yet one of you is a devil." He was speaking of Judas son of Simon Iscariot, for he, though one of the twelve, was going to betray him.

There are tantalizing parallels with the Synoptic story of Peter's confession on the road to Caesarea Philippi and, perhaps, with the rejection of Jesus at Nazareth. Another example of a sign that functions in the context of opposition to Jesus is the healing of the man born blind. The story ends with Jesus' observation, "I came into this world for judgment so that those who do not see may see, and those who see may become blind" (John 9:39). The Pharisees rightly see this as an attack on them.

The most obvious use of a sign in the dramatic structure of the Gospel is the way John tells of the raising of Lazarus (John 11). When Jesus hears of Lazarus's illness, instead of going immediately to Bethany he tarries for two days. He then summons his disciples for the journey, despite their conviction that this is courting trouble, and tells them that "Lazarus has fallen asleep, but I am going there to awaken him." The disciples misunderstand the euphemism, and Jesus then tells them plainly that Lazarus is dead. Thomas says to his fellow disciples, "Let us also go, that we may die with him." Thomas is apparently referring to Jesus and to the certain fate that awaits him in Judaea. He urges the disciples not to desert their master but to follow him and share in his fate. But at a deeper level life and death are intertwined in an ironic fashion. Jesus' raising of Lazarus to life is the dramatic straw that breaks the camel's back. It is what provokes Jesus' arrest and execution. So life for Lazarus brings death for Jesus. But the death of Jesus is really life not only for him but for the world. Dramatically, however, the Jews who witness the miracle are divided. Some believe in Jesus, but others report what has happened to the Pharisees. They and the chief priests assemble a meeting of the Sanhedrin. Caiaphas, inadvertently prophesying, argues that "it is better for you to have one man die for the people than to have the whole nation destroyed." And so they make the decision to have Jesus put to death, and the drama moves toward its conclusion.

The thematic and dramatic structures just examined make it clear that John's Gospel is an artfully constructed narrative, moving inexorably toward the climax of Jesus' fate. At the same time it is equally clear that it is the deeper meaning of the narrative that represents the true message of the Gospel. The orientation to a temporal framework tends to yield to the contrast between an earthly and time-bound sequence of events and the heavenly and eternal realities toward which they point. One example may be found in John's account of Jesus' trial before Pilate (John 18:25–19:16). Jesus is taken inside the praetorium, while the Jews remain outside. Pilate goes outside to ascertain the charges brought by the Jews, who say that Jesus is a criminal but that they are not allowed to execute capital sentences. Pilate goes back inside the praetorium to ask Jesus whether he is the King of the Jews. The pattern is repeated. A second time Pilate goes out to the Jews and says that he finds no case against Jesus. He appeals to the custom of releasing a prisoner at Passover, but the Jews demand the release of Barabbas rather than Jesus. Pilate returns to Jesus inside the praetorium and has him flogged and mocked. Then a third time he goes out to the Jews, this time bringing Jesus crowned with thorns and wearing a purple robe. Pilate says, "Here is the man!" And twice more he pronounces Jesus innocent. Taking Jesus back inside the praetorium, Pilate asks where he is from. Despite his attempt to release Jesus Pilate finally takes him out and hands him over to be crucified. The narrative is moving and dramatic. But its meaning concerns what has been called "the dualism of decision." Pilate moves back and forth from the Jews to Jesus, and so he hesitates between allying himself with the "world" and faith in the savior and redeemer. So, too, all must choose whether to accept or to reject the revelation.

A second example of the way in which John's narrative tends to dissolve into its timeless and heavenly meaning may be found in the narrative of Jesus' crucifixion, which immediately follows the trial before Pilate (John 19:17-30). Jesus, carrying his own cross, goes to Golgotha. The soldiers place the inscription bearing the charge on which he is to be crucified on the cross—"Jesus of Nazareth, the King of the Jews." Despite the Jews' objections, Pilate refuses to change the inscription. The soldiers then do what they always do; they divide Jesus' clothes among themselves. But they cast lots on his seamless robe. Jesus' mother and the beloved disciple are among the friends standing by the cross. Jesus' last thoughts are for them, and he says, "Woman, here is your son" and to his friend, "Here is your mother." He then says, "I am thirsty." Some pitying bystanders give him some wine to help him bear the agony of the cross. Then Jesus says, "It is finished," bows his head and dies. We can read the story as the death of a righteous man, unjustly executed but noble in accepting his fate. He thinks not so much of himself as of his mother and friend, and the scene concludes with his words, "It is all over." But, of course, there is another way of reading the story. Jesus is the universal king; Pilate has written the title in Hebrew, Latin, and Greek. He is also the universal priest, since the seamless robe is described so as to suggest this identification. This king and priest then accomplishes his work by creating a new family not based on blood ties but on his own divine command. He then calls for the cup of death, which he drinks voluntarily; and he pronounces the verdict—"it has been perfected." The redeemer's work has been accomplished.[47]

In the same way the story of Jesus' death and resurrection and of the risen Lord's gift of the Spirit dissolves into the timeless reality of the hour of glory. The cross, of course, represents Jesus' death. But it is also his exaltation in the resurrection. John's identification of the cross with the hour of glory suggests this. So, too, does the verse we have already encountered: "And I, when I am lifted up [exalted] from the earth, will draw all people to myself" (John 12:32). The earthly lifting up of Jesus by death on the cross is really his ascent from earth to heaven in the resurrection. The cross, then, stands not so much for Jesus' death as for his resurrection. And this was the way the early church understood the cross. It is never a symbol of death, and even when we find Jesus portrayed on the cross, he is very much alive with eyes wide open. The cross is always a sign of victory and is often given a cosmological meaning to show that it orders and perfects the new creation. The ascension of Christ is, of course, Luke's idea and cannot be found elsewhere in the New Testament. For John the resurrection is the ascent of Jesus to heaven. The cross for John is not only death, resurrection, and ascension; it is also the hour when Jesus breathes forth the Spirit. Instead of describing the mighty acts by which God in Christ has effected salvation as a series of events chronologically ordered the way they are in Luke's two volumes and in the church year, John treats these acts as aspects of a single hour of glory, an hour that becomes a timeless reality.

There are a number of passages that help establish this conclusion. The glory of the cross is tied to the eternal glory the redeemer has as God's Son and Word. In the prologue to the Gospel we read: "And the Word became flesh and tabernacled among us, and we have seen his glory, the glory as of the Father's only Son, full of grace and truth." John identifies the redeemer with the eternal Word of God, through whom

God made the world. That explains his true glory. But that eternal glory "tabernacled" among us. Just as God's presence was located in the Temple, so the Son's glory becomes in Jesus the presence of God in the human context. It is possible that John is thinking of Jesus as identical with God's Shekinah. For rabbinic Judaism the Shekinah is the presence of the transcendent God with his people. The word is formed from the word for "tabernacle" and is often translated "glory" in the Septuagint. Moreover, the references in John to "name" may well be associated with the idea. Deuteronomy describes the one Temple as "the place that the Lord will choose as a dwelling for his name."[48] And when Solomon dedicates the Temple in Jerusalem, he prays to God whom even "heaven and the highest heaven cannot contain . . . much less this house that I have built." But his prayer is that this transcendent God's "eyes may be open night and day toward this house, the place of which you said, 'My name shall be there'" (1 Kings 8:27-30).

John transforms this idea by applying it to Jesus. As the Redeemer he is God's name, dwelling no longer in the Temple but in his people When Jesus prays the Father to glorify his name, he is praying that the Father will glorify the Son (John 12:28).[49] God's name, of course, is the I AM revealed to Moses in the burning bush. Consequently, we can understand the texts where Jesus says I AM as references to his identity as God's name. What substantiates this interpretation most clearly is John's account of Jesus' arrest. When the soldiers and police come to the garden, Jesus takes the initiative and says, "Whom are you looking for?" They say, "Jesus of Nazareth," and Jesus replies, "I AM." The speaking of the divine name causes them to step back and fall to the ground (John 18:3-6). The divine name identifies Jesus with God, an identification made quite explicit in the prologue to the Gospel and in Thomas' confession, "My Lord and my God." The Son and the Father are one (John 10:30). But the full revelation of Jesus' identity falls in the context of the glory of the cross (John 8:28):

> So Jesus said, "When you have lifted up the Son of Man, then you will realize that I AM, and that I do nothing on my own, but I speak these things as the Father instructed me."

As the I AM, Jesus is bread, light, the door of the sheep, the good shepherd, the true vine, the resurrection and the life, and the way, the truth, and the life.[50] In all these ways the glory Jesus had from eternity with the Father is revealed in his ministry on earth and specifically in the glory of the cross. Like Paul, John employs what we now call "the Redeemer myth," the story of a divine figure who appears on earth and, having effected salvation, returns to heaven. But unlike Paul, who treats the earthly revelation as a humility and emptying that conceals glory, John sees the cross *as* the revelation of eternal glory.

The hour of glory, then, though it is clearly tied to the time of Jesus' death and resurrection, is really a timeless Now. No longer bound by time the hour of glory is what Abraham and Isaiah saw. Jesus, arguing with the Jews, says (John 8:56-58):

> "Your ancestor Abraham rejoiced that he would see my day; he saw it and was glad." Then the Jews said to him, "You are not yet fifty years old, and have you seen Abraham?" Jesus said to them, "Very truly, I tell you, before Abraham was, I AM."

We might be able to understand Jesus' claim as one that treats Abraham as a prophet, foreseeing the cross. Or we might suppose that what is involved is Abraham's vision of the Word of God apart from the incarnation. The better interpretation, however, is that Abraham sees Jesus' "day" as the timeless hour of glory.

The same conclusion suggests itself regarding the passage that concerns Isaiah, where one of the texts cited is from Isaiah's inaugural vision of the Lord "high and lifted up." The passage reads (John 12:37-41):

> Although he had performed so many signs in their presence, they did not believe in him. This was to fulfill the word spoken by the prophet Isaiah: "Lord, who has believed our message, and to whom has the arm of the Lord been revealed?" [Isa 53:11] And so they could not believe, because Isaiah also said, "He has blinded their eyes and hardened their heart, so that they might not look with their eyes, and understand with their heart and turn—and I would heal them." [Isa 6:10] Isaiah said this because he saw his glory and spoke about him.

In his vision Isaiah sees the arm of the Lord stretched out on the cross and the glory of the Lord high and lifted up. And he also sees Jesus' rejection by his own. Once again, the emphasis seems to be not so much on prophecy as on Isaiah's vision of a timeless pattern. The glory Isaiah sees is the glory of the cross, but this glory is really the same as the Son's eternal glory. In the high priestly prayer Jesus prays the Father to "glorify me in your own presence with the glory that I had in your presence before the world existed" (John 17:5).

In some respects John adopts the same perspective we found in Paul's writings. Jesus' death and resurrection, while remaining events that took place in a certain time and place, become the "there and then." That is, the dead and risen Lord supplies a perspective that lies outside the world of our experience in such a way as to give a meaning to that world it could not otherwise have. Yet, Paul's understanding of this fundamental pattern is tied to a temporal perspective that tends to locate the dead and risen Lord in the future. He is the firstborn of the dead, the first fruits of those who sleep; and so he belongs in the context of the general resurrection, which will be future and bodily and will not take place until this world has ended. In contrast, John's understanding drives toward a spatial perspective. He sees the glorified Lord as an eternal reality, located in heaven so as to be available on earth. Both perspectives seek to affirm the tension between the "there and then" and the "here and now." Christians must live in the tension between fulfillment and consummation. But for Paul the tension is primarily one of "then and now," whereas for John it is basically one of "there and here."

We can see John's way of discerning the tension most easily by examining chapter 14. Chapters 13-17 in the Gospel are usually called the Supper Discourses and are primarily concerned with Jesus' teaching. Suddenly we leave the larger scene and find ourselves within the community. John places Jesus' private and esoteric teaching *before* the passion and resurrection narratives. Some would argue that this placement is meant to refute gnostic ideas about esoteric revelations given by the risen Lord. We need not make too much of this idea, since the more obvious function of that placement is to supply us with the heavenly meaning of the story that is about to be completed. To return, then, to chapter 14, Jesus begins his discourse with a summary of the common understanding of the last things with its time-oriented perspective (John 14:1-4):

> "Do not let your hearts be troubled. Believe in God, believe also in me. In my Father's house there are many dwelling places. If it were not so, would I have told you that I go to prepare a place for you? And if I go and prepare a place for you, I will come again and will take you to myself, so that where I am, there you may be also. And you know the way to the place I am going."

These words must certainly refer to the risen Lord's ascent to his Father in heaven and to his return at the end of the world, when the resurrection of the dead will usher his followers into heaven. Moreover, John's Gospel, at least as we have it, does not deny the usual Christian view of the last things.[51]

Jesus' discourse, however, goes on to reinterpret the meaning of the usual view. Thomas responds to the passage I have cited above by saying that the disciples do *not* know where Jesus is going and so cannot possibly know the way. Jesus replies by saying, "I AM the way, and the truth, and the life." This could mean several different things. Is Jesus the way that leads to truth and life? Is he the way and truth that leads to life? Or are the three words simply different expressions of the same idea? I should prefer the last possibility. Perhaps what the statement means is that so soon as one embraces Jesus as the way, one is immediately united with truth and life. As one commentator has put it, Jesus is simultaneously the way and the goal. We step on the road and with no interval of time attain the journey's end. We see the Son and immediately know the Father. And this is what Jesus says (John 14:7, 9):

> "If you know me, you will know my Father also. From now on you do know him and have seen him." [And in answer to Philip's request:] "Whoever has seen me has seen the Father."

The vision of God is no longer located in a future beyond the confines of this world. Instead, because of Jesus it becomes a present reality, a heavenly destiny brought to earth.

The discourse underlines this promise by reinterpreting the coming of Jesus. We need not think of this as what will take place only at the end of the world. In fact Jesus' *going* to the Father does not need to mean his absence on earth, since the glory located "there" in heaven is poured out "here" on earth (John 14:12-14):

> "Very truly, I tell you, the one who believes in me will also do the works that I do and, in fact, will do greater works than these, because I am going to the Father. I will do whatever you ask in my name, so that the Father may be glorified in the Son. If in my name you ask me for anything, I will do it."

Jesus goes on to reinterpret his coming again. We need no longer think only of his return at the end of this age, but can understand that coming as his presence in the community. The Son will ask the Father, and "he will give you another Advocate." The "Spirit of truth" will be another Jesus, known to the community and abiding with it. In this way, Jesus promises, "I will not leave you orphaned; I am coming to you." The coming of the Spirit, then, is also the coming of Jesus. And it is also the coming of the Father (John 14:23): "Those who love me will keep my word and my Father will love them, and we will come to them and make our home with them." The "coming again" of Jesus at the end of the world has become the coming of the Spirit with the Son and the Father, a perennial presence of the glorified Jesus with his followers.

Jesus' discourse in chapter 14 turns the opening verses upside down. Not only is his coming again transformed into a present reality, the heavenly dwelling places have become the dwelling of Father, Son, and Spirit in the hearts of the disciples. The reassuring words that open the discourse occur again toward its end (John 14:27): "Peace I leave with you; my peace I give to you. I do not give to you as the world gives. Do not let your hearts be troubled, and do not let them be afraid." The temporal references tend to disappear, and the emphasis is on the way in which the heavenly glory, perfectly revealed in the hour of the cross, defines and protects the community of believers on earth. "My Father is glorified by this, that you bear much fruit and become my disciples" (John 15:8; cf. 16:14). What is "there" is also "here." The resurrection is not only located in the future; it is a present reality. Jesus reassures Martha that her brother, Lazarus, "will rise again." Martha understands him to mean "that he will rise again in the resurrection on the last day." But Jesus says, "I AM the resurrection and the life. Those who believe in me, even though they die, will live, and everyone who lives and believes in me will never die" (John 11:21-26). Thus, "the hour is coming, and is now here, when the dead will hear the voice of the Son of God, and those who hear will live" (John 5:25).

The narrative of the footwashing at the Last Supper that introduces the Supper discourses treats the meaning of the presence of Jesus' love in the band of disciples and, hence, in the community in a double way. First, that love washes and cleanses (John 13:1-11). The redeemer is a light that reveals sin and takes it away for those who turn toward the light (John 3:17-21; cf. 15:22):

> Indeed, God did not send the Son into the world to condemn the world, but in order that the world might be saved through him. . . . And this is the judgment, that light has come into the world, and people loved darkness rather than light because their deeds were evil. For all who do evil hate the light and do not come to the light, so that their deeds may not be exposed. But those who do what is true come to the light, so that it may be clearly seen that their deeds have been done in God.

Jesus, as John the Baptist says, is "the Lamb of God who takes away the sin of the world" (John 1:29, 36). We learn more about what this means in the passion narrative, where John underlines the irony that at the very moment the Jews are slaughtering the paschal lambs in the Temple, the true Lamb of God is slaughtered on Golgotha.[52] That this is what John implies is confirmed by his claim that the soldiers did not break Jesus' legs because it was necessary for the prophecy to be fulfilled that says, "None of his bones shall be broken."[53] The Old Testament text is part of the instructions for preparing the paschal lamb, and so just as the blood of the lambs preserved Israel from the destroying angels, so the sacrifice of the true paschal Lamb preserves believers from sin and death.

The second meaning of the footwashing also echoes throughout the Gospel. This meaning has to do with Jesus' example (John 13:14-17):

> "So if I, your Lord and Teacher, have washed your feet, you also ought to wash one another's feet. For I have set you an example, that you

also should do as I have done to you. Very truly, I tell you, servants are not greater than their master, nor are messengers greater than the one who sent them. If you know these things, you are blessed if you do them."

The example is one that illustrates the new commandment—"Just as I have loved you, you also should love one another" (John 13:34).[54] The command to love one another is rooted in Jesus' love for his disciples, just as the command to love the neighbor is rooted in the love of God in the Synoptic Jesus' summary of the Law. Jesus, "having loved his own who were in the world, . . . loved them to the end" (John 13:1). The disciples are to abide in Jesus' love the way the branches must abide in the vine in order to have life and produce fruit. In this way they will no longer be servants but instead will be friends (John 15:1-17).

The two meanings of the footwashing, then, are initially a double promise. The presence of Jesus' love among the disciples cleanses them of sin and effects full unity with the Son and, through him, with the Father. The promise establishes the new family of God, but it also becomes an imperative by which the members of that new family seek to love one another. John can understand what this means in much the same way that Paul understands the relationship between reconciliation with God through Christ and the moral response implied by that reconciliation. John's Jesus says, "If you love me, you will keep my commandments" (John 14:15, 23). Unlike Paul, however, John can reverse the logic (John 14:21):

"They who have my commandments and keep them are those who love me; and those who love me will be loved by my Father, and I will love them and reveal myself to them."

Perhaps what this means is that John recognizes the virtually impossible idealism of the "indicative-imperative" schema central to Paul's moral teaching. In this life it is not always the case that our moral life springs spontaneously from the religious or personal relationships that we hold dear. And so there may be times when the relationship seems less vivid and real. Those are times when we can keep going by obeying the commands that have been given us in the hope that by doing so the sense of joy in the relationship will return.

John recognizes the difficulty of preserving the "there" as something the disciples have "here." The present possession of the abundant new life brought by the Redeemer and of the full fellowship of the new family of God find a real threat in the world's hatred of Jesus and his disciples (John 15:18-20):

"If the world hates you, be aware that it hated me before it hated you. If you belonged to the world, the world would love you as its own. Because you do not belong to the world, but I have chosen you out of the world—therefore the world hates you. Remember the word that I said to you, 'Servants are not greater than their master.' If they persecuted me, they will persecute you; if they kept my word, they will keep yours also."

These words are a reassurance that the obstacle of hatred and persecution need not be either surprising or finally destructive. And in the last words we find a key to a hope articulated in the high priestly prayer of chapter 17. The possibility remains that the world will turn from its hatred and by keeping the disciples' word cease to be the "world." Jesus prays for his disciples, not asking the Father to take them out of the world, but "to protect them from the evil one." He prays also for those who will believe in him through the disciples' word and that their unity may mirror his own unity with the Father. But the unity of the new family of God is not an end in itself but is rather a means "so that the world may believe that you have sent me and have loved them even as you have loved me" (John 17:20-23). It is at least the will of the Father and the Son that the world will cease to be and that all will be brought into the family created by the redeemer.

What we begin to discover is that even though the "there" of the hour of glory is a timeless and heavenly now, the "here" that the cross and Jesus' love shapes is one of change and growth. The new family must learn to love one another despite persecution and temptation, and it must continue Jesus' mission and revelation, seeking to persuade the world to turn from its darkness to the light. The dynamic character of the Christian life finds clear expression in the way John's Gospel treats faith. The noun never occurs in the Gospel; John always uses the verb "to believe," "to have faith." This fact alone indicates a fundamental way in which he differs from Paul. For Paul faith tends to be an event, a sudden intervention of Christ into the life of a believer. For John faith is really a journey, and it has different levels. As we have seen, there are those who believe because they see Jesus' signs as no more than miracles. But there are also those who see and believe because they understand what the signs point toward. There is an example of seeing and believing that helps us understand more fully this higher stage of faith. When Mary Magdalene tells Peter and the other disciple that she has found Jesus' tomb empty, the two disciples run to it. They see the linen wrappings and the cloth that had been around Jesus' head lying separately from the wrappings (John 20:8-9): "Then the other disciple, who reached the tomb first, also went in, and he saw and believed; for as yet they did not understand the scripture, that he must rise from the dead." These verses are very puzzling. We should expect to hear that they both saw and believed because they *remembered* the scriptural predictions of the resurrection. We should probably understand that the other disciple's belief is based not on external proofs but on his love of Jesus. The "other" disciple is almost surely the "beloved" disciple. Jesus' love for him awakens his love for Jesus, and that is what explains his faith, not the scriptural proof he does not yet understand.

If believing should move from outward attraction to Jesus as a wonder-worker to a faith that appears in the context of the mutual love between the disciple and his Lord, there is one further stage John would have us understand. Thomas was not present when the risen Lord first appeared to the disciples, and he refused to believe unless he could see and touch Jesus' wounds. When Jesus appears to the disciples a second time, Thomas is there. Jesus challenges him to touch his wounds, but Thomas without doing so responds by confessing, "My Lord and my God!" (John 20:24-29) Jesus concludes the scene by saying, "Blessed are those who have not seen and yet have come to believe." The story almost certainly has many meanings, but one of them is that belief must in the long run rest on a willingness to accept the testimony of the disciples who were witnesses of the resurrection. Doubting Thomas, who failed to believe his fellow disciples, supplies a cautionary tale. John recognizes that the risen Lord appeared only to those who already believed in him (John 14:22). And he treats his Gospel as the apostolic testimony that must represent the basis for believing (John 21:24-25):[55]

> This is the disciple who is testifying to these things and has written them, and we know that his testimony is true. But there are also many other things that Jesus did; if every one of them were written down, I suppose that the world itself could not contain the books that would be written.

Believing, then, has many facets. It presumably begins by accepting the apostolic witness to Christ and by incorporation into his new family. But this is no more than the beginning of the journey.

When John tells the story of Jesus' healing of the man born blind (John 9), he is also telling us something about that journey. The story is artfully constructed as a series of scenes, rather like a slide show than a movie.[56] The first scene is the healing itself. We next see the man who had been blind together with his neighbors, who are divided about his identity. The third scene is an interrogation of the man by the Pharisees;

the fourth, an interrogation of the man's parents. The fifth scene is a second appearance of the man before the Pharisees. In the final scene Jesus reappears and speaks with the one he has healed. In each of these scenes, save for the first and the fourth, the healed man ventures an opinion about his healer, and these opinions are ordered as an increasing recognition of who Jesus is. To begin with, the healer is "the man called Jesus," who anointed the blind man's eyes with mud and told him to wash in Siloam. And the man healed does not know where Jesus is. Next, the man says that his healer is "a prophet." After his second interrogation by the Pharisees, he denies that Jesus is a sinner, acquiesces in the Pharisees' accusation that he is Jesus' disciple, and concludes, "If this man were not from God, he could do nothing." In the final scene Jesus asks the man whether he believes in the Son of Man and identifies himself as that Son of Man. The man says, "Lord, I believe." And he worships Jesus. What we are meant to understand by the story is that believing is a movement further and further into the reality of Jesus' identity and into the significance of what he has done.

John really goes no further in specifying the character of the Christian life. He sees that life in a dynamic way, but his emphasis is on the Christian community as a fellowship and family of love, responding to the love evidenced by the hour of glory and the heavenly meaning of the cross. We look in vain for specific moral norms, however much they may be assumed by John. To be sure, there are references to sin. But sin seems largely a question of rejecting the Redeemer and so refusing to enter the new family he has created. What we notice most about John's Gospel, however, is the way in which the spatial pattern of the relationship of heaven to earth has eclipsed the temporal pattern of that between future and present. The Christian hope remains a present possession, but it is oriented toward heaven and eternity rather than toward the future. It seems to me possible to argue that this sea change is designed to preserve the tension between the "there and then" and the "here and now." As we can see in Luke's Gospel and in Acts, the temporal framework runs the risk of relegating the first act of the final drama to the past, to Jesus' death and resurrection as having taken place long ago and far away. And equally, the second act of the drama—the end of the world, the general resurrection, and the establishment of the new age—tends to be placed in a distant and harmless future. John's schema of the intersection of heaven and earth can be thought to restore the tension between what is proximate and what is ultimate. Christians are caught between two worlds, torn between who they are and their destiny.

Conclusion

My argument has been meant to drive toward two conclusions. First, the New Testament is basically concerned to establish a dialectic between the "there and then" and the "here and now." The Christian hope, while it is certainly a present possession that informs and shapes the Christian life, is nonetheless oriented to what lies beyond the world of our experience. Even though the Kingdom of God is breaking into the present, its consummation lies in the age to come after the destruction of this world. Similarly, the death and resurrection of Christ, understood as a single process the way we can understand the labor pangs of a woman and the birth of her child as a single event, stands partly in history and partly outside history. There is no reason to doubt that the crucifixion is something that happened fully within the historical context of our world. But the resurrection, since it is the raising of Jesus to the life of the age to come and not merely the resuscitation of a dead body, is by definition something that lies outside the historical realm. The risen Lord, then, breaks through the confines of this age. And it is he that in one way or another becomes the focus of the Christian hope. The second conclusion I have wished to suggest is that despite the general rubric I hope to have established, there are many different ways in which the New Testament seeks to explain the basic conviction. The resurrection of Christ is a guarantee and promise of the general resurrection, and the promise means many different things. All the evils of our present life will disappear—grief, the abuse of power, injustice, war. Christ will abolish those social and economic dimensions of our lives that now divide us from one another. We shall find reconciliation not only with one another but also with God himself through our solidarity with the risen Lord. Death itself will become the entrance to this consummation. But the promise is also a present possession. Sometimes it is a hope that anticipates what will be in the age to come, a hope that enables us to discern in this life what will last, what will finally triumph. And so we can live in anticipation of the future beyond all futures, beyond death itself. Sometimes the promise is a hope that enables us to participate in our destiny, to discern heaven on earth in an imperfect and partial way. Moreover, the promise is also a challenge, an imperative to live new lives by standards that spring from the destiny for which we hope. Our perfected love of God and neighbor is reserved for that destiny. But here and now we can anticipate that love; or, to put the point another way, we can see the eternal norms of love at work in our lives. The promise, then, is a challenge to mission.

In a sense, my conclusion is that the New Testament gives no easy or complete understanding of Christian destiny or of the kind of life in this world that destiny makes possible. Instead, we find many themes— inklings that represent struggles to understand what will be and what can already be the case. I rejoice that this is so, since there is a profound sense in which the way we define our hope always falls short of its object. We cannot fully grasp it, since we walk by faith and not by sight. And yet we do apprehend it in manifold ways. The very rich variety or various richness of New Testament attempts to come to grips with the significance of Christ means that Christian thinkers after the New Testament have considerable grist for their mills. The four writers I have chosen to consider in one way or another all build on the foundation established by the New Testament. They treat scripture as a point of departure for their own speculations about Christian destiny and its relation to this life. The New Testament by no means restricts the imagination of its interpreters. It unfolds its meaning and so constantly renews itself. The treasures of the Gospel are hidden and limitless. They are beyond articulation, and yet they invite the raids to be examined in the following chapters.

Notes

1. See Helmut Koester, "One Jesus and Four Primitive Gospels," in *Trajectories through Early Christianity*, ed. J. M. Robinson and H. Koester (Philadelphia: Fortress Press, 1971), 158–204.

2. Cf. Mark 4:12, where Isa 6:9-10 is cited to explain why the parables are designed to harden the hearts of those who hear them.

3. Cf. Sirach 24:23; Matt 11:19; 11:25-30; 23:37-39. See M. Jack Suggs, *Wisdom, Christology, and Law in Matthew's Gospel* (Cambridge, MA: Harvard University Press, 1970).

4. Cf. Rom 8:22, where Paul speaks of the whole creation travailing with the birth of the children of God.

5. Cf. Mark 15:11, 13 (the Longer Ending); Matt 28:17; Luke 24:11; John 14:22; 20:24ff.

6. I am thinking, of course, of doubting Thomas in John 20. Thomas's error was his failure to believe the apostolic witness to the resurrection of Jesus.

7. See Luke T. Johnson, *The Real Jesus: The Misguided Quest for the Historical Jesus and the Truth of the Traditional Gospels* (New York: HarperCollins Publishers, 1996).

8. For the argument that follows see John A. T. Robinson, *Twelve New Testament Studies: Studies in Biblical Theology 34* (Naperville, IL: A. R. Allenson, 1962).

9. See Malachi 3:1-4; 4:1-5. The fiery Elijah will come "before the great and terrible day of the Lord."

10. See Willi Marxsen, *Mark the Evangelist: Studies on the Redaction*

History of the Gospels (1956; ET Nashville and New York: Abingdon, 1969), especially "Study Three: Euangelion," 117–50.

11. Acts 8:12; 14:22; 19:8; 28:23.

12. Rom 14:17; 1 Cor 4:20; 6:9-10; 15:50; Gal 5:21; Eph 5:5; Col 4:11; 2 Thess 1:5.

13. "Kingdom"—Gospel of Thomas 3, 22, 82, 107, 109, 113; "Kingdom of heaven"—Gospel of Thomas 19, 54, 114; "Kingdom of the Father"—Gospel of Thomas 57, 76, 96, 97, 98, 99, 113. The emphasis appears to be on the presence of the Kingdom. For example, "His disciples said to him: On what day does the kingdom come? <Jesus said:> It does not come when one expects (it). They will not say, Lo, here! or Lo, there! But the kingdom of the Father is spread out upon the earth, and men do not see it" (113). It is also worth noting that the kingdom is often associated with Jesus' parables (20, 57, 76, 96-98, 107, 109).

14. See John 1:49; 6:15; 12:13, 15; 18:36-37; 19:14-15. But see also Matt 16:28; 20:21; Luke 1:33; 22:30; 23:42; 1 Thess 2:12; 2 Tim 4:1.

15. See, e.g., Acts 23:23-35, where Paul argues for his "orthodoxy" regarding the resurrection.

16. Cf. Matt 16:28, Luke 9:27. See also Mark 13:30; Matt 24:34; Luke 21:32; and Matt 10:23. It would be possible to get round these texts by referring them to the resurrection of Jesus, but their obvious meaning seems more likely.

17. See the parallels in Matt 13:11 and Luke 8:10.

18. See the parallel in Luke 7:28.

19. Cf. Matt 6:33.

20. Cf. the parallel in Luke 13:28-29, also Matt 21:31.

21. The parallel in Mark 10:29 has "for the sake of the good news"; in Matt 19:29, "for my name's sake."

22. See the parallel in Luke 11:20.

23. Matt 8:13; 9:22, 29; 15:28 and parallels.

24. E.g. Matt 4:23ff.; 8:14ff.; 10:1.

25. See the parallels in Matt 9:1-8 and Luke 5:17-26.

26. See the parallels to the second passage in Matt 13:31 and Luke 13:18.

27. See the parallel in Luke 13:20.

28. See the parallel in Luke 14:15.

29. See the parallels in Matt 19:23-30 and Mark 10:23-31. Matthew and Mark omit the reference to the Kingdom.

30. See the parallels in Matt 18:6-9 and Luke 17:1-2. See also Mark 10:14-15 and the parallels in Matt 19:14 and Luke 18:16-17. Also Matt 18:3-4 and the parallel in Luke 9:47.

31. Mark 12:28-34 and parallels in Matt 22:34-40 and Luke 10:25-28.

32. Lucian, "The Passing of Peregrinus," LCL 5:12-14.

33. Note that he adds himself to the list of people to whom the risen Lord appeared, but this appearance was "last of all, as to one untimely born" (1 Cor 15:8). Moreover, it is this vision of the risen Lord that qualifies him as an apostle (1 Cor 9:1). He cannot, of course, claim the second qualification for

apostolic office, sc. to have "accompanied us during all the time that the Lord Jesus went in and out among us, beginning from the baptism of John until the day when he was taken up from us" (Acts 1:21-22)"

34. Cf. "The voice of one crying, 'In the wilderness prepare the way of the Lord'" (Isaiah 40:3) as opposed to "The voice of one crying in the wilderness, 'Prepare the way of the Lord'" (Mark 1:3 and parallels).

35. "Forgiveness of our trespasses" occurs in Eph 1:7 and Col 1:14; "whose iniquities are forgiven" in the Old Testament citation of Rom 4:7; "forgave us all our trespasses" in Col 2:13. See also Hebrews 9:22 and 10:18.

36. Sifra 112b, ed. Isaac Hirsch Weiss (reprint, New York: OM Publishing Co., 1946).

37. Here we can note the problem that in Romans 5 it is the *fallen* Adam that defines humanity, while in 1 Corinthians 15 it is the *created* Adam. There follow a good many problems and puzzles. Does redemption simply reverse the fall, or does it complete creation? If we say the second, does this mean that God created Adam fallen?

38. See Col 2:12-13.

39. Ignatius, *Romans* 2-3, in *Early Christian Fathers,* ed. Cyril C. Richardson (The Library of Christian Classics; Philadelphia: Westminster, 1953), 1:103–4.

40. 1 Cor 11:21.

41. For the tradition see not only Gal 3:28 but also 1 Cor 12:13, where "neither male nor female" is omitted, perhaps because the Corinthians have built too much on this part of the formula.

42. Cf. the parallel passage in Eph 6:5-9. See also 1 Tim 6:1 and Titus 2:9.

43. John 2:22; 12:16; 14:26. See also John 7:39.

44. Cf. Rev 19:9: "Blessed are those who are invited to the marriage supper of the Lamb."

45. See R. E. Brown, *The Gospel According to John* (Anchor Bible 29; Garden City, NY: Doubleday, 1966), 1:326, 343.

46. Jesus' words can also call the reader's attention to the climax of the story. See John 2:19; 3:14; 7:33; 8:21; 10:11.

47. See R. E. Brown, *The Gospel According to John* (Anchor Bible 29A; Garden City, NY: Doubleday, 1970), vol. 2, ad loc.

48. See Deut 12:5, 11, 21; 14:23, 24; 16:2, 6, 11.

49. Cf. 17:6, 11, 26; 5:43; 10:25.

50. John 6:35, 41, 48, 51, 54; 8:12 and 12:46; 10:7, 9; 10:11, 14, 17; 11:25; 14:6; 15:1, 5.

51. See, e.g., John 6:39, 40, 44, 54; 12:48.

52. See the time reference in John 19:14.

53. John 19:36, citing Exod 12:46.

54. Cf. John 15:12, 17; 1 John 3:11; 2 John 5.

55. Cf. 20:30-31; 19:35.

56. John 9:1-7, 8-12, 13-17, 18-23, 24-34, 35-38.

2

Gregory of Nyssa–
The New Creation

GREGORY, WHO WAS BORN in 335 C.E., must have been in his early twenties when he received an unwelcome summons from his mother, Emmelia. A widow, she had presided over a household on the family estate in Pontus at Annisa on the Iris river not too far from Neocaesarea. Her daughter Macrina and several other women were already living as dedicated virgins in the household; and Emmelia finally allowed herself to be persuaded to join them in their monastic routine. It may well be that at this time Emmelia decided to place relics of the Forty Martyrs of Sebaste in a tomb constructed for the use of her family. Her summons to Gregory was an invitation to attend the ceremonies attached to the deposition of the relics. The invitation was a command and not a welcome one. Gregory was living at a distance, was a young man and still "numbered among the laity." He was not particularly interested in ecclesiastical ceremonies. He was "busy," and as he confessed in retrospect "thoughtless." Grudgingly and privately complaining, he obeyed the summons, since it seems that his mother was not the kind of woman to be refused. He arrived the day before the ceremony was to take place and discovered an all-night vigil taking place before the relics. Uninterested in the psalm singing, he took refuge in a small house near the garden where the vigil was taking place.

While Gregory was sleeping, a dream and a vision came to him. In his dream he decided to go back to the garden and the vigil. But the door to the garden was blocked by soldiers sitting there—the Forty Martyrs of Sebaste. When he approached, they all stood up, brandishing their staffs against him in a threatening way. Had one of the soldiers not taken pity on him, they would have beaten him. Waking up, Gregory understood the dream as a rebuke. He realized that he was at fault and sinful in his attitude toward his mother and the religious observances taking place. He attended the deposition of the relics, shedding bitter tears for his folly, beseeching God to be kindly and the holy soldiers to grant him pardon. The story Gregory tells is scarcely an account of his conversion; indeed, he recounts his dream to demonstrate the power of the Forty Martyrs rather than to say anything about himself. But his experience must have contributed to his becoming more than a nominal Christian.[1] Despite the fact that his family had been Christian for several generations—or perhaps because of that fact—Gregory began his life in a purely secular fashion as a school teacher and a married man.

In an early work Gregory supplies us with a brief glimpse into his life as it appears to him from the perspective of a fully committed Christian. He is writing a treatise on virginity both to explain its significance for the spiritual life and to recommend it. And he laments the fact that it is an ideal to which he cannot aspire:[2]

> As it is, this my knowledge of the beauty of virginity is in some sort vain and useless to me, just as the corn is to the muzzled ox that treads the floor, or the water that streams from the precipice to a thirsty man when he cannot reach it. Happy they who still have the power of choosing the better way, and have not debarred themselves from it by engagements of the secular life, as we have, whom a gulf now divides from glorious virginity: no one can climb up to that who has once planted his foot upon the secular life. We are but spectators of others' blessings. . . . Even if we strike out some fitting thoughts about virginity, we shall not be better than the cooks and scullions who provide sweet luxuries for the tables of the rich, without having any portion themselves in what they prepare.

Gregory may exaggerate. In any case, later in the treatise he backtracks and denies any wish to disparage marriage. He may well imply that virginity is a spiritual ideal that can be realized even in the married state.[3] We know nothing of his wife or of what became of her.[4]

Gregory's gradual conversion from a nominal to a real Christianity almost certainly owes much to his family. He calls his older sister Macrina "teacher," and he acknowledges his debt to his brother Basil, who was probably five or six years older. Gregory's progress is tied to Basil's career. Basil, as a young man, studied in Athens, where he met his lifelong friend Gregory Nazianzen. He returned to Caesarea in Cappadocia about 356 as a teacher of rhetoric. But he soon became intrigued with the spiritual life and with what he had heard about the monks in Egypt and the Near East. He took the grand tour of the monasteries and returned to the family estate in Pontus, where he established a hermitage not far from Annisa. Friends joined him there, including the two Gregorys. And it was there that he and Nazianzen compiled the anthology of Origen's writings known as the *Philocalia*. The hermitage seems to have been at one and the same time a monastery and a school. Origen, who died in 253, was a Christian Platonist. Basil and his friends admired his writings but did not hesitate to correct his opinions. Their view of the spiritual life underlined the importance of the life of the mind as well as the life of the heart and soul.

One of Basil's letters, written about 362, supplies some idea of the context in which Gregory of Nyssa's Christian formation took place. Basil is writing to Gregory Nazianzen and begins by telling of his brother Gregory's letter with its wish to pay a visit. He goes on to describe the place he has found for his hermitage, seeking to persuade his reluctant friend to follow him:[5]

> There is a high mountain, covered with a thick forest, watered on its northerly side by cool and transparent streams. At its base is outstretched an evenly sloping plain, ever enriched by the moisture from the mountain. A forest of many-coloured and multifarious trees, a spontaneous growth surrounding the place, acts almost as a hedge to enclose it, so that even Kalypso's isle, which Homer seems to have admired above all others for its beauty, is insignificant as compared with this. . . . Adjoining my dwelling is another neck of land, as it were, which supports at its summit a lofty ridge, so that from the former the plain below lies outspread before the eyes, and from the elevation we may gaze upon the encircling river. . . .

Here in this romantic and peaceful place Basil and his companions made progress in the spiritual life and prepared themselves for the years ahead, which would not prove peaceful at all.

Basil was too well known to enjoy rustication for long. In 364 Eusebius, the metropolitan bishop of Caesarea in Cappadocia, ordained him priest; and he began his career as an ecclesiastical politician. When Eusebius died in 370, Basil succeeded him as bishop. He used his office to care for his people by persuading those who had hoarded grain to open their supplies during a famine and by establishing a large hospice and hospital outside Caesarea. He also fostered the development of monasticism and drew up rules for this purpose. Basil also played a central role in resolving the Arian controversy. It was Arius, a priest in Alexandria, who opened the controversy by arguing that the Son of God is less than God and a creature. The basic difficulty, of course, was how to reconcile belief in monotheism with the claim that Christ is divine. Far from settling the question, the Council of Nicea in 325 represents the beginning of disputes that lasted until 381, when the Council of Constantinople established the dogma of the Trinity—God is one substance but three persons. Let me reserve discussion of the theological issues till later and turn here only to a rough outline of the way in which the solution of 381 was the outcome of ecclesiastical politics and compromise.

No sooner had the Council of Nicea ended than the "Arians" gained the upper hand in the church. The council had affirmed that the Son of God is "of one substance" or "one in being" with the Father. It had also identified two Greek terms with one another—*ousia* and *hypostasis*. As a consequence, the council's creed looked to most people like a revival of what was called Sabellianism—the idea that there is only a single God capable of manifesting himself in three guises. There was no way of affirming the distinct and divine identity of God's Son and no way of distinguishing Father, Son, and Spirit. Prejudices, of course, were involved. And there were parties in the church that sought to solve the problem by rejecting Nicea and by arguing that the Son was "of like substance" or "like" or even "unlike" the Father. The emperor's role as patron of the church was crucial, and for the most part the emperors from 325 until 379 stood against the creed of Nicea. Basil was one of the people who saw that the way to defend Nicea was to modify it. And so the slogan "one *ousia* and three *hypostaseis*" replaced the "one *ousia*" slogan. Basil's work can be seen in his letters, and it partly involved the creation of a "new Nicene" party strong enough to defy the anti-Nicene parties and to withstand the emperor himself.

Another aspect of this work was to appoint bishops in the various cities within his jurisdiction on whose support Basil could rely. As well, the emperor had made new civil jurisdictions by dividing the province of Cappadocia; and there were those who thought that the ecclesiastical boundaries should be redrawn accordingly. Basil disagreed, and his appointments were also designed to shore up his metropolitan authority within the traditional area. Both Gregory Nazianzen and Gregory of Nyssa found themselves caught up in Basil's enterprise. Our Gregory became bishop of Nyssa in 371, but within five years a synod of Arianizing bishops and civil officials deposed him. Basil's "new Nicene" party really had no hope of success so long as Valens remained emperor in the East. But in 378 the Goths, driven south by the expansion of the Huns, crossed the Danube into Roman territory. Valens, failing to wait for reinforcements, engaged the Goths in battle at Hadrianople, where he was defeated and killed. Theodosius the Great, his successor, turned out to be an ardent supporter of the new Nicenes; and Basil's party poised itself for the triumph that it achieved at Constantinople in 381. In 378 Gregory returned to Nyssa.

Gregory tells the story of his return in one of his letters.[6] There was a cold drizzle of rain followed by thunder and lightning as he and his companions drew near the town. The storm broke just as they were entering:

> because of the storm our entrance was very quiet, no one being aware of our coming. And then, as we reached the covered porch of the bishop's house, the sound of the carriage wheels along the hard dry earth was heard, and the people poured out to meet us, as though they had been expelled from nowhere. . . . [T]he crowd surrounded us and would have crushed us with excessive kindness, and I was near fainting. When we were well within the covered porch, we saw a river of fire pouring into the church, and this came from the choirs of virgins carrying wax candles in their hands as they marched in file through the open doors of the church, kindling a blaze of splendor.

Reading between the lines we can discern Gregory's love for his people and theirs for him. He must have been a compassionate bishop, but he scarcely seems to have been a strong and effective one. In one of his letters Basil contemplates the possibility of sending Gregory to Rome, to enlist help in resolving a schism in Antioch between the old and the new Nicene parties. But Basil is not very confident. "I know that he [Gregory] is quite inexperienced in ecclesiastical matters; and that although his dealings would inspire respect with a kindly man and be worth much, yet with a high and elevated personage, one occupying a lofty seat, and therefore unable to listen to men who from a lowly position on the ground would tell him the truth—what advantage would accrue to our common interests from the converse of such a man as Gregory, who has a character foreign to servile flattery?"[7]

Basil's attitude toward Gregory may in part stem from an episode that took place in 371, four years before the letter I have just cited. Their uncle, a bishop, had taken sides against Basil in an ecclesiastical dispute of some kind. Gregory attempted to effect a reconciliation by forging letters from the uncle to Basil, apparently asking forgiveness. Needless to say, Gregory's "white lies" became known to Basil; and Gregory found that he had poured oil on troubled fires rather than troubled waters. One of Basil's letters is his scathing rebuke of his brother.[8] Gregory himself seems to have realized that he was not cut out for ecclesiastical politics at a high level. In his *Life of Macrina* Gregory recounts his conversations with his dying sister and at one point complains to her of his difficulties—expulsion from his see and the confusion in the church that dragged him into controversies and wearisome squabbles. Macrina strongly rebukes him, arguing that his involvement in the affairs of the church is a gift that brings him honor throughout the world in contrast to their father's provincial renown.[9] Though he does not say so, Gregory seems quite unconvinced of the blessings of ecclesiastical preferment.

Gregory, however, took a prominent part in the Council of Constantinople in 381, and he went on several missions designed to straighten out ecclesiastical troubles of one kind or another. Some of his writings also addressed the controversies of his day.[10] But I think we can argue that his heart was not fully engaged in all this. His real interest was in prayer and in thinking through the meaning of the Christian life. His best-known works are either Christianized philosophical treatises or lectures and homilies on the spiritual life. After Basil's death in 379 Gregory wrote *On the Making of Man*, which purports to complete Basil's *Homilies on the Six Days of Creation* at a theoretical rather than a homiletical level. *On the Soul and the Resurrection* is a dialogue between Gregory and his sister and teacher, Macrina, who is on her death bed. Gregory must have written this work shortly after Macrina's death in 380. He wrote the *Catechetical Oration* as a set of instructions for catechists, probably in 385. It is neither easy nor necessary to distinguish Gregory's exegetical from his spiritual works. *On Virginity*, *On the Lord's Prayer*, and *On the Beatitudes* are probably early writings, while the *Life of Moses* and the *Homilies on Song of Songs* appear to be quite late. These works, as well as a number of smaller ones, can be regarded as Gregory's attempt to create a kind of ideology for monasticism, a monasticism regarded as no more than an attempt to live the Christian life in its fullest and most ideal fashion. The year of his death is probably 394.

Gregory had the advantage of outliving the worst of the controversies of his time. He has, therefore, left us writings that are more concerned to articulate his faith positively than to refute the errors of others. It has also seemed to me that Gregory may have been lucky to escape the kind of formal education that Basil and Nazianzen received. To be sure, he received an education; but he did not go to Constantinople or to Athens to find it. I suspect that he was in part self-taught and that he felt free to find his own way of expressing what he learned. Like the rest of the church fathers Gregory made no attempt to create a system of doctrine. Truth, for him, was elusive and could never be available in its fullness in this world. As a result, his ideas are designed to establish paths that lead toward truth, to describe facets of a truth that in its unity escapes our grasp. In what follows I want to describe three of these paths, all of which represent hopeful visions of human destiny beyond this world and yet also seek to show how our destiny can shape our lives in their present experience. The first path is his vision of a transfigured and divinized physical universe—the resurrection writ large. The second is his idea of *epectasy*, perpetual progress in the good. The third revolves around his idea of human nature as the communion of all people with one another. The three paths are contrary, if not contradictory of one another. I think he believes that they will not converge until the whole of creation arrives at its final end.

The New Creation: The Resurrection Writ Large

There can be little doubt that Gregory treats Christ's resurrection as central to the meaning of Christian faith, but he also understands it as the climax and the completion of the incarnation:[11]

> Christ, then, rose today, the God, the unsuffering, the undying . . . not having suffered by necessity nor compelled to come down from heaven nor experiencing the resurrection as an unexpected benefit beyond his hopes, but knowing the end of all things and in that knowledge making the beginning. With eyes of godhead he had knowledge of what lay ahead, and saw, before his descent from heaven, the uproar of nations, the stubbornness of Israel, Pilate seated before him, Caiaphas tearing his clothes apart, the rebellious mob seething, Judas betraying, Peter fighting for him, and himself soon after transfigured by the resurrection into the glory of incorruption.

The incarnation, then, is not simply Christ's birth, nor is it the impossible and timeless puzzle of a christological definition. Instead, it is the entire story that begins with the babe in Mary's womb and ends with the resurrection itself. Gregory can reflect on the details of Christ's death and resurrection. His death is the separation of his soul and body; but the divine Word remains united to both. This explains how Christ could both have descended into hell and taken the penitent thief to paradise. And there are solutions to the problem of enumerating three days between his death and his resurrection.

Gregory's emphasis, however, is on the idea that Christ, the firstborn from the dead, by his resurrection establishes the possibility of the general resurrection:[12]

> Now just as the principle of death had its origin in a single person and passed to the whole of human nature, similarly the principle of the resurrection originated in one Man and extends to all humanity. He who united again the soul he had assumed, with his own body, did so by means of his own power which was fused with each element at their first formation. In the same way he conjoined the intelligible and sensible nature on a larger scale, the principle of the resurrection extending to its logical limits. For when in the case of the man in

whom he was incarnate the soul returned once more to the body after
the dissolution, a similar union of the separated elements potentially
passed to the whole of human nature, as if a new beginning had been
made.

We can scarcely read this passage without thinking of Paul's comparison
of Christ with Adam in Romans 5 and 1 Corinthians 15. The logic is
that of the one and the many, or better, of the individual and universal
humanity. From this point of view the Christian hope, based on Christ's
death and resurrection, finds its reference in the general resurrection of
the dead that will take place at the end of this age.

Gregory must argue for this possibility. As we have seen, for the earliest Christians, who were Jews, the problem was why Christ should
have been raised ahead of time. But in the Gentile world the problem
was defending the idea of the resurrection itself. To be sure, there were
pagan ideas of an afterlife; but none of them went beyond an insistence
on the immortality of the soul. The strange idea that our physical bodies, which obviously disintegrated in corruption after death, could be
reassembled was one that flew in the face not only of cultural assumptions but also of common sense. Gregory, then, marshals the traditional
Christian arguments for the resurrection. God's goodness requires him
to save all that he created, including the body. Moreover, if God could
create bodies, it is far easier for him to recreate them. Jesus' raising of
Jairus' daughter, the widow of Nain's son, and Lazarus are signs of this
divine power. Gregory also uses arguments from nature. We are not surprised at the miracle of the creation of a child from a moist and shape-
less seed, so why should we be surprised at the resurrection? The
mystery of death and rebirth undergirds the potter's art, the growth of
seeds to wheat, the new life of trees in the spring, the waking of serpents
from their hibernation, the phases of human life, and our very sleeping
and waking.[13]

Of course, there are serious objections that Gregory must answer.
How are we to believe that people can be raised from the dead when
they have been reduced to ashes or have been eaten by wild beasts or
fish?[14] Moreover, how are we to understand the resurrection of those
who have died in extreme old age when "our bodies shrivel up and
change into something repulsive and hideous, with the flesh all wasted
in the length of years, the skin dried up about the bones till it is all in
wrinkles, the muscles in a spasmodic state from being no longer
enriched with their natural moisture, and the whole body consequently
shrunk, the hands on either side powerless to perform their natural
work, shaken with an involuntary trembling?"[15] What about those who
have died of consumption or leprosy, those who have been in some way

mutilated, or infants who have died at birth? Even apart from these cases we must recognize that human beings constantly change:[16]

> If, then, a particular man is not the same even as he was yesterday, but is made different by this transmutation, when so be that the Resurrection shall restore our body to life again, that single man will become a crowd of human beings, so that with his rising again there will be found the babe, the child, the boy, the youth, the man, the father, the old man, and all the intermediate persons that he once was.

Gregory does not attempt to give a full answer to all these questions, since the "true explanation . . . is still stored up in the hidden treasure-rooms of Wisdom, and will not come to the light until that moment when we shall be taught the mystery of the Resurrection by the reality of it."[17] Indeed, Gregory sometimes articulates a highly spiritual doctrine of the resurrection that differs from Origen's problematic view only by seeking to insist that the continuity between this body and the resurrection body must include a continuity of bodily elements.[18]

Nevertheless, he insists that the dissolution of our bodies in death is no impediment to the divine power that will raise them. The dispersal of our bodily parts is like that of a common herd of animals scattered but easily brought back together. Or it is like quicksilver that when poured out "forms small globules and scatters itself over the ground" but flows quickly back together if there is no hindrance.[19] God uses the soul to restore the body, since the soul is what gives life and order to the body. Those who deny the immortality of the soul are like "a man . . . imprisoned in a cabin, whose walls and roof obstruct the view outside [and who] remains without a glimpse of all the wonders of the sky."[20] The soul cannot be limited by the body it permeates, since "that which is intelligent and undimensional is not liable to the circumstances of space." Gregory modifies the usual understanding of death as the separation of soul and body by arguing that even after death the soul maintains its attachment to the body in its dissolution. It is as though death were a shipwreck with the "vessel . . . scattered in many directions." And just as the sailor "when his ship has been wrecked and gone to pieces, cannot float upon all the pieces at once," so the soul "if she finds it hard to be parted from the body altogether, [will] cling to some one of [its pieces]." Gregory seems to think of this as a kind of nucleus for the resurrection, and we can remember his idea that after Jesus' death the Word of God remains united to his separated body and soul.

Gregory does not regard any of his arguments as demonstrative proofs of the general resurrection. They are merely ways of showing that *faith* in the resurrection need by no means be considered senseless. And he recognizes that what primarily produces that faith is belief in the risen Lord:[21]

> For it behoved Him, when He had accustomed men to the miracle of the resurrection in other bodies, to confirm His word in His own humanity. Thou sawest the thing proclaimed working in others—those who were about to die, the child which had just ceased to live, the young man at the edge of the grave, the putrefying corpse, all alike restored by one command to life. Dost thou seek for those who have come to death by wounds and bloodshed? does any feebleness of life-giving power hinder the grace in them? Behold Him Whose hands were pierced with nails: behold Him Whose side was transfixed with a spear. . . . If He then has been raised, well may we utter the Apostle's exclamation, "How say some that there is no resurrection of the dead?"

The risen Lord, then, is the true guarantee of the general resurrection, which represents at least one dimension of human destiny. Moreover, the resurrection of Christ is not only a paradigm of human redemption. It also functions as the basis for understanding the destiny of the whole creation. Gregory can think of that larger redemption as "the reconstitution of our nature in its original form."[22] It is by no means easy to discern what Gregory means, but let me attempt one way of trying to make sense of what he says. Doing so involves interpreting chapter 16 of *On the Making of* Man, a chapter that in all likelihood defies interpretation.

In the letter to his brother Peter that introduces the treatise Gregory outlines his argument. It will examine "what we believe to have taken place beforehand and what we hope will ultimately come to pass." And it will also address "what is seen at the present time."[23] The contrast is one between the ideal portrait of humanity he draws in the first fifteen chapters and his recognition that the ideal does not exist in the present:[24]

> Moreover, the same characteristics are not to be seen in [human] nature as it came to be from the beginning and as it now exists. Consequently, what seems to be contradictory concerning humanity must be reconciled through some necessary logic [akolouthia] on the basis of the scriptural meaning and an understanding found through reasoning. In this way the entire account will have coherence in its definition and order, bringing the apparent contradictions to one and the same goal—provided the divine power finds a hope for what is beyond hope and a way for what is perplexing.

It is in chapter 16 that Gregory addresses the problem directly. He poses the question as follows:[25]

> How then is man, this mortal, passible, shortlived being, the image of that nature which is immortal, pure, and everlasting? The true answer

to this question, indeed, perhaps only the very Truth knows: but this is what we, tracing out the truth so far as we are capable by conjectures and inferences, apprehend concerning the matter.

Gregory goes on to say that scripture cannot lie when it says that humanity was created in the image of God, but that we cannot deny our own experience of humanity. We cannot say that "the pitiable suffering of man's nature [is] like to the blessedness of the impassible Life."

We must, he says, examine scripture more carefully. And he finds a contrast or even a contradiction between v. 26 and v. 27 of the first chapter of Genesis. God says, "Let us make humankind in our image, according to our likeness." But what he actually does is to create humankind male and female. "So God created humankind in his image, in the image of God he created them; male and female he created them." Verse 26 refers to the "creation" (*ktisis*) of the image of God; v. 27, to the "fashioning" (*kataskeuē*) of the image together with the male–female distinction.[26] Even though there are difficulties involved in my argument, I want to suggest that "male and female" in *On the Making of Man* 16.7-17 refers primarily to the body rather than to procreation.[27] From one point of view the fact that the image is incorporated indicates that humanity is *created* and thus *like* but not identical with God:[28]

> As the Gospel calls the stamp upon the coin "the image of Caesar" (Matt 22:20-21), whereby we learn that in that which was fashioned to resemble Caesar there was a resemblance as to outward look, but difference as to material, so also . . . when we consider the attributes contemplated both in the Divine and human nature, in which the likeness consists, . . . we find in what underlies them the difference which we behold in the uncreated and the created nature.

God's intention (Gen 1:26), then, must be actualized (Gen 1:27) by creating humanity in the divine image but with that image incorporated so as to be the governing principle of the body.

The body, then, is good and a necessary addition to the image of God.[29] Gregory, however, makes two other points in chapter 16. First, he argues that the words "male and female" used by scripture convey to us "a great and lofty doctrine":[30]

> While two natures—the Divine and incorporeal nature, and the irrational life of brutes—are separated from each other as extremes, human nature is the mean between them: for in the compound nature of man we may behold a part of each of the natures I have mentioned,—of the Divine, the rational and intelligent element, which

does not admit the distinction of male and female; of the irrational, our bodily form and structure, divided into male and female: for each of these elements is certainly to be found in all that partakes of human life.

By "divine" Gregory must mean "god-like," and the distinction he makes is precisely the sort of distinction Platonists would make between the intelligible and the sensible, the incorporeal and the bodily. Humanity, then, is amphibious. The human soul belongs in the intelligible realm, while the human body is clearly sensible. The psychosomatic union of the human person, then, bridges the gulf between these two orders of creation. I shall return to this theme after completing my discussion of chapter 16.

The second point Gregory makes is that when scripture says that God created and fashioned humanity, it uses the "indefinite" term to indicate "that in the Divine foreknowledge and power all humanity is included in the first fashioning (*kataskeuē*)." This means that God created "the entire plenitude of humanity."[31] Gregory defines this plenitude as "human nature" and can in some sense identify it with humanity in the age to come:[32]

> the man that was manifested at the first fashioning (*kataskeuē*) of the world, and he that shall be after the consummation of all are alike: they equally bear in themselves the Divine image.

As we have seen, in *On the Soul and the Resurrection* Gregory defines the resurrection as "the reconstitution of our nature in its original form."[33] The implication is that just as the final condition of human nature will include the body, so too the first fashioning of that nature included the body as well as the image of God.[34]

The likeness of the first fashioning of human nature to its final destiny, then, includes the idea of bodily creation and of the resurrection of the body. But there is one major difference between the beginning and the end. The nature God fashioned did not include individuation. Consequently, it was a sort of potentiality designed to find actualization in the production of a finite number of human beings.[35] This idea leads Gregory to a conclusion that will astonish the modern reader and that creates some real puzzles for anyone attempting to describe his thought. What he says is that if Adam had not fallen, human nature would have multiplied into the number of individuals fixed by God, but would have done so in an angelic fashion:[36]

> whatever the mode of increase in the angelic nature is (unspeakable and inconceivable by human conjectures, except that it assuredly

exists), it would have operated also in the case of men . . . to increase mankind to the measure determined by its Maker.

God, however, foresaw the fall of Adam and the consequent impossibility of this angelic form of multiplication. Therefore, he added the male–female distinction as a "contrivance for increase which befits those who had fallen into sin, implanting in mankind, instead of the angelic majesty of nature, that animal and irrational mode by which they now succeed one another."[37] Thus, human sexuality is a consequence of the fall. Moreover, Gregory's idea implies several extremely difficult questions. If, as I have argued, the male–female distinction refers to the body and to the positive function of the body to assist the soul in binding together the invisible and the visible creations, how can the same distinction, understood to have the restricted meaning of procreation, have what appears to be a negative assessment? If God created humanity with the male–female distinction as a remedy for the fall, how can we avoid the implication that he created humanity with the occasion for the fall, or as already fallen?

It seems to me unlikely that we can resolve these difficulties. At the same time, it does seem reasonably clear that Gregory thinks that the original fashioning of human nature included the body and that he can regard the body as a necessary instrument whereby the image of God can function to harmonize the entire creation. He often returns to this idea. In the *Catechetical Oration* he points out that "despite the strong opposition between the elements, a certain harmony of these contraries has been contrived by the wisdom which governs the universe." In a similar fashion "the bond of concord" we find in the sensible creation has a larger counterpart in the universe as a whole:[38]

> In the same way the divine wisdom also provides a blending and admixture of the sensible with the intelligible nature, so that all things equally partake in the good, and no existing thing is deprived of a share in the higher nature. . . . In that way, as the apostle says, "no part of creation is to be rejected," and no part fails to share in the divine fellowship.

The angels, of course, comprise the intelligible, invisible creation. They dwell in heaven, while humans dwell on earth. And yet the human soul is allied to the angelic creation. God's will is "to bring the whole creation into relationship with itself, so that neither the lower portion should be without part in the heavenly heights, nor heaven wholly without a share in the things pertaining to earth."[39]

At the same time, by the body humanity finds a bond with the sensible creation. Gregory correlates this idea with God's will and intention that humanity should "have dominion over the fish of the sea, and over the birds of the air, and over the cattle, and over all the wild animals of the earth, and over every creeping thing that creeps upon the earth" (Gen 1:26). He raises the question why God should have created humanity last of all. It would have been unsuitable "that the ruler should appear before the subjects of his rule." And so God prepares the whole of creation as "a royal lodging for the future king," like a good host preparing his house and the feast before introducing the guest of honor.[40] Humanity, then, orders and harmonizes the lower creation— beasts, plants, and even lifeless things. The peaceable kingdom is, as it were, writ large. The entire creation, visible and invisible, is brought into a perfect hierarchical harmony with humanity as the linchpin. Gregory's idea, of course, is not a novel one. Even Cicero could think of humanity's role in this way. And in a Christian context Irenaeus thought that Christ as the risen Lord headed up and united all things in himself, while Theodore of Mopsuestia treated Adam as the "pledge" but Christ as the "bond" of universal harmony.

It seems to me important to recognize that the dominion of humanity over the rest of creation finds expression in Genesis 1:26, which Gregory understands as God's eternal intention, a purpose that must be actualized in the intervals of time and space that define the created order. We can think of a process that will find its completion only in the age to come. It is with this in mind that we can examine Christ's place in the structure of Gregory's vision of a perfected physical creation. One peculiar feature of Gregory's discussions of Christ is that he can sometimes speak of his humanity in generic and corporate terms, but sometimes treats that humanity as individual and particular. For example, the eternal Word of God is the Good Shepherd who places the lost sheep of humanity on his shoulder. Or take another example:[41]

> Our whole nature had to be brought back from death. In consequence he stooped down to our dead body and stretched out a hand, as it were, to one who was prostrate. He approached so near death as to come in contact with it, and by means of his own body to grant our nature the principle of the resurrection, by raising our total humanity along with him by his power.

But the passage I have just cited goes on to speak of "the God-bearing man" as taken "from the lump of our humanity." We can make sense of the apparent contrast between Christ's corporate and individual humanity by distinguishing the result of a process from the process itself. The metaphor implied by Gregory's reference to "lump" supplies the key to this understanding. The man Jesus, united to God the Word, is like leaven introduced into the total lump of humanity. That leaven is still at work, but when the leavening is completed, the distinction between leaven and lump will vanish. To expand the metaphor, we might suggest that Gregory sees the whole story of creation and redemption on the analogy of making bread. What we call creation is the assembling of the ingredients, say, the flour and the milk. The incarnation is the introduction of the yeast into the mixture. The time after the incarnation and before the end of the world is when the dough is kneaded and leavened. The end of the world is like putting the loaf in the oven, and the age to come is like the baked bread.

The idea of Christ's individual humanity as a leaven introduced into the whole of human nature is one that Gregory repeats with some frequency. In Song of Songs the bride explains her beloved to her maidens, the daughters of Jerusalem. Gregory paraphrases her explanation by interpreting the parable of the Good Samaritan allegorically:[42]

> This is the one I am seeking. By rising from Judah to become our brother he became the neighbor of the man who fell among thieves. He healed his wounds with oil and wine and bandages. He placed him upon his own ass. He gave him rest at the inn. He furnished two denarii for his living and promised that when he returned he would pay whatever additional cost fulfilling his orders required.

The focus of the interpretation is on the identification of the Word of God with human nature. He "clothed himself with the whole of human nature through the first fruits of the lump of dough in which there was a portion of every race—Jew, Samaritan, Greek, and all humanity at once." This description of Christ's individual humanity as a first fruits including all races implies the universal scope of the incarnation.

Gregory's hope that salvation will be universal lies behind the way he interprets the common and popular understanding of Christ as the victor over Satan. Satan deceived Adam by a specious good which baited the "fishhook of evil." Like Aesop's dog, which dropped the real bone in its mouth to get its reflection in the stream, so Adam chose the false good of Satan's promise he would be like God and became, quite justly, Satan's prisoner. Christ gave Satan a dose of his own medicine by deceiving the deceiver:[43]

> By the principle of justice the deceiver reaps the harvest of the seeds he sowed with his own free will. For he who first deceived man by the bait of pleasure is himself deceived by the camouflage of human nature. For the one practiced deceit to ruin our nature; but the other, being at once just and good and wise, made use of a deceitful device to save the one who had been ruined. And by so doing he benefited, not only the one who had perished, but also the very one who had brought us to ruin.

Satan took the bait—the human Christ—and was caught on the fish-hook of the divinity. That is, Satan was willing to exchange all human-ity for the one glorious human being he saw in Christ. His defeat not only freed humanity but also had the possibility of saving him, since all divine punishments are remedial and educative. Thus, Christ "freed man from evil, and healed the very author of evil himself." Universal salva-tion extends even to Satan. At least this is Gregory's hope.

The universal salvation brought by the incarnate Word who died and rose again undid what was done in Adam. Gregory can think of sal-vation as a healing and purification of human nature, which had been marred by the fall. But he can also, as I have suggested, understand sal-vation as the completion of God's creative purpose. At one point in the *Catechetical Oration* Gregory speaks of the way in which God pervades the whole of the created order as what we should call its "ground of being." The cross makes the point clear:[44]

> In shape it is divided into four parts in such a way that the four arms converge in the middle. Now He who was extended upon it at the time God's plan was fulfilled in his death is the one who binds all things to himself and makes them one. Through himself he brings the diverse natures of existing things into one accord and harmony.

Gregory is saying, I suggest, that the cross, which represents Christ's death and resurrection and which is the climax of his incarnate life, brings to perfection and completion God's plan to bind all creation into total harmony. We find the same idea in Gregory's allegorical interpre-tation of the heavenly tabernacle Moses sees.[45] A tabernacle is some-thing that "encompasses" what is in it. Christ, then, encompasses the universe in two ways. As uncreated and divine he encompasses every-thing in himself. But when he pitched his tabernacle among us the divine power used the created Christ to encompass the world. "For the power which encompasses the universe, in which *lives the fullness of divinity*, the common protector of all, who encompasses everything within him-self, is rightly called 'tabernacle.'"[46]

In a number of ways, then, Gregory writes Christ's resurrection large and views it as the basis of one of his visions of human destiny. Christ's resurrection guarantees the general resurrection, which is uni-versal in scope. All human souls will be empowered so to govern their bodies that they will become incorruptible and glorious. It may even be that somehow the evil angels and Satan himself will be healed, though, of course, since they are spiritual, the resurrection does not apply to them. Moreover, the general resurrection will complete the process by which Christ's individual humanity leavens the whole lump of human nature. Christ's humanity will become corporate, and I shall later want to turn to the implications this idea has for another of Gregory's visions of human destiny. The point I wish to make here is that the humanity of the new creation will finally be empowered to fulfill God's purpose that humanity should have dominion over the created order. Gregory understands this to mean that humanity will have the task of binding together the angelic and intelligible creation with the sensible and visible creation of beasts, plants, and lifeless things. Salvation, then, is an idea that attaches not only to human beings, but also to the entire creation, visible and invisible. We might imagine this the way C. S. Lewis imagines the destiny of Narnia at the end of his stories—where the "real" Narnia finally appears with all its beauty and order. Finally, since human nature is united with the divine Word of God, it will be enabled to divinize as well as harmonize creation. The new creation will be transfigured, totally permeated with God's power and love.

Of course, this vision is beyond imagining; nor can we know how the new creation will be perfected. The vision springs from faith and not from sight, and the only thing Gregory wants us to be sure of is that the divinization of the physical creation will surpass anything we might guess or imagine. At the same time, he is convinced that the new creation is already in the womb of the old one. The process leading to the destiny of all creation is already at work, and we can at least catch glimpses of it. The same almost romantic sensibility we saw in Basil's description of his hermitage finds expression in Gregory's writings. He wrote a letter to his friend Adelphius, who had allowed him to stay at his country estate in Vanota. His praise of Adelphius's home is a kind of thanks, but it also betrays his ability to discern the dawn of the new creation in the old one:[47]

> The river Halys gleams like a ribbon of gold through a deep purple robe, and scarlet sand is washed down from the bank to touch the river with redness. High up lie the oak-crowned ridges of the hills, all green, and worthy of some Homer to sing their praises; and as the oaks wander down the slopes they meet the saplings planted by men. All over the foothills are vines, some green, others ripe with grape clusters. Here at Vanota the fruit is ripe, but it is otherwise in the nearby villages. . . . Homer never saw the apple trees with such gleaming fruit as we have here, the apples themselves almost the color of appleblossom, so white and shining. Have you ever seen pears as white as newly polished ivory? And what shall we say of the immense heap of peaches? And what of the pathways beneath the climbing vines, and the sweet shade under the cluster of grapes, and the new wall where the roses climb and the vines trail and twist and form a

kind of protecting fortress against invaders, and what about the pond which lies at the very top of the pathway and the fish that are bred there?

Gregory's description includes the buildings on the estate—a chapel for the martyrs under construction and the house itself with its gardens. And he tells how one of the youths on the estate entered the fish pool and brought up fish as he pleased. The "fish seemed no strangers to the fisherman's touch, being tame and submissive under the artist's hands, like well-trained dogs." Eating the fish would, of course, spoil the effect; but we seem almost to be in the peaceable kingdom or in Eden.

It is his appreciation of the beauty and order of his own world that informs Gregory's description of the ideal creation held in God's bounteous intention and, as it were, fresh from his hands:[48]

> Now all things were already arrived at their own end: "the heaven and the earth," as Moses says, "were finished," and all things that lie between them, and the particular things were adorned with their appropriate beauty; the heaven with the rays of the stars, the sea and air with living creatures that swim and fly, and the earth with all varieties of plants and animals, to all which, empowered by the Divine will, it gave birth together; the earth was full, too, of her produce, bringing forth fruits at the same time with flowers; the meadows were full of all that grows therein, and all the mountain ridges, and summits, and every hillside, and slope, and hollow, were crowned with young grass, and with the varied produce of the trees . . . and all the beasts that had come into life at God's command were rejoicing . . . and skipping about . . . while every sheltered and shady spot was ringing with the chants of the song-birds. And at sea . . . the sight to be seen was of the like kind, as it had just settled to quiet and calm in the gathering together of its depths, where havens and harbours spontaneously hollowed out on the coasts made the sea reconciled with the land; and the gentle motion of the waves vied in beauty with the meadows, rippling delicately with light and harmless breezes that skimmed the surface. . . .

I shall not apologize for these lengthy citations, since they convey better than I can the way in which Gregory's hope for the new creation is bound together with his appreciation of the old one. The leaven of creation's destiny is already at work.

Gregory also sees the physical beauty of human beings. In one passage of *On Virginity* he makes the somewhat repugnant argument that marriage has no value because of the difficulties and accidents that inevitably beset it. If the paths of glory lead but to the grave, so too the beauty of the bride will "melt away and become as nothing, turned after all this show into noisome and unsightly bones, which wear no trace, no memorial, no remnant of that living bloom." But the argument is a stock one, and Gregory sees the beauty all too well to dismiss it easily:[49]

> Whenever the husband looks at the beloved face, that moment the fear of separation accompanies the look. If he listens to the sweet voice, the thought comes into his mind that some day he will not hear it. Whenever he is glad with gazing on her beauty, then he shudders most with the presentiment of mourning her loss. When he marks all those charms which to youth are so precious and which the thought-less seek for, the bright eyes beneath the lids, the arching eyebrows, the cheek with its sweet and dimpling smile, the natural red that blooms upon the lips, the gold-bound hair shining in many-twisted masses on the head, and all that transient grace, then, though he may be little given to reflection, he must have this thought also in his inmost soul, that some day all this beauty will melt away....

The force of this passage depends on the stark contrast between the bride's beauty and the inevitability of her death. But what if we take death away? The beauty then becomes a sign of what will be in the new creation. Gregory's vision is really, I think, a kind of this-worldly portrait of the next world. What he finds of beauty and order here and now he posits of what will be then and there. At the same time, it probably works in both directions. Gregory's ultimate optimism about the there and then is what gives him the possibility of being optimistic about much of his present world. Once more we find a dialectic between hope and present experience. And it is this conjunction that enables Gregory to believe that the new creation is in embryo in his own world. To be sure, there is much that is savage and destructive both in nature and in human life. But this is not what will have the last word.

The New Creation: Perpetual Progress in the Good

In discussing Gregory's vision of the physical dimension of salvation I have started with his hope and moved toward the way he sees that hope foreshadowed in his present experience. Turning to his ideas about the spiritual dimension of salvation and his reworking of the Christian Platonist conviction that the soul is destined to ascend to God, I want to begin with his understanding of the Christian life here and now. The *Life of Moses* is Gregory's advice "concerning the perfect life," and he compares himself to a spectator of a chariot race, cheering the contestants on and urging them to greater speed. Gregory is writing to a young man as what we should now call a spiritual director:[50]

> For if we who have been appointed to the position of fathers over so many souls consider it proper here in our old age to accept a com-

mission from youth, how much more suitable is it, inasmuch as we have taught you, a young man, to obey voluntarily, that the right action of ready obedience be confirmed in you.

Gregory cites the Lord's command to "be perfect, just as your heavenly father is perfect"; but he understands that command in the light of the apostle Paul's injunction to perfection in Philippians 3, where he urges his readers to "strain forward toward those things that are still to come." He concludes that "the perfection of human nature consists perhaps in its very growth in goodness."[51]

Gregory also points out that scripture supplies us with many models of the perfect life, and different models suit different people. One important difference is the distinction between the sexes:[52]

> Human nature is divided into male and female, and the free choice of virtue or of evil is set before both equally. For this reason the corresponding example of virtue for each sex has been exemplified by the divine voice, so that each, by observing the one to which he is akin (the men to Abraham and the women to Sarah), may be directed in the life of virtue by appropriate examples.

Gregory means that the Christian life is, in principle, the same for men and women, and indeed for all people; but the particular conditions of that life may well differ from person to person. Thus, there is room for a distinctive female piety; but the distinction is not one that abolishes the basic ideals involved. Furthermore, Gregory's choice of Moses as the example is to some degree arbitrary. He does, however, have at his disposal Philo's lives of Moses; and they provide him with a partial basis for his discussion. He begins with the narrative (*historia*) of Moses' life as we find it in scripture and in midrashic elaborations found in the tradition; he then turns to his spiritual reading (*theoria*) of that story.

The ghost of Origen's construal of the Christian life informs Gregory's advice. That is, Gregory does not explicitly employ Origen's description of the stages of that life; but I am convinced that he has them in mind, however much he refuses to apply them in a systematic way. Origen's ideas, which remind us of Clement of Alexandria's view, are to be found in the prologue to his commentary on Song of Songs. There he points out that Solomon wrote three books—Proverbs, Ecclesiastes, and Song of Songs. These three books correspond to three of the traditional divisions of Greek philosophy—ethics, physics, and "enoptics." With this in mind he argues for three stages in the Christian life. The first is moral in character and involves the repudiation of vice and the acquisition of virtue. Solomon's Proverbs supply a basis for this stage. Ecclesiastes represents the second stage. Here Solomon surveys the entire creation and pronounces his verdict, "Vanity of vanities, all is vanity."

This means, first, that all creation is contingent on God and could not exist without participating somehow in God's power and providence. But the idea also seems to be that God's presence permeates the whole of the created order. Thus, at this stage we can discern that presence in all our world. This is why a Christian Platonist spirituality sometimes appears to be almost pantheistic, though the coined word "panentheistic" seems a better way of putting the point. Finally, Solomon's third book has as its theme "My beloved is mine, and I am his." The union of the believer with God through his Word is Origen's point. These three stages, of course, become a fixture in the history of Christian spirituality. In the Latin medieval period they appear as the purgative, illuminative, and unitive stages.

One basis for my conviction that Gregory has this schema in mind is a brief description he gives of the image of God in *On the Making of Man*.[53] He employs the metaphor of an artist painting a portrait of himself:

> so I would have you understand that our Maker also, painting the portrait to resemble His own beauty, by the addition of virtues, as it were with colours, shows in us His own sovereignty: and manifold and varied are the tints, so to say, by which His true form is portrayed: not red, or white, or the blending of these, whatever it may be called, nor a touch of black that paints the eyebrow and the eye, . . . but instead of these, purity, freedom from passion, blessedness, alienation from all evil, and all those attributes of the like kind which help to form in men the likeness of God: with such hues as these did the Maker of His own image mark our nature.

Here "virtue" must refer to the moral virtues, even though Gregory can certainly use the term, which means "excellence," to describe more broadly the spiritual life. The colors, then, represent the moral virtues associated with the first stage of the Christian life. Gregory goes on to speak of the Godhead as "mind and word." And so "you see in yourself word and understanding, an imitation of the very Mind and Word." Here he thinks of the second or illuminative stage, which is an intellectual contemplation of the created order. Finally, God is love; and his image must include love, since "love is of God."[54] Thus, God created humanity—or more properly the human soul—with the moral virtues, with the understanding, and with love. We can think of these three as natural potentialities that must be actualized by the Christian life.[55]

In the *Life of Moses* Gregory allegorizes Moses' early career as the development of the moral stage of the Christian life. His birth is a birth to virtue; his education is a training in pagan philosophy, useful at this level. And his retirement to the desert prepares him for the second stage and his vision of the burning bush. Nevertheless, Gregory's emphasis is on the moral progress of the people. The crossing of the Red Sea represents the break with evil and vice effected by baptism; "after we have drowned the whole Egyptian person (that is every form of evil) in the saving baptism we emerge alone, dragging nothing foreign in our subsequent life."[56] If someone has crossed the Red Sea of baptism and discovers that Pharaoh and his host—the passions—are still pursuing him, then he has not rightly received the grace of baptism.[57] The break with the old life, however, is not easy; we tend to long for the fleshpots of Egypt and a return to the old slavery. Thus, no sooner have the people crossed the Red Sea than they come to the bitter waters of Marah. The new life seems at first "difficult and disagreeable":[58]

> But if the wood be thrown into the water, that is, if one receives the mystery of the resurrection which had its beginning with the wood (you of course understand the "cross" when you hear "wood"), then the virtuous life, being sweetened by the hope of things to come, becomes sweeter and more pleasant than all the sweetness that tickles the senses with pleasure.

The moral life begins with the repudiation of vice, but it finds completion in the acquisition of virtue. The twelve springs and seventy palms at Elim represent the teaching of the Twelve and the Seventy, and the camps in the wilderness that follow stand for the virtues. The moral stage, then, makes the people "capable of receiving God."[59]

The second stage, represented by Ecclesiastes, is one of the allegorical meanings Gregory gives to Moses' vision of the burning bush:[60]

> It seems to me that at the time the great Moses was introduced in the theophany he came to know that none of those things which are apprehended by sense perception and contemplated by the understanding really subsists, but that the transcendent essence and cause of the universe, on which everything depends, alone subsists.

The burning bush also stands for the incarnation and for "the mystery of the Virgin." It might not be going too far to suggest that it is the incarnation that enables us to understand God's presence in the world he made. Later in the treatise Gregory allegorizes the trumpet that sounds as Moses ascends Mount Sinai to receive the Law as a teacher. "For the wonderful harmony of the heavens proclaims the wisdom which shines forth in the creation and sets forth the great glory of God through the things which are seen."[61]

Gregory contrasts the revelation given Moses in the burning bush with that he receives when he enters the "dark cloud where God was":[62]

What is now recounted seems somehow to be contradictory to the first theophany, for then the Divine was beheld in light but now he is seen in darkness. Let us not think that this is at variance with the sequence of things we have contemplated spiritually. Scripture teaches by this that religious knowledge comes at first to those who receive it as light. Therefore what is perceived to be contrary to religion is darkness, and the escape from darkness comes about when one participates in light. But as the mind progresses and, through an ever greater and more perfect diligence, comes to apprehend reality, as it approaches more nearly to contemplation, it sees more clearly what of the divine nature is uncontemplated.

Gregory means that it is one thing to perceive God's presence in creation but quite another thing to see God himself. Indeed, as John teaches in the first chapter of his Gospel, "No one has ever seen God." And so the "darkness" stands for "the seeing that consists in not seeing." Moses enters the darkness which is God's "hiding place," and so enters "the inner sanctuary of divine knowledge." This, in turn, enables him to enter the tabernacle not made with hands.

Moses' entrance into the dark cloud (Exod 20:21) seems very like his ascent of Mount Sinai (Exod 19:16ff.) and his vision of God's back parts while standing on the rock (Exod 33:17ff.). The scriptural narrative, of course, distinguishes these episodes from one another. And it is certainly possible that Gregory wishes to distinguish their spiritual meaning.[63] In that case we should have a series of stages that press beyond the burning bush and the revelation in light. While I can certainly see that Gregory resists any easy systematization and does not apply Origen's schema in such a fashion, I prefer to think of his allegorization of the three episodes as differing dimensions of the third or unitive stage. Perhaps that stage is sufficiently beyond our present capacities that it can only be characterized by a series of disparate guesses. At any rate, it is certainly the case that one passage in the narrative can have many spiritual meanings, while a single spiritual meaning can find expression in a number of different narratives. The relation of the two levels of meaning is highly complex:[64]

> If, while trying to parallel completely the historical [narrative] account to the sequence of such intellectual contemplation, someone should somehow discover something in the account which does not coincide with our understanding, he should not reject the whole enterprise. He should always keep in mind our discussion's goal, to which we are looking while we relate these details.

Consequently, I prefer to see the three allegories as indicating different dimensions of the third stage in which the believer passes beyond the discernment of God's presence in creation to a mystical union with God.

Gregory understands Moses' ascent of Sinai as his climbing the mountain of divine knowledge. Moses' "way to such knowledge is purity":[65]

> This means that the one person who would approach the contemplation of Being must be pure in all things so as to be pure in soul and body, washed stainless of every spot in both parts, in order that he might appear pure to the One who sees what is hidden and that visible respectability might correspond to the inward condition of the soul.

The moral stage, then, is the purification that must prepare the Christian for the contemplation of God that is the end of the journey. The fact that no irrational animals were allowed on the mountain means "that in the contemplation of the intelligibles we surpass the knowledge which originates with the senses."[66] This kind of knowledge "is a mountain steep indeed and difficult to climb." Indeed, Gregory would be happy with the idea that the only true knowledge of God is to know that he is incomprehensible. This conviction finds roots in the Christian Platonist tradition in which Gregory belongs, but it is intensified by the Cappadocians' controversy with the Eunomians, the neo-Arians who believed that God could in fact be known. It seems important to me to recognize that the people who first clarified the Christian doctrine of the Trinity were committed to the doctrine that God is incomprehensible.

The third story that Gregory uses to explain what we can call the unitive stage is the one in which Moses sees God's back parts. In Gregory's text of the Old Testament God says that there is "a place with himself" where there is "a rock with a hole in it." Moses enters the rock, and when God summons him, he sees God's back. The story signifies the ascent of the soul to God:[67]

> If nothing comes from above to hinder its upward thrust (for the nature of the Good attracts to itself those who look to it), the soul rises ever higher and will always make its flight yet higher—by its desire of the heavenly things straining ahead for what is still to come, as the Apostle says. Made to desire and not to abandon the transcendent height by the things already attained, it makes its way upward without ceasing, ever through its prior accomplishments renewing its intensity for the flight. Activity directed toward virtue causes its capacity to grow through exertion; this kind of activity alone does not slacken its intensity by the effort, but increases it.

The highest knowledge of God, then, becomes a desire and a love that moves toward the Good without ceasing. The "straining ahead" of Philippians 3 is an endless ascent. God is infinite, and so movement toward him is a kind of counting to infinity. It can have no term. Moreover, the soul's desire constantly expands. Presumably, God satisfies that desire, but in doing so creates a larger one. We are in the presence of a redeemed becoming.

Part of Gregory's idea stems from his reading of Plato's *Symposium,* in which Diotima instructs Socrates in the mysteries of love. The lover ascends from the love of a beautiful body to the love of the soul and, finally, to a vision of Beauty itself:[68]

> And the bold request which goes up the mountains of desire asks this: to enjoy the Beauty not in mirrors and reflections, but face to face. The divine voice granted what was requested in what was denied, showing in a few words an immeasurable depth of thought. The munificence of God assented to the fulfillment of his desire, but did not promise any cessation or satiety of the desire.

Gregory reinterprets what Paul says concerning the "face-to-face" vision of God in 1 Corinthians 13:12. "This truly is the vision of God: never to be satisfied in the desire to see him."[69] The experience is the opposite of the one people have when they try to climb uphill in sand. They move and toil but make no progress. But Moses *stands* on the rock and makes perpetual progress toward the Beloved. The vision of God, then, is an endless following in which the Christian constantly keeps the back of God in view.

"Epectasy," then, is perpetual progress in the knowledge and love of God. Gregory roots his idea in his understanding both of God and of the human soul. With respect to God:[70]

> we believe that the divine nature is unlimited and incomprehensible, and hence we do not conceive of its being comprehended. But we declare that the nature is in every way to be thought of as infinite. What is altogether infinite is not limited in one respect and not in another, but infinity entirely transcends limitation.

Understanding God this way means that the names we use for him are at best analogical. God transcends the intervals of time and space within which we exist. He is Being, while all created things are constantly becoming. Since God is infinite, no finite being can ever exhaust his being.

When Gregory turns his attention to the soul, he must take seriously the strong distinction he makes between the creator and his creatures. Such a distinction, of course, was unnecessary in Greek philosophy for which the rational soul is identical in nature with the gods, simply appearing at a different level in the hierarchy of being. But scripture and the Christian tradition insist that the human soul is created and merely *like* God. These considerations prompt Gregory to make an important change in the Greek idea of the soul. To be sure, we cannot speak of a single understanding of the soul. Even within the Platonic dialogues there are somewhat differing views. But, on the whole, the philosophers thought of the soul as a constant and unchanging principle that gave life and movement to the body and as something that could ultimately find its destiny by returning to its divine place of origin. The conditions under which the soul existed might change, but the soul itself did not. Indeed, in much of later Platonism the ascent of the soul to the divine represented a stripping away of its bodily experience. Gregory, however, defines the soul as a nature that grows and develops, just as the body does.

Even though, as we shall see, Gregory will ultimately think the soul capable of breaking all ties with the body, his view of the soul as growing organically finds it basis in his insistence on the close union of soul and body and his understanding of the human person as a psychosomatic unity. He points out "that we must think that the point of commencement of existence is one and the same for body and soul."[71] The soul neither preexists the body, as Origen supposed, nor is it newly created by God and implanted in the body formed from our parents, as Methodius said. Rather, body and soul are together passed down from our parents. Gregory employs the analogies of saplings that grow into trees and seeds that grow into wheat:[72]

> As, then, in the case of those growing seeds the advance to perfection
> is a graduated one, so in man's formation the forces of his soul show
> themselves in proportion to the size to which his body has attained.

Gregory reapplies Aristotle's distinctions of the vegetative, sentient, and rational souls to his idea. For Aristotle the soul can be the life force or animating principle. In this sense plants and animals have "souls." But human beings have a rational soul. Gregory treats the vegetative and sentient souls as stages in the soul's growth toward rationality. It is simply the next logical step to think of the soul's growth as a perpetual becoming.

One implication of this idea is Gregory's conviction that all will be saved. We need, however, to add another teaching to make the point. For Gregory good is without limit, whereas evil is the privation of good:[73]

> Now change is a perpetual movement toward a different state. And it
> takes two forms. In the one case it is always directed toward the good;
> and here its progress is continual, since there is no conceivable limit
> to the distance it can go. In the other case it is directed toward the
> opposite, the essence of which lies in non-existence.

Gregory does not mean that evil does not exist; he simply wants to say that it has no *independent* existence, since it is always a deprivation or a depravation of the good. Moreover, since the soul is always moving and since there is a limit to evil, bounded as it is by good, in the long run all souls will move toward good. Gregory uses the analogy of an eclipse to make the point. The conical shadow cast by the eclipse stands for evil. Even if we enter that shadow, sooner or later our movement will take us back to the light. He concludes "that on passing the limit of wickedness we shall again have our conversation in light, as the nature of the good, when compared with the measure of wickedness, is incalculably super-abundant."[74] Evil, then, is nonexistent not only because it has no *independent* existence, but also because it will have no *final* existence.

Up to this point in the argument, I have treated epectasy as the third and final stage in Gregory's construal of the Christian life. It is now time to make several qualifications and additions. The first qualification has to do with the idea of "stages." It might be better to argue that Gregory, at least if we confine our attention to the Christian life in this age, treats the three stages as no more than three dimensions. Like Origen before him he treats the contemplative life and the active life of virtue in a dialectical relationship with one another:[75]

> Religious virtue is divided into two parts, into that which pertains to the Divine and that which pertains to right conduct (for purity of life is a part of religion). Moses learns at first the things which must be known about God (namely, that none of those things known by human comprehension is to be ascribed to him). Then he is taught the other side of virtue, learning by what pursuits the virtuous life is perfected.

Gregory writes this in the context of his discussion of Moses' entrance into the dark cloud. And yet he treats Moses' knowledge of God as prior to his knowledge of what "pertains to right conduct." Let me suggest that we can solve the puzzle thus created by appealing to the broader structure of the *Life of Moses*. Moses' active life of virtue and his vision of God's presence in the burning bush are what prepare him for the epectatic contemplation of God. But his vision of God enables his active life of virtue. In the treatise Moses, after climbing the mountain of divine knowledge, after entering the dark cloud, and after seeing God's back, returns to the people to guide them to the Promised Land.[76] And Gregory says that this is the aim of the spiritual life, to be the servant of God. We are to understand that the active life is a preliminary purification enabling the contemplative life, but that it is equally clear that the contemplative life is a vision that enables virtue. The better we have our life in order, the better we can pray; but the better we pray, the better we can put our life in order.

Gregory gives what amounts to a philosophical explanation of the way in which the contemplative life plays itself out in the active life of moral virtue in *On the Making of Man*:[77]

> we therefore say that the mind, as being in the image of the most beautiful, itself also remains in beauty and goodness so long as it partakes as far as is possible in its likeness to the archetype; but if it were at all to depart from this it is deprived of that beauty in which it was. And as we said that the mind was adorned by the likeness of the archetypal beauty, being formed as though it were a mirror to receive the figure of that which it expresses, we consider that the nature which is governed by it is attached to the mind in the same relation, and that it too is adorned by the beauty that the mind gives, being, so to say, a mirror of the mirror; and that by it is swayed and sustained the material element of that existence in which the nature is contemplated.

It is the task of the mind or soul to govern the body and the bodily passions. The passions can rebel against the mind, just as slaves can revolt against their master. But these passions or emotions "lie in the power of their possessors for good or ill, to be either virtue or vice."[78] Rightly ordered the passions are love and courage; wrongly ordered, lust and anger. The mind, however, cannot fulfill its task without assistance. Thus, to the degree that the mind mirrors God, to that degree it is empowered to govern the body and the bodily passions. Vision and virtue are in a dialectic that cannot be broken, at least in this life.

The vision is in one sense a human attainment, but it is more properly a divine gift. We can, therefore, argue that the notion of the mind's being empowered by its relation to God introduces the problem of Gregory's account of the relation between divine grace and human free choice. In the *Life of Moses* he worries with the scriptural passages that speak of God hardening Pharaoh's heart. He begins by insisting:[79]

> People live differently—some live uprightly in virtue while others slide into vice. One would not reasonably attribute these differences in their lives to some divine constraint which lies outside themselves. It lies within each person's power to make this choice.

Pharaoh cannot blame God for his hardened heart. That would be like someone blaming the sun for making him fall into a ditch. The hardened heart is God's punishment of Pharaoh, a punishment that Pharaoh brought on himself. Similarly, the plagues suffered by the Egyptians are a punishment caused by their wickedness. "[E]ach man makes his own plagues when through his own free will he inclines toward these painful experiences."[80] Gregory, following Philo, bases his point on his under-standing that the Hebrews and the Egyptians are living in the same places and that the Hebrews are unaffected by the plagues. Pharaoh, then, really hardens his own heart by his choice of evil, a choice that rep-resents the misuse of God's providence. God's providence is there before Pharaoh makes his choices, however much those choices determine the *effects* of providence.

Gregory understands God's providence to be a general and univer-sal activity, and one that has differing effects depending on how it is received. Rightly received, providence assists and benefits us. Wrongly received, it has a punitive effect—one that we bring on ourselves. It is as though when we rightly use someone's love of us, that love helps us; but when we misuse that love, we bring upon ourselves misfortune. Gregory takes one further step. God's punishments are always remedial and educative; they are meant to enable us to learn by our mistakes. For this reason "someone, taking his departure from the fact that after three days of distress in darkness the Egyptians did share in the light, might be led to perceive the final restoration which is expected to take place later in the kingdom of heaven of those who have suffered condemna-tion in Gehenna."[81] Elsewhere Gregory will say that punishments after this life will purify those who have failed to live rightly in this world. There will be a sort of purgatory before the final end. One problem with Gregory's view is that it includes the theme that later characterized Pelagius's heresy, namely that if we take the first steps in turning toward God, he will come to our assistance. A synergistic view of grace appears to result; God cooperates with our efforts.

Gregory interprets Moses' meeting with Aaron this way. Aaron stands for Moses' guardian angel, who comes to his assistance because he has made progress in virtue:[82]

> For truly the assistance which God gives to our nature is provided to those who correctly live the life of virtue. This assistance was already there at our birth, but it is manifested and made known whenever we apply ourselves to diligent training in the higher life and strip our-selves for the more vigorous contests.

The second sentence in this passage is decisive. Little or no distinction obtains between grace and nature. Our nature is a grace that God gives us, and our lives are always lived in the context of God's providential love. Our capacity for virtue is itself gracious, and God constantly nur-tures that capacity by his love. God's providence and our capacity for free choice need not conflict for the simple reason that they are forces operating at different levels simultaneously. Moreover, we cannot think of God's providence as coercive both because love cannot compel but

only persuade and because God's love determined that we should have
the freedom to choose virtue. To be sure, Gregory's view of grace is quite
different from Augustine's insistence on the sovereignty of grace. But he
would certainly resist any attempt to characterize his view as one that
put the possibility of salvation in our own hands. Our choices matter
and make a difference. But just as the lover's choices, while free, by no
means exclude the more mysterious and gratuitous aspects of the love
relationship, so the choices we make encounter the mysterious way God
uses them for our benefit and the benefit of all.

Another qualification or addition I must make has to do with the
degree to which the Christian life as Gregory describes it may be related
to the age to come as well as to life here and now. If we regard the moral
virtues, the discernment of God's presence in the created order, and the
epectatic union with God as different dimensions of the spiritual life,
then we might argue that these dimensions will be fully actualized only
in the age to come but are ideals that find at least partial expression here
and now. Looked at this way, the ideal would appear to make little distinction between this world and the next. Our partial participation in
our destiny here and now will simply be amplified and made complete
in the there and then. Up to a point I do not think such a view would be
far from the mark. Nevertheless, at least in terms of his understanding
of the mystical union with God in epectasy Gregory does in fact make a
distinction between what is possible now and what will be hereafter.[83]
However much he insists on the continuities between our present experience and our destiny, Gregory balances this insistence with a recognition of a basic discontinuity which treats epectasy as the final goal rather
than merely a dimension of the Christian life.

In *On the Soul and the Resurrection* Gregory and his teacher, Macrina, worry with the problem of the passions or emotions. Initially, Macrina argues that the soul's destiny must involve the abolition of the
passions. The passions, says Macrina, are on the "borderland" between
the soul and the body. They are "accretions from without, because in the
Beauty which is man's prototype no such characteristics are to be
found." In this way "the peculiar conditions of the brute creation are
blended with the intellectual part of the soul."[84] These considerations
explain what Macrina has already said. The passions are not properly
part of the soul but are "like warts growing out of the soul's thinking
part, which are reckoned as parts of it because they adhere to it, and yet
are not that actual thing which the soul is in its essence." And there are
examples of people who have removed these warts by stripping themselves of the passions.[85] Nevertheless, Macrina yields to Gregory's view
that the passions need not be simply identified with vice, but can be

thought to be emotions which, when rightly ordered, are virtuous. She does so on the understanding that so long as the soul remains embodied, it requires sensations and emotions that ally it to the brute creation. In this life, then, the issue is the moderation and governance of the passions, making them virtues rather than vices.

The discussion reaches a further stage with Macrina's interpretation of the parable of Lazarus and Dives. Lazarus's soul fixes itself firmly on his present blessings, while Dives remains cemented to the goods of this life. The moral of the parable is[86]

> that those still living in the flesh must as much as ever they can separate and free themselves in a way from its attachments by virtuous conduct, in order that after death they may not need a second death to cleanse them from the remnants that are owing to this cement of the flesh, and, when once the bonds are loosed from around the soul, her soaring up to the Good may be swift and unimpeded, with no anguish of the body to distract her.

The soul's destiny, then, is to be altogether freed from the body. This view, of course, flatly contradicts the doctrine of the resurrection and Gregory's physical notion of salvation. But it is one that Gregory accepts at this point in the dialogue. He does, however, notice a contradiction in Macrina's argument. On the one hand, she is arguing that the soul's destiny takes it beyond this bodily life when the passions are to be moderated to a life outside the body, which would presumably mean a life without the passions. On the other hand, the discussion has focused on "desire" as that movement of the soul which assists it in its ascent toward God. "[T]hrough desire above all we are brought nearer God, drawn up, by its chain as it were, from earth towards Him."[87]

The solution of this dilemma revolves around the idea that in the age to come desire will be transformed into love:[88]

> Whenever the soul, then, having divested itself of the multifarious emotions incident to its nature, gets its Divine form and, mounting above Desire, enters within that towards which it was once incited by that Desire, it offers no harbour within itself for hope or for memory. . . . [A]nd thus the soul copies the life that is above, and is conformed to the peculiar features of the Divine nature; none of its habits are left to it except that of love, which clings by natural affinity to the Beautiful.

This is the love that "never fails," and it is the principle of epectasy. Love remains constantly active since there is no limit to Beauty and the Good. We are obliged to conclude that epectasy in its proper sense is relegated to the age to come, and we must remain puzzled at the contradiction between this totally spiritual articulation of salvation and Gregory's equal insistence on the physical character of the resurrection writ large.

Gregory does not, however, wish to exclude epectasy entirely from our present experience. At least I wish to suggest that this is the case. If we can think of epectasy as our enjoyment of God found in our imperfect knowledge of the Good and our imperfect love of Beauty, then Gregory is unwilling to deny the possibility of our anticipating the perpetual progress of the age to come:[89]

> When the soul's gaze penetrates the marvelous world of appearances, it reasons to the one known through his works and understands that he exists. Something similar will happen in the age to come when everything seen will pass away according to the Lord's utterance, saying that "heaven and earth will pass away" (Matt 24:35), and when we shall pass over to that life which is above sight, hearing, and understanding. Then we shall no longer know the nature of the Good in part through his works as we do now (1 Cor 13:12), nor will that which is transcendent be known through the working of what appears, but in a completely different way the form of ineffable blessedness will be grasped, and there will be a different manner of enjoyment.

We might read this passage as though our "enjoyment" of God in this life is confined to discerning his presence in creation, placing the second "stage" in this life and the third "stage" in the life to come. But I am not sure that this is what Gregory wishes to say. In another of his *Homilies on Song of Songs* he says that "the soul, when it looks towards God and renews that good longing for the incorruptible beauty, always has a new desire for what transcends it, never blunting the longing by satiety." He then goes on to say that when the bride is "beaten" (Song of Songs 5:7), this can mean her death but really refers to the immortality that lies beyond death. "Thus, the mantle of her despair was taken away and she saw the invisible and unbounded beauty of the beloved, always found better in every eternity of the ages. She stretches herself forward in more zealous longing and tells her beloved through the daughters of Jerusalem her heart's condition."[90] Gregory locates contemplation and the enjoyment of God on both sides of the divide and watershed of death, but he also argues for a qualitative as well as a quantitative transformation by the passage from this life to the next.

There is one final consideration I wish to add. In discussing epectasy I have said virtually nothing about the role of Christ. The mystical union with God that must be understood as perpetual progress in the good often seems to one side of Gregory's Christology. I do think it possible, however, to argue that Christ plays a double role in Gregory's doctrine of epectasy. In the first place, *The Life of Moses* allegorizes the trumpets that prepare Moses for his ascent of Mount Sinai as sounding "the divine mystery of the incarnation."[91] More clearly, Christ is the rock on which Moses must stand in order to see God's back parts.[92] Gregory at least implies that it is Christ who gives the possibility of the highest stages of the Christian life and their consummation in the age to come. He suggests a second role for Christ in passages where he apparently sees Christ as the object and goal of epectasy. The "crown of righteousness" that Paul mentions in 2 Timothy 4:7 is the "prize" of the Christian life; and even though the word Gregory uses differs from the word for prize in Philippians 3:14, it is difficult to avoid hearing an echo. The prize has many designations in scripture, including the "prize of calling" in the passage from Philippians. Gregory continues:[93]

> We say, then, that Moses' entrance into the rock has the same significance as these descriptions. For, since Christ is understood by Paul as the rock, all hope of good things is believed to be in Christ, in whom we have learned all the treasures of good things to be. (Col 2:3, Eph 1:3) He who finds any good finds it in Christ who contains all good.

Moses' epectasy, then, is an entrance into Christ. Christ is not only the rock on which Moses must stand, but also the rock he enters.

Earlier in *The Life of Moses* Gregory allegorizes Moses' entrance into "the dark cloud where God was" (Exod 20:21). To begin with Moses is "initiated into the mysteries in the same *inner sanctuary* (*adyton*)" of which David speaks in Psalm 17:12. Here he receives the Decalogue and the divine knowledge that includes both "the things which must be known about God" (sc. that he is incomprehensible) and "by what pursuits the virtuous life is perfected." Only then does he leave the inner sanctuary and enter "the *tabernacle* (*skēnē*) not made with hands."[94] In sections 170–83 Gregory describes the heavenly tabernacle, which he identifies with Christ:[95]

> Taking a hint from what has been said by Paul, who partially uncovered the mystery of these things, we say that Moses was earlier instructed by a type in the mystery of the tabernacle which encompasses the universe. This tabernacle would be *Christ who is the power and the wisdom of God* (1 Cor 1:24), who in his own nature was not made with hands, yet capable of being made when it became necessary for this tabernacle to be erected among us. Thus, the same tabernacle is in a way both unfashioned and fashioned, uncreated in preexistence but created in having received this material composition.

Moses, then, is first initiated into the incarnation; and then he passes through the sanctuary into the tabernacle of the uncreated Christ.

The tabernacle, then, is Christ himself, "the Only Begotten God, who encompasses everything in himself but who also pitched his own tabernacle among us."[96] The "curtain of the lower tabernacle is the flesh of Christ" (Heb 10:20), and we may suppose that passing through that curtain we enter the divine presence of Christ, "the power which encompasses the universe, in which *lives the fullness of divinity* (Col 2:9), the common protector of all, who encompasses everything within himself."[97] The journey begins and ends with Christ's summons. Following him means obedience to his demands but also a gradual ascent that culminates in the stable motion of perpetual progress in the good:[98]

> But when the Lord who spoke to Moses came to fulfill his own law, he likewise gave a clear explanation to his disciples, laying bare the meaning of what had previously been said in a figure when he said, *If anyone wants to be a follower of me* (Luke 9:23) and not "If any man will go before me." And to the one asking about eternal life he proposes the same thing, for he says *Come, follow me* (Luke 18:22). Now, he who follows sees the back.

Epectasy, then, is Gregory's reworking of Origen's contemplative ideal. Contemplative union with God is a redeemed becoming, perpetual progress in the good. And, if my suggestion has merit, it is also union with Christ.

My conclusion, then, is that Gregory treats the spiritual life as an ideal fully realized in the age to come but an ideal in which Christians can in some degree participate in this life. The one exception would be epectasy in its true form and mode. Perhaps we can say that in this life the mystical union with God is a fleeting thing and must always drive the Christian back to the active life of virtue, while in the age to come there will no longer be a need for the moral struggle involved in the active life. I want to suggest one final point. Gregory's ideal, I think, can be correlated with his understanding of monasticism. The monk is not a special kind of Christian. On the contrary, monks and virgins are simply Christians seeking to actualize the Christian ideal in the fullest possible way. Monastic rules are not meant to be restrictive barriers but are thought to establish the external conditions in which living out the ideal will be possible. Gregory's monks must strive for moral perfection, and we can suppose that at least in some cases the setting of the monastery will enable them to see God's presence in the created order. Presumably, their prayer represents some approximation of the soul's movement of desire and love toward God. And the fact that the monks are given tasks—supplying hospitality, establishing schools, caring for the poor and sick—means that their life is meant to embody the dialectic between contemplation and action. Finally, the corporate life of the monastery seems to me related to Gregory's third vision of human destiny, to which I shall now turn.

The New Creation: Christ's Humanity as the Plenitude of Our Nature

One striking feature of the various ways in which the New Testament and the early church fathers articulate the Christian hope is an insistence on the corporate character not merely of the Christian church but of all humanity. At its best early Christianity combined strong community solidarity with an openness to the stranger that reflected the church's sense of mission. Gregory seeks to express this hope and ideal by sketching what I wish to call a theomorphic definition of humanity, a definition that builds on his doctrine of the plenitude of humanity, which I have already examined. Of course, the doctrine of the Trinity developed in large part as a response to those who denied the divinity of Christ or who failed to make any real distinction between Father, Son, and Spirit. It was designed to supply language that would enable the church to maintain its insistence on the monotheism that was its heritage from Judaism and at the same time to protect the distinct and divine status of Christ. It was, I think, a Christocentric piety that required these early theologians to avoid the "Sabellian" error of regarding the three persons of the Trinity as no more than three aspects or modes of the one God. But if the doctrine of the Trinity was primarily designed to rule out error and to protect what was regarded as essential to the piety of the church, it was—and is—a doctrine that can have a number of different functions. To put the point as simply as possible, Gregory concludes that the Godhead is a single incomprehensible nature, but a nature or essence that must be understood as "communion" because of the three persons or *hypostaseis* that are "relations" or "modes of being" of the one essence. This view is, then, a mean between Jewish monotheism and pagan polytheism and between Sabellianism and Arianism. It lies between the error of making no distinctions in the Godhead and regarding those distinctions as divisions of the Godhead.

Gregory articulates this mean in *On Not Three Gods* by saying that Ablabius's question, to which he is responding, is posed in such a way that he is faced with an impossible dilemma:[99]

> Either we must say that there are three gods, which is blasphemy; or else we must deny divinity to the Son and the Holy Spirit, which is irreligious and absurd.

Gregory's treatise seeks to show that the truth enables us to deny these false conclusions. Granted that "our rather feeble powers of reason [may] prove unequal to the problem, we must guard the tradition we have received from the Fathers." His arguments, in other words, are not demonstrative and are only meant to show that the middle ground he seeks is not entirely senseless. Gregory begins by suggesting that using the plural for "the nature of those who do not differ in nature, and to speak of 'many men' is a customary misuse of language."[100]

The analogy seems somewhat forced, since we do not in fact address individuals by the name of their nature, but as "Luke" or "Stephen." Otherwise there would be considerable confusion in ordinary life. But the distinctions we make by no means compromise the unity of human nature:[101]

> Rather does the distinction of persons arise from the individual differences we observe in each. When we see them together, we can count them. Yet the nature is one, united in itself, a unit completely indivisible, which is neither increased by addition nor diminished by subtraction, being and remaining essentially one, inseparable even when appearing in plurality, continuous and entire, and not divided by the individuals who share in it.

It is tempting to suppose that Gregory is appealing to the Platonic idea or form "humanity," a universal in which individual human beings participate. But this, I think, cannot be his meaning. The Cappadocians are well aware of the fact that the philosophical models available to them from Greek philosophy fall short of supplying a way of defining the Trinity. If we say that the one God is a Platonic form, then the three persons will not be "real" in any sense save that they participate in the Godhead. Similarly, if we understand Aristotle's "primary essence" to refer to the three, then the "secondary essence" of the Godhead will be no more than an abstraction. As well, the Stoic distinction between matter as a substratum and individuated matter would define God as one *or* three, but not one *and* three. The one humanity, then, is not a Platonic universal, but is equated by Gregory with what he calls the "plenitude of humanity," that is, all humans who have ever been, are, or ever will be.

Gregory's argument employs his analysis of human nature to define the Trinity as a single ineffable nature with individuation, but the logic that lies behind that argument depends on assuming that human nature must be defined the same way we define the Godhead. That is, if human nature is the image of the Trinity, then we must find a way of understanding that nature as both one and individual. The older interpretation of the image of God found in the language of the first chapter of

Genesis defined the archetype as the Father and the "image" as the Son or Word. God created humanity "after his image," that is, modeled according to the Son. But this view, of course, introduces a division into the Godhead and so plays into the hands of Arianizing views. Gregory is quite clear that the image must be the image of the Trinity:[102]

> He Who said, "Let us make after our image," and by the plural signification revealed the Holy Trinity, would not, if the archetypes were unlike one another, have mentioned the image in the singular.

Thus, the single image of human nature corresponds to the single archetype of the one God. But this does not exclude the idea of an individuation that does not compromise unity. The "us" and the "our" in the scriptural text imply the three persons of the Trinity.

It is, then, Gregory's trinitarian theology that determines and shapes his understanding of humanity as the image of God, an image that is single and yet corporate in character. In this sense the Son of God by becoming incarnate united to himself the human image of God: ". . . so that he might make you again the image of God he himself became the image of the invisible God through his love for humanity."[103] The operative word in this citation is "became." Gregory implies that the incarnate Lord is God's image in two senses. As the Son of God he is the natural image of the Father; as the incarnate Son he adds to the image in that sense the image of God represented by human nature. The expression "image of the invisible God," of course, comes from Colossians 1:15. There it must be understood to refer to the Son as the natural image of the Father, the way a human son can be the "spit and image" of his father. But Gregory also applies the expression to human nature, a created image of God, the way a painting can be the image of a person and yet not be the same in nature as that person.

We have already seen that Gregory can speak of the humanity of Christ in corporate or generic terms. It is the totality of human nature that the Son of God unites to himself. The Son as the Good Shepherd takes the lost sheep of human nature on his shoulder in order to rescue it. But I have also argued that when he speaks this way he is calling attention to the end of a process and is locating that end in the age to come. The process begins with Christ's union with an individual human being, thereby becoming the leaven of the new humanity, leavening the entire lump of dough. The obvious conclusion to draw is that his ideal of a corporate humanity, perfecting the image of God, attaches to God's creative intention for humanity and to the ultimate actualization of that intention in the age to come:[104]

> In saying that "God created man" the text indicates by the indefinite
> character of the term all mankind. . . . [T]he name given to the man
> created is not the particular [Adam], but the general name: thus we
> are led by the employment of the general name of our nature to some
> such view as this—that in the Divine foreknowledge and power all
> humanity is included in the first creation; for it is fitting for God not
> to regard any of the things made by Him as indeterminate, but that
> each existing thing should have some limit and measure prescribed by
> the wisdom of its Maker.

Thus, God foreknows "the entire plenitude of humanity"; and he also
foreknows "the time co-extensive with the creation of men" so that
"when the generation of men is completed, time should cease together
with its completion."[105] Creation, then, extends from the forming of
Adam until the end of this world; and the new age will introduce not
only the general resurrection but also the perfected corporate character
of humanity.

Gregory's vision of this corporate humanity, while tied to the new
creation of the age to come, finds allegorical expression in a number of
places. Solomon's "litter" or "chariot" in Song of Songs 3:7 can stand
for "the universal Church, its parts . . . divided among persons according to their different functions." This is why the apostle Paul speaks of
"apostles, prophets, and teachers" and then "every person."[106] Gregory
alludes to 1 Corinthians 12:27ff. and Ephesians 4:11ff. and to Paul's use
of the metaphor of Christ's body:[107]

> The whole church is the one body of Christ, but in one body, as the
> apostle says, there are many members and not all the members have
> the same function. Instead, God has fashioned one person as the eye
> in the body; another has been implanted as the ear; some have become
> hands because they work mighty deeds; and some are said to be feet
> because they carry burdens. We can find in the common body of the
> church lips, teeth, tongue, breasts, stomach, and throat.

This interpretation explains the crown placed on the bridegroom's head
in Song of Songs 3:11. The eternal Son of God has as his crown the corporate humanity expressed in the common life of the church. Elsewhere
he treats that common life as a sign of the beginning of the new creation,
and points toward the time when we shall "all come to the unity of the
faith and of the knowledge of the Son of God, to maturity, to the measure of the full stature of Christ" (Eph 4:13). Gregory takes the contin-
uation of the text from Ephesians as his prayer: "May we grow up in all
things into him, who is the head, namely Christ; from whom the whole
body, joined and knit together by every ligament with which it is

equipped, as each part is working properly, promotes the body's growth in building itself up in love."[108]

The other metaphor Gregory employs to express his idea is that of the temple or tabernacle. In the *Life of Moses* the heavenly tabernacle has its earthly counterpart in the church.[109] The pillars and lights are apostles, teachers, and prophets. The lavers are those who wash away sin. The interconnecting courts "are fittingly understood as the harmony, love, and peace of believers." "The skin dyed red and the coverings made of hair" symbolize the ascetics and those dedicated to virginity. Gregory clearly finds the two Pauline metaphors of the body and the temple congenial. He understands them in his own way, but he surely does not distort their meaning by equating them with the common life of the church as established and guided by the incarnate Lord. Moreover, it is possible to argue that Ephesians and Colossians tend to think of the church as destined to be equatable with all humanity. Ephesians 1:10 speaks of God's mystery set forth in Christ "as a plan for the fullness of time, to gather up all things in him, things in heaven and on earth." Gregory does not frequently cite this text, one that was central to Irenaeus's theology. But its sense is one that fits his hope that in the new creation there will be a single corporate humanity that will not abolish individual differences and his conviction that the hope can already be seen in the life of the church.

Some three centuries after Gregory's time there was a Christian theologian called Maximus the Confessor, who in many ways elaborated Gregory's theology without departing from the spirit of Gregory's thought. Maximus's discussions of Christ's corporate humanity help clarify the ideas I have been explaining. He is writing after the Council of Chalcedon in 451 drew up its definition of Christ's person. The two errors chiefly condemned were Nestorianism, which *divided* Christ's divine from his human nature, and Eutychianism, which *confused* Christ's natures. Thus, Maximus understands *unity* to be a middle term between division and confusion; and he equates unity with *difference*, a difference that unites the two natures without abolishing their distinction from one another:[110]

> Therefore when the wise man makes affirmation of the union by negation of the division between the divine and human [properties], he does not ignore the natural difference between what has been united. For the union, in refusing division, does not harm the difference.

Maximus applies his idea more broadly. He argues that there are five divisions that we can perceive in the universe—the ignorance that divides the creation from God, the division between the intelligible and the sensible, that between heaven and earth, that between paradise and the inhabited world, and that between male and female. Salvation requires that these divisions be overcome. And, in principle, "humanity has the power of naturally uniting at the mean point of each division since it is related to the extremities of each division in its own parts."[111]

It is the incarnate Son of God who abolished these divisions without at the same time eliminating the differences involved. In Christ there is "neither male nor female," as the apostle Paul says in Galatians 3:28. His promise to the thief, "Today you will be with me in paradise" (Luke 23:43), reconciled the world we inhabit with paradise, while his ascension into heaven united heaven and earth. Next, "by passing with his soul and body, that is, with the whole of our nature, through all the divine and intelligible ranks of heaven, he united the sensible and the intelligible":[112]

> And finally, considered in his humanity, he goes to God himself, having clearly *appeared,* as it is written, *in the presence of God* the Father *on our behalf* (Heb. 9:24), as a human being. As Word, he cannot be separated in any way at all from the Father; as man, he has fulfilled, in word and truth, with unchangeable obedience, everything that, as God, he has predetermined is to take place, and has accomplished the whole will of God the Father on our behalf.

With respect to the corporate nature of humanity what is decisive is the removal of the division between male and female, by which Christ "showed us as properly and truly to be simply human beings, thoroughly transfigured in accordance with him, and bearing his intact and completely unadulterated image, touched by no trace at all of corruption."

Maximus's rather complicated idea of a distinction between the "gnomic" and the "natural" will further explains how he understands the community of human nature. In the incarnate Lord there are two natural wills but no difference of gnomic wills. The fathers of the church "knew that it was only this difference of *gnomic* wills that introduced into our lives sin and our separation from God. For evil consists in nothing else than this difference of our *gnomic* will from the divine will. . . ."[113] What he means is that our natural will is an activity of the soul or personality that orients us toward God. In principle, then, our choices and God's purposes should coincide. The gnomic will, however, represents an orientation that divides us from God's will. In Christ the gnomic will has no place, and so his purposes as human are completely in agreement with his purposes as God. Presumably, we can also argue that salvation means the abolition in us of any purpose that divides us from God or from one another. This does not mean that we cease to be individuals, but it does mean that we find our individuality fulfilled in perfect relation to one another and to God by our fundamental relation to the corporate humanity of Christ.

Maximus thinks of the church this way. In *The Church's Mystagogy* he raises the question how the church can be an image and figure of God:[114]

> For numerous and of almost infinite number are the men, women, and children who are distinct from one another and vastly different by birth and appearance, by nationality and language, by customs and age, by opinions and skills, by manners and habits, by pursuits and studies, and still again by reputation, fortune, characteristics, and connections: All are born into the Church and through it are reborn and recreated in the Spirit. To all in equal measure it gives and bestows one divine form and designation, to be Christ's and to carry his name. In accordance with faith it gives to all a single, simple, whole, and indivisible condition which does not allow us to bring to mind the existence of the myriads of differences among them, even if they do exist, through the universal relationship and union of all things with it.

Maximus continues by citing an expanded version of Galatians 3:28, but he also cites the description of the Jerusalem church in Acts 4:32: "For all had but one heart and one mind." Though the ideal he is describing is one located in the age to come, it nonetheless finds some expression in the present life of the church.

Maximus, of course, has elaborated Gregory's vision of Christ's corporate humanity as including the plenitude of humanity; and we should not simply identify his theology with Gregory's. Nevertheless, what he says helps us to understand the implications of Gregory's idea. In the age to come the theomorphic definition of human nature will find its perfection. Individuals and their differences will continue to exist so that salvation will not compromise our identity as particular persons. But the distinction of persons will not affect the mysterious unity of our nature. We shall be relations of one another in the single nature and image of God in a way correlative with the way the three divine persons are relations within the single divine nature and essence. It has seemed to me that the idea is a difficult one for us who live in a post-Cartesian world. I suspect that we tend to think of ourselves as centers of consciousness— Leibnizian monads, so to speak. But this habit of thought runs the risk of being dualistic and imposing on the subject the task of creating meaning for itself in a meaningless world. Gregory's idea is that, properly speaking, we are individuals because of our relationships. Like Tennyson's Ulysses we are "part of all we have met." What we mean as persons is the product of the relations we have had with people and places.

And, of course, the Christian believes that the one relation we all have in common is participation in Christ.

Gregory, I think, would recognize that the fullness of our corporate identity belongs in the age to come and at the time of the completion of the leavening process begun when the Son of God united himself with the first fruits of our nature. But he surely sees signs of what will be in the here and now. The communal life of the monastery is almost certainly what he has in mind, a life not special in character but different only because it attempts to put the ideal into practice. We learn from Gregory Nazianzen's panegyric of Basil the Great that Basil reconciled the solitary life of hermits with the common life of the monasteries. While it is not entirely clear what he means by this, it seems likely that the common practice of many Eastern monks enables us to understand his remark. The hermits on Mount Athos, for example, are solitary and yet are bound together in community by a common liturgy. Even if we think of the monastery and its common life, it seems clear that the common life, far from designed to eliminate individuality, was meant to enable individual growth in the spiritual life. More broadly, perhaps we can think of the idea this way. For the most part we experience ourselves as divided from one another. Nevertheless, we all have experiences in which the barriers between individuals briefly disappear. Our experience of love is probably the best example of what I mean. It is these moments that give us a partial experience of the there and then, a harbinger of our destiny as relations within the one corporate humanity of Christ.

Conclusion

Gregory has three rather different, but equally powerful, understandings of human destiny and of the Christian hope. We shall be physically transfigured by the resurrection and shall be a central part of a transfigured new creation. Humanity will be enabled by the incarnation to fulfill its mediatorial role by harmonizing and divinizing the entire physical creation. Next, we shall be so oriented toward God that we shall make perpetual progress in the good. It will be a redeemed becoming in which God satisfies our yearning for him and in doing so creates in us an ever greater yearning. Finally, we shall see ourselves no longer divided from one another but as relations of one another in Christ's humanity. Gregory clearly treats these three visions as visions of the future, of the age to come when the new creation will be accomplished. At the same time, he also identifies the new creation with God's creative purpose for the world he makes. And since this divine purpose or intention is eternal, there is a real sense in which Gregory's hopes are heavenly and eternal in character. The two perspectives we found in the New Testament by contrasting Paul and John are in some sense bound together in Gregory's thought. Just as in the letter to the Hebrews the "good things" that constitute salvation are both "heavenly" and "to come," so Gregory's hopes are both future and heavenly.

Up to a point the three hopes described by Gregory represent implications of his theology. The incarnate Word unites divinity and humanity, and this union finds its climax and perfection in the resurrection of Christ. And so, writ large, the resurrection becomes the first of the hopes and is tied to Gregory's Christology and to his trinitarian theology, which protects the distinct divinity of the Son of God. It is more difficult to discern these dogmatic themes in Gregory's notion of epectasy, since here we really have an imaginative reworking of the common theme of the soul's ascent to God and its perfect contemplation of God. Nevertheless, the catalyst that explains Gregory's idea of a redeemed becoming is his insistence on the importance of the scriptural distinction between God and the created order. Moreover, as I have suggested, there are passages in Gregory's writings that mean we can think of Christ as both the gracious cause enabling epectasy and as the mysterious goal of perpetual progress. Finally, the hope of a corporate humanity is clearly tied to Gregory's treatment of Christ's humanity and to his definition of that humanity as an image of the Trinity. In these ways Gregory seeks to make his theology functional. That is, theology is not just a kind of cobweb spinning. Rather, the theological themes are tied to aspects of the Christian life and touch the heart as well as the mind.

I need to add that Gregory's three hopes do not cohere with one another in any systematic way. He makes no real attempt to tie his notion of epectasy, which seems oriented to the individual, to his convictions about the corporate character of humanity. More strikingly, there appears to be a flat contradiction between epectasy and the physical dimension of his hope. Epectasy involves a movement freeing the soul from its involvement in the body and the bodily passions. Yet, Gregory can insist on the psychosomatic character of the human person and on the resurrection of the body. In other words, there is an apparent contradiction between a purely spiritual understanding of salvation and a physical one. There may well be ways of seeking to make the conflicting views coherent, but I suggest that the contradiction is one that Gregory both sees and accepts. As a Christian Platonist he remains true to the definition of a philosopher as someone who loves and seeks wisdom rather than as someone claiming its possession. Truth eludes our grasp, and Gregory remains convinced that we shall find it only at the consummation of all things. The best we can hope for here and now is to find paths that lead toward truth. So perhaps we can say that Gregory's three hopes are three such paths. They lead in the right direction, but we cannot now understand how they will converge when they arrive at their goal. In a sense, this way of interpreting Gregory's thought seems to me one that fits the theological method of the Cappadocians. Gregory Nazianzen says that "faith gives fullness to reason." That is, the theologian begins with careful reasoning, but knows that sooner or later his task must find completion in the appeal to the faith of the church, particularly as found in scripture.

The three hopes I have tried to describe are, of course, located in the then and there. But they can be found foreshadowed and instantiated in the here and now. Gregory's lively appreciation of the beauty and order of nature and of human beauty supplies an inkling of the resurrection writ large. Moments of contemplation and prayer point toward the redeemed epectasy of our destiny. And the common life of the monastery and the church, at least that life at its best, suggests what the completion of the plenitude of humanity will involve. These hopes are, of course, from one point of view ways of articulating the meaning of the New Testament. There as in Gregory's thought we find salvation described both in physical terms as the resurrection and in spiritual terms that revolve around relationship—the knowledge, vision, and love of God, reconciliation and justification. Moreover, what I take to be the emphasis of the New Testament on the community and the implicit universalism of the Christian hope both find expression in Gregory's thought. Finally, Gregory takes a fundamentally hopeful view of the present. The leaven of salvation is already at work, and we can take comfort and assurance from that conviction. Salvation is fundamentally the completion of God's creative purpose, and the Christ of the incarnation is the consummator of creation. The fall does no more than interrupt the total process; indeed, God so integrates the fall and evil into the process that it contributes to it. When we turn to Augustine, we shall find a very different perspective, one that fastens our attention on the tragic character of human life in the present and that notices more fully the obstacles to hope that beset us.

Notes

1. Gregory of Nyssa, *In XL Martyres*, Jaeger 10.1, pp. 167f.
2. *On Virginity* 3; NPNF 2.5, p. 345.
3. Ibid. 8; NPNF 2.5, pp. 352f.
4. This assumes that Gregory Nazianzen's Letter 197, consoling Gregory for the death of Theosebeia, sends sympathy for the death of his sister rather than of his wife.

5. Basil, Letter 14; LCL 1:107f.

6. Gregory of Nyssa, Letter 3, Jaeger 8.2.

7. Basil, Letter 215; LCL 3:236ff.

8. Basil, Letter 58; LCL 1:356ff.

9. *Life of Macrina* 21; Pierre Maraval, *Grégoire de Nysse: Vie de sainte Macrina* (Sources chrétiennes 178; Paris: Éditions du cerf, 1971), 211.

10. E.g., *Against Eunomius, Antirrheticus against Apollinaris, To Ablabius.*

11. "Discourse on the Holy Pascha" in *The Easter Sermons of Gregory of Nyssa: Translation and Commentary,* ed. A. Spira and C. Klock (Cambridge, MA: Philadelphia Patristic Foundation, 1981), 7.

12. *Address on Religious Instruction;* LCC 3:293f. (this is the title given in LCC to the *Catechetical Oration*).

13. *Discourse on the Holy Pascha* 254.12–263.20; *Easter Sermons,* 11–18. *On the Making of Man* 25–27, NPNF 2.5, pp. 414ff. *On the Soul and the Resurrection;* NPNF 2.5, pp. 460ff.

14. *On the Making of Man* 26; NPNF 2.5, p. 417.

15. *On the Soul and the Resurrection;* NPNF 2.5, p. 462. Cf. *On Virginity* 3; NPNF 2.5, p. 346.

16. Ibid.; NPNF 2.5, p. 463.

17. Ibid.; NPNF 2.5, p. 464.

18. See J. T. Dennis, "Gregory on the Resurrection of the Body," in *The Easter Sermons of Gregory of Nyssa,* 55–80. Dennis persuasively argues that Gregory's views of the resurrection are by no means consistent, ranging from Origenizing to fairly materialistic speculations.

19. *On the Making of Man* 27; NPNF 2.5, p. 418.

20. *On the Soul and the Resurrection;* NPNF 2.5, p. 432.

21. *On the Making of Man* 25; NPNF 2.5, p. 417.

22. *On the Soul and the Resurrection;* NPNF 2.5, pp. 464, 467.

23. My translation. The English translation in NPNF 2.5, p. 387, reverses the order of the Greek and lists the topics in the order of past, present, and future. This translation fails to understand that Gregory makes an identification of some sort between the original and the eschatological state of humanity and contrasts both with the present state of humanity.

24. Again my translation. Cf. NPNF 2.5, p. 387.

25. *On the Making of Man* 16.4; NPNF 2.5, p. 404.

26. The English translation in NPNF 2.5 fails to distinguish between *ktisis* and *kataskeuē* both here (16.7, p. 405) and elsewhere, rendering both words by "creation."

27. See NPNF 2.5, pp. 405–6. The first difficulty is Gregory's reference in 16.7 to the "fashioning" as a "departure from the Prototype: for 'in Christ Jesus,' as the apostle says, 'there is neither male nor female.'" The second is his statement in 16.9 that "his community and kindred with the irrational is for man a provision for reproduction."

28. *On the Making of Man* 16.13; NPNF 2.5, pp. 405–6.

29. In *On the Making of Man* 16.8 Gregory says "the creation of our nature is in a sense twofold: one made like to God, one divided according to this

[male–female] distinction . . . [and] alien from our conception of God." Cf. 29.2 (NPNF 2.5, p. 421), where Gregory insists on the psychosomatic unity of the human person.

30. Ibid. 16.9; NPNF 2.5, p. 405.

31. Ibid. 16.16-17; NPNF 2.5, p. 406. Cf. 22.4 and 29.1-2; NPNF 2.5, pp. 411, 420f.

32. Ibid. 16.17; NPNF 2.5, p. 406.

33. NPNF 2.5, pp. 464, 467 (*apokatastasis eis to archaion tēs physeōs*).

34. Cf. *On the Making of Man* 17.2 and 18.9; NPNF 2.5, pp. 407, 409. The resurrection is a life "closely related to that of the angels" and "a restoration of the fallen to their ancient state."

35. Ibid. 22.5-6; NPNF 2.5, p. 412. Cf. *On the Soul and the Resurrection*; NPNF 2.5, pp. 465, 467.

36. *On the Making of Man* 17.2; NPNF 2.5, p. 407.

37. Ibid. 17.4; NPNF 2.5, p. 407.

38. *Address on Religious Instruction* 6; LCC 3:278f.

39. *On the Lord's Prayer* 4; ACW 18, p. 61.

40. Gen 1:26; *On the Making of Man* 2; NPNF 2.5, p. 390.

41. *Address on Religious Instruction* 32; LCC 3:310.

42. *Homily 14 on Song of Songs*, commenting on 5:16; Jaeger 6, pp. 427–28.

43. *Address on Religious Instruction* 22, 26; LCC 3:298, 303f.

44. Ibid. 32; LCC 3:311.

45. *Life of Moses* 174–77, commenting on Exod 25:40; CWS, pp. 98–99.

46. Ibid. 177, citing Col 2:9; CWS, p. 99.

47. Gregory of Nyssa, Letter 15; Jaeger 8.2, p. 20.

48. *On the Making of Man* 1.5; NPNF 2.5, pp. 389f.

49. *On Virginity* 3; NPNF 2.5, p. 346.

50. *Life of Moses*, Prologue 2; CWS, p. 29.

51. Ibid., Prologue 9 (citing Matt 5:48), 5 (citing Phil 3:13), and 10; pp. 30–31.

52. Ibid., Prologue 12; CWS, p. 32.

53. *On the Making of Man* 5; NPNF 2.5, p. 391.

54. 1 John 4:7-8.

55. It is not impossible to argue that Gregory here implies a psychological analogy of the Trinity. Does he mean to correlate understanding with the Word and love with the Spirit? Nevertheless, it seems to me unlikely that we can press his language in this direction. In general, as we shall see, the human analogy to the Trinity is located in the plenitude of humanity. The social analogy for the Trinity dominates.

56. *Life of Moses* 126; CWS, p. 84.

57. Ibid. 125; CWS, p. 84. Cf. *Address on Religious Instruction* 39; LCC 3, p. 322: "For what happens in the sacrament of Baptism depends upon the disposition of the heart of him who approaches it."

58. *Life of Moses* 132; CWS, p. 86.

59. Ibid. 133–36; CWS, pp. 86–87. For Elim see Exod 15:27.

60. Ibid. 24; CWS, p. 60.

61. Ibid. 168; CWS, p. 96. Gregory's proof texts are Ps 19:1—"the heavens declare the glory of God"—and Ecclus 46:17—"The heavens trumpeted from above."

62. Ibid. 162–69; CWS, pp. 94–97, based on Exod 20:21. Gregory equates the "thick darkness" of this verse with the "cloud" of Exod 24:15, 18.

63. See *Homilies 11 and 12 on Song of Songs*; Jaeger 6, pp. 322ff. And 354ff. The first passage does seem to distinguish the "cloud" from the "thick darkness," but the second passage appears to be a summary of the narrative meaning.

64. *Life of Moses* 48; CWS, p. 65.

65. Ibid. 154; CWS, p. 92.

66. Ibid. 156; CWS, p. 93.

67. Ibid. 225–26; CWS, p. 113.

68. Ibid. 231–32; CWS, pp. 114f.

69. Ibid. 239; CWS, p. 116.

70. *To Ablabius on Not Three Gods*; LCC 3:264.

71. *On the Soul and the Resurrection*; NPNF 2.5, p. 459.

72. Ibid.

73. *Address on Religious Instruction* 21; LCC 3:298.

74. *On the Making of Man* 21.3; NPNF 2.5, p. 411.

75. *Life of Moses* 166; CWS, p. 96.

76. Cf. Plato's philosopher-king in the Republic.

77. *On the Making of Man* 12.9; NPNF 2.5, p. 399.

78. *On the Soul and the Resurrection*; NPNF 2.5, p. 443.

79. *Life of Moses* 74; CWS, p. 71.

80. Ibid. 86; CWS, p. 74.

81. Ibid. 82; CWS, p. 73.

82. Ibid. 44; CWS, p. 64.

83. For this discussion I am indebted to Warren Smith, whose 1999 dissertation carefully and persuasively examines Gregory's doctrine of epectasy.

84. *On the Soul and the Resurrection*; NPNF 2.5, p. 441.

85. Ibid.; NPNF 2.5, p. 440.

86. Ibid.; NPNF 2.5, p. 448.

87. Ibid.; NPNF 2.5, p. 449.

88. Ibid.; NPNF 2.5, p. 450.

89. *Homily 11 on Song of Songs*; Jaeger 6, pp. 335–36.

90. Ibid., pp. 361, 366, and 370.

91. *Life of Moses* 159; CWS, pp. 93–94. Cf. the allegorical meaning of the burning bush in 20–21; CWS, p. 59.

92. Ibid. 243–44; CWS, p. 117. Gregory employs Paul's identification of Christ with the rock that followed Israel in the wilderness and supplied them with water. (1 Cor 10:4).

93. Ibid. 248; CWS, p. 118. The scriptural expression listed in the preceding section are: Gen 2:15; 3:23f.; 2 Cor 5:1; John 14:2, 23; Luke 16:22f.; Ps

26:13; 114:9; 22:2; Gal 4:26; Matt 13:44; Phil 3:14; Prov 1:9; 4:9; Isa 62:3; Ps 60:4; Isa 65:11-14; Prov 25:4, 8; Luke 22:30; Deut 12:5; Ps 26:5.

94. Ibid. 164, 166, 167; CWS, pp. 95, 96.

95. Ibid. 174; CWS, p. 98.

96. Ibid. 175; CWS, pp. 98–99. The allusion is to John 1:14.

97. Ibid. 177; CWS, p. 99.

98. Ibid. 251; CWS, p. 119.

99. *To Ablabius on Not Three Gods*; LCC 3:256.

100. Ibid., p. 257.

101. Ibid., p. 258.

102. *On the Making of Man* 6.3; NPNF 2.5, p. 392.

103. *De perfectione*; Jaeger 8.1, pp. 194–95.

104. *On the Making of Man* 16.16-17; NPNF 2.5, p. 406.

105. Ibid. 16.16-17 and 22.5; NPNF 2.5, p. 412.

106. *Homily 7 on Song of Songs*; Jaeger 6, p. 211.

107. Ibid., p. 216.

108. *Homily 13 on Song of Songs*, citing Eph 4:11-13, 15-16; Jaeger 6, pp. 382–83.

109. *Life of Moses* 184–88; CWS, pp. 101ff.

110. Maximus, *Difficulty 5*; Louth, p. 177.

111. Ibid. 4; Louth, pp. 156ff.

112. Ibid. 41; Louth, pp. 159–60.

113. Maximus, *Opuscule 3*; Louth, p. 197.

114. Maximus, *The Church's Mystagogy* 1; CWS, p. 187.

3

Augustine–The Pilgrim of Hope

MORE THAN ANYTHING ELSE Augustine was a seeker. He portrays himself as one longing for God, for knowledge of himself, for truth, for peace, and above all for happiness in the fulfillment of all these quests. We could illustrate the point by any number of passages from his writings, but one selection from the *Confessions* will suffice:[1]

> How, then, do I look for you, O Lord? For when I look for you, who are my God, I am looking for a life of blessed happiness. I shall look for you, so that my soul may live. For it is my soul that gives life to my body, and it is you who give life to my soul. How, then, am I to search for this blessed life? For I do not possess it until I can rightly say, 'This is all that I want. Happiness is here.' Am I to seek it in memory, as though I had forgotten it but still remembered that I had forgotten it? . . . Some people are happy in the sense that they have actually achieved a state of happiness. Others are happy only in the hope of achieving it. . . . Yet even these others must possess happiness in a certain sense, otherwise they would not long for it as they do. . . .

Augustine clearly thinks of himself as happy only by hope and not by a sense of achieved happiness. But where is that hope to be located? It appears to be in the memory, but is it the memory of a time in his experience that is now lost? Or is it a memory of the time "we were all happy in Adam, the first sinner, in whom we all died and from whom we all descended in a heritage of misery"? The remembered happiness is, paradoxically, absent and yet not utterly forgotten. It is like the coin the woman in the parable has lost but is still able to look for everywhere.

Like Gregory of Nyssa Augustine thinks of this longing as a desire for God implanted in us by him and consequently central to our being. For Gregory the Christian life represents a gradual growth and purification of this desire, and Christian destiny is the transformation of the desire to that love which will enable us to make perpetual progress toward God, who is infinite good. His emphasis is on the positive character of our longing, and he sees our destiny in dynamic terms as a "stable motion." To be sure, he can recognize the way in which our longing expresses itself in a fallen world. Human desires can be self-defeating. When we long for what takes us away from God, it is as though we were making bricks in Egypt. The fulfilled desire leaves us empty, just as the finished bricks taken from the mould leave it empty. But for Gregory the redirection of our desires remains an open if not an easy possibility. In contrast Augustine sees the beginning of our longing primarily in negative terms:[2]

> Man is one of your creatures, Lord, and his instinct is to praise you. He bears about him the mark of death, the sign of his own sin, to remind him that you *thwart the proud* (Ps 145:3). But still, since he is a part of your creation, he wishes to praise you. The thought of you stirs him so deeply that he cannot be content unless he praises you, because you made us for yourself and our hearts find no peace until they rest in you.

Augustine clearly retains the idea that God has created human beings with a natural longing for him. The soul as the image of God must find its destiny in its likeness to God and its union with him. But he hedges the longing with the dark recognition that it belongs to fallen beings, trapped in death. The longing becomes a kind of home-sickness. It is the restless heart that finds no peace in this life and that will cease from its tragic restlessness only in the eternal peace of the age to come. Of course, I do not wish to exaggerate the contrast between the two figures. Both of them recognize the difference between the Christian life in this age and Christian destiny in the age to come. And both have ways of speaking of how our destiny works its way into our present experience. Nevertheless, granted this pattern of continuity and discontinuity between this age and the next, it seems clear to me that Gregory stresses the continuity, while Augustine sees the discontinuity more clearly. There is a sense for Gregory in which we can even now *participate* in the new age, but for Augustine the best we can hope for is an *anticipation* of the rest in eternal peace.

From one perspective Augustine understands this anticipation as a possibility graciously bestowed on him at the moment of his conversion. At least this is the way he looks back on his experience in the garden in Milan. Ten years later he remembers what happened in 386. He and his friend Alypius were in the small garden of the house where they lodged, and he found himself torn between his desire to commit himself to becoming a baptized Christian and his incapacity to make that decision. "I was in torment, reproaching myself more bitterly than ever as I twisted and turned in my chain. I hoped that my chain might be broken once and for all, because it was only a small thing that held me now. All the same it held me."³ The rest of the story is well known. The child's voice chants "Take it and read," and Augustine turns at random to Romans 13. In his account Augustine cites the concluding verses of the passage—"not in reveling and drunkenness, not in debauchery and licentiousness, not in quarreling and jealousy. Instead, put on the Lord Jesus Christ, and make no provision for the flesh, to gratify its desires." But the passage almost certainly has baptismal associations. "Besides this, you know what time it is, how it is now the moment for you to wake from sleep. For salvation is nearer to us now than when we became believers; the night is far gone, the day is near. Let us then lay aside the works of darkness and put on the armor of light." Surely it is not too much to say that Augustine sees what has happened as God's interruption of his life and as God's gracious overruling of his hesitation in offering himself for baptism.

Augustine, then, understands his conversion as a Damascus road experience. He articulates its meaning by citing Psalm 116:16-17: "Lord, I am your servant, born of your own handmaid. You have broken the chains that bound me; I will sacrifice in your honour."⁴ But this, as it were, punctiliar understanding of his conversion is not his only perspective. He also sees the experience as a stage in the midst of a long journey. The journey began in a real sense when, while studying at Carthage, he read Cicero's *Hortensius*. Nineteen years old, he decided to pursue philosophy, the quest for truth. This meant abandoning his mother's ambitions for him. Instead of preparing himself for a career in the Roman imperial civil service, Augustine decided to become a teacher. His pursuit of truth took him to the Manichees, whose motto was "truth and truth alone." Their truth, of course, involved a commitment to cosmological myths and speculations, to cult practices, and, above all, to a dualism that identified evil with matter and the body. Looking back on his early career Augustine sees his path as one like that of the prodigal son, wandering far from his father:⁵

> Where were you in those days? How far away from me? I was wandering far from you and I was not even allowed to eat the husks on which I fed the swine. For surely the fables of the poets and the penmen are better than the traps which those imposters set! There is certainly more to be gained from verses and poems and tales like the flight of Medea than from their stories of the five elements disguised in various ways because of the five dens of darkness. These things simply do not exist and they are death to those who believe in them. Verses and poems can provide real food for thought, but although I used to recite verses about Medea's flight through the air, I never

maintained that they were true; and I never believed the poems which I heard others recite. But I did believe the tales which these men told.

The wandering continued, and Augustine can describe it by alluding to Plotinus's description of the soul in exile from its heavenly home.[6] After teaching school in Thagaste, his hometown, and in Carthage, he decided that prospects were better in Rome. In 383 he went there and found his Manichaean connections useful in seeking preferment.

The next year, when Augustine was thirty years old, Symmachus, a leading pagan and the urban prefect of Rome, secured for him the chair of rhetoric in Milan. By this time Augustine found himself disillusioned with the Manichees, whose views did not accord with what he knew of natural philosophy and science. At loose ends in his intellectual and spiritual development, he had two encounters that prepared him for his conversion. The first was with Ambrose and the church in Milan. Ambrose preached a Christian Platonism that was learned and convincing to Augustine, largely because it enabled him to see the possibility of an allegorical interpretation of passages in the Old Testament that he found offensive and immoral. Augustine also learned the stories of Marius Victorinus and Antony. Victorinus, a pagan philosopher, converted to Christianity and insisted on being baptized publicly. Antony, whose life had been written by Athanasius and translated into Latin, was a paradigm of the ascetic and eremitical life. Augustine treats both as models. The second encounter was with the "Platonic books," Latin translations of some of Plotinus's neo-Platonic treatises. "These books served to remind me to return to my own self."[7] Like the prodigal son, Augustine began to come to his senses. The double dose of Platonism he received from Ambrose and the Platonic books gave him a Christian road map. He could see where he wanted to go, but as we have seen, he was unable to take the first step by himself. Only God's grace in the child's chant and in the passage from Paul enabled this prodigal to embark on his return journey. Augustine's conversion, then, does not so much represent the welcoming of the prodigal son and the killing of the fatted calf as it does the decision of the son to turn back to his father's house.

In a lyrical passage that must be his meditation on the meaning of his conversion Augustine begins by treating his experience as a massive breakthrough:[8]

> I have learnt to love you late, Beauty at once so ancient and so new! I have learnt to love you late! You were within me, and I was in the world outside myself. I searched for you outside myself and, disfigured as I was, I fell upon the lovely things of your creation. You were with me, but I was not with you. The beautiful things of this world

kept me far from you and yet, if they had not been in you, they would have had no being at all. You called me; you cried aloud to me; you broke my barrier of deafness. You shone upon me; your radiance enveloped me; you put my blindness to flight. You shed your fragrance about me; I drew breath and now I gasp for your sweet odour. I tasted you, and now I hunger and thirst for you. You touched me, and I am inflamed with love of your peace.

The God who has broken his chains has also broken into all his senses, his ears, his eyes, his senses of smell and taste and touch. And yet he goes on to make it clear that the breakthrough, though it is an end of his wandering in a far country, is not so much an ending as a beginning. God has graciously turned him in the right direction. This *peregrinus*, this resident alien in exile from his homeland, can at least see the road to his true country; but the journey still lies ahead. Or, to shift the metaphor, God has given him the medicine that will cure him; but he has no wish to confuse the medicine with the cure. He will remain a convalescent until the completion of the cure in the age to come. Augustine continues his meditation by saying,[9]

> When at last I cling to you with all my being, for me there will be no more sorrow, no more toil. Then at last I shall be alive with true life, for my life will be wholly filled by you. . . . Have pity on me, O Lord, in my misery! My sorrows are evil and they are at strife with joys that are good, and I cannot tell which will gain the victory. Have pity on me, O Lord, in my misery! I do not hide my wounds from you. I am sick, and you are the physician. You are merciful: I have need of your mercy. Is not our life on earth a period of trial? . . . Is not man's life on earth a long, unbroken period of trial?

It is as though Augustine's conversion is the climax of a Shakespearean play. The rising action has reached its completion, and the rest of the drama is the falling action that moves toward the denouement of the age to come.

After his conversion in 386 Augustine went to a country house at Cassiciacum, returning to Milan in April of the next year, when he was baptized together with his son, Adeodatus, and his friend, Alypius. From there he went to Ostia, the port of Rome, intending to return to North Africa with Monica, his mother. She, however, died; and he spent some time in Rome. By August of 388 we find him in his hometown, Thagaste, where he established a community of ascetics. Three years later Valerius, the bishop of Hippo, persuaded him to be ordained priest; and in 396 he became a bishop, assisting Valerius, who died a year later and whom he succeeded. The journey continued. Returning to Africa as a Christian Platonist and an ascetic, a servant of God, he found himself unexpectedly and perhaps reluctantly a bishop. For more than thirty years he served the church, tirelessly presiding over legal squabbles in his flock, preaching and teaching. He wrote against the Manichees. He involved himself in ecclesiastical and theological disputes, and he wrote and wrote. His works defended Catholic Christianity against the Donatists, who had become schismatics after the Diocletian persecution at the beginning of the fourth century and who were in the majority when Augustine returned home from Italy. And they attacked what he regarded as the novel opinions of Pelagius and his followers. But works like the *City of God* and *On the Trinity* went beyond polemic to a full and positive articulation of his understanding of the Christian faith, an articulation that in various ways stands at the ground floor of the development of Western Christianity. Augustine's journey also took place as the Roman Empire in the West began to yield to a network of barbarian kingdoms. His early life was in a Christian empire that was largely peaceful and ordered. He died in 430 while the Vandals were besieging Hippo. It is certainly easier for us to see the changes from a pagan to a Christian empire and from Roman to barbarian rule than it would have been for Augustine. But his life puts us in touch with the way these changes may have appeared to him as simultaneous rather than successive changes. He was obliged to deal with the remnants of paganism not only in relation to specific squabbles but also in the larger issues he raises in the *City of God*. The aristocratic pagans who fled from Rome when the city was sacked by Alaric the Visigoth blamed the disaster on Rome's having become Christian. Augustine's defense becomes more than that, since he places the events of his time in the broader perspective of what amounts to a deep and thoughtful theodicy. He places himself and his world, so to speak, in an eternal perspective. Our journeys twist and turn, but what matters is the destination God will give them by his own mysterious but just judgment. Looking back on his life Augustine the bishop spoke of God's providence by saying, "You were guiding me as a helmsman steers a ship, but the course you steered was beyond my understanding."[10] Putting the point more broadly, what our journeys and the course of human history mean will only be made clear in the age to come. Augustine's emphasis is on the gap between the here and now and the there and then. And yet he is unwilling to make the gap an absolute, bridging it not with knowledge and fulfillment but with faith, hope, and charity.

The Vision of God: A Journey in Thought

It appears to be a common understanding that Augustine's conversion was a double one—first to Platonism and then to Christianity. But it seems to me that the doubling is unnecessary and that Augustine's first instinct is to regard Platonism and Christianity as compatible if not largely identical. As late as 390, when he wrote *Of True Religion*, he comes close to identifying his understanding of Plato's message with that of the church. He imagines himself—or one of Plato's disciples— addressing Plato with an affirmation and a question:[11]

> You have persuaded me that truth is seen not with the bodily eyes but by the pure mind, and that any soul that cleaves to truth is thereby made happy and perfect. Nothing hinders the perception of truth more than a life devoted to lusts, and the false images of sensible things, derived from the sensible world and impressed on us by the agency of the body, which beget various opinions and errors. There- fore the mind has to be healed so that it may behold the immutable form of things which remains ever the same, preserving its beauty unchanged and unchangeable . . . . You, my master, have persuaded me to believe these things. Now, if some great and divine man should arise to persuade the peoples that such things were to be at least believed if they could not grasp them with the mind, . . . would you not judge that such a man is worthy of divine honours?

The implication is that the one thing Plato needs is Christ. Platonism is, as it were, an unpersuasive and churchless Christianity. It has failed to persuade the common people and so remains the possession of an elite. And it has failed to establish a community throughout the world. But Plato's message, understood as a religious one, is virtually identical with that of Christianity. Becoming a Christian can mean entering on a period of moral purification that will prepare the soul for its ascent to God and for its spiritual vision of God. We have found the bare bones of the idea in aspects of Gregory of Nyssa's thought. Indeed, we can say that at least in broad terms the Christianity to which Augustine was converted is the kind of Christian Platonism we see not only in Gregory but also in Ambrose and, presumably, in an understanding of Christianity widely accepted in the later fourth century.

We can find both Augustine's commitment to this view and his dif- ficulty with it in one of his earliest works. He wrote *The Soliloquies* at Cassiciacum shortly after his conversion in 386; and in it he puts into words his own inner dialogue, presenting his thoughts as a conversation between himself and Reason. His thoughts focus on an earnest quest for knowledge of himself, his chief good, and the evil he should avoid. Rea- son mysteriously appears to him and instructs him to pray and to write down his conclusions briefly. "Do not look to attract a multitude of readers. This will be sufficient for the few who share your fellowship."[12] Augustine's prayer reflects this elitist view. The Christian Platonist paradigm, though widely accepted by the leadership of the church, is available to the few rather than to the many. The prayer addresses God, who shows "that evil is nothing to the few who take refuge in the truth." A little later Augustine prays: "Hear me, hear me, in thine own way known to but few."[13] Let me suggest in passing that this elitist view will prove an important aspect of the Pelagians' understanding of Christianity and that Augustine will repudiate such a view. Indeed, we can argue that his reaction to Pelagius stems in part from his repudiation of his early stance toward the faith he embraced. More important, however, than Augustine's emphasis on the "few" is his articulation of what the few can expect. Reason explains what this is quite succinctly:[14]

> Reason who speaks with you promises to let you see God with your mind as the sun is seen with the eye. The mind has, as it were, eyes of its own, analogous to the soul's senses. The certain truths of the sciences are analogous to the objects which the sun's rays make visible, such as the earth and earthly things. And it is God himself who illumines all. I, Reason, am in minds as the power of looking is in the eyes.

The mind, then, is so constituted by God as to have the possibility of contemplating God. And this contemplative ideal is at the heart of the Christian Platonism to which Augustine was converted.

Nevertheless, Reason's promise has one condition. Before the mind's eyes can see God they must be healed. That is, a period of moral purification must precede the pure contemplation of God. Only those who have put their lives in order can find for themselves the vision of which Reason speaks. Reason goes on to say,[15]

> The eye of the mind is healthy when it is pure from every taint of the body, that is, when it is remote and purged from desire of mortal things. And this, faith alone can give in the first place. It is impossible to show God to a mind vitiated and sick. Only the healthy mind can see him. But if the mind does not believe that only thus will it attain vision, it will not seek healing. Even if it believes that this is true, and that only so will it attain the vision, but at the same time despairs of healing, will it not abandon the quest and refuse to obey the precepts of the physician? . . . Suppose it believes all this is true and hopes that healing is possible, but does not love and desire the promised light, and thinks it must meantime be content with its darkness which through habit has become pleasant, will it not, no less, spurn the physician?

Faith, hope, and love are necessary for healing. And even at this point in the dialogue we begin to suspect that Augustine remains uncertain about the possibility of his healing. Reason puts him to the test, requiring him to say how far he has been healed. At first his answers are satisfactory. He is no longer tempted by riches, honors, a wealthy marriage, food, drink, the baths. Reason warns him, however, that a "spent pestilence is a very different thing from one that is merely quiescent."[16] A dung heap does not stink until someone stirs it. And, indeed, when the dialogue is resumed the next day, it turns out that Augustine's dream of "imagined fondlings" has demonstrated how far he is from being healed. He asks Reason for a "shortcut" to the light, to a place where he can bear its brightness, "so that I may be reluctant to go back to the darkness which I have left—if indeed I may be said to have left it—and which soothes my blindness."[17]

The conclusion I wish to draw from this discussion of *The Soliloquies* is that Augustine betrays a considerable degree of discomfort with the conventions of the Christianity he has embraced. He is by no means confident that healing will be easy for him, and Reason's promise of the vision of God seems correspondingly remote. Indeed, we gain the impression that he is reluctant to abandon his "darkness" for the simple reason that it "soothes his blindness." Why would he fail to seek the healing and the moral purification that would bring him to his goal? My guess is that he does not himself know the answer to the question. There is, I suppose, always the risk of imposing our own perspectives on ancient texts; but it has seemed to me that Augustine recognizes in himself what we should call unconscious compulsions and obsessions. Could it be that certain forms of modern psychiatry are secularized forms of Augustine's insights? However that may be, it does seem clear to me that Augustine increasingly finds the Christian Platonist conventions uncongenial. They do not fit his own experience, largely because they do not take account of the dark forces within him that represent obstacles to the healing that must precede the vision of God. In this way, I think, Augustine begins to transform Christian Platonism into the theological structure we find in his mature writings. I say "transform" advisedly, since it is obvious that a great many Platonizing themes remain even in his latest works. One way of putting the point as simply as possible is to suggest that Augustine's doctrines of original sin and operative grace qualify and so alter the fundamental pattern I have noted. That is, the soul or mind is capable of moving toward or away from God, and its healing represents a turning of the soul toward God. Original sin, however, means that all humans are born moving away from God, while operative grace means that only a sovereign act of God can reverse this movement. It is these ideas that explain why Augustine will relegate the vision of God to the age to come, to the there and then. And so it makes sense for me to say something about the two doctrines by which, as I think, Augustine introduces novelties into the Christian theological tradition.

The pessimistic sensibility that I suggest can be found in *The Soliloquies* informs the argument of Augustine's later treatise *On Free Will*. He wrote this work over a long period of time, beginning it before he returned to Africa in 388 and completing it possibly as late as 396. Some have sought to explain the difficulties of the treatise by suggesting that by the time of its completion Augustine's views had changed. But it seems to me this is quite unnecessary and implies that Augustine did not understand what he was writing. In any case, *On Free Will* is really an attempt to think through the problem of evil and to examine what can be called the free will defense as carefully as possible. The view to be examined is easy enough to explain. Properly speaking, evil is what we do rather than what we suffer, since suffering is a just punishment for our sins. Next, the evil we do is a voluntary violation of an "eternal law as it is stamped upon our minds."[18] It is a movement away from God and the good. Consequently, evil must be the privation or the depravation of good. And it is "non-being" not because it does not exist, but because it has no independent existence, since it is a corruption of the good. This view, in its essential aspects, is the same as the one we found in Gregory of Nyssa's thought.

Augustine's difficulty with the view stems primarily from its positive implications. If God is good and the author of all good, and if free will is a good God has given human beings, then it ought to follow that we can easily make good use of this good gift. Augustine makes the point repeatedly in book 1. "Nothing makes the mind a companion of cupidity, except its own will and free choice."[19] "We believe that man has been created perfect by God and has been allotted a happy life so that it is by his own will that he has fallen to the miserable condition of this mortal life."[20] "Whoever does not have it [a good will], lacks that which is more excellent than all the goods which are not in our power, and yet he can have it by willing it simply."[21] The climax of the argument, which is a dialogue with Evodius, reads as follows:[22]

> *Augustine*—If we love and embrace this good will and prefer it to all the things which we cannot retain by willing, those virtues . . . which together constitute right and honourable living, dwell in our souls. Hence it follows that whoever wishes to live rightly and honourably, if he prefers that before all fugitive and transient goods, attains his object with perfect ease. In order to attain it he has to do nothing but to will it. *Evodius*—Truly I can hardly refrain from shouting for joy, when I find I can so quickly and so easily obtain so great a good. *Augustine*—This very joy which comes from attaining this good, espe-

cially when it keeps the mind calm and tranquil and stable, is what we call the happy life. . . .

Evodius's joy, however, is short-lived. If the happy life is what all of us will and if it is so easily attained, "Why, then, do not all obtain it?" Augustine's conclusion is that "when we say that men are unhappy voluntarily, we do not mean that they want to be unhappy, but that their wills are in such a state that unhappiness must follow even against their will."

What does Augustine mean? It seems to me important to remember that the Latin word we translate as "will" also means "wish" or "desire." Augustine is making a distinction between free choice and the "will" or "desire" that lies behind our choices and motivates them. Thus, he thinks of the "will" as the basic movement or orientation of the mind—the fundamental posture of the person. We might even think of his idea in terms of a commonsense understanding of character. The actions and choices a person makes are in many ways determined by that person's basic character. Indeed, the moral life is not necessarily tied to the conscious choices we must constantly make. Much of what goes to make up our lives as moral beings has to do with the unconscious and habitual unfolding of our character in our lives. If this is so, then what matters more than our actions and choices is the character that undergirds them. It is not so much that we must judge actions by their motive as that we must attend to the basic posture of persons in making judgments about their behavior. It is something like this that I think Augustine is suggesting. He does not think of the will as a faculty of the mind to be distinguished from the intellect, even though his ideas appear to lead to that sort of philosophical development. Rather, the "will" is the tree that produces the fruits of our actions; and it is planted in the soil of the mind. That soil is always good, but the tree can be good or evil. And the good tree will always produce good fruit, while the evil tree will always produce evil fruit. It may be that in *On Free Will* Augustine has not arrived fully at his mature view. But at least he sees that our failure to attain the joy of the happy life is by no means the product of our conscious choices. Instead, it has to do with the condition of our basic "willing" or "desiring." There is something in our character that trips us up. We are somehow our own worst enemies. Augustine explains this by arguing that we find ourselves in a "penal state":[23]

> It is not to be wondered at that man, through ignorance, has not the freedom of will [*arbitrium liberum voluntatis*] to choose to do what he ought; or that he cannot see what he ought to do or to fulfill it when he will, in face of carnal custom which, in a sense, has grown as strong, almost, as nature, because of the power of mortal succession.

It is the most just penalty of sin that man should lose what he was unwilling to make a good use of, when he could have done so without difficulty if he had wished. It is just that he who, knowing what is right, does not do it should lose the capacity to know what is right, and that he who had the power to do what is right and would not should lose the power to do it when he is willing. In fact there are for every sinful soul these two penal conditions, ignorance and difficulty. . . . These do not belong to the nature of man as he was created. They are the penalty of man as condemned.

The context makes it clear that Augustine is thinking of Adam and Eve and arguing that all human beings inherit their penalty in such a way as to be ignorant of the good and impotent to do it.

In *On Free Will*, then, we have a radical view of human incapacity. Even though Augustine does not articulate his idea in quite the same way he does in the *City of God*, we certainly find what functions as a doctrine of original sin. We do not, however, encounter a doctrine of operative or sovereign grace. In the passage just examined Augustine goes on to raise the obvious objection that it seems unfair to blame us for the sin of Adam and Eve. He silences the question by saying it would be admissible only "if no man had ever been victorious over error and lust." At first this makes it seem as though we retain the power of ourselves to free ourselves from the penal state. But that is not quite what Augustine thinks. Our problem is the failure to turn to the divine physician who will heal our "wounded members."[24] We cannot heal ourselves. We are radically incapacitated, but we do retain one capacity:[25]

But if any of Adam's race should be willing to turn to God, and so overcome the punishment which had been merited by the original turning away from God, it was fitting not only that he should not be hindered but that he should also receive divine aid.

Though we cannot help ourselves, we can ask for God's help. And it seems likely that we can assume that God will not fail to respond to our request. Augustine will, of course, change his mind. As he hardens his view of human incapacity into his mature doctrine of original sin, he will follow this logic to a view that insists on God's total sovereignty. No longer can we summon grace. Instead, grace says, "Do not call me, I shall call you."

One way of explaining Augustine's mature doctrine of original sin is to examine his treatment of the story of the fall, particularly in books 12–14 of the *City of God*. I suggest that he makes three significant changes in what was in his time the usual understanding of Adam's sin and its consequences. The first change has to do with his assessment of Adam and Eve before the fall. They are "upright," and so are capable of knowing the good and doing it. There is, of course, a certain instability. Adam has "the possibility of not sinning," whereas the saints in the next age will have the "impossibility of sinning." Redemption represents an increment on creation; the *posse non peccare* will be stabilized into the *non posse peccare*. Nevertheless, the first humans had knowledge of the good and had only one simple command to obey—not to eat of the tree of the knowledge of good and evil. Their fall, then, cannot find its explanation in their immaturity. And the failure to find such an explanation means that we cannot understand why they sinned. Why would beings who knew the good fail to act on that knowledge? That they did so means that Augustine is obliged to repudiate a central axiom of Platonism, that knowledge is virtue, that to know the good is to do it. The second change correlates with the first by making it impossible to explain the fall. Adam's sin lies not in his choice to eat the forbidden fruit but in the evil will that motivates that choice. We can think of Augustine's story in the *Confessions* of how he and his companions robbed pears and threw them at pigs. The way he tells the story makes it appear to be paradigmatic of human evil. But why should such an insignificant peccadillo have so vast a function? The answer, I think, is that Augustine sees the horror of evil located in the motive more than in the act, in our complicity in evil, and in the very meaninglessness of evil. Adam's sin, likewise, is not a murder or a rape. Its horrendous character lies in its motive and in its inexplicability. There is no "efficient cause" of the evil will, only a "deficient cause." This is Augustine's way of underlining the simple fact that we cannot explain why Adam fell.

These two changes, I think, treat the fall as an unmitigated disaster—a view that seems to me somewhat novel in the early church. We are at any rate a long way from Irenaeus, who regards the fall as a childish mistake and one that in the long run represents an almost inevitable part of growing up. The third change that Augustine makes turns Adam's disaster into a universal catastrophe. We inherit Adam's penalty. Of course, this was the usual view in the early church. At the same time, that penalty meant no more than that we inherit mortality. This can mean that we inherit an unstable relationship between the soul and the body, or between our personality and our emotions and impulses. And so some would say that our mortality explains why we have a tendency to sin. But no one before Augustine would argue that we are born spiritually dead. In other words, Augustine expands the meaning of Adam's penalty. God tells him that "in the day that you eat of it [the tree of the knowledge of good and evil] you shall surely die." Augustine points out that Adam and Eve live hundreds of years after the day they ate of the tree. And so death must be more than physical death. The point finds confirmation in Augustine's text, which reads "you will die by death." The moment Adam and Eve eat the forbidden fruit they die spiritually in the sense that they have separated their souls from God. As a just penalty, their bodies refuse to serve their souls. In the end their souls are separated from their bodies, and they die in the ordinary sense of the word. Moreover, they are liable to the "second death," eternal damnation and torment. Thus, we inherit from Adam and Eve two deaths. The first is a process that begins with the death of the soul and ends with what we normally call death. The spiritual death involved is the impossibility of doing good—not necessarily because we cannot perform good deeds but because even our good deeds are wrongly motivated by pride and the perverse love of self. The noble deeds of the pagans are just that, but when examined more closely, they are really nothing but "splendid sins." The second death will be the reunion of soul and body for eternal punishment. Thus, we are all born incapable of good in any true sense, mortal, and doomed to eternal torment. We could scarcely find a more radical assessment of the human predicament.

This is not, of course, where Augustine leaves the story. We might expect him to complete it the way Paul does. Paul, too, believes that all stand condemned and are subject to God's wrath. But, if I read Paul correctly, the logic of his thought requires us at least to leave open the possibility that God's aim in condemning all is to redeem all. As I have argued, the logic both of justification by faith and of the Adam typology is universalist. But this is not the way Augustine continues the story. Indeed, he can argue that even if God had chosen to save no one, he still would have brought good out of evil. God does this by ordering evil together with good in order to make up a total good. His idea takes us into what seems to me the most puzzling aspect of his theology. Even though he accepts the Platonizing idea of evil as the deprivation of good when he seeks to explain its origin, nevertheless he turns to a different idea when he explains how God responds to evil. This second idea treats evil as the antithesis of good and even as something necessary for the total good. The beautiful picture requires shadows as well as light.[26] It would follow that God, had he so chosen, could have maintained the goodness of the universe by his sovereign ordering of evil with its antithesis good without saving any from the human "mass of perdition." But Augustine goes on to say that God, having demonstrated his justice by condemning all, demonstrates his mercy by electing *some* and rescuing them from damnation. We can now see what he means by operative grace. Grace is the absolutely sovereign act of God, a sovereignty that means we cannot complain that it is also selective. Augustine arrives at this view considerably before the outbreak of the Pelagian controversy, so we cannot argue that his theology is the product of any polemic against what he regards as error. To be sure, the Pelagians will oblige Augustine to sharpen and develop his theology. Operative grace will not only come before—be prevenient of—election, but will also be tied to perseverance. And what he begins by thinking of as election will be tied to the notion of predestination. Nevertheless, the basic view seems to me the product of the religious sensibility implied even by his earliest writings, a sensibility that underlines the radical incapacity of human beings and, correspondingly, the radical sovereignty of God. Put this way, we can begin to appreciate what he is trying to say. He is not really interested in setting the tables in heaven and hell. Indeed, it is Pelagius who puts heavy emphasis on God's wrath and judgment and who probably thinks that fewer will be saved than Augustine supposes. Instead, the true function of Augustine's theology is to underline what seems to him the miracle that God saves those who cannot save themselves. I have wondered whether the selective character of operative grace may not be tied to the realities of Augustine's world, where it was easy to be a Christian and where many in his flock must have been quite nominal in their Christian commitment. Perhaps what he really supposes is that any one who has been baptized and who takes his baptism seriously belongs in the ranks of the elect.

A final point about operative grace will take my argument from this rather long digression back to the issue of the vision of God. Grace, as we have seen, must be equated with the medicine that *will* effect the cure for original sin and not with the cure itself. Like Paul in Romans 7 the graced Christian is no more than a convalescent, however much assured of eternal life in the age to come. To return to the argument of the *Soliloquies*, Augustine increasingly believes that the healing that would enable him to have the vision of God can never be completed in this life. Consequently, the vision of God tends to be located in the age to come. There are two passages in the *Confessions* that might appear to contradict this conclusion, and it is worthwhile to examine them briefly. The first is in the context of his reflections on the Platonic books. They remind him "to return to my own self":[27]

> Under your guidance I entered into the depths of my soul. . . . And with the eye of my soul, such as it was, I saw the Light that never changes casting its rays over the same eye of my soul, over my mind. It was not the common light of day that is seen by the eye of every living thing of flesh and blood, nor was it some more spacious light of the same sort. . . . What I saw was something quite, quite different from any light we know on earth.

It is tempting to read this as though Augustine is claiming to have found the vision of God. But what he means becomes clearer when we read the rest of the passage. "I gazed on you with eyes too weak to resist the dazzle of your splendour." He is aware of the Light, but it blinds him. The vision, if there is one at all, is far too momentary to fulfill the promise Reason gave him in the *Soliloquies*.

The second passage from the *Confessions* is often called the "Ostia vision." But, as we shall see, the metaphors Augustine uses are speaking and touching rather than seeing. He and his mother, Monica, are in the courtyard of the house in Ostia where they are lodging:[28]

> I believe that what I am going to tell happened through the secret working of your providence. For we were talking alone together and our conversation was serene and joyful. *We had forgotten what we had left behind and were intent on what lay before us* [Phil 3:13]. In the presence of Truth, which is yourself, we were wondering what the eternal life of the saints would be like, that life which *no eye has seen, no ear has heard, no human heart conceived* [1 Cor 2:9].

Their words and thoughts ascend higher and higher, and Augustine's language skillfully mimics this ascent in one of his most dazzling passages. Their thoughts "ranged over the whole compass of material things in their various degrees, up to the heavens themselves." They come to their own souls and, beyond them, "to that place of everlasting plenty, where you feed Israel for ever with the food of truth." This life is from God's eternal Wisdom. "And while we spoke of the eternal Wisdom, longing for it and straining for it with all the strength of our hearts, for one fleeting instant we reached out and touched it. Then with a sigh . . . we returned to the sound of our own speech, in which each word has a beginning and an ending—far, far different from your Word, our Lord, who abides in himself for ever, yet never grows old and gives new life to all things." The experience is one that takes Augustine out of time and the multiplicity of our present life to the unity of eternity, and "touch" is the way he describes it. But his emphasis, I think, is on the momentary and incomplete character of the experience. It is a hint of what will be in the age to come, but it is no more than that.

Augustine treats the question of contemplating God in book 12 of the *De trinitate*. Here he is concerned to move beyond the lower forms of knowledge which are tied to sense perception to the higher forms not dependent on the perceptible world, and in this way he continues his search for an image of the Trinity in the soul. He notes that Paul in 1 Corinthians 11:7 treats the man as the image of God but appears to exclude the woman from this honor. It is clear to him that we cannot understand what Paul says in any obvious and literal way, since there can be no doubt that the soul does not partake of the bodily distinction of male and female and that women are the image of God in precisely the same way men are. There must be a deeper meaning, and part of that meaning appears indicated by the apostle's distinction of knowledge from wisdom in 1 Corinthians 12:8. This distinction finds precision in Job 28:28: "Behold piety is wisdom, while to abstain from evil things is knowledge." In other words, Augustine concludes, "action by which we make good use of temporal things differs from contemplation of eternal things, and this is ascribed to wisdom, the former to knowledge." To be sure, Paul can sometimes use the word "knowledge" to refer to "the contemplation of God which is to be the supreme reward of the saints," as in 1 Corinthians 13:12. But Augustine insists on his distinction. "Piety" in the verse from Job translates the Greek word *theosebeia*, the worship of God:[29]

> And what among eternal things is more excellent than God whose nature alone is unchangeable? And what is the worship of him but the love of him by which we now desire to see him, and believe and hope that we will see him? And however much progress we make, we see now *in a puzzling reflection in a mirror, but then it will be* "in clear"; for this is what the apostle Paul means by *face to face.* . . . (1 Cor 13:12)

Augustine contrasts our *present desire* to see God with the contemplation and vision by which we *will* see him. As he says earlier in the passage, the vision of God will be "the supreme reward of the saints." In the present we see God only in the sense that we love him and because we believe and hope we shall see him in the age to come when faith will yield to sight and hope to its fulfillment. Augustine repeatedly cites 1 Corinthians 13:12 with its contrast of our present vision "in a mirror and in an enigma" and the face to face vision of the age to come.

In book 15 of the *De trinitate* Augustine tries to understand the meaning of the "mirror" and the "enigma." The mirror implies the image it reflects, and he thinks of 2 Corinthians 3:18: "But we with face unveiled, looking at the glory of the Lord in a mirror, are being transformed into the same image from glory to glory as by the Spirit of the Lord." "From glory to glory" might mean from faith to sight or from being children of God to being like him. But the meaning he selects is "from the glory of creation to the glory of justification."[30] What we see in the mirror of the soul is the beginning of God's saving work but not its completion. Nor do we find the vision of God. Turning to "enigma" Augustine points out that the term refers to a figure of speech or to what the Greeks would call a "trope." He designates "allegory" as a general trope that includes "various species, and among them the one called enigma." Thus, an "enigma, to put it briefly, is an obscure allegory." The final step in the argument is to say that "mirror" and "enigma" occur in a single sentence and that, therefore, the two words must define one another. He concludes:[31]

> As far as I can see then, by the word "mirror" he wanted us to under-stand an image, and by the word "enigma" he was indicating that although it is a likeness, it is an obscure one and difficult to penetrate.

Our present vision, then, points toward the face-to-face vision of God in the age to come, but Augustine's emphasis seems to be on its disconti-nuity with the destiny of the saints. Later in book 15 of the *De trinitate* he draws this conclusion:[32]

> So then, when this image is renewed to perfection by this transforma-tion, we will be like God *because we shall see him,* not through a mirror but *as he is* (1 Jn 3:2); what the apostle Paul calls *face to face* (1 Cor 13:12). But now, in this mirror, in this puzzle, in this likeness of whatever sort, who can adequately explain how great the unlike-ness is?

The vision of God, then, promised by Reason to Augustine in the *Solil-oquies,* no longer remains a possibility for this life but is firmly located as a destiny in the life to come for those whom God has freed from the bonds of original sin.

Augustine's conclusion, however, does not prevent him from trying to imagine that destiny. At the end of the *City of God* he meditates on the meaning of the saints' future face to face vision of God, and he does so with the full realization that this knowledge, like the peace of God, surpasses his understanding (Phil 4:7). The passage from 1 Corinthians 13 dominates his discussion.[33] Because of the resurrection of the body it is clear that "the saints will see God *in* the body; but whether they will see *through* the body . . . is no easy question." For one thing the saints will have a kind of vision that transcends bodily sight. Elisha's vision of Gehazi, whom he sees even though not present, supplies an analogy (2 Kings 5:26). Another consideration is that God, of course, is incor-poreal and could presumably be seen only by the eyes of the heart or the soul. When Paul uses the expression "face to face," "that does not com-pel us to believe that we shall see God by means of this corporal face, with its corporal eyes. We shall see God by the spirit without any inter-ruption." Nevertheless, Augustine is uncomfortable with the direction his thoughts are taking. Part of the reason for this has to do with the way bodily eyes, even though belonging to the "spiritual" resurrection body, begin to seem superfluous. It may be, as well, that he is uncomfortable with the idea of a complete vision or knowledge of God. He concludes his reflections as follows:

> God then will be seen by those eyes in virtue of their possession (in this transformed condition) of something of an intellectual quality, a power to discern things of an immaterial nature. Yet it is difficult, if not impossible, to support this suggestion by any evidence of passages in holy Scripture. An alternative suggestion is easier to understand: perhaps God will be known to us and visible to us in the sense that he will be spiritually perceived by each one of us in each one of us, perceived in one another, perceived by each in himself; he will be seen in the new heaven and the new earth, in the whole creation as it then will be; he will be seen in every body by means of bodies, wherever the eyes of the spiritual body are directed with their penetrating gaze.

It is not easy to understand what he means, but I suggest that he is reinterpreting the "face to face" vision of God as a way of talking about the saints' vision of God's *presence* in themselves, in one another, and in the whole of the new creation. When the soul finds its perfection there and then, it will become a perfected mirror. The image reflected in the soul's mirror will be God's likeness and the presence of God in the soul. The mirror will no longer reflect the image enigmatically. And the saints will perfectly "see" God's presence not only in themselves but also in the corporate life of the saints and in the City of God itself. If my suggestion makes sense, then as Augustine's thought develops and matures, his understanding of the vision of God not only defers that vision until the age to come but also qualifies its meaning so that what the saints will see is not so much God himself as God's presence.

It seems to me that this understanding of Augustine's mature view makes it easier to discover that, however much he establishes a gap between the here and now and the there and then, he by no means wishes to eliminate a degree of continuity, at least for those whom God has elected and freed from the bondage of sin. In an interesting passage from book 2 of the *De trinitate* he worries with a problem created by his version of Exodus 33:11ff. In v. 11 we read "The Lord spoke to Moses face to face, as a man speaks to his friend." But in v. 13 Moses says, "If I have found favor in your sight, show yourself to me openly." The first "face to face" vision must not be "a true spiritual vision of God."[34] Instead, the better vision is of God's back (Exod 33:20), and Augustine refers to the story of Moses standing on the rock in order to see God's back. The usual understanding of the passage, he says, refers the story to Christ, interpreting the "back" as his flesh or human nature. Christ's "face" is the form of God to which Philippians 2:6 refers, and the reason we cannot see it "is perhaps that we shall see him, as the apostle says, *face to face* only after this life." Nevertheless,[35]

> This is the sight which everyone yearns to behold who aims to *love God with all his heart and with all his soul and with all his mind* (Matt 22:37); and as far as possible he also builds up his neighbor by encouragement and good example to behold it, since he *loves his neighbor as himself; the two commandments on which the whole law depends and the prophets* (Matt 22:39). . . . This then is the sight which ravishes every rational soul with desire for it, and of which the soul is the more ardent in its desire the purer it is; and it is the purer the more it rises again to the things of the spirit; and it rises more to the things of the spirit, the more it dies to the material things of the flesh. But while *we are away from the Lord and walking by faith and not by sight* (2 Cor 5:6), we have to behold Christ's back, that is his flesh, by this same faith; standing that is upon the solid foundation of faith, which is represented by the rock, and gazing at his flesh from the security of the lookout on the rock, namely the Catholic church, of which it is said, *And upon this rock I will build my church* (Matt 16:18). All the surer is our love for the face of Christ which we long to see, the more clearly we recognize in his back how much Christ first loved us.

Though we must distinguish the road and the journey's end, we can walk by faith toward the fuller vision of Christ. And to do so means also walking in love.[36]

This walking is also a seeking. Indeed, the *De trinitate* is all a seeking, one that fails in its quest for understanding the church's faith in the Trinity but one that succeeds in moving both writer and reader along the path that leads not only to understanding but also to the full vision of God. Augustine obeys the command of Psalm 105:3-4: "Let the heart of those who seek the Lord rejoice; seek the Lord and be strengthened; seek his face always." The fact that the seeking cannot cease in this life and the realization that the journey must continue need not discourage the believer:[37]

> Why then look for something when you have comprehended the incomprehensibility of what you are looking for, if not because you should not give up the search as long as you are making progress in your inquiry into things incomprehensible, and because you become better and better by looking for so great a good which is both sought in order to be found and found in order to be sought? It is sought in order to be found all the more delightfully, and it is found in order to be sought all the more avidly.

There is a gap between the here and now and the there and then. But God has supplied a path from the present to that future which is beyond all imagination. And so the saints on pilgrimage in this world can walk and seek in faith and love, rejoicing in hope.

The same idea, together with the same use of the verses from Psalm 105, occurs earlier in the *De trinitate*. Here Augustine cites 1 Corinthians 8:2: "If anybody thinks he knows anything, he does not yet know as he ought to know. But anyone who loves God, this man is known by him." Paul does not presume to say he knows, but is willing to claim that he *is known*. He makes the same point in Galatians 4:9. The final text Augustine cites is the most important one:[38]

> Above all there is this text: *Brothers*, he says, *I do not consider that I myself have got there; one thing, though, forgetting what lies behind, stretching out to what lies ahead I press on intently to the palm of our upward calling from God in Christ Jesus. As many of us therefore as are perfect, let us set our minds on this* (Phil 3:13). Perfection in this life, he is saying, is nothing but forgetting what lies behind and stretching out to what lies ahead intently. The safest intent, after all, until we finally get where we are intent on getting and where we are stretching out to, is that of the seeker. And the right intent is the one that sets out from faith. The certitude of faith at least initiates knowledge; but the certitude of knowledge will not be completed until after this life when we see *face to face* (1 Cor 13:12). Let this then be what we set our minds on, to know that a disposition to look for the truth is safer than one to presuppose that we know what is in fact unknown. Let us therefore so look as men who are going to find, and so find as men who are going to go on looking.

The text from Philippians 3 is as important for Augustine as we found it to be for Gregory of Nyssa, and we shall encounter it again in the next section. Let me now, however, conclude my discussion of Augustine's understanding of the vision of God. Two general points occur to me. First, by looking at the ways in which he treats the theme we can discern the fundamental development of his thought, a development that effects an astonishing sea change in the Christian Platonism to which he was converted. He abandons the hope that in this life a period of moral purification will lead to the vision of God. Reason must relocate his promise in the age to come. Original sin means that Augustine has no power to heal himself; and operative grace, though it gives him the medicine that will heal him, reserves the cure for what lies beyond death. Only then will there be any vision of God. Second, Augustine's mature view of the vision of God implies, I think, two further themes. One is that the future vision of God will more likely be a perfected vision of

God's presence than a "face to face" vision in any literal sense. The other is that despite the gap between the here and now and the there and then, those who have been delivered from the "mass of perdition" have been given a road and the possibility of walking and seeking.

Time and Eternity

I wish to turn now to the way Augustine understands time and eternity and to argue that the pattern of his thought about this theme correlates with the structure I hope to have discerned in his reflections on the vision of God. I need to begin with the way he treats the topic in books 11 and 12 of the *City of God*. The immediate issue that concerns him is God's creation of the world, and he is obliged to attend not only to the difficulties of the scriptural account in the first chapter of Genesis but also to the philosophical problems as they appeared to him in his own time. In broad terms we can say that the Greek philosophical tradition did not have any true notion of creation. Instead, Platonists would argue that God merely ordered and gave form to preexistent matter. But some Christians, while arguing that God created matter, would retain many of the Platonizing cosmogonic themes. Particularly important was the question whether the universe was eternal. Augustine refers to "some who admit that the world is created by God, but refuse to allow it a beginning in time, only allowing it a beginning in the sense of its being created, so that creation becomes an eternal process."[39] In other words, while the world is co-eternal with God, it remains logically dependent on him. This view attempts to integrate the usual Platonic incorporation of Aristotle's judgment that the world is eternal into a Christian framework, and whether or not he is correctly understanding Origen, Augustine almost certainly has the Alexandrian's opinions in mind. The idea of an eternal creation has some merit in Augustine's eyes, since it functions to exclude any change of plan or alteration in God's eternal changelessness. Yet, to say that the soul is eternal is to make it impossible to understand how it could change; and it is obvious that the soul can change by turning to misery or felicity.

It is, he says, equally absurd to argue that the world came to be *in* time, since that might imply that there were infinite times before creation.[40] The question thus raised also appears in the *Confessions*:[41]

> My answer to those who ask "What was God doing before he made heaven and earth?" is not "He was preparing Hell for people who pry into mysteries." This frivolous retort has been made before now, so we are told, in order to evade the point of the question. But it is one thing to make fun of the questioner and another to find the answer.

> . . . You are the Maker of all time. . . . If there was no time before heaven and earth were created, how can anyone ask what you were doing "then"? If there was no time, there was no "then." Furthermore, although you are before time, it is not in time that you precede it.

Augustine's solution both here and in the *City of God* is to say that "the world was not created *in* time but *with* time."[42] Thus, the distinction between eternity and time is equated with that between the creator and his creation. God's eternity is quite beyond our understanding. He does not "look ahead to the future, look directly at the present, look back to the past. He sees in some other manner, utterly remote from anything we experience or could imagine."[43] It is not probable that we can purge our language about God from temporal notions, but we can at least remember that he is quite outside anything having to do with time or space. Once again we can see Augustine's concern to draw as sharp a line as possible between God and what he made.

Granted this basic perception and its equation of creation and time, there are a good many further problems that stem in large measure from the puzzles to be found in the first chapter of Genesis. One obvious difficulty is that this account of creation makes no mention of angels, even though it is abundantly clear from other passages in scripture that the angels are God's creation. Augustine's suggestion is that "Let there be light" in Genesis 1:3 refers to the creation of the angels on the "one day" that begins creation, while God's separation of the light from the darkness in the next verse means the separation of the evil angels—Satan and his host—from the blessed angels. His reasoning is that God pronounces the light good but fails to give this verdict after the separation of light and darkness. The point is clinched by the fact that on the fourth day when God separates the light from the darkness (v. 18), he "saw that it was good." In other words, it was good that there should be day and night; but it was not good that the evil angels had to be separated from the blessed ones.[44] There are other difficulties. Why is the first day called "one day"? Most important of all, if it is the sun, moon, and stars that enable us to distinguish evening and morning, and if these luminaries were not created until the fourth day, how can there be evening and morning in the first three days?[45] Augustine appears to answer the first of these questions by his understanding of the created wisdom of God. The "Beginning" in which or through which God made heaven and earth is the eternal Wisdom and Word of God, the second person of the Trinity, "your Word uttered eternally in whom all things are uttered eternally."[46] What the Word of God utters is God's first creature, "a sublime creature which is bound to the true God, the truly eternal God, by so pure a love that, though it is not co-eternal with him, it never parts

from him." This creature is the created wisdom of God, "that intellectual nature which is light because it contemplates Light." It is to be identified with the City of God, the heavenly Jerusalem, and the "heaven of
heavens" referred to in Genesis 1:1.[47]

Augustine's solutions are, of course, speculative; and they may not
hold together as neatly as I am trying to suggest. Nevertheless, the idea
of the one day as a reference to the creation of the angels and of the
heaven of heavens as the created wisdom of God helps explain Augustine's solution of the problem how there can be evening and morning
before the creation of the luminaries on the fourth day. He speaks of the
angels as follows:[48]

> They have existed for all time: so much so that they were created
> before all measured time, if we accept it that measured time began
> with the creation of the sky, and they existed before that. But time, we
> suppose, did not begin with the sky, but existed before it; though not
> indeed in hours, days, months and years. For these measurements of
> temporal spaces, which are by usage properly called "times," evi-
> dently took their beginning from the motion of the stars. . . . Time, we
> suppose, existed before this in some changing movement, in which
> there was succession of before and after, in which everything could
> not be simultaneous. If then before the creation of the sky there was
> something of this sort in the angelic motions, and therefore time
> already existed and the angels moved in time from the moment of
> their creation, even so they have existed from all time, seeing that time
> began when they began.

Here Augustine seems simply to make a distinction between measured
time and time in a more fundamental sense as the angelic movements. In
the *Confessions*, however, he denies that measured time is a viable concept. It is not the movement of the heavenly bodies that measures time.
Rather, time measures "the movement of bodies." Even though the sun
stood still for Joshua at Gibeon (Josh 10:13), "time continued to
pass."[49] There may be other differences between his discussion of time
in *Confessions* 11 and the *City of God* 11-12. The created wisdom of
God that is the heaven of heavens occurs only in *Confessions*, while the
angelic motions that constitute true time are found only in the *City of
God*. It may also be that in *Confessions* he emphasizes a *timeless* time,
while in the *City of God* he is thinking of a timeless *time*. Nevertheless,
in broad terms the time beyond measured time is located at the very
beginning of creation and is defined as something close to but not identical with God's eternity.

In *Confessions* 11 Augustine tries to think through the meaning of
time, and for the most part he does so not in the context of a cosmology

of some kind but rather from the perspective of our human experience of time. "What, then, is time? I know well enough what it is, provided that nobody asks me: but if I am asked what it is and try to explain, I am baffled."[50] It is not clear what we mean by "a short time" or "a long time." Such observations stem from our present perspective. But it is not easy to understand what the present is. This century? This year? This month? This day? This hour? This minute? "In fact the only time that can be called present is an instant, if we can conceive of such, that cannot be divided even into the most minute fractions, and a point of time as small as this passes so rapidly from the future to the past that its duration is without length."[51] Looked at this way, the present is no more than the constantly changing point at which the future turns into the past. Or we could think of the present in a slightly different way as something that encompasses all times, "a present of past things, a present of present things, and a present of future things."[52] That is, the "present" encompasses memory, attention, and expectation. These considerations press Augustine to the conclusion that time in its proper sense is somehow "an extension of the mind itself."[53] It does not seem to me to be going too far to suggest that this psychological understanding of time correlates with the equation of time with the angelic motions. In both cases we are dealing with the changing movements of a spiritual creature. And we can think of the idea for ourselves in terms of a commonsense understanding of what we mean when we speak of a long time, a short time, a good time, a bad time. We have all attended social events that seemed longer than they were, or that were longer than they seemed. In this way time seems to correlate with the desires and choices of the person. Granted that this is the sort of thing Augustine is speaking of, we can go on to recognize that time has become a moral problem for him. The question is not merely an abstract, cosmological one. It has to do with the tyranny of time, with why time often seems to be the petty pace of tomorrow and tomorrow and tomorrow.

Toward the end of *Confessions* 11 this pessimistic view of time appears most clearly. Augustine sees retrospectively that his life has been "wasted in distractions." The word he uses is *distentio*, which can have the connotation of "scattering" or "tearing apart." He makes its meaning clear when he goes on to say,[54]

> You are my eternal Father, but I am scattered in times whose order I do not understand. The storms of incoherent events tear to pieces my thoughts, the inmost entrails of my soul, until that day when, purified and molten by the fire of your love, I flow together to merge into you.

At first it looks as though the contrast is between the eternity of God and the time-bound predicament of humanity in this life. But this reading involves impossible implications. If the distinction of eternity from time correlates with the distinction of our redeemed and our unredeemed condition as well as with the distinction of the creator from his creation, then it might follow that God created humanity fallen and that redemption means crossing the line between creator and created and actually becoming God. Augustine surely sees that even though redemption involves insisting on the closest possible union between God and humanity, it cannot be defined in such a way as to undermine the distinction between God and what he has made. Consequently, the contrast Augustine is drawing in this passage is between our present "scattering" in time and the "gathering" that in the age to come will enable us to cleave to God's eternity without becoming co-eternal with him. Augustine's pessimism in the passage I am examining finds a balance in his conviction that he has been upheld by God's right hand (Ps 18:35) "in my Lord, the Son of man who is mediator between you the One and us the many, who live in a multitude of distractions by many things; so 'I might apprehend him in whom also I am apprehended' (Phil. 3:12-14), and leaving behind the old days I might be gathered to follow the One. . . ."

This "gathering," I wish to argue, must be understood as the entrance of the elect in the next life into "the heaven of heavens" so that they may enter the City of God in fellowship with the blessed angels. God's first creation was of the heaven of heavens and of unformed matter, the heaven and earth of the first verse of Genesis. "From nothing, then, you created heaven and earth, distinct from one another; the one close to yourself, the other close to being nothing; the one surpassed only by yourself, the other little more than nothing."[55] This heaven of heavens, though "it is in no way co-eternal" with God, nonetheless "partakes" of God's eternity:[56]

> Through the rapture and joy of its contemplation of God it has power to resist the propensity to change, and by clinging to you unfailingly ever since its creation it transcends every vicissitude of the whirl of time.

The character of the heaven of heavens also represents the destiny of the saints. In his own way Augustine appears to be thinking of a redeemed becoming not altogether unlike Gregory of Nyssa's doctrine of epectasy. Both theologians are concerned to articulate a view of redemption that will allow for an overcoming of our predicament and even of the incompleteness of this creation without at the same time losing the basic conviction that God transcends the world he seeks to redeem. In sum, it seems to me that Augustine's fundamental contrast in his discussion at the end of *Confessions* 11 is between the *distentio* that characterizes our predicament and the *intentio* that will be the destiny of the saints.

We must, however, take one further step. If this were all Augustine were saying, then it would be impossible to suppose that God's redeeming work could ever inform our present existence. We should be left with nothing but a gap between the here and now and the there and then. There would be no bridge or road across that gap. But Augustine supplies us with a view of such a road for the pilgrim to take. The incarnate Lord, mediating between the One and the many, has so apprehended Augustine that[57]

> leaving behind the old days I might be gathered to follow the One, "forgetting the past" and moving not towards those future things which are transitory but to "the things which are before" me, not stretched out in distraction [*distentus*] but extended in reach [*extentus*], not by being pulled apart [*secundum distentionem*] but by concentration [*secundum intentionem*]. So I "pursue the prize of the high calling" where I "may hear the voice of praise" and "contemplate your delight" (Ps 25:7; 26:4) which neither comes nor goes.

We find a middle term between *distentio* and *intentio*; "stretching forth" (*extentus*) is a movement from the scattering and distraction of our fallen condition toward the "concentration" of our destiny. And, of course, Augustine borrows the term from the passage in Philippians 3, which supplies the same term for Gregory of Nyssa's idea of epectasy. But while Gregory attaches the full significance of the stretching forth to the age to come, Augustine sees in it a reference to the movement of pilgrims toward the rest that, to mix the metaphor, will complete their cure.

I want to conclude, then, that Augustine's reflections about time and eternity correlate quite completely with his mature understanding of the vision of God. He begins by drawing what seems a virtually total contrast between our present predicament and the destiny that awaits the saints in the there and then. Now we are blind, scattered in the distractions and incoherence of time. Then we shall see God and cleave to his eternity. From one perspective the contrast is between multiplicity and a partaking of unity, and we can discern the impact on Augustine of his reading of Plotinus. More properly, however, the contrast is between the spiritual death that represents our heritage from Adam and Eve and the eternal life that is the Christian hope. That hope is really what supplies the road that bridges the gap between the present and the future beyond all futures. And it expresses itself as the enigmatic apprehensions of God vouchsafed to us primarily in the inner life of the soul and as our stretching forth toward eternal life, rest, and peace. We must not forget that the hope and the road are the unexpected and undeserved gift of God. Augustine's retrospective understanding of his conversion and his consequent doctrine of operative grace are decisive aspects of the picture. In what follows this is where I want to begin. Then my argument will continue by describing the "stretching forth" of Philippians 3 as remembering, knowing, and loving.

God's Gift: Stretching Forth

My argument has led me to focus on the way in which Augustine understands the life in this world of those destined for the City of God. In other words, we need to turn directly to what he says about the Christian life. There can be no better point of departure than the *De trinitate*. Even though the work remains in one sense an attempt to expound the Christian faith of the Trinity and to seek ways of understanding the doctrine, much of it is really concerned with examining the character and growth of the soul, or what we should call the personality. That this is so is a factor of the form of Augustine's argument. It may be the case that we cannot treat the entire work as "faith seeking understanding," nevertheless his articulation of the church's trinitarian faith dominates the first seven books, while in book 8 he turns to an attempt to understand the Trinity by examining its image in the soul. His discussion presupposes two conclusions: God is the Trinity; the human soul is the image of God. Consequently, by seeking for triune structures in the soul we can begin to understand the Trinity as we move from the image to the archetype. In one sense the enterprise is doomed from the start. The basic problem is that the image is not yet perfected; the soul has not yet acquired that full likeness to God that will bring it completion. This conviction finds full articulation toward the end of book 14:[58]

> Those who do, on being reminded, turn to the Lord from the deformity which had conformed them by worldly lusts to this world are reformed by him; they listen to the apostle saying, *Do not conform to this world, but be reformed in the newness of your minds* (Rom 12:2). And thus the image begins to be reformed by him who formed it in the first place. It cannot reform itself in the way it was able to deform itself. . . . To be sure, this renewal does not happen in one moment of conversion, as the baptismal renewal by the forgiveness of sins happens in a moment, so that not even one tiny sin remains unforgiven. But it is one thing to throw off a fever, another to recover from the

weakness which the fever leaves behind it. . . . The first stage of the cure is to remove the cause of the debility, and this is done by pardoning all sins; the second stage is curing the debility itself, and this is done gradually by making steady progress in the renewal of this image.

Augustine continues by citing 1 Corinthians 13:12, 2 Corinthians 3:18, and 1 John 3:2. This last text reads: "Beloved, we are now sons of God, but that which we shall be has not yet appeared. We know that when he appears we shall be like him, because we shall see him as he is." The text may well refer in part to the resurrection of the body, but it contributes to the conclusion that "the image of God will achieve its full likeness of him when it attains to the full vision of him."[59]

What this means is that Augustine's treatment of the soul in *De trinitate* has primarily to do with his understanding of the stretching forth of those elected out of the mass of perdition by prevenient grace. There is, I think, a temptation to read the work as though Augustine's mature framework has disappeared and so to fail to understand that what he says of the soul must be restricted to the predestined saints. But he is writing the *De trinitate* partly at the same time he is writing the *City of God*, and we surely cannot saddle him with a fundamental inconsistency. Moreover, there are a good many passages in the *De trinitate* that allude to original sin and prevenient grace. It would seem to me better to argue that in this work we see the true function of his idiosyncratic doctrines. They are meant to underline the miraculous way in which God has chosen to reform the souls of the saints. Of course, he speaks of that way by appealing to God's grace. But it is obvious that he regards this grace as made available by Christ and, particularly by Christ's death and resurrection. One puzzling feature of Augustine's thought is the relative absence of extended discussion of the incarnation or of Christ's person. I think that this can be explained by arguing that Augustine firmly accepts the church's faith in Christ but that his concern is to explore what Christ has done rather than to raise questions concerning who he is. At least this is the conclusion I should draw regarding two lengthy discussions in the *De trinitate* that attempt to explain Christ's saving work. These discussions are of particular interest because they betray Augustine's acceptance of the standard patristic notion of *theōsis* and at the same time sow the seeds of what at least from the time of Anselm will become the standard Western doctrine of the atonement. And so before turning to the ways Augustine characterizes the stretching forth of those being healed let me turn to the way he understands Christ to have given the gift of healing.

The two discussions I have in mind appear in books 4 and 13, and Augustine himself perceives them as related.[60] In book 4 the basic idea derives from a musical analogy; Christ's "single" matches our "double." That is, his death and resurrection somehow harmonize our spiritual and physical deaths and resurrections. The metaphor really depends on Paul's distinction between the inner and the outer humanity and on his treatment of the believer's death and resurrection with Christ in baptism (Rom 6). Christ's death and resurrection is both a "sacrament" (*sacramentum*) and a "model" (*exemplum*).[61] That is, it is a mysterious sign which effects the inner, spiritual death and resurrection that represents a deliverance from sin and the birth of a new vision and a new way of walking; and it is also a model of the actual death and resurrection of the believer that will be completed in the age to come. In book 13 this contrast appears in the context of Augustine's definition of the happy life. He argues that all people desire this life and says that "no one is happy but the man who has everything he wants, and wants nothing wrongly."[62] To have what we want is *power*; to want what is right is *justice*. Our problem is that we put power before justice. Christ's death and resurrection demonstrate the proper order. His death took place in weakness but in justice, while his resurrection was with power.

By way of digression let me make one comment about the argument in book 13. Augustine puts it as follows:[63]

> Unless he [Christ] had been man he could not have been killed; unless he had been God no one would have believed he did not want to do what he could do, but they would simply have thought that he could not do what he wanted to; nor would we have imagined that he was preferring justice to power, but simply that he lacked power. As it is, however, he suffered human pains for us because he was man, though if he had not wanted to he would have been able not to suffer so, because he was God. In this way the justice of humility was made more acceptable, seeing that the power of divinity could have avoided the humiliation if it had wanted to; and so by the death of one so powerful we powerless mortals have justice set before us and power promised us. He did one of these two things by dying, the other by rising.

From the perspective of the New Testament and the early church the way Augustine appears to divide Christ's death from his resurrection is extremely peculiar. I argue that the New Testament treats the two as a single event. We can no more separate Christ's death from his resurrection than we can divide the labor pangs of a woman from the birth of her child. Moreover, the earliest liturgical celebration of Christ's death and resurrection seems to have been the Christian Passover rather than the distinction we are familiar with between Good Friday and Easter. I can think of no one else in the early church who would attribute one effect to Christ's death and another to his resurrection. I suggest that Augustine's idea is far more a factor of the argument he is making about the happy life than it is a doctrine about Christ's death and resurrection. Nevertheless, in the West what he said helped lead to a division between Christ's death and resurrection. Launcelot Andrewes, for example, will say in the seventeenth century that Christ saved us mercifully by his death and mightily by his resurrection.

To return to the main line of my argument, Augustine relates these two discussions to two rather different theological understandings of the role of Christ in redemption. The first is usually called *theōsis*, divinization. It means that the eternal Son of God became human that human beings might become the children of God. The idea, of course, depends on passages in the New Testament that modern scholars associate with the "redeemer myth." We find it in the writings of Irenaeus toward the end of the second century, and Athanasius gives it classical expression in his treatise *On the Incarnation*. The divinization involved by no means suggests that the redeemed actually become God. The redeemed become "as like God as possible."[64] This likeness involves both spiritual and moral conformity to God and the resurrection of the body that gives the redeemed a created likeness of God's changelessness. So it is that Augustine can say that Christ by "becoming a partaker of our mortality . . . made us partakers of his divinity."[65] Toward the end of book 4 he turns to a citation from Plato's *Timaeus*: "As eternity is to that which is originated, so truth is to faith."[66] The Son of God, then, who is "truth itself, co-eternal with the Father," became incarnate as the Son of man and sought to accomplish two things. First, his aim was "to capture our faith and draw it to himself, and by means of it to lead us on to his truth." Second, "the eternal allied himself to us in our originated condition, and so provided us with a bridge to his eternity." In this way the incarnate Lord fulfilled his promise that we should know the truth and that it would set us free (John 8:31). And this freedom will be "from death, from perishability, from liability to change."[67] One final passage from book 13 reflects Augustine's use of the common theme of *theōsis*:[68]

> For surely if the Son of God by nature became son of man by mercy for the sake of the sons of men (that is the meaning of *the Word became flesh and dwelt amongst us*), how much easier it is to believe that the sons of men by nature can become sons of God by grace and dwell in God; for it is in him alone and thanks to him alone that they

can be happy, by sharing in his immortality; it was to persuade us of this that the Son of God came to share in our mortality.

Augustine employs the conventional doctrine of *theōsis* in his own way, but to say this by no means undermines the conclusion that he belongs to his own time.

The second way in which Augustine understands Christ's redeeming work also depends on previous understandings, even though I wish to suggest that his emphasis on and his development of these conventions represent a decisive shift in the Christian theological tradition. The understandings to which I refer revolve around the idea of Christ as the victor over Satan, and they make use of several metaphors that are often mixed with one another—sacrifice, the payment of a debt, and the liberation of captives. We are really in the presence of a story rather than a theological concept, and we have already had a glimpse of the story in our examination of Gregory of Nyssa's *Catechetical Oration*. Satan conquered Adam in paradise, and since then all humans have been subject to him. Christ, however, conquered Satan in turn and delivered humanity from his power. The story as usually told treats Satan's power primarily as death. Hebrews 2:14-15 reads, "Since, therefore, the children share flesh and blood, he himself likewise shared the same things, so that through death he might destroy the one who has the power of death, that is, the devil, and free those who all their lives were held in slavery by the fear of death." The association of the devil with death had already been made by the *Wisdom of Solomon* (2:23) where we learn that God created humanity for "incorruption," but that through the "envy of the devil death entered the world." As we have seen, however, Augustine extends the meaning of "death" to include spiritual and eternal death. While I think this move is a real departure from the tradition, we do need to recognize that Satan can also be treated as the power of sin by Augustine's predecessors and contemporaries. In any case, Augustine sees Christ's victory over Satan as the binding of the strong man which enables his goods to be plundered (Matt 12:29). But, as I have implied, he sees that victory as a double one. "So he overcame the devil with justice first and power second." He goes on to say,[69]

> It is not difficult then to see the devil overcome when the one who was killed by him rose from the dead. It calls for greater and more profound understanding to see the devil overcome when he thought he himself was overcoming, that is when Christ was killed. That is when this blood of his, of one who had no sin at all, was shed for the remission of our sins, and the devil, who once held us deservedly under sentence of death as we were guilty of sin, was deservedly obliged to give

us up through him he had most undeservedly condemned to death, though guilty of no sin.

Christ's victory, then, is a freeing of those held captive; but Augustine tends to think of two other metaphors. His language of obligation and justice seems to me to imply the idea of a debt, while his reference to the blood of Christ makes the sacrificial metaphor explicit.

Christ's victory over the devil, then, is from one point of view the payment of a debt. He went to his passion "to pay for us debtors the debt he did not owe himself."[70] John 14:30 establishes a basis for what Augustine says, "Behold the prince of this world is coming and in me he finds nothing." That is, since the devil can find no sin in Christ, he has no power over him. By putting Christ to death, the devil has forfeited his claim on humanity:[71]

> And so why after all should Christ's death not have happened? Why indeed should the Almighty not have set aside all the other countless ways which he could have employed to set us free, and chosen this one specially, in which his divinity suffered no change or diminution, and the humanity he took on conferred such a great benefit on men; in which a temporal death he did not owe was paid by the everlasting Son of God who was at the same time Son of man, in order to deliver them from the everlasting death they did owe?

Again we seem to have Christ's victory in this sense restricted to his death. Moreover, it seems to me important to note that the debt Christ pays is given to the devil. Finally, the passage I have just cited goes on the equate that debt with Christ's blood. And so the payment of the debt begins to yield to the metaphor of Christ's sacrifice. This is where Augustine's emphasis lies.

Let me begin with Augustine's discussion in *De trinitate* 4.15-19. He points out that we are wrong to fear death more than sin:[72]

> The truth is, men were more inclined to avoid the death of the flesh which they could not avoid, than the death of the spirit; that is, they shrank more from the punishment than from what deserved the punishment. Few, after all, care—or care very much—about not sinning; but they make a great fuss about not dying, though it is in fact unobtainable. So then, in order that *as by one man came death so by one man there might come the resurrection of the dead* (1 Cor 15:21), the mediator of life came to show us how little we should really fear death, which in our human condition cannot now be avoided anyway, and how we should rather fear ungodliness which can be warded off by faith. And to do this he came to meet us at the end to which we had come, but not by the way we had come. We came to death by sin, he

came by justice; and so while our death is the punishment of sin, his death became a sacrifice for sin.

Augustine repeats the point a little later. "By his death he offered for us the one truest possible sacrifice, and thereby purged, abolished, and destroyed whatever there was of guilt, for which the principalities and powers had a right to hold us bound to the payment of the penalty; and by his resurrection he called to new life us who were predestined, justified us who were called, glorified us who were justified."[73]

Though once again we find a mixing of the metaphors of debt and sacrifice, the second metaphor dominates and is tied to Christ's death. What does Augustine mean by this sacrifice? He contrasts Christ's true sacrifice with the false sacrifices of the pagans and argues that not only is true sacrifice owed to the one true God but also that "true sacrifice can only be correctly offered by a holy and just priest, and only if what is offered is received from those for whom it is offered, and only if it is without fault. . . ."[74] Christ, of course, is the holy and just priest, and what he offers is pure human flesh "born in and from a virgin's womb." And he offers this for us. Three of the "four things to be considered in every sacrifice" are clear—by whom it is offered, what is offered, and for whom it is offered. Despite the fact that Augustine describes Christ as the "one true mediator . . . reconciling us to God by his sacrifice of peace" he falls short of telling us explicitly that Christ offers the sacrifice to God, the fourth consideration in any sacrifice.[75] This is not entirely surprising, since the New Testament in speaking of Christ's sacrifice seldom says that it was offered to God. Indeed, the only clear passage is Ephesians 5:2, which says that Christ "gave himself up for us, a fragrant offering and sacrifice to God." It seems to me instructive that nowhere in the *De trinitate* does Augustine cite this verse. Indeed, in the passage to which I have just called attention, he speaks of reconciling *us* and not of Christ reconciling God. I think he sees the problem I am raising. In *De trinitate* 13.15 he asks what Paul means by saying we are "justified in his blood" (Rom 5:9):

> Is it really the case that when God the Father was angry with us he saw the death of his Son on our behalf, and was reconciled to us? Does this mean then that his Son was already so reconciled to us that he was even prepared to die for us, while the Father was still so angry with us that unless the Son dies for us he would not be reconciled to us?

The answer is obvious, and Augustine finds it in Romans 8:13. "Would the Father have not spared his own Son but handed him over for us, if he had not already been reconciled?" To think of Christ's sacrifice as one offered to God would be to imply that somehow God needed to be appeased and reconciled to us. But the true situation is that we were those who had to be reconciled, and it is this that makes it difficult to press the sacrificial metaphor too far.

There may be a degree of ambiguity in Augustine's treatment of the sacrificial theme. It seems to me that he does wish to transform the metaphor into a theological concept and that he argues for the view that the only true sacrifice is Christ's death. But he also seems to me to recoil from pressing the concept too far. In fact, there is at least one passage in which he argues that Christ's sacrifice is offered not to God but to Satan, an idea that will become repellent in later Western Christianity for the simple reason that the devil does not deserve the sacrifice. Here is what Augustine says:[76]

> In this act of redemption the blood of Christ was given for us as a kind of price, and when the devil took it he was not enriched by it but caught and bound by it, so that we might be disentangled from his toils. No longer would he drag down with him to the doom of the second and everlasting death, rolled up in the nets of their sins, any of those whom Christ, free of every debt, had redeemed by shedding the blood he did not owe. But those who belong to the grace of Christ, foreknown and predestined and chosen before the foundation of the world, would simply die as Christ himself had died for them, that is to say with the death of the flesh alone and not of the spirit.

The idea of a sacrifice made to an evil spirit is, of course, foreign to scripture. The Old Testament treats all the temple sacrifices as offered to God. But in Greek religion sacrifices often aimed at appeasing malign gods and were apotropaic in character. "We give that you may go away." Consequently, it is not uncommon for the church fathers to treat the metaphor of Christ's sacrifice as an aversion sacrifice. For example, since Christ may be identified with the lamb of God and since the lamb's blood averted the destroyer from the houses of Israel in Egypt, this true lamb averts Satan from those who are his own, freeing them from sin and death.

Augustine's mixed metaphors and the different ways he construes the redemption brought by Christ suggest to me that his real interest lies in the effect that redemption has on the elect. To be sure, we can equate the work of prevenient grace with the first death and resurrection and with the justice that must begin the saints' journey toward the age to come. But what does this really mean? Augustine understands the first dying and rising with Christ as follows:[77]

By the crucifixion of the inner man is to be understood the sorrows of repentance and a kind of salutary torment of self-discipline, a kind of death to erase the death of ungodliness in which God does not leave us. . . . The Lord's bodily resurrection is a sacrament of our inner resurrection. . . . To this mystery corresponds what the apostle says, *If you have risen with Christ, seek the things that are above, where Christ is seated at God's right hand; set your thoughts on the things that are above.* (Col 3:1)

Repentance seems to me his way of speaking of the turning around that is conversion, a turning away from the old humanity condemned to death in its widest sense and toward the new humanity that can now "dwell" in God.[78] Just as both Adam's sin and our inheritance of his penalty begin with the death of the soul by its separation from God, so overcoming the penalty means restoring the soul to its fellowship with God. Sin, then, is not so much the violation of a law as the breach of a relationship. The forgiveness of sins and its consequent reconciliation is, therefore, the restoration of a right relationship with God through Christ. Augustine underlines the gratuitous character of what happens. We neither deserve nor have the capacity to move toward reconciliation. Indeed, in conversion God does not so much heal us as raise us from the dead so that we can be healed. Moreover, the restoration of the relationship, no matter how crucial it is, remains the beginning of a life completed only in the next age. In his homilies on 1 John Augustine worries with the apparent contradiction between the scriptural affirmation that those born of God do not sin (3:9) and the recognition that "if we say that we have no sin, we deceive ourselves, and the truth is not in us" (1:8). His solution depends on distinguishing the inviolability of the relationship with God given to the saints and the fact that they can sin against that relationship without destroying it. Convalescence need not mean the total disappearance of the fever.

So we can say that Augustine understands Christ's saving work as a reorientation, one that turns the elect from their old predicament and enables them to stretch forth toward God. He can call this faith, since doing so focuses attention on the motivational character of the new life, the "will" that is the fundamental desire of the elect:[79]

So now we accord faith to the things done in time for our sakes, and are purified by it; in order that when we come to sight and truth succeeds to faith, eternity might likewise succeed to mortality. Our faith will then become truth, when we come to what we are promised as believers. . . .

Faith, then, is the trust given us in what Christ has done for us. And it is not to be severed from love. In Galatians 5:6 Paul speaks of "faith

working through love." Augustine argues that Paul sees this as a possibility because "the love of God has been poured into our hearts through
the Holy Spirit which has been given to us" (Rom 5:5). The love of God,
of course, is for Augustine also the love of neighbor. Appealing to
Christ's high priestly prayer in John 17, he says,[80]

> he wants his disciples to be one in him, because they cannot be one in
> themselves, split as they are from each other by clashing wills and
> desires, and the uncleanness of their sins; so they are cleansed by the
> mediator that they may be one in him, not only by virtue of the same
> nature whereby all of them from the ranks of mortal men are made
> equal to the angels, but even more by virtue of one and the same
> wholly harmonious will reaching out in concert to the same ultimate
> happiness, and fused somehow into one spirit in the furnace of
> charity.

The one will "reaching out" must refer not only to the binding of the
elect "in the fellowship of the same love" but also to the stretching forth
in faith and love that characterizes the life of the saints on their pilgrimage. We can add hope to the picture and suggest that one way of char-
acterizing the stretching forth given those whom God has chosen is to
speak of faith, hope, and love.

Stretching Forth as Remembering, Knowing, and Loving

The richness of Augustine's thought, I think, lies partly in the multiplicity of the ways he seeks to articulate his understanding of the Christian
life, but partly in how those differing ways intersect with one another.
We have already seen that Augustine thinks of the Christian life—at
least for the elect—as the gradual growth to perfection of the triune
image of God found in the soul. In the De trinitate he finds a great many
triads that might disclose the image or at least put us on its track. The
one that seems to work best is that of remembering, knowing, and loving or willing. And I am tempted to make correlations with faith, hope,
and love. Perhaps remembering is a kind of hope, faith a kind of knowledge; and, of course, love always remains love. Nevertheless, it seems
wiser to me to avoid imposing too narrow a structure on what Augustine says. To be sure, his prayer at the end of the De trinitate is in part
an apology for his multitude of words, words which have not taken him
to the end of his quest:[81]

> If only I only spoke when preaching your word and praising you! Not only would I avoid sin, I would acquire good merit, however much I spoke like that. Nor would a man blessed by you have enjoined a sin upon his own son in the faith, to whom he wrote to say, *Preach the word, be urgent in season, out of season* (2 Tim 4:2). Can it be said that this man did not speak much, who did not keep quiet about your word out of season, let alone in season? But perhaps it was not really much, because it was so necessary. Deliver me, my God, from the much speaking which I suffer from inwardly in my soul, which is so wretched in your sight and flies to your mercy for refuge. My thoughts are not silent even when my voice is.

His prayer for deliverance from much speaking is something of a surprise. Part of what he means is that not all his speech is preaching God's word and praising him. Another part may have to do with his recognition that so long as we are trapped in the multitude of words we can never arrive at the unity of God's Word. Meanwhile, however, the much speaking has a function. So, earlier in the prayer, he asks: "Let me remember you, let me understand you, let me love you. Increase these things in me until you refashion me entirely."

How does Augustine understand remembering? In *De trinitate* 10 he suggests that the mind, while it does not know itself, knows how good that would be:[82]

> But this is passing strange, not yet to know oneself, and already to know how beautiful it is to know oneself. Perhaps then the mind sees some excellent end, that is its own security and happiness, through some obscure memory which has not deserted it on its travels to far countries and it believes it can only reach this end by knowing itself. Thus while it loves this end it seeks knowledge of itself, and it is on account of the known thing it loves that it seeks the unknown. But why in this case could the memory of its happiness remain with it while the memory of itself could not . . . ?

His explanation is that the mind in this way knows itself as seeking but not as knowing. He makes sense of this by appealing to our experience of "looking for something to come back to our minds that has slipped out of them." Though he gives no examples, we might think of trying to remember someone's name or trying to remember where we have put what we have lost. The appeal is to common sense, but it drives beyond our ordinary experience to the mysterious character of memory. What Augustine says in the *De trinitate* comes close to the conclusion he reaches in his lengthy discussion of memory in book 10 of the *Confessions* as I have sought to summarize it at the beginning of this chapter.

Augustine begins book 10 by pondering the possible reactions of those who will read his work. He implies that they may be disappointed because of their expectation that he will tell them how he has achieved sanctity and Christian perfection. Instead, he presents himself as still far from any goal of this kind. Citing 1 Corinthians 13:12 he confesses that "as long as I am away from you, during my pilgrimage, I am more aware of myself than of you." Nevertheless, he hopes for something better:[83]

> I shall therefore confess both what I know of myself and what I do not know. For even what I know about myself I only know because your light shines upon me; and what I do not know about myself I shall continue not to know until I see you face to face and *my dusk is noonday* (Isa 58:10).

And so he turns to himself and, specifically to his memory, "which is like a great field or a spacious palace, a storehouse for countless images of all kinds which are conveyed to it by the senses."[84] His memory is a "great power," a power of his mind. Indeed, "the mind and the memory are one and the same."[85] It retains all the sense perceptions he has had, sounds, smells, tastes, and touches as well as sights. And these images "are there ready to present themselves to our thoughts when we recall them."[86] In this way the mind can have *conceptions* which spring from revived sense *perceptions*. The memory also contains remembered emotions, and Augustine points out that he "can be glad to remember sorrow . . . and sorry to remember happiness that has come to an end."[87] His memory, then, includes the whole of his life's experience.

But Augustine moves beyond this commonsense understanding of memory and so disengages it from its association with the past. He finds in his memory "all that I have ever learnt of the liberal sciences, except what I have forgotten."[88] Nevertheless, this knowledge has not come to him from the senses and has a special place. He does not know where the facts he has assembled came from:[89]

> It was my own mind which recognized them and admitted that they were true. I entrusted them to my own mind as though it were a place of storage from which I could produce them at will. Therefore they must have been in my mind even before I learned them, though not present to my memory.

Similarly, his memory contains the science of numbers. Finally, though he does not say so explicitly, the most important reality stored up in his memory is the image of God that is his soul and his true identity. He employs the parable of the woman seeking the lost coin as a way of describing his own search for self-knowledge and, consequently, the knowledge of God, the archetype of his image.

Remembering, then, becomes a search for one's identity and, simultaneously, a search for God. This quest, of course, never comes to its conclusion in this life. And it is one that involves knowing. In this way remembering and knowing intersect one another and can even be thought of as two aspects of the same activity. The memory, as we have seen, helps explain the two lower forms of knowledge that are tied to the senses—immediate sense perception and the revival of the images that come from perception when we conceive something. Augustine uses Carthage, which he has seen, as his stock example of perception, and Alexandria, which he has not seen, as his way of explaining conception. Both these forms of knowledge are subject to error. The higher forms of knowledge depend on what Augustine thinks of as illumination. Just as the sun illuminates the visible world, making sight possible, so God illumines the mind so that it can know the spiritual principles that are stored within it. We cannot help being reminded of Plato's *Meno*, where Socrates by careful questioning elicits from the slave boy a sophisticated knowledge of geometry. Plato, of course, supposes that knowledge of this kind is the awakening of the soul's memory of its previous existence, a memory that lies dormant but that can be awakened by careful questioning. Augustine does not wish to commit himself to this Platonic doctrine of "recollection" or *anamnesis*, but his doctrine of illumination is in a real sense a "demythologization" of Plato's idea. That is, he purges the doctrine of what we should regard as its mythological elements, but retains the idea of some transcendental aspect of the soul or mind that prepares it for the gift of knowledge by divine illumination. Perhaps this helps explain why Augustine never comes to a firm conclusion about the origin of the soul. His doctrine of illumination might drive toward arguing for the preexistence of the soul, while his doctrine of original sin might seem to require the traducionist view that our souls are passed down to us together with our bodies from our parents. However that may be, in the *De trinitate* Augustine explores the activity of knowing. Book 11 treats the two lower forms of perception and conception, while book 12, as we have seen, treats the higher forms of knowing as "knowledge" and "wisdom." The first has to do with the active life of virtue, while the second involves the contemplation of God. Only when the two are "one flesh" can we speak of an image of God. In other words, only when the moral life is tied to our relationship with God can it have its true significance.

Augustine, I think, at least implies that remembering is tied to the hope that attaches to our destiny as the perfected image of God. More clearly, he argues for some relationship between knowledge and faith. He distinguishes between the faith *that* we believe and the inner faith *by which* we believe:[90]

> We certainly say very truly that faith has been impressed from one single teaching on the hearts of every single believer who believes the same thing, but what is believed is one thing, the faith it is believed with is another.

In *De trinitate* 8 he points out that since God is truth and unchanging good, the soul will find its destiny only by participating in God. "So the good the soul turns to in order to be good is the good from which it gets its being soul at all. This is when the will accords with nature to perfect the soul in good, when the will turns in love towards that good. . . ."[91] If, then, loving God who is the good is what alone can make the soul happy, we must first know God in order to love him. The capacity to love presupposes a knowledge of what we love. Perhaps the inner faith by which we believe is the way we can know God in order to love him.

Augustine seems to recognize truth in this conclusion, but he points out that "the spirit which believes what it does not see must be on its guard against fabricating something that does not exist, and thus hoping in and loving something false."[92] Just as we can argue that commitment is a good thing, but fail to see that commitment to something false can be evil, so faith without being bound to what is true can be deceptive. An analogy derives from an examination of how we can know the apostle Paul in order to love him. The knowledge involved can have nothing to do with his physical features because we have no clear idea of how Paul appeared. Instead, we somehow know Paul in accordance with the standard of justice implanted in our minds:[93]

> So then a man who is believed to be just is loved and appreciated according to that form and truth which the one who is loving perceives and understands in himself. . . . Whoever therefore loves men should love them either because they are just or in order to be just. This is how he ought to love himself, either because he is just or in order to be just; in this way he can love *his neighbor as himself* (Mark 12:33) without any danger.

Thus, the true basis for our knowledge of Paul and, indeed, of anyone is the standard of justice by which we know them and ourselves not necessarily as we and they are, but as we and they ought to be. In this way our love will be creative and will aim toward the perfection of those we love.

These reflections lead to a final step in what we should perhaps call a meditation rather than an argument. We learn from 1 John 4:7 that "love is from God" and that "God is love." There is, then, no need to "go running round the heights of the heavens and the depths of the earth looking for him who is with us if only we should wish to be with him." We can find the knowledge we are looking for more simply:[94]

> Let no one say "I don't know what to love." Let him love his brother, and love that love; after all, he knows the love he loves with better than the brother he loves. There now, he can already have God better known to him than his brother, certainly better known because more present, better known because more inward to him, better known because more sure.

It is, I suppose, a profound simplicity to point out that we know our love for another better than we know the other. But this idea enables Augustine to treat our loving as that form of knowledge by which we know God in order to love him. Book 8, then, ends in this paradox. But the paradox means that just as we cannot draw any firm line between our remembering and our knowing, so our knowing and our loving are in a real sense two ways of speaking of the same thing.

Augustine, of course, recognizes that loving is a more complicated activity than this conclusion would suggest. The love that is from God is not necessarily the love that we have in our fallen condition. In *Confessions* 4 he explains how he learned this lesson. When he first began to teach in Thagaste, he had "a very dear friend" who fell sick and died. Augustine's grief was compounded by that fact that his friend had been baptized while unconscious in his final illness and, when he temporarily regained consciousness, refused to join Augustine in making fun of the ceremony:[95]

> He looked at me in horror as though I were an enemy, and in a strange, new-found attitude of self-reliance he warned me that if I wished to be his friend, I must never speak to him like that again.

Despite the hope of recovery the friend died. Augustine's grief knew no measure. "My heart grew sombre with grief, and wherever I looked I saw only death. . . . All that we had done together was now a grim ordeal without him. . . . I was sick and tired of living and yet afraid to die."[96] Retrospectively he recognizes that his excessive sorrow was "because I had poured out my soul upon him, like water upon sand, loving a man who was mortal as though he were never to die."[97] The lesson he draws is that "no friends are true friends unless you, my God, bind them fast to one another through that love which is sown in our hearts by the Holy Ghost, who is given to us."[98]

To think of the love that is from God requires understanding that only God can be the ultimate and absolute object of our love. It is the love of God that must order all our other loves, and Augustine can speak of this as the one love to be "enjoyed." All other loves may only be "used," that is, treated as falling short of what can be thought an end in itself. At first he seems to oppose the love of God to our very real and human loves and to give those loves no value. But that is not what he means:[99]

> For when love of God is placed first and the character of that love is seen to be described so that all other loves must flow into it, it may seem that nothing has been said about the love of yourself. But when it is said, "Thou shalt love thy neighbor as thyself" at the same time, it is clear that love for yourself is not omitted.

When we treat our human loves as ends in themselves, we open ourselves in the short run to disappointment and in the long run to the loss of the destiny God intends for us. In this way human loves have no final value if only for the simple reason that their objects must inevitably perish. Yet, when we allow our human loves to "flow into" the love of God, they take on a meaning and value they could not otherwise have. They partake in some sense of God's eternity. Augustine, of course, identifies the love of God and the love of neighbor; and as the passage I have just cited shows, we can add the love of self, understood properly. I think what he means is that by loving God we so identify ourselves with his love of all his creatures that we can at least in part love ourselves and others not as we or they are now but as all are seen in God's purpose for our lives. In some small way we share in his creative love.

We can, then, distinguish remembering, knowing, and loving as three activities that characterize our stretching forth toward our destiny. At any rate, these three movements of the soul, of the person, are possibilities for those whom God has freed from original sin. They are capacities that God helps us to actualize more and more as we make progress. Perhaps most important of all they are activities that intersect one another. In the last book of the *De trinitate* Augustine points out that when he remembers, he also finds knowing and loving. The same can be said of knowing and loving. The three cannot be separated from one another:[100]

> To put it in a nutshell we can say: "It is I who remember, I who understand, I who love with all three of these things—I who am not either memory or understanding or love, but have them."

What I think he implies is that the distinction of these three movements represents a recognition of their multiplicity, while realizing that they

drive toward one another is a way of saying that they are meant ultimately to characterize the unitary movement of the soul toward God in
its redeemed state. In other words, Augustine no longer understands the
spiritual life as one that proceeds through a period of moral purification
toward a contemplative ideal. He certainly can employ this conventional
understanding, as we have seen. But his final understanding, I think,
treats the spiritual life as a movement from diversity toward unity. It has
seemed to me that we can here find the influence of Plotinus' contrast
been the many and the One. But, if I am correct in seeing Augustine's
view of the soul's destiny as one that enables it to cleave to God's eternal unity, it needs to be added that the soul's unity will never be equatable with God's. Our three activities are activities of a single person. And
yet,[101]

> It is certainly a marvelously inexpressible and an inexpressibly mar-
> velous thing that while this image of the trinity is one person and that
> supreme trinity is three persons, that trinity of three persons should
> still be more inseparable than this trinity of one.

The stretching forth of the soul toward God, whether we think of it in
terms of faith, hope, and love or as a remembering, knowing, and loving, is one that increasingly drives toward that unitary movement
toward God that will represent cleaving to his eternity and having the
face to face vision promised.

Conclusion

In reflecting on Augustine's treatment of the relation of the there and
then to the here and now I am tempted to suggest we have in some
respects a new perspective. Paul in the New Testament seems to me to
argue for the simultaneity of the two. The believer is at one and the same
time living in the new age and in the old one. John, in contrast, thinks
of the simultaneity of heaven and earth—the there and here, so to speak,
rather than the then and now. Gregory of Nyssa, despite the fact that he
sees the importance of making a distinction between this life and that to
come, nonetheless seems to me to underline the ways in which we can at
least in part already participate in our destiny. But Augustine makes so
sharp a distinction between the pilgrimage of the citizens of the heavenly
city in this life and their destiny in the age to come that it makes more
sense to me to think of his understanding of the Christian hope as an
anticipation of what will be. In other words, he treats the Christian
life—the life made possible by God's operative grace—as a bridge
between our fallen condition and the redemption that awaits the saints.

The bridge is hope, but we have seen that it is also the broken vision found in the mirror in which we now know God. And it is the stretching forth that takes us from the "distraction" of our fallen estate toward the "concentration" of the age to come.

It is this hope, as Augustine says toward the end of the *City of God*, that enables us to see that God's "goodness has filled even this misery with innumerable blessings of all kinds."[102] In the passage that follows this statement he focuses on God's command at creation to be fruitful and multiply. And so blessings flow from this gift of propagation and the conformation of creation to its first beginning. He thinks of the crops and the birth of living creatures, the "manifold diversity of beauty in sky and earth and sea," but also of the human capacity for virtue and the good life, for the "arts discovered and developed by human genius":

> I have here made a kind of compressed pile of blessings. If I decided to take them singly, to unwrap each one, as it were, and examine it, with all the detailed blessings contained within it, what a time it would take!

I have added reference to this passage from the *City of God* because it enables me to make two final points that represent some qualification of my discussion in this chapter. My focus has been on Augustine's understanding of the spiritual life and consequently on what people have called his "introspective piety." The introspective route toward God advocated by Augustine, then, runs the risk of misleading us with respect to his understanding of creation and of neglecting the corporate character of the Christian life.

It does seem to me true that Augustine tends to see the path to God as one that leads primarily through the soul. The conventions of his time would add to that route the idea that the creation itself betrays the presence of God, who fills and informs it. We have seen this "panentheistic" piety in Gregory of Nyssa's thought. It is, however, far more difficult to find the idea in Augustine's writings. It is almost as though he blocked the road to God through creation and insisted that the only right way is through the soul. There are probably several reasons for this impression, one of which is his reliance on Plotinus's injunction to seek the divine within oneself. But it also seems to me that Augustine is wary of using the visible creation as a path to God for another reason. It is not, I think, that he disparages the sensible world or the body and so sees the soul's destiny as a repudiation of its bodily condition. Certainly his account of human destiny in the last three books of the *City of God* presses the physical character of eternal doom and bliss in a surprising way. He may well take this approach because he knows that his pagan readers will find the physical character of human destiny hard to understand and accept. The other reason to which I have alluded is what I take to be Augustine's deep sense of the beauty and order of the visible world. It is so very beautiful that he wonders whether it is really possible to avoid idolizing it, worshiping the creature rather than the creator. Consequently, though I agree that Augustine treats the Christian life introspectively, I do not see this as in any way a repudiation of the visible creation or of the bodily aspects of our life here on earth.

It is still easier to show that his view of the Christian life by no means neglects its corporate character. Indeed, even in his most Platonizing moods, when he stresses the ascent of the soul to God, he is mindful of the fact that human souls are not monadic but are bound together by common innate ideas. For Plotinus the individual soul is a "portion" of the world Soul. For Augustine all souls properly belong in the created wisdom of God, the heaven of heavens that is God's first creation. They all "remember" a common destiny. And the faith that individual Christians hold is a common faith, held by all in some such way as all of us hold in our minds the wish to be happy. And, most of all, the love Christians are given by God is one that binds them together in community. Indeed, the two cities find their constitution in two loves. The "love of self" that is to be understood as pride forms the earthly city, while the love of God is the basis for the City of God. We could go further and examine what we might call Augustine's political theology. Particularly in book 19 of the *City of God* he makes it clear that we cannot simply identify the earthly city with the Roman Empire or the City of God with the church. The two cities are inextricably mixed in this life, mixed in such a way that there can be no true commonwealth in this world. Only the perfected City of God in the age to come will meet an idealistic definition of what a city is. But there are human cities and commonwealths made up of people united in their loves. One might suppose that Augustine, because he weighs all human associations in the balance and finds them wanting, would adopt a sectarian stance in practice. On the contrary, he argues that the heavenly citizens should make use of the peace of Babylon. They can at least make the best of a bad bargain and so seek to ameliorate human societies. I need to say much more to make all this persuasive. But the conclusion toward which I am driving is that Augustine really is a pilgrim of hope. His pessimistic understanding of human life has a vivid awareness of our tragic predicament. But he gives the last word to God and to the hope God has given us in Christ.

Notes

1. *Confessions* 10.20.
2. Ibid. 1.1.
3. Ibid. 8.11.
4. Ibid. 9.1.
5. Ibid. 3.6.
6. Cf. ibid. 1.18, where he refers to the prodigal son and alludes to Plotinus. See also 7.10, 8.8.
7. Ibid. 7.10.
8. Ibid. 10.27.
9. Ibid. 10.28.
10. Ibid. 4.14.
11. *Of True Religion* 3.3; LCC 6:226f.
12. *Soliloquies* 1.1; LCC 6:23.
13. Ibid. 1.2, 4; LCC 6:24-25.
14. Ibid. 6.12; LCC 6:30.
15. Ibid. 6.12; LCC 6:30-31.
16. Ibid. 11.19; LCC 6:35.
17. Ibid. 14.26; LCC 6:39.
18. *On Free Will* 6.15; LCC 6:121.
19. Ibid. 1.11.21; LCC 6:125. (*propria voluntas, liberum arbitrium*)
20. Ibid. 1.11.23; LCC 6:126.
21. Ibid. 1.12.26; LCC 6:127.
22. Ibid. 1.13.29-30; LCC 6:129-30.
23. Ibid. 3.18.52; LCC 6:202.
24. Ibid. 3.19.53; LCC 6:202.
25. Ibid. 3.20.55; LCC 6:203. Cf. 2.20.54; LCC 6:169: "But since man cannot rise of his own free will as he fell by his own will spontaneously, let us hold with steadfast faith the right hand of God stretched out to us from above, even our Lord Jesus Christ."
26. We can already see the basic idea in ibid. 3.15.44; LCC 6:197-98: "There is no interval of time between failure to do what ought to be done and suffering what ought to be suffered, lest for a single moment the beauty of the universe should be defiled by having the uncomeliness of sin without the comeliness of penalty."
27. *Confessions* 7.10.
28. Ibid. 9.10.
29. *De trinitate* 12.22.
30. Ibid. 15.14.
31. Ibid. 15.16.
32. Ibid. 15.21.
33. *City of God* 22.29.
34. *De trinitate* 2.27.

35. Ibid. 2.28.

36. Cf. *De trinitate* 14.4 and 8.6.

37. Ibid. 15.2.

38. Ibid. 9.1.

39. *City of God* 11.4. The last phrase in the Latin is *semper sit factus.*

40. Ibid. 11.5.

41. *Confessions* 11.12-13.

42. *City of God* 11.6.

43. Ibid. 11.21.

44. Ibid. 11.9, 19-20.

45. Ibid. 11.7.

46. *Confessions* 11.7.

47. *Confessions* 12.15.

48. *City of God* 12.16.

49. *Confessions* 11.23.

50. Ibid. 11.14.

51. Ibid. 11.15.

52. Ibid. 11.20.

53. Ibid. 11.26.

54. Ibid. 11.29, using Chadwick's translation.

55. Ibid. 12.7.

56. Ibid. 12.9. Cf. 12.11: ". . . not even the Heaven of Heavens, your creature, is co-eternal with you. Though it delights in you alone and enjoys your savour in untiring purity, at no time and in no way does it shed its mutability. But being always in your presence and clinging to you with all its love, it has no future to anticipate and no past to remember, and thus it persists without change and does not diverge into past and future time."

57. Ibid. 11.29.

58. *De trinitate* 14.22. See the entire discussion in 14.22-26.

59. Ibid. 14.23-24. See his use of 1 John 3:2 in 1.17, 2.28, 4.5 (where the reference to the resurrection is employed), 12.22, 14.23 and 25, 15.21.

60. Ibid. 13.25.

61. Ibid. 4.6.

62. Ibid. 13.8.

63. Ibid. 13.18.

64. See Plato, *Theaetetus* 176A. Cf. 2 Pet 1:4: "participants of the divine nature."

65. *De trinitate* 4.4.

66. *Timaeus* 29C, probably in Cicero's translation. The Greek reads "As being is to becoming, so is truth to belief."

67. *De trinitate* 4.24.

68. Ibid. 13.12.

69. Ibid. 13.18-19.

70. Ibid. 13.18.

71. Ibid. 13.21.

72. Ibid. 4.15.

73. Ibid. 4.17.

74. Ibid. 4.19.

75. I think the same ambiguity obtains in his discussions of Christ's sacrifice in *City of God* 10.6, 20. These discussions make it clearer that the church's sacrifice is made to God than that Christ's is offered to God.

76. *De trinitate* 13.19.

77. Ibid. 4.6.

78. Ibid. 13.12.

79. Ibid. 4.24.

80. Ibid. 4.12.

81. Ibid. 15.51.

82. Ibid. 10.5.

83. *Confessions* 10.5.

84. Ibid. 10.8.

85. Ibid. 10.8, 14; cf. 10.17: "Yet it is my mind."

86. Ibid. 10.8.

87. Ibid. 10.14.

88. Ibid. 10.9.

89. Ibid. 10.10.

90. *De trinitate* 13.5.

91. Ibid. 8.5.

92. Ibid. 8.6.

93. Ibid. 8.9.

94. Ibid. 8.11-12.

95. *Confessions* 4.4.

96. Ibid. 4.4-5.

97. Ibid. 4.8.

98. Ibid. 4.4.

99. *De doctrina christiana* 1.27. See the whole discussion in book 1.

100. *De trinitate* 15.42.

101. Ibid. 15.43.

102. *City of God* 22.24.

4

John Donne–the Sorrowing but Joyful Penitent

SHIFTING OUR ATTENTION from Augustine to John Donne represents an enormous leap. After all there are more than a thousand years between Augustine's death in 430 and Donne's birth in 1572. Nevertheless, Izaak Walton's life of Donne at the least implies the opinion that Donne was a second Augustine. He ties this interpretation to Donne's ordination in 1615, an event he treats as a conversion experience. Donne had resisted attempts to persuade him to be ordained for some years, and Walton tells us that King James was finally successful. God wrestled with Donne the way the angel wrestled with Jacob at the brook of Jabbok. But the story that really explains what happened is that of Augustine's conversion:[1]

> Such strifes St. Austin had, when St. Ambrose endeavoured his conversion to Christianity; with which he confesseth he acquainted his friend Alipius. Our learned author—a man fit to write after no mean copy—did the like. And declaring his intentions to his dear friend Dr. King, then Bishop of London . . . that reverend man did receive the news with much gladness; and, after some expressions of joy, and a persuasion to be constant in his pious purpose, he proceeded with all convenient speed to ordain him first Deacon, and then Priest not long after.

In what we must regard as a forced way Walton hints that a strange experience Donne had in 1612 had an affinity with Augustine's life. Donne had accompanied Sir Robert Drury to Paris in connection with Lord Hay's embassy to the French king. Unexpectedly he had "a dreadful vision." His wife had passed by him twice in his room "with her hair hanging about her shoulders, and a dead child in her arms." Sir Robert discovers that this apparition took place at precisely the time that Anne had delivered a stillborn child. Walton reflects that the story is hard to believe, but that we should not discount the wonders that can spring from "a sympathy of souls." We can remember that "both St. Austin, and Monica his mother, had visions in order to his conversion."[2]

It is, of course, extremely difficult to understand Donne's ordination as his conversion. My impression is that Donne never quite arrived at the point of thinking that he had been sufficiently converted. Or at least it seems to me that he reached that point only at the time of his death. Moreover, it is reasonably clear that part of his motive in offering himself for ordination had to do with the necessity of abandoning hope of preferment at court in a civil way. Nevertheless, I do not think it entirely beside the point to associate Donne with Augustine, not so much in his life as in his theology. At a general level, there can be little doubt that most of Western theology betrays the heavy influence of Augustine's thought; and there is much to be said for thinking of Luther, Calvin, and the Reformers of the sixteenth and seventeenth centuries as people writing footnotes to Augustine. The doctrines of original sin, the atonement, and operative grace—expressed both in predestination and in justification—all find their roots in Augustine's writings. And it is clear that Donne was committed to the doctrines of the Church of England as expressed in the Articles of Religion, which place weight on the central authority of scripture and the importance of justification by faith. More important, as it seems to me, is the conclusion that Donne in many ways has an affinity with Augustine's basic religious sensibility—a radical distrust of himself and an equally radical reliance on God, who is his sole help. Putting the point another way, Donne like Augustine tends to sever the here and now from the there and then. The distance between our present predicament and the destiny for which we hope seems at times infinite. Sin and its consequence, death, represent a barrier humans cannot breach. But, for Donne, there is a bridge that God has provided in his mercy. The Christian life, then, is a precarious walking along that bridge.

If we are to believe Walton, even as a youth Donne took the religious questions of the day seriously. It certainly must have been the case that it was difficult for him to repudiate the Roman Catholic loyalties of his family and upbringing. And I shall want to return to this question. Nevertheless, it seems equally clear that Donne had youthful ambitions and that it was obviously necessary for him to conform to the Church of England in order to fulfill those hopes. That conformity, of course, need not have meant more than escaping the penalties of the law by attending church. It is likely enough that Donne first distanced himself from the Church of Rome by adopting a skeptical and humanist point of view and only gradually took seriously a loyalty to the Church of England. However we try to settle the hard questions that attach to his religious development, the outward circumstances of his life betray his secular hopes. In 1592 at the age of about seventeen he was admitted to Lincoln's Inn, where he began the study of law. Four years later he joined the Earl of Essex's expeditions to Cadiz and the Azores. One of his companions on the second of these failed attempts to bring Spain to its knees was Thomas Egerton, the eldest son of the Lord Keeper of the Great Seal of England. By November of 1597 Donne's friend succeeded in securing for him from his father, also named Thomas, the post of secretary to the Lord Keeper. It looked as though Donne were on his way. Sir Thomas was a powerful patron, and it seems likely enough that Donne would have succeeded in his ambitions to find a place at court. Unfortunately, at least from this perspective, he fell in love with Anne More, who was the niece of Sir Thomas's second wife. Donne was neither sufficiently wealthy nor sufficiently advanced in his career for such a marriage to be acceptable, and Anne's father sought to take her out of harm's way. But in December of 1601 the two young people were secretly married. The secret did not last long, and Anne's father saw to it that Donne was imprisoned and dismissed from Sir Thomas Egerton's service. Even though Donne finally secured his release from prison and, in April of 1602, the validation of his marriage, his hopes of preferment were effectively dashed.

From 1602 until his ordination in 1615 Donne sought to retrieve himself, but without much success. During those years he lived with Anne in poverty and on the kindness of friends. She bore ten children during these years, of whom six were still alive in 1615. If we are to trust Walton, Anne's father relented and sought to restore Donne to his position as secretary to the Lord Keeper; but he had no success and was unwilling to support the growing family himself. During this period, probably from 1605–1607, Donne assisted Dr. Thomas Morton, who was chaplain to the Earl of Ruthford and who later became Dean of Gloucester and then Bishop of Durham. Morton apparently tried to persuade Donne to seek ordination, but Donne declined, as Walton says, on the grounds of "irregularities of my life." It is not easy to know what this means—wild oats sown before his marriage? the marriage with Anne More itself? his religious opinions? In 1610 he published *Pseudo-Martyr*, a work in which he opposed Roman Catholics who refused to take the oath of allegiance to the king. The next year *Ignatius His Conclave* appeared, an attack on the Jesuits. Perhaps Donne supposed that these writings would free him from suspicion on religious grounds and so pave the way for preferment. As we have seen, Sir Robert Drury did become his patron, taking him to Paris as part of the English embassy and giving him a house on Drury Lane in London. King James, however, made it clear that Donne's only hope of preferment lay in ordination; and Donne consented. He preached at court, took part in an embassy to Germany at the beginning of the Thirty Years' War, and in 1621 was appointed Dean of St. Paul's Cathedral.

If one aspect of Donne's life is his quest for preferment, a quest that found success only in his ordination and deanship, another revolves around his love poetry and his marriage. In his own time Donne was the preacher; in our time he is best known as the poet, particularly through his secular poems. Walton conveys the impression that Donne's ordination represents the conversion of the dissolute Jack Donne to the devout Dean of Saint Paul's. The transition is one from his early poems, "those pieces that had been loosely—God knows, too loosely—scattered in his youth," to the "divine sonnets" of his maturity.[3] The year after his ordination Donne became the Reader of Divinity at Lincoln's Inn. Walton describes his acceptance of the lectureship by saying he was[4]

> glad to renew his intermitted friendship with those whom he so much loved, and where he had been a Saul,—though not to persecute Christianity, or to deride it, yet in his irregular youth to neglect the visible practice of it,—there to become a Paul, and preach salvation to his beloved brethren.

Is there an echo here of a conventional understanding of Augustine's conversion? The "irregular youth" suffers an amazing conversion and becomes the chaste and ascetic saint. But this convention really fits neither Augustine nor Donne. To be sure, we can probably assume that Donne was no different from any other young man about town. But to suppose that he was a rake goes beyond the evidence. The love poetry is really quite conventional and Petrarchian in character; the lover is alternately successful, disappointed, raving mad, and cynical. It surely does betray Donne's own emotions; but that he was no more than a profligate finds refutation in his marriage, which remained stable despite all the forces brought against it. Moreover, it is by no means clear that we can separate the love poetry from the religious poetry chronologically.

Despite Walton's view that Donne's "marriage was the remarkable error of his life,"[5] he faithfully reports Donne's constancy to Anne and hers to him. Walton supposes that "A Valediction forbidding mourning" was Donne's message to Anne in 1611, when he left for Paris with Sir Robert Drury. The poem begins by asking that their parting be like a quiet death—"So let us melt, and make no noise, / No tear-floods, nor sigh-tempests move. . . ." But the parting is really no parting at all. The two lovers' souls "endure not yet / A breach, but an expansion, / Like

gold to aery thinness beat." Or it is like a compass with Anne'
fixed foot." "Thy firmnes makes my circle just, / And mak__
where I begun."[6] Holy Sonnet 17 is Donne's tribute to Anne after her
untimely death in 1617. The octave reads:[7]

> Since she whom I lov'd hath payd her last debt
> To Nature, and to hers, and my good is dead,
> And her Soule early into heaven ravished,
> Wholly on heavenly things my mind is sett.
> Here the admyring her my mind did whett
> To seeke thee God; so streames do shew their head;
> But though I have found thee, and thou my thirst hast fed,
> A holy thirsty dropsy melts mee yett.

The second line is ambiguous, but it could mean that Anne is dead both
to her own good and to Donne's. The poet has followed her soul to
heaven. On earth his love for her drew him toward the love of God. Perhaps he means that following her soul to heaven ought to be a finding
of God, but that his grief is a thirst that cannot be satisfied. The sestet,
which ought to be the resolution of the poem, seems to me almost an
accusation that God has jealously taken Anne so that his love for God
need no longer be shared with her. I want to read the poem as a bitter
lament that cannot be assuaged either by a belief in Anne's immortality
or by a recognition that only the love of God can be enjoyed.

Donne's great love, I think, while it thwarted his ambitions, gave
him what was immeasurably more important. And by accident it gave
him the gift of ordination and his ecclesiastical career. We must, then,
turn to the difficult question of Donne's religious development. Is it
really the case that he accepted ordination only for want of a better kind
of preferment? Or can we suppose that he was conscientious and in his
own way devout and religious in seeking it? Questions such as these are
ones that we ask ourselves and often find impossible to answer. Can any
of us claim that our motives are unmixed or even entirely clear to us?
Suffice it to say that to argue that Donne saw ordination as a way of
gaining preferment is by no means to deny that he also saw it as a way
to serve and as a genuinely religious vocation. The earliest religious
dilemma Donne must have faced had to do with his Roman Catholic
upbringing. His grandfather, John Heywood, fled to Louvain in 1564
not very many years after the accession of Elizabeth to the throne. His
sons, Ellis and Jasper, Donne's uncles, became Jesuits. Jasper came to
England as a missionary in 1581 and within two years was imprisoned
in the Tower of London. Years later, in 1593, Donne's brother Henry

was arrested for harboring a Roman Catholic priest. Henry was released, but the priest was executed. Donne's recusancy, then, was more than a nostalgia for the old religion; it implied a willingness to undergo persecution. It was certainly for religious reasons that Donne went up to Hart Hall, Oxford, in 1584 when he was no more than eleven years old. Since students were not obliged to subscribe to the Articles of Religion and the royal supremacy until the age of sixteen, Catholic boys sought to complete their education before that time, even though, of course, they could not take a degree. Donne apparently remained close to his family. His mother lived with him in the deanery of St. Paul's and died only three months before he did. And it is not likely she abandoned her ancestral faith. Donne's difficulty, then, was to repudiate his family's religion but not his family.

There is no reason to doubt Walton's view that when Donne was admitted to Lincoln's Inn in 1592, about nineteen years old, he was "unresolved what religion to adhere to."[8] Walton may, however, exaggerate when he says that Donne already at this time engaged in a close study of divinity as a way of resolving his doubts. His study of Cardinal Bellarmine's writings, which defended Roman Catholicism, may possibly be dated somewhat later when he was assisting Dr. Morton. What cannot be doubted at this stage of his development is Donne's doubt. He probably wrote Satyre III in 1597. The poem begins:[9]

> Kind pity chokes my spleen; brave scorn forbids
> Those tears to issue which swell my eye-lids;
> I must not laugh, nor weep sins, and be wise,
> Can railing then cure these worn maladies?
> Is not our mistress fair religion,
> As worthy of all our soul's devotion,
> As virtue was to the first blinded age?

He does not know whether to laugh or cry when he looks at religion; but true religion surely ought to transcend these reactions. The different sects of his day—Rome, Geneva, Canterbury, and the separatists—all claim truth. But "on a huge hill, / Cragged, and steep, Truth stands, and he that will / Reach her, about must, and about must go." Like flowers washed away by a raging stream, "So perish souls, which more choose men's unjust / Power from God claimed, than God himself to trust."

Donne must have resolved some of his doubts by the time he published *Pseudo-Martyr* in 1610, and within five years his ordination obliged him to accept the doctrine, discipline, and worship of the Church of England. We might argue, however, that he understood doing so not as a commitment to any closed system of religion but rather as a way of seeing his vocation in the church as one that did indeed enable him to put his trust in God rather than in any human system. While it may have been written before his ordination, I like to think that Holy Sonnet 18 represents his settled view of religion. The poem begins with a prayer: "Show me deare Christ, thy spouse, so bright and clear."[10] Which·church is the bride of Christ? The only answer is a repetition of the prayer:

> Betray kind husband thy spouse to our sights,
> And let myne amorous soule court thy mild Dove,
> Who is most trew, and pleasing to thee, then
> When she'is embrac'd and open to most men.

The idea appears to be that the church ought not to be restricting and restricted but ought to leave room for a variety of views and vocations. If this is what Donne means, then we can think of the character of the Elizabethan Settlement and of Richard Hooker's defense of it. As a *politique* Elizabeth thought of the religious settlement as one that would best preserve the unity of the commonwealth by including all but the religious extremists. Uniformity of public worship was the guarantee of unity, but the Book of Common Prayer left room for a comprehension of differing Protestant views. Hooker sought to think through this policy of comprehension. He does so in part by making a distinction between what is necessary for salvation and what is a matter of indifference, between the divine law which is immutable and infallible and positive human law which is neither. The polity and liturgy of the Church of England belong in the second category and so, of themselves, cannot claim infallibility and function properly only when they point beyond themselves to the divine law itself.

Donne, I think, must have found Hooker's point of view congenial. For one thing both writers attempt to keep together what the English Revolution was to pull apart. Let me explain what I mean. In book 5 of the *Laws of Ecclesiastical Polity* Hooker carefully and slowly establishes the conclusion that Christ is present and that he has made it possible for human beings to participate in him and so find salvation as union with God. The question then becomes *how* this possible participation can be made actual for the individual. Hooker thinks first in terms of predestination and the way predestination works itself out for a particular person in terms of justification and sanctification. The Protestant doctrines clearly appear, but without any close questioning about who is predestined and justified. Hooker follows the caution of the Articles of Reli-

gion. But one path by which God bestows the benefits of Christ's aton-
ing death on people is the mysterious one of his grace, which is not tied
to any human or ecclesiastical arrangement. Nevertheless, Hooker goes
on to speak more fully of another path, that of the sacraments of baptism and the eucharist. In other words, Hooker wants to keep together
justification and baptism, sanctification and the eucharist. The English
Revolution will take place in part because there will emerge a tendency
to make the question either-or rather than both-and. The High Calvin-
ists will increasingly insist on conversion and justification, whereas the
so-called Arminians (or anti-Calvinists) will give pride of place to the
church and the sacraments. Like Hooker, Donne accepts the Protestant
doctrines without seeking to pry too deeply into them; and he places an
equal emphasis on the church and the sacraments as the ordinary context and means by which God justifies and sanctifies his own.

In his sermons Donne seldom engages in polemics; his concern is not
so much to attack what he regards as errors as to proclaim the gospel as
he finds it in scripture. Nevertheless, the occasional glimpses we get of
what he opposes help us to understand what he means by a church
"embrac'd and open to most men." In one of his Christmas sermons he
meditates on the abundant life promised by Christ in John 10:10.[11] He
speaks of God's mercy, which has such a proportion above his justice
"as that there is no cause in him, if all men be not partakers of it." On
this basis he finds fault with those who would expunge from the Litany
the petition "That thou wouldst have mercy upon all men." God made
no one for damnation, and Donne cites Augustine's opinion as a war-
rant for his own. What he implies is that the High Calvinist view that
makes God's eternal decrees of election and reprobation the cause of
damnation as well as of salvation is one that denies scripture's insistence
on God's mercy. These extreme Protestants make narrow what God
would make broad. In other passages Donne attacks the Roman
Catholic use of indulgences and the Inquisition.[12] The church in this
way blocks the way to God, making itself an obstacle to God's grace.
Similarly, without humiliation, "without holinesse, no man shall see
God, though he pore whole nights upon the Bible; so without that, without humility, no man shall heare God speake to his soule, though hee
heare three two-houres Sermons every day."[13] Protestants as well as
Roman Catholics can turn the means of grace into ends in themselves
and so thwart their purpose. It is "an abuse of Gods grace, not to
emprove it." And it is equally dangerous "to rely upon that portion of
grace, which I thinke I had in my election, or that measure of Sanctification, which I came to in my last sicknesse."[14] Part of what he means
is that there is grave danger for Christians who fail to see that their

graced life is a journey toward God and that they ought not suppose they have ever come to the end of grace or to the end of their journey. Another part of his meaning may be what he says just before the passage I have cited. Appealing to Gregory Nazianzen, he says that the Christian religion

> is a plain, an easy, a perspicuous truth, but that the perverse and uncharitable wranglings of passionate and froward men, have made religion a hard, an intricate, and a perplexed art; so that now that religion, which carnal and worldly men, have by an ill life discredited and made hard to be believed, the passion and perverseness of schoolmen, by controversies, hath made hard to be understood.

In various ways, then, human beings seek to close what God would have open. It is not that Donne has any wish to challenge the doctrines of the church he serves. It is merely that he wants to be sure that those doctrines function to assist the Christian life and to keep open the bridge by which God's grace reaches sinners, enabling them to begin their journey. God's grace is really his mercy, and Donne's piety draws on what he finds in the Book of Common Prayer. If one goes through the prayers Donne used in public worship and underlines every occurrence of the words "sin" and "mercy," the point becomes immediately apparent. The Prayer Book harps on human sinfulness, but the counterweight is not God's judgment or wrath but God's mercy. If I am correct, then human sin and divine mercy are the very heart of Donne's religion. And it is in this way that he articulates Augustine's basic religious sensibility, a sensibility that obliges him to confess both his own incapacity for good and to confess in praise the God who has given him all the good he has. Walton's account of Donne's death echoes, I think, the points I am making.

Although he was gravely ill, Donne was determined to honor his appointment to preach at Saint Paul's "upon his old constant day, the first Friday in Lent." It may be that his determination was in part designed to counter complaints that he was too much absent from London, but there is no reason to doubt Walton's judgment that "as he had long thirsted for it, so he resolved his weakness should not hinder his journey." Donne's friends were appalled at his condition when they saw him. And when he appeared in the pulpit to preach, many people "thought he presented himself not to preach mortification by a living voice, but mortality by a decayed body, and a dying face." The sermon he preached was the one that came to be known as "Death's Duel," and those whom Walton describes as "many" drew the conclusion from his tears and his weakened voice that "Dr. Donne had preached his own Funeral Sermon."[15] The next day one of Donne's friends came to visit him and, struck by his weakness, asked him why he was so sad. Walton tells us that Donne replied "with a countenance so full of cheerful gravity, as gave testimony of an inward tranquility of mind, and of a soul willing to take a farewell of this world." I suppose that we cannot entirely trust Walton; his concern is more with constructing a panegyric of Donne than in giving us an objective and considered biography. Nor can we be sure that the words he goes on to attribute to Donne are words Donne actually used. Nevertheless, it seems to me that Walton rightly understands the basic religious attitude of Donne when he speaks of his "cheerful gravity." And even if Donne did not give the brief speech Walton attributes to him, what he is supposed to have said is an excellent summary of Donne's deepest convictions.

Donne's response to his friend, then, begins by a denial that he is sad. Instead, he has been thinking of friends who have passed from this life and whom he expects to join shortly. He has been preparing for death and is restless only because of his infirmities. He then continues,[16]

> But at this present time, I was in a serious contemplation of the providence and goodness of God to me; to me, who am less than the least of His mercies: and looking back upon my life past, I now plainly see it was His hand that prevented me from all temporal employment; and that it was His will I should never settle nor thrive till I entered into the Ministry; in which I have now lived almost twenty years—I hope to His glory,—and by which, I most humbly thank Him, I have been enabled to requite most of those friends which shewed me kindness when my fortune was very low. . . . And though of myself I have nothing to present to Him but sins and misery, yet I know He looks not upon me now as I am of myself, but as I am in my Saviour, and hath given me, even at this present time, some testimonies by His Holy Spirit, that I am of the number of His Elect: I am therefore full of inexpressible joy, and shall die in peace.

Like Augustine Donne sees the work of God's grace in his life retrospectively. To use Augustine's own metaphor, the sentence that is his life has almost ended with death about to put the period to it. And in that completed sentence Donne finds meaning. What he sees most clearly is the paradox that he has himself nothing worth offering to God, but that God's mercy has accepted him. His confession, like Augustine's, is a double one—a confession of his sins and a confession of praise to God.

In the Shadow of Thy Wings

To describe Donne's theology is immediately to run the risk of imposing some kind of system on writings that are not at all systematic or even primarily concerned with articulating a theology in the strict sense. Of course, Donne's holy poems, his sermons, and the *Devotions upon Emergent Occasions* reflect the Elizabethan Protestantism we find most carefully expressed in Hooker's *Laws of Ecclesiastical Polity*; there can be no doubt of Donne's commitment to this middle way between Geneva and Rome. Nevertheless, his writings do not expound doctrines so much as they represent reflections on what those doctrines mean for the religious life. What occasions them are various religious emotions and a wide range of scriptural texts. The rhetoric of the sermons, while it sometimes appears to be expository and didactic, really seems more concerned with drawing the listeners into a structure of thought designed to press them further toward the more mysterious referents of that structure. Walton's account of Donne's preaching, I think, captures the point. Donne was[17]

> a preacher in earnest; weeping sometimes for his auditory, sometimes
> with them; always preaching to himself like an angel from a cloud, but
> in none; carrying some, as St. Paul was, to Heaven in holy raptures,
> and enticing others by a sacred art and courtship to amend their lives:
> here picturing a vice so as to make it ugly to those that practised it;
> and a virtue so as to make it beloved, even by those that loved it not;
> and all this with a most particular grace and an unexpressible addi-
> tion of comeliness.

Donne's preaching, then, was a kind of poetry in prose, designed more to move the heart than to instruct the mind.

Another way of making the point is to say that there is a meditative character to both Donne's poetry and his prose. Needless to say, many scholars have noticed this and have explained in some detail the way the meditative conventions of his time inform his writings. Of course, we see those conventions most clearly in his *Devotions upon Emergent Occasions*, twenty-three meditations on the serious illness he experienced in 1623. These meditations follow the basic structure best know from Ignatius of Loyola's *Spiritual Exercises*. The method depends on Augustine's triad of memory, intellect, and will. The first step is memory, an exercise by which the person meditating seeks to compose a mental portrait of the object of meditation. This portrait is a composition of place, and involves locating oneself in the portrait created. Donne calls this step the meditation proper. The second step requires standing back from the portrait and reflecting on it with the intellect. How are we to understand the portrait we have drawn? Donne's word for this stage of the meditation is "expostulation," and he sees it as "debatements with God." The final stage involves turning to the will and forming resolutions designed to apply the meditation to the active Christian life.

Donne's prayers serve this function. The peculiar feature of the *Devotions* is that the object of his meditation is his own illness rather than a scriptural passage or a religious mystery. In the holy poems and the sermons, however, we can discern the spirit if not the letter of this meditative technique applied to scripture and to the doctrines Donne supposes that scripture teaches.

In sum, it is difficult to know where to begin in describing Donne's theology. But despite the absence of system, there are, I think, patterns that repeat themselves; and, as I have suggested, there is a central point of view that revolves around human sinfulness and divine mercy. Let me begin by examining one of Donne's sermons. At St. Paul's Cathedral on January 29, 1625, Donne preached on the text from Psalm 63:7—"Because thou hast been my help, therefore in the shadow of thy wings will I rejoice." He begins by suggesting that the psalms are "the manna of the Church." The legend was that the manna took the form of whatever those who ate it liked best. Similarly, the psalms adapt themselves to every human condition and speak to the condition of each individual. But "there are some certain psalms that are imperial psalms, that command over all affections and spread themselves over all occasions, catholic, universal psalms that apply themselves to all necessities."[18] In this way the entire Psalter is "contracted" into Psalm 63, and the verse Donne has chosen is itself a contraction of the whole psalm. The key to its meaning, as Jerome suggested, lies in its title, which tells us that David composed it "when he was in the wilderness of Judah." It surveys time past, present, and future. Thinking specifically of David, Donne writes,[19]

> First, his distress in the wilderness, his present estate, carried him upon the memory of that which God had done for him before; and the remembrance of that carried him upon that of which he assured himself after. Fix upon God anywhere and you shall find him a circle. He is with you now; he was with you before, for he brought you to this fixation; and he will be with you hereafter, for, "He is yesterday, and today, and the same forever." (Hebr 13:8)

The line that represents the course of our journey can intersect the circle of God's eternity at any point, but in this text the movement is from the present, to the past, and finally toward the future. We can bear present affliction because of the assurance that comes from the past, and this gives us confidence for the future. In this way Donne sets forth the structure of the sermon, a structure carefully based on his meditative and careful reading of the text.

The first part of the sermon asks us to reflect on our predicament as one of affliction. Job and others speak of the burden of affliction. And

even though we may find no one affliction too heavy to bear, the cumu-
lative weight of many afflictions is a "sand-hill of crosses." Donne
speaks of children, servants, and wives who "suffer under the anger, and
moroseness, and peevishness, and jealousy of foolish masters, and parents, and husbands." The afflictions are not extraordinary; they are ones
that few of us can avoid. God understands this, and his view trumps
what David and Solomon have said:[20]

> David and Solomon have cried out that all this world is vanity and
> levity; and God knows all is weight, and burden, and heaviness, and
> oppression; and if there were not a weight of future glory to counter-
> poise it (2 Cor 4:17), we should all sink into nothing.

Temporal affliction can certainly harden our hearts and separate us from
God, but they are of no significance when compared to spiritual affliction—"all this that is temporal is but a caterpillar got into one corner of
my garden, but a mildew fallen upon one acre of my corn." Spiritual
affliction is far worse because God withdraws "his spiritual blessings,
his grace, his patience." Donne speaks of various times when this happens, for example, "when I shall think to refresh myself in the serenity
and sweet air of a good conscience and God shall call up the damps and
vapors of hell itself and spread a cloud of diffidence and an impenetra-
ble crust of desperation upon my conscience."

Spiritual affliction, then, leads to our supposing that God's hand is
against us and that we are utterly cast off:[21]

> I shall see that because I have given myself to my corrupt nature, thou
> hast changed thine; and because I am evil towards thee, therefore thou
> hast given over being good towards me; when it comes to this height,
> . . . that mine enemy is not an imaginary enemy (fortune) nor a tran-
> sitory enemy (malice in great persons), but a real, and an irresistible,
> and an inexorable, and an everlasting enemy, the Lord of Hosts him-
> self, the Almighty God himself—the Almighty God himself only
> knows the weight of this affliction. And except he put in that *pondus
> gloriae,* exceeding weight of an eternal glory, with his own hand, into
> the other scale, we are weighed down, we are swallowed up, irrepara-
> bly, irrevocably, irrecoverably, irremediably.

Donne's reference to his "corrupt nature" must certainly be an allusion
to original sin; but, as we shall see, the predicament he describes is one
that still obtains even when the bondage of original sin has been broken.
To use Augustine's metaphor, receiving the medicine has by no means
obliterated the disease. The despair of which Donne speaks remains a
possibility for the baptized and justified Christian, and it can lead to a
kind of self-excommunication. David's greatest affliction in the wilder-

ness of Judah was his exclusion from the tabernacle and the prayers of God's congregation. And so we should not absent ourselves from the church, nor should the church close its doors to us. "[C]ertainly there is much tenderness and deliberation to be used before the Church doors be shut against any man."[22]

Granted this virtually overwhelming picture of our present predicament, what can we do? Where can we turn for the assurance that will enable us to bear our afflictions? The answer David gives in the psalm is "because thou hast been my help." Donne begins the second part of his sermon by arguing that our actions ought to be based on clear patterns:[23]

> If I pretend to serve God, and he ask me for my idea, how I mean to serve him, shall I be able to produce none? If he ask me an idea of my religion and my opinions, shall I not be able to say, It is that which thy word and thy Catholic Church hath imprinted in me? If he asks me an idea of my prayers, shall I not be able to say, It is that which my particular necessities, that which the form prescribed by the Son, that which the care and piety of the church in conceiving fit prayers hath imprinted in me? If he ask me an idea of my sermons, shall I not be able to say, It is that which the analogy of faith, the edification of the congregation, the zeal of thy work, the meditations of my heart have imprinted in me?

The alternative to these appeals to the past and to what precedes the individual's experience is an "extemporal" prayer, preaching, faith, and religion. And the consequence will be "an extemporal Heaven, a Heaven to be made for me; for to that Heaven which belongs to the Catholic Church I shall never come, except I go by way of the Catholic Church, by former ideas, former examples, former patterns. . . ."

Donne moves from this digression, or, if we prefer, from these general considerations to the theme of his sermon:[24]

> Something then I must propose to myself to be the rule and the reason of my present and future actions . . . and . . . I can propose nothing more availably than the contemplation of the history of God's former proceedings with me, which is David's way here.

Those former proceedings are summed up in God's help, and Donne argues that God "hath been my help, but he hath left something for me to do with him and by his help." This is because "help always presumes an endeavor and co-operation in him that is helped."[25] What does he mean? At first it looks as though he is discarding the usual Protestant understanding of justification by faith with its emphasis on the sovereignty of God's grace. Richard Hooker defined the righteousness we receive in justification as perfect but not inherent (that is, not our own because it is Christ's perfect righteousness imputed to us), while the righteousness we receive in sanctification is inherent but imperfect (that is, our own but never the complete sanctification reserved for the age to come). Moreover, in justification even the faith by which we are enabled to receive Christ's righteousness is God's gift and not within our own power. By saying that we have cooperated with God in his help, is Donne overturning the view we find in Hooker and in the Articles of Religion?

The answer to this question must be no. It is obvious that Donne sees the problem and wants to make it clear that God's "help" belongs in the context of sanctification rather than in that of justification. He does not employ the technical or conventional language, but we cannot mistake his meaning:[26]

> God did not elect me as a helper, nor create me, nor redeem me, nor convert me by way of helping me; for he alone did all, and he had no use at all of me. God infuses his first grace, the first way, merely as a giver, entirely, all himself; but his subsequent graces, as a helper; therefore we call them auxiliant graces, helping graces; and we always receive them when we endeavor to make use of his former grace. "Lord, I believe," says the man in the Gospel to Christ, "help mine unbelief." (Mark 9:24) If there had not been unbelief, weakness, imperfectness in that faith, there had needed no help; but if there had not been a belief, a faith, it had not been capable of help and assistance, but it must have been an entire act, without any concurrence on man's part.

We can easily see that Donne has no intention of denying the absolutely gratuitous character of "the first grace," presumably justification by faith. He would agree with Hooker's understanding. At the same time there are two points that occur to me to make. The first is that Donne at least implies that he is speaking to a congregation of justified sinners. Or perhaps his association of justification with baptism is what enables him to suppose that the people have already received the first grace. The second point has to do with his understanding of faith. It is not something given complete and once for all. The gift of faith that God gives in justification is no more than a point of departure. One way of construing the Christian life is to think of it as the working out—or the failure to work out—one's conversion. The point of reference is the new birth of justification. But Donne's way is to think of the past as a beginning and to locate the Christian's identity in that future beyond all futures. The Christian life is the line, the path that leads to God in his eternal circle. I shall want to return to Donne's understanding of justification by faith, but should wish to keep these points in mind.

The third and last part of the sermon focuses on "confidence for the future." Donne wants to make it very clear that the assurance we gain from thinking of how God has been our help in the past by no means represents an immunity from affliction. When we read the words in the text, "In the shadow of thy wings," we must not suppose this refers so much to "an absolute immunity, that we shall not be touched, as [to] a refreshing and consolation when we are touched, though we be pinched and wounded."[27] The consolation is really little more than something enabling us to stand firm in our afflictions. "If I have refreshing and respiration from them [God's wings], I am able to say as those three confessors did to Nebuchadnezzar, 'My God is able to deliver me.'" In other words confidence for the future means that we have the assurance that our afflictions will not have the final word:[28]

> Though God do not actually deliver us, not actually destroy our enemies, yet if he refresh us in the shadow of his wings, if he maintain our subsistence (which is a religious constancy) in him, this should not only establish our patience (for that is but half the work), but it should also produce a joy, and rise to an exultation: "Therefore in the shadow of thy wings, I will rejoice."

In this way Donne's meditation finally reaches the last phrase of his text. The joy of which it speaks is a counterweight to "a new spiritual disease" God has let loose on the land, a disease accompanied by "an extraordinary sadness, a predominant melancholy, a faintness of heart, a cheerlessness, a joylessness of spirit."[29] In some ways Donne's piety is a gloomy one, preoccupied with sin and death. But here we find its deeper orientation, a joy that does not deny the tragic character of human life but that is confident that God's mercy takes us beyond tragedy.

Joy in its fullness, of course, belongs in heaven, in the there and then. But Donne, though he agrees, wants to locate it, as well, in the present. He employs a metaphor to make his point. A map of the world has two hemispheres; and if we "crush heaven into a map," we shall find two hemispheres. One half heaven will be "joy"; the other, "glory":[30]

> And as of those two hemispheres of the world, the first has been known long before but the other (that of America, which is the richer in treasure), God reserved for later discoveries; so though he reserve that hemisphere of heaven which is the glory thereof, to the Resurrection, yet the other hemisphere, the joy of heaven, God opens to our discovery and delivers for our habitation even while we dwell in this world.

To be sure, this joy is not complete. "The everlastingness of the joy is the blessedness of the next life, but the entering, the inchoation is afforded here." God bids us "come" in this world; "there in the next he shall bid us, 'Welcome.'" Any soul that by a true confession is "washed in the tears of true contrition, embalmed in the blood of reconciliation, the blood of Christ Jesus" can never be cast down or disquieted:[31]

> Howling is the noise of hell, singing the voice of heaven; sadness the damp of hell, rejoicing the serenity of heaven. And he that has not this joy lacks one of the best pieces of evidence for the joys of heaven, and has neglected or refused that earnest by which God uses to bind his bargain, that true joy in this world shall flow into the joy of heaven, as a river flows into the sea.

So shall Christ's promises be fulfilled: our joy shall be full, and no one shall take it away from us (John 16:24, 22).

Donne's sermon gives us the broad pattern of his understanding of the Christian life. He accepts an Augustinian understanding of original sin, and so we can argue that he posits a radical gap between the here and now and the there and then, between the doom into which we are born and a destiny we can never achieve for ourselves. But his concern is to establish a bridge between now and then. God's mercy expressed in Christ's death makes that bridge. God may sometimes appear as our enemy, barring us access to the bridge. But that is not what his mercy desires. Instead, the Christian life represents a walking along that bridge with God's help. The Christian life is, as it were, a line—perhaps not a straight one, but a line nonetheless. The "first grace" is the point that begins that line and is solely within God's power. But the line reaches forward by common stages. Afflictions, both temporal and spiritual, are part of the picture; but so is God's help. Assurance and confidence for the future follow. Most important of all is the joy that gradually swells until the day it will flow into the oceanic joy of life to come. To pursue the metaphor of the line, it seems to me necessary to add that Donne sees us as obliged to begin our journey on that line over and over again. The line actually consists of repeated points of departure, and it is to this dimension of Donne's thought that I wish now to turn.

Repeated Beginnings and Points of Departure

Even though he seldom expounds a doctrine of justification by faith in conventional language, we have seen that Donne by no means wishes to deny this "first grace." Thus, one point of departure for the Christian life is justification. The doctrine presupposes both original sin and the atonement. In the *Devotions* Donne has all these doctrines in mind as he meditates on the onset of his illness. He punctuates the meditation proper with "O miserable condition of man!" The immediate misery, of course, is the suddenness of his sickness. But the larger misery is original sin:[32]

> O miserable condition of man! Which was not imprinted by God, who, as he is immortal himself, had put a coal, a beam of immortality into us, which we might have blown into a flame, but blew it out by our first sin; we beggared ourselves by hearkening after false riches, and infatuated ourselves by hearkening after false knowledge.

The penalty inherited through original sin is not only death itself but the apprehensions of death to be found in the earthquakes, lightnings, eclipses, and rivers of blood of sickness in the "little world" that human beings are. And in the Expostulation Donne shifts his attention to sin, which is the sickness of the soul and lacks the apprehensions of death found in physical sickness:[33]

> O height, O depth of misery, where the first symptom of the sickness is hell, and where I never see the fever of lust, of envy, of ambition, by any other light than the darkness and horror of hell itself, and where the first messenger that speaks to me doth not say, "Thou mayest die," no, nor "Thou must die," but "Thou art dead." . . .

Donne may not be speaking of total depravity, but he surely is thinking of death as physical, spiritual, and eternal.

Nevertheless, he quickly turns to the remedy of God's grace. Just as no watchmaker leaves out the spring, so God has not failed to supply his grace. He makes a spring and surely will not fail to wind it up:[34]

> [Will God] Infuse his first grace, and not second it with more, without which we can no more use his first grace when we have it, than we could dispose ourselves by nature to have it?

Again we encounter Donne's reference to the "first grace," which we are bound, I think, to equate with justification by faith. The end of his Prayer suggests the role of Christ, "who knows our natural infirmities, for he had them, and knows the weight of our sins, for he paid a dear price for them."[35] Christ's death, then, is the atonement that establishes the possibility of the forgiveness of original sin, the "first grace." Notice, however, that Donne treats this first grace as an "infusion" rather than an "imputation." He appears to say that, while justification is wholly the work of God, it is a work that gives us something we can possess as our own. Moreover, the first grace is clearly necessary but far from sufficient. With God's help we must use the first grace wisely. However much he accepts justification by faith, Donne treats it as no more than a point of departure. He focuses his attention on sanctification.

In his Prayer in this first station of his illness Donne makes the familiar comparison of God and a circle, but goes on to say that "considered in thy working upon us, [thou] art a direct line, and leadest us from our beginning, through all our ways, to our end." He prays for God's grace to enable him to see God's mercies all along the line of his life, both backward and forward. In the past he sees his "beginning in this world," his planting in the Christian church, "in the beginning of all my actions here: that in all the beginnings, in all the accesses and approaches, of spiritual sicknesses of sin, I may hear and hearken to that voice, *O thou man of God, there is death in the pot* (2 Kings 4:40), and so refrain from that which I was so hungerly, so greedily flying to." The line is a constant series of beginnings. But when he looks forward he sees another kind of beginning, "thy mercy in the beginning in the other world, when thou writest me in the book of life, in my election."[36] What really matters is what lies between the completion of his election in the next world and the first grace that planted him in the church in this world. In one of his sermons Donne says,[37]

> This life is not a Parenthesis, a Parenthesis that belongs not to the sense, a Parenthesis that might be left out, as well as put in. More depends upon this life, then so: upon every minute of this life, depend millions of yeares in the next, and I shall be glorified eternally, or eternally lost, for my good or ill use of Gods grace offered to me this houre.

He makes the same point in one of his prayers in *Essays in Divinity*. "Nor can we pass from the prison of our mother's womb, to thy palace, but we must walk (in that pace whereto thou hast enabled us) through the streets of this life, and not sleep at the first corner, nor in the midst."[38] However much he treats the first grace as God's sovereign act, Donne's true concern is with holy living, which he treats as a proper use of God's grace.

Let me reinforce this conclusion by turning to a sermon on one of the penitential psalms. Donne's text is Psalm 32:1-2: "Blessed is he whose transgression is forgiven, whose sin is covered; blessed is the man, unto whom the Lord imputeth not iniquity, and in whose spirit there is no guile." The text and, particularly, its use of the word "imputeth" looks like an obvious basis for a sermon on justification by faith. And, indeed, Donne does remember that St. Paul cites this text in his discussion of justification in Romans 4:5. The psalm speaks of blessedness:[39]

Of all these fruits of this Blessednesse, there is no other root but the goodnesse of God himselfe; but yet they grow in no other ground, then in that man, *In cujus spiritu non est dolus* ["in whose spirit there is no guile"]. The Comment and interpretation of S. *Paul*, hath made the sense and meaning of this place cleare: *To him that worketh, the reward is of debt, but to him that beleeveth, and worketh not, his faith is counted for righteousnesse, Even as David describeth the blessednesse of Man*, says the Apostle there, and so proceeds with the very words of this Text. Doth the Apostle then, in this Text, exclude the Co-operation of Man? . . . Doth S. *Paul* require nothing, nothing out of this Text, to be done by man? Surely he does. . . . To attribute an action to the next Cause, or to the Cause of that Cause, is, to this purpose, all one. And therefore, as God gave a Reformation to his Church, in prospering that Doctrine, that Justification was by faith onely: so God give an unity to his Church, in this Doctrine, That no man is justified, that works not; for, without works, how much soever he magnifie his faith, there is . . . *Guile in his spirit*.

Presumably what Donne means is that what he can call the first grace has as its cause only God's goodness, but that this grace must in turn cause the good works meant to flow from faith. Cranmer's Homily on Justification makes the same point. The faith that God gives in justification is a *lively* faith, productive of works. There ought to be no contradiction between Paul and James.

In his sermon, however, Donne does not in fact stress a works righteousness. Rather, he treats the different parts of his text as references to considerations that will show how God's mercy enables us to use his grace and so move toward the destiny of perfect blessedness:[40]

In the first Act ["whose transgression is forgiven"], we consider God the Father to have wrought; He proposed, he decreed, he accepted too a sacrifice for all mankind in the death of Christ. In the second, The Covering of sinnes, we consider God the Sonne to worke, *Incubare Ecclesiae*, He sits upon his Church, as a Hen upon her Eggs, He covers all our sinnes, whom he hath gathered into that body, with spreading himselfe, and his merits upon us all there. In this third, The not Imputing of Iniquity, we consider God the Holy Ghost to worke, and, as the Spirit of Consolation, to blow away all scruples, all diffidences, and to establish an assurance in the Conscience. The Lord imputes not, that is, the Spirit of the Lord, The Lord the Spirit, The Holy Ghost, suffers not me to impute to my selfe those sinnes, which I have truly repented.

When the psalm speaks of forgiving transgressions, it refers to the atonement; and it seems likely that the covering of sins has to do with the word and sacraments administered in the church. We should expect the non-imputation of sins to refer to justification, but Donne does not give it that meaning. Instead, it refers to the way in which the Spirit guarantees to the believer the fruits of his repentance. If "our part," then, is to use God's grace rightly, Donne wants to understand this primarily in terms of our response to God's mercies. The holy living he urges on the congregation is not a set of moral duties so much as it is a determination to allow God's grace to shape our lives.

Another way of explaining Donne's view is to say that he tends to conflate justification and sanctification. What matters to him is not a quibbling over the nice points of theology but a religious understanding that will underline the mysterious and sovereign character of God's grace—understood as his mercy—without at the same time eradicating our part in responding to God. In this sense, justification becomes, as it were, a perennial dimension of the Christian life. We could say that we are repeatedly justified, just as we have repeated beginnings. Or we could say that the work of justification will never be complete till the next life. Some of Donne's Holy Sonnets seem to me to drive in this direction. For example, in Sonnet 3 he speaks of his "playes last scene," and reflects on the "gluttonous death" that will soon claim him. The octave ends with his expectation that death may bring sleep, "But my'ever-waking part shall see that face, / Whose feare already shakes my every joint. . . ." The resolution of the sestet reads as follows:[41]

> Then, as my soule, to'heaven her first seate, takes flight,
> And earth-borne body, in the earth shall dwell,
> So, fall my sinnes, that all may have their right,
> To where they'are bred, and would presse me, to hell.
> Impute me righteous, thus purg'd of evill
> For thus I leave the world, the flesh, the devill.

It is only in death that he can expect to be imputed righteous, justified by faith. And only death will make good his baptismal renunciation of the world, the flesh, and the devil. The poet's religious destiny is firmly tied to the life to come rather than to any real experience of new birth in the past. Donne's is not a "conversion" sensibility.

In the other mode I have suggested, Donne sees the Christian life as one perennially invaded by God's grace, or at least this is his hope and prayer. Holy Sonnet 10 begins with such a prayer: "Batter my heart, three person'd God; for you / As yet but knocke, breathe, shine, and seeke to mend." The poet needs more forceful means—breaking, blowing up, burning. Only if God overthrows him will he be able to stand upright. The poem continues by the metaphor of a captured town. Donne is that town, and his reason is the "viceroy" of God, who is the true ruler of the town. But Satan has captured Donne, and even though he wishes to open the gates and admit God's besieging forces, he cannot, for his reason "is captiv'd, and proves weake or untrue." The prayer is that God will enable him to do what he wills but is unable to do. The sestet repeats and elaborates the opening prayer:[42]

> Yet dearely'I love you, 'and would be loved faine,
> But am betroth'd unto your enemie:
> Divorce mee, 'untie, or breake that knot againe,
> Take mee to you, imprison me, for I
> Except you' enthrall mee, never shall be free,
> Nor ever chaste, except you ravish mee.

The phrase "breake that knot againe" seems to me telling. The battering ram of God's grace must work repeatedly. The town that is Donne will in all likelihood be captured and recaptured over and over again.

If "the first grace" is one way Donne speaks of the beginning of his beginnings, another way revolves around various meanings of "resurrection." In the *Devotions* he finally comes to the time when his doctors call him out of bed just as Christ called Lazarus out of his tomb. He thinks of his recovery as a resurrection:[43]

> My God, my God, how large a glass of the next world is this! As we have an art, to cast from one glass to another, and so to carry the species a great way off, so hast thou, that way, much more; we shall have a resurrection in heaven; the knowledge of that thou castest by another glass upon us here; we feel that we have a resurrection from sin, and that by another glass too; we see we have a resurrection of the body from the miseries and calamities of this life. This resurrection of my body shows me the resurrection of my soul; and both here severally, of both together hereafter.

In the prayer that follows he makes his thought a little clearer; God has "made this bodily rising, by [his] grace, an earnest of a second resurrection from sin, and of a third, to everlasting glory."[44] In one of his sermons Donne repeats this threefold resurrection, "First, a Resurrection from dejections and calamities in this world, a Temporary Resurrection; Secondly, a Resurrection from sin, a Spiritual Resurrection; and then a Resurrection from the grave, a finall Resurrection."[45] We can discount the resurrection from worldly calamities, since the Christian must imitate Job's claim that he will trust God though he slay him. "[T]hough he kill me, kill me, kill me, in all these several deaths, and give me no Resurrection in this world, yet I will trust in him."[46] What counts is the spiritual resurrection; "be so mercifull to thy selfe, as to take away that life [of sin] by mortification, by repentance, and thou art come to this Res-

urrection. . . . An infallible seale of the third resurrection too, to a ful-
nesse of glory in body, as well as in soule."[47]

Here the spiritual resurrection lies in some degree within the power
of the Christian, and so Donne does not seem to identify it with "the
first grace." And yet he can understand it as the effect of conversion:[48]

> First then, Christ saies, *Ne miremini, Marvaile not at this,* not at your
> spiritual resurrection, not that a Sermon should worke upon man, not
> that a Sacrament should comfort a man, make it not a miracle, nor an
> extraordinary thing, by hearing to come to repentance, and so to such
> a resurrection. For though S. *Augustine* say, That to convert a man
> from sin, is as great a miracle, as Creation, yet S. *Augustine* speaks
> that of a mans first conversion, in which the man himself does noth-
> ing, but God all; then he is made of nothing; but after God hath
> renewed him, and proposed ordinary meanes in the Church still to
> worke upon him, he must not looke for miraculous working, but
> make Gods ordinary meanes, ordinary to him.

Donne does not deny what he elsewhere calls the first grace, and from
God's perspective this is the true beginning. But the spiritual resurrec-
tion is its consequence and the beginning for us. Once again we find
Donne's emphasis on what can be called sanctification.

In another sermon Donne speaks more emphatically of our spiritual
resurrection as the work of God's grace:[49]

> Death is the Divorce of body and soul; Resurrection is the Re-union
> of body and soule: And in this spirituall death, and resurrection,
> which we consider now, and which is all determined in the soule it
> selfe, Grace is the soule of the soule, and so the departing of grace, is
> the death, and the returning of grace is the resurrection of this sinful
> soule.

He goes on to say that just as the grave is the ordinary means to the resurrection of the body, so "to the resurrection of the soul, there is an ordinary way too, the church." At first he seems to be equating the spiritual
resurrection with baptism. And, indeed, the church is "the wombe
where my soule must be mellowed for this first resurrection." But his
emphasis is on "Reconciliation to God, and the returning of the soule of
our soule, Grace, in his Church, by his Word, and his seales there."[50]
Thus, from our perspective the spiritual resurrection is not so much an
event as a process representing repeated beginnings and points of departure. The same sensibility informs his treatment of baptism:[51]

> Upon those words of our Saviour to Nicodemus (John 2:3), *Oportet
> denuo nasci,* speaking of the necessity of Baptisme, *Non solum denuo,
> sed tertio nasci oportet,* saies S. *Bernard,* He must be born againe, and

againe; againe by baptisme, for Originall sin, and for actuall sin,
againe by repentance. . . .

What matters is not so much baptism itself, but the baptized life. God's
points of departure, then, are wholly in his hands—the first grace of justification and baptism. But our points of departure represent the use we
make of that free grace; and the Christian life, while governed by grace,
is a constant beginning all over again. Moreover, Donne tends to associate our repeated points of departure with repentance.

In his poem "Goodfriday, 1613. Riding Westward" Donne ties
dying and rising with Christ to repentance. The poem begins by identifying the soul with a sphere meant to lose its own motions toward pleasure or business and find its first mover in devotion. Thus, on this Good
Friday Donne himself is "carryed towards the West . . . when my Soule's
form bends towards the East." The East is where we can locate the dead
and risen Lord:[52]

> There I should see a Sunne, by rising set,
> And by that setting endless day beget;
> But that Christ on this Crosse, did rise and fall,
> Sinne had eternally benighted all.

Christ, the sun and Son, died by "rising" on the cross. And we can think
of Christ's words in John 12:32: "And I, when I am lifted up from the
earth, will draw all people to myself." That death was in fact a resurrection, a sunrise that brings "endless day." But Donne turns to the doctrine of the atonement, Christ's "fall" in death that eradicates the night
of sin. He is afraid to turn from west to east, since if looking on God's
face brings death, how much more must God's death appall us. Even
nature reacted this way to Christ's death. Yet he keeps all this in his
memory:

> For that looks towards them; and thou look'st towards mee,
> O Saviour, as thou hang'st upon the tree;
> I turn my backe to thee, but to receive
> Corrections, till thy mercies bid thee leave.
> O thinke mee worth thine anger, punish me,
> Burne off my rusts, and my deformity,
> Restore thine Image, so much, by thy grace,
> That thou may'st know mee, and I'll turne my face.

If by repentance he is able to receive the benefits of Christ's death, he can
turn toward him and share in his resurrection. Or, putting it another
way, repentance becomes the first resurrection that will make possible

his true resurrection in the next life. In various ways, then, we see the importance Donne attaches to repentance; and it is to that theme we must now turn.

Repentance

In the passage cited immediately above Donne equates repentance not with the forgiveness of original sin in baptism or in justification but with the forgiveness of actual sin after baptism. As we shall see, this conclusion requires some qualification; but in thinking of repentance Donne has partly in mind the conventions of Roman Catholic moral theology, which was tied to the confessional and to private penance. He clearly disapproves of the distinction this moral theology would make between mortal and venial sins. He realizes that there are "some sins so rooted, so rivetted in men, so incorporated, so consubstantiated in the soul, by habitual custom, as that those sins have contracted the nature of ancient possessions." As well, there are "less sins, light sins, vanities; and yet even these come to possess us, and separate us from Christ." Because both sorts of sins have the same effect, the distinction makes no difference whatsoever:[53]

> You heare of one man that was drowned in a vessell of Wine; but how many thousands in ordinary water? And he was no more drowned in that precious liquor, than they in that common water. A gad of steele does no more choake a man, then a feather, then a haire; Men perish with whispering sins, nay with silent sins, sins that never tell the conscience they are sins, as often as with crying sins. . . .

He has a second objection. While he accepts the distinctions of contrition, confession, and satisfaction,[54] he by no means accepts the conclusions some moral theologians would draw. We should not accept the ideas "That man should be able to satisfie God, nor that delusion upon Gods act, That God should pretend to pardon, and yet punish. Wee are not disposed to wrangle about words, and names; The Schoole may admit that exercise, but not the Pulpit."[55]

Nevertheless, Donne by no means repudiates the basic structures of Roman Catholic moral theology, and he seeks to tie those structures to a scriptural and Protestant basis. Let me make these points by examining the sermon he preached, probably at St. Paul's in 1623, on Psalm 32:5: "I acknowledged my sin unto thee, and mine iniquity have I not hid. I said, I will confess my transgressions unto the Lord, and thou forgavest the iniquity of my sin." The first words of the sermon are,[56]

> This is the Sacrament of Confession. So we may call it in a safe mean-
> ing. That is, the mystery of confession: for true confession is a myste-
> rious art.

By "sacrament" he means mystery, and so the sermon does not confine
confession to private penance. Later in the sermon he rejects the
Roman Catholic practice of bringing people to the confessional "in
chains"; and he appeals to the rubric in the Prayer Book office of the
Visitation of the Sick which allows sick persons, "if they feel their consciences troubled with any weighty matter, to make a special confession
and to receive absolution at the hands of the priest."[57] But this is simply a special case in the broader structure of the two parts of the psalm
verse, "David's act and God's act, confession and absolution." Both
these acts, however, can be subdivided so as to make their significance
clear. David's act of confession takes place in three stages. First, we find
"I acknowledged my sin"; then, "I have not hid my iniquity"; finally,
"I said I will confess."

The first of these stages is David's "reflected" and "preparatory" act
by which he "came to a feeling in [himself] what [his] sinful condition
was. This is our quickening in our regeneration and second birth." As
Donne continues it becomes evident that he is indeed thinking of the first
grace and consequently of justification:[58]

> And till this [the regeneration] come a sinner lies as the chaos in the
> beginning of the creation, before the "Spirit of God had moved upon
> the face of the waters, dark" and "void," and "without form." He
> lies, as we may conceive out of the authors of natural story, the slime
> and mud of the river Nilus to lie, before the sun-beams strike upon it;
> which after, by the heat of those beams, produces several shapes and
> forms of creatures. So till this first beam of grace, which we consider
> here, strikes upon the soul of a sinner, he lies in the mud and slime, in
> the dregs and lees and tartar of his sin.

The sinner cannot even wish that the sun would shine on him, indeed,
cannot even know that there is a sun. But once the sun of the first grace
shines on him "his sins begin to take their forms, and their specifica-
tions, and they appear to him in their particular true shapes. . . . "

This stage, I suggest, is not yet repentance. But it is the necessary
basis for repentance, which would be impossible if God had not applied
the benefits of Christ's atonement to the sinner, freeing him from original sin. In this way Donne ties his doctrine of repentance to the Augustinian framework that lies at the heart of the theology to which he is
committed. Nevertheless, the first stage is only the place where grace
must begin. The first grace reveals to the sinner his sins, and the second
stage represents a right use of that grace:[59]

> Blessed be thy name, O Lord, that hast brought me to this *notum feci*,
> to know mine own name, mine own miserable condition. He will also
> say, may that blessing of thine enlarge itself farther, that as I am come
> to this *notum feci*, to know that I mistook myself all this while, so I
> may proceed to the *non operui*, to a perfect sifting of my conscience,
> in all corners. . . .

It would not be misleading, I think, to understand this stage as contrition.
The final stage, of course, is the actual confession of sin, which is always
made to God even when it is made to a priest. The confession must be of
true sins, all sins, his own sins and not those of others, and on the understanding that all sins are sins against God. True confession, Donne seems
to be saying, is a mean between over-scrupulosity and indifference.

The next part of the sermon considers God's act of absolution,
which has "two leaves . . . the fulness of God's mercy . . . and the sea-
sonableness, the acceleration of his mercy." The first leaf precedes confession; the second follows it:[60]

> These will be the two leaves of this door. And let the hand that shuts
> them be this "and," this particle of connection which we have in the
> text, "I said, and thou didst." For though this remission of sin be not
> presented here as an effect upon that cause of David's confession . . .
> yet it is at least as a consequence from an occasion, so assured, so
> infallible, as let any man confess as David did, and he shall be sure to
> be forgiven as David was. For though this forgiveness be a flower of
> mercy, yet the root grows in the justice of God. If we acknowledge our
> sin, he is faithful and just to forgive us our sin. (1 John 1:9) It grows
> out of his faithfulness, as he hath vouchsafed to bind himself by a
> promise, and out of his justice, as he hath received a full satisfaction
> for all our sins. So that this hand, this "and," in our text, is as a liga-
> ment, as a sinew, to connect and knit together that glorious body of
> God's preventing grace and his subsequent grace. If our confession
> come between and tie the knot, God that moved us to that act will
> perfect all.

In one sense God's absolution is the consequence of David's confession.
But when we examine the picture more carefully, we find that it is the
promise of God's mercy, rooted in the atonement effected by Christ's
death, that comes before the confession itself. The absolution completes
God's mercy for the sinner. The prevenient grace, I think, is not quite the
same thing as the first grace. Donne goes on to cite Revelation 3:20:
"Behold I stand at the door and knock." God wishes to come and sup
with us and "feast us with his abundant graces." But he does not give us
those graces at the door, but only when "we have let him in, by the good
use of his former grace."[61] We can conclude, I think, that God's grace is

always present. It is the first grace that allows the very possibility of repentance. And God's subsequent graces remain prevenient of our repentance, and follow it by bestowing absolution. Moreover, our repentance must be repeated over and over again—repeated beginnings and points of departure along the line of our lives.

In one of his prayers from *Essays in Divinity* Donne makes the last point explicit. He asks God to "hide us in the wounds of thy Son, our Savior Christ Jesus; and though our sins be as red as scarlet, give them there another redness, which may be acceptable in thy sight." The prayer continues with a series of renunciations—of confidence in this world, in our own merits, even in our own confessions and accusations of ourselves:[62]

> Yea we renounce all confidence even in our repentances, for we have found by many lamentable experiences that we never perform our promises to thee, never perfect our purposes in our selves, but relapse again and again into those sins which again and again we have repented. . . . We have no confidence in our own confessions and repentances, but in that blessed Spirit, who is the author of them and loves to perfect his own works and build upon his own foundations, we have.

The mercy of God "in the merits of Christ" is "a sea of mercie, that as the Sea retaines no impression of the Ships that passe in it, (for Navies make no path in the Sea) so when we put out into the boundlesse Sea of the blood of Christ Jesus, by which onely wee have reconciliation to God, there remains no record against us."[63] And yet we must sail that sea again and again.

In another sermon, preached on the shortest verse in the Bible—"Jesus wept" (John 11:35)—it is Christ's tears rather than his blood that represent the sea. Donne divides Jesus' tears into three kinds—the tears for Lazarus, those for Jerusalem (Luke 19:41), and the tears of blood at his passion. These last tears are the ones important for us:[64]

> And if Christs looking upon *Peter*, made *Peter* weep, shall not his looking upon us here, with teares in his eyes, such teares in such eyes, springs of teares, rivers of teares, seas of teares, make us weep too? *Peter* who wept under the waight of his particular sin, wept bitterly: how bitterly wept Christ under the waight of all the sins of all the world? In the first teares, Christs humane teares (those we called a spring) we fetched water at one house, we condoled a private calamity in another; *Lazarus* was dead. In his second teares, his Prophetical teares, wee went to the condoling of a whole Nation; and those we called a River. In these third teares, his pontificall teares, teares for sin,

for all sins (those we call a Sea) here is *Mare liberum*, a Sea free and open to all; Every man may saile home, home to himselfe, and lament his own sins there.

The grace of Christ gives Peter the tears of repentance, and the story is paradigmatic for us. Indeed, Donne concludes the sermon by exhorting the people to wash themselves in all of Christ's tears. But repentance here is not so much an act as an attitude. Donne calls it a "godly sorrow." And he is concerned to argue that godly sorrow and joy are one and the same. "To conceive true sorrow and true joy, are things not onely contiguous, but continuall; they doe not onely touch and follow one another in a certaine successione, Joy assuredly after sorrow, but they consist together, they are all one, Joy and Sorrow."[65]

It seems possible to me to keep this point in mind even when we examine some of Donne's poetry. The Holy Sonnets seem at first gloomy and almost despairing, but the attitude that prevails is a confidence in God's repeated mercies. Holy Sonnet 2 begins as the poet sees himself "summoned / By sicknesse, deaths herald, and champion." In the octave he compares himself to a pilgrim and a prisoner. But the pilgrim is a traitor, who has committed treason "abroad" and has been justly forbidden his homeland. And the prisoner, though wishing for release, prefers imprisonment to execution. Donne fears that death will bring him condemnation. But the resolution in the sestet reads,[66]

> Yet grace, if thou repent, thou canst not lacke;
> But who shall give thee that grace to beginne?
> Oh make thy selfe with holy mourning blacke,
> And red with blushing, as thou art with sinne;
> Or wash thee in Christ's blood, which hath this might
> That being red, it dyes red soules to white.

Repentance, then, would resolve the poet's anguish and allow him not to fear death. Grace will follow repentance, but it must also precede it. And the grace that will enable him "to beginne" is available in Christ's blood, shed for the forgiveness of sin. Here it may well be that the godly sorrow is not quite a joy; but it is a confidence, not in himself, but in the mercy of God made effective in Christ's death.

Holy Sonnet 4 makes, I think, a similar point. The poem opens with a description of judgment day, when the angels will blow their trumpets at the "imagin'd corners" of the "round" earth and when all the dead will be raised, and even those who have lived till the end of the world (1 Cor 15:51-52) will behold God. But the poet is not ready and is unwilling to face God's judgment. His prayer is:[67]

> But let them sleepe, Lord, and mee mourne a space,
> For, if above all these, my sinnes abound,
> 'Tis late to aske abundance of thy grace,
> When we are there; here on this lowly ground
> Teach mee how to repent; for that's as good
> As if thou' hadst seal'd my pardon, with thy blood.

Once again repentance clears the way, and once again grace—Christ's teaching—makes repentance possible. The Christian life, then, is a line. Only God can place the point from which the line stems. But the other points along that line, while constantly informed by God's helping graces, are points at which we must do our part to use grace wisely. These repeated points are best understood as repeated repentances. Or, we could say that the Christian is a pilgrim who walks with a godly sorrow and yet, paradoxically, with a joy that will find its fulness at the end of the journey.

Seeing, Knowing, and Loving

As we have seen, Donne knows Augustine's thought and can reflect the Augustinian triad of memory, understanding, and will. The structure of the *Devotions* makes this apparent. Indeed, in Expostulation 5 he says: "I cannot fear but that thou wilt reckon with me from this minute, in which, by thy grace, I see thee; whether this understanding, and this will, and this memory may not decay, to the discouragement and the ill interpretation of them that see that heavy change in me, I cannot tell."[68] But the reference is a passing one. I should draw the same conclusion regarding section IV: The Trinity of "A Litanie":[69]

> As you distinguish'd undistinct
> By power, love, knowledge bee,
> Give mee a such selfe different instinct
> Of these; let all mee elemented bee,
> Of power, to love, to know, you unnumbered three.

It is interesting that power appears instead of memory or mind, and the power is simply what enables the loving and knowing. I suggest that what we found central in Augustine's thought is peripheral in Donne's. Nevertheless, he does have a good deal to say about the vision and knowledge of God, and something to say about the love of God.

In a sermon preached at St. Paul's on Christmas Day, 1621, Donne worries with the question of knowledge and with its relation to natural reason. His text is John 1:8: "He was not that light, but was sent to bear witness of that light." The text is in the context of John's account of Christ's divinity, and yet it also refers to Christ's "offices, and to his calling of his apostles."[70] If we ask *who* is the light, the answer can only be Christ. But scripture refers to other "lights"—John the Baptist, the apostles, and, indeed, all the faithful. The troubling verse in John's prologue, however, is the fourth one: "In it was life, and that life was the light of men." Many understand the reference to be "only that natural light, natural reason, which distinguishes us men from other creatures." Donne thinks that this interpretation does not reach "home, for it reaches not to the essential light which is Christ Jesus, nor to the supernatural light, which is faith and grace."[71] The conclusion with which he begins and ends the sermon is that Christ alone is "that light, the true light. . . . The fountain of all lights," and that "in our regeneration, when we are made new creatures, the Spirit of God finds us in natural darkness, and by him we are made light in the Lord":[72]

> All other men, by occasion of this flesh, have dark clouds, yea nights, yea long and frozen winter nights of sin, and of the works of darkness. Christ was incapable of any such nights or any such clouds, any approaches toward sin; but yet Christ admitted some shadows, some such degrees of human infirmity, as by them, he was willing to show, that the nature of man, in the best perfection thereof, is not *"vera lux, tota lux,* true light, all light,". . .

Properly speaking, it is Christ in his divinity who is that true light. That "essential" light begets the "supernatural" light of faith and grace.

Donne continues by meditating on the relation of natural light and natural reason to faith. Reason can, of course, quench the light of Christ. "We may search so far and reason so long of faith and grace as that we may lose not only them but even our reason too, and sooner become mad than good."[73] Yet, "It is but a slack opinion, it is not belief, that is not grounded upon reason." Attempting to convert a heathen person by threatening him with the fires of hell if he refuses to believe the articles of the Christian faith is doomed to failure, since the obvious way out for the prospective convert is to refuse to believe in hell. "The reason therefore of man, must first be satisfied." But we must do this persuasively, beginning with an argument from providence for the existence of God and only then moving on to scripture. Donne sees both sides of the question, and his basic conclusion is that "[k]nowledge cannot save us, but we cannot be saved without knowledge; faith is not on this side knowledge but beyond it; we must necessarily come to knowledge first, though we must not stay at it when we are come thither."[74] The issue is what use we make of the common light of reason:

> Divers men may walk by the seaside and the same beams of the sun
> giving light to them all, one gathereth by the benefit of that light peb-
> bles or speckled shells for curious vanity, and another gathers precious
> pearl or medicinal amber by the same light.

People have discovered many important and beneficial wisdoms and
crafts by their use of natural reason, but in the long run this is but the
gathering of pebbles.

The important task is to use the light of reason as a starting point.
In a long and highly rhetorical passage Donne explains what he
means:[75]

> But, if thou canst take this light of reason that is in thee, this poor
> snuff that is almost out in thee, thy faint and dim knowledge of God
> that riseth out of this light of nature, if thou canst in those embers,
> those cold ashes, find out one small coal and wilt take the pains to
> kneel down and blow that coal with thy devout prayers, and light thee
> a little candle (a desire to read that book which they call the Scrip-
> tures, and the Gospel, and the Word of God); if with that little candle
> thou canst creep humbly into low and poor places; if thou canst find
> thy Savior in a manger, and in his swathing clouts, in his humiliation,
> and bless God for that beginning . . . if according to that example thou
> canst contain thyself in that station and vocation in which God hath
> planted thee, . . . if with this little poor light, these first degrees of
> knowledge and faith, thou canst follow him into the garden and
> gather up some of the drops of his precious blood and sweat which he
> shed for thy soul; if thou canst follow him to Jerusalem and pick up
> some of those tears which he shed upon that city and upon thy soul;
> . . . Thou shalt see that thou by thy small light hath gathered pearl
> and amber, and they by their great lights nothing but shells and
> pebbles. . . .

Natural reason, then, supplies a beachhead for faith; and grace does not
so much supplant nature as transform it. But the transforming power of
faith is itself the beginning of a journey of redeemed knowing rather
than an event.

Donne completes the sermon by meditating on four pairs of lights.
The second pair implies that the light of nature, though fainter, directs
us to the light of faith the way the light of the moon points toward the
light of the sun.[76] The third pair contrasts the light of the heavenly luminaries with that of combustible things on earth. The luminaries are
found in the Christian Church, "the proper sphere in which . . . the
essential light Christ Jesus moves by that supernatural light of faith and
grace." Christians are the combustible things of earth that catch fire by
"the zeal of God's glory, and compassion of other's misery."[77] Donne

must here be thinking of the love of God and neighbor. The final pair of lights is that of precious stones and their reflections, which Donne equates with good works, which profit not only those who do them but also those who see them done.[78] These three pairs revolve around the progress Christians make from faith to a right will and finally to right actions. But the first pair contrasts the present life of Christians with the life to come. The *lux essentiae*, as God's own essential light, is unattainable:[79]

> yet by the light of faith and grace in sanctification we may come to such a participation of that light of essence, or such a reflection of it in this world, that it shall be true of us which was said of those Ephesians, "You were once darkness, but now are light in the Lord." (Eph 5:8)

The other light in the pair is "the light of glory. . . . That glorification which we shall have at the last day of which glory we consider a great part to be in that denudation, that manifestation of all to all . . . this laying open of ourselves to one another, which shall accompany that state of glory, where we shall see one another's bodies and souls, actions and thoughts." Donne here seems to reflect Augustine's guess as we found it in the last chapter but one of the *City of God*. But he goes on to argue that this "denudation" of the next life in glory is one that can be anticipated by the "denudation" of repentance in this life. Thus, the Christian journey along the line that leads to God involves the growth and unfolding of faith and vision, but faith is itself tied to repentance.

Donne covers much of the same ground in another sermon, preached at St. Paul's on Easter Day, 1628, on the text from 1 Corinthians 13:12 that we saw played a key role in Augustine's thinking: "For now we see through a glass darkly, but then face to face; now I know in part, but then I shall know, even as also I am known." The basic contrast he sees in the text is that between "now" and "then," that is, in this life and in that to come. He organizes the sermon around the further distinction between vision and knowledge. In this life the whole world is the theater in which by natural reason we see "the Book of Creatures."[80] The church, then, is the academy in which we find by faith the knowledge of God. And he points out that this knowledge is necessary in order for us to love God. Later in the sermon he contrasts present faith with future vision and says,[81]

> this knowledge of God, by this faith, may be diminished and increased, for it is but *in aenigma,* says our text, darkly, obscurely; clearly in respect of the natural man but yet obscurely in respect of that knowledge of God which we shall have in heaven; for, says the

Apostle, "As long as we walk by faith, and not by sight, we are absent from the Lord." (2 Cor 5:6) Faith is a blessed presence, but compared with heavenly vision it is but an absence; though it create and constitute in us a possibility, a probability, a kind of certainty of salvation, yet that faith which the best Church hath, is not so far beyond that sight of God which the natural man hath, as that sight of God which I shall have in heaven is above that faith which we have now in the highest exaltation.

This is why Paul says we now know only "in part." And "the best knowledge that we have of God here, even by faith, is rather that he knows us, than that we know him."[82]

When he turns to the "then" of his text, Donne is obliged to be more speculative, and he is consequently briefer in his meditation. He stumbles on the question what it will mean to see God "face to face." At first all he can say is that "[w]e shall see whatsoever we can be the better for seeing." Seeing God will mean "[n]othing but the sight of the humanity of Christ, which only is visible to the eye."[83] He finds more to say about our knowledge of God in the next life. Obviously, this knowledge cannot be "a comprehensive knowledge of God." Instead, following Thomas, Donne defines our future knowledge of God as follows:[84]

It cannot be such a knowledge of God as God hath of himself, nor as God hath of us; for God comprehends us and all this world and all the world that he could have made, and himself. But it is, *nota similitudinis, non aequalitatis*. As God knows me, so I shall know God; but I shall not know God so as God knows me. It is not *quantum*, but *sicut*; not as much, but as truly. . . .

Thus, knowledge in the there and then will have serious strictures placed on it. But this knowledge will be enough, for "it shall be a knowledge so like his knowledge, as it shall produce a love like his love, and we shall love him as he loves us." What seems to me a little surprising is that Donne does not pursue the point. He is far from rejecting the idea that the journey of faith and repentance is a journey of love as well as of knowledge, but that is not where his emphasis lies. Loving God somehow seems less important than accepting his mercy, the mercy that destroys sin and death.[85] Or perhaps we could say that loving God becomes the resolutions of Donne's will, his moral intent to please God.

Nevertheless, Donne does accept Augustine's idea of the ordering of loves. In a sermon preached on Trinity Sunday he takes 1 Corinthians 16:22 as his text: "If any man love not the Lord Jesus Christ, let him be anathema, maranatha." The emphasis of the sermon is on the object of our love rather than on the loving itself. Donne does, however, argue that in the first instance we should love Christ because he is God:[86]

> God forbids us not a love of the creature, proportionable to the good
> that that creature can do us; to love fire as it warms me, and meat as
> it feeds me, and a wife as she helps me; but because God does all this,
> in all these several instruments, God alone is centrically, radically,
> directly to be loved, and the creature with a love reflected and derived
> from him; and Christ to be loved with the love due to God himself.

To love Christ as Lord is to love him as God. But we can also love him
"as he hath loved us." And so we must love him not only when we shout
"hosanna" or behold him transfigured, but also in his crucifixion.
Donne's exhortation is that we should love Christ

> not only in spiritual transfigurations, when he visits thy soul with
> glorious consolations, but even in his inward eclipses, when he with-
> holds his comforts and withdraws his cheerfulness, even when he
> makes as though he loved not thee, love him. Love him all the way, to
> his end, and to thy end too, to the laying down of thy life for him.[87]

Only occasionally does Donne address the theme of love in his religious poetry, and we have already looked at the sonnet he wrote after
his wife's death, where he plays on the ambiguity attached to the relation of that love to his love of God. Two of the other Holy Sonnets seem
to have in mind his love poetry and his "profane love." Holy Sonnet 15
is a kind of lament and confession. Donne begins by wishing that "those
sighes and teares" might return, presumably that he might once more
find himself in the bittersweet anguish of the Petrarchian lover of his secular poetry. But this wish is that the attitude of the crossed lover may be
applied to repentance:[88]

> That I might in this holy discontent
> Mourne with some fruit, as I have mourn'd in vaine;
> In mine Idolatry what showres of raine
> Mine eyes did waste? What griefs my heart did rent?
> That sufferance was my sinne; now I repent;
> 'Cause I did suffer I must suffer paine.

The drunkard and the lecher at least have the memory of "past joyes"
to console them; but for the poet the past joys are the sins that cause him
to deserve punishment. The comparison of the poem is not one relating
profane to sacred love, but one that compares and contrasts the lover's
sighs with the Christian's penitence.

Holy Sonnet 19 compares the inconstant lover with the inconstant
penitent. Donne begins by speaking of how "contrayes meet in one."
The allusion appears to be to Romans 7, where Paul complains that the
good he wills he cannot do:[89]

> Inconstancy unnaturally hath begott
> A constant habit; that when I would not
> I change in vowes, and in devotione.

The inconstancy of his contrition is "As humorous . . . As my prophane Love, and as soone forgott." His condition is a spiritual chill and fever:

> So my devout fitts come and go away
> Like a fantastique Ague: save that here
> Those are my best dayes, when I shake with feare.

Here too Donne avoids any comparison of secular to divine love. Indeed, the only Holy Sonnet that speaks directly of the love of God is Sonnet 11. The question of the poem is how to fulfill the desire to love God. The answer is to meditate on how God the Spirit "doth make his Temple in thy brest." That this miracle has happened is the effect of Christ's incarnation and death:[90]

> 'Twas much, that man was made like God before,
> But, that God should be made like man, much more.

Presumably, we can love God because he first loved us by sending his Son to die for us, enabling the Spirit to dwell in our hearts. But Donne's emphasis is far more on God's love for us than on ours for him. And the word "love" occurs only once in the poem. It is difficult to escape the conclusion that in considering the line of human life as the bridge that God has built enabling us to journey from the here and now to the there and then Donne's emphasis is on a life of repentance and faith. That life includes a progress in vision and knowledge, and he does not deny that it is also a life of love. But, oddly enough, loving God does not fully capture his imagination. Perhaps this is because it is easier for him to see himself as the undeserving beloved than as one who dares to love God.

Death

In Donne's time people were preoccupied with death, probably because it was so frequent and, from our perspective, so very public. Death was not necessarily associated with old age as it is with us. We can remember that only six of Donne's children were still alive at the time of his death. In Holy Sonnet 4 he refers to the dead: "All whom the flood did, and fire shall o'erthrow, / All whom warre, dearth, age, agues, tyrannies, / Despair, law, chance, hath slaine. . . . "[91] Moreover, death led to hell and eternal torment as well as to heaven and to God. It became important to practice the "art of dying." And, of course, this art really began with learning how to live so that one's death would be an entrance to heaven. Donne speaks, as we have noted, of human life as a line. God himself has provided such a line, a bridge that serves to lead us to him. Rightly understood, the Christian life must be a journey along that bridge, and the way the Christian conducts himself is crucial. For Donne, as we have seen, there must be a constant reliance on God's grace and a good use of the first grace that establishes the first point on the line. We can illustrate the first of these points by Holy Sonnet 13.[92] The first line is a question: "Thou hast made me, And shall thy worke decay?" The answer would seem to be, certainly not. But in the first part of the sonnet the poet has no certainty whatsoever. His end, death, hastens to meet him; and he runs just as fast toward it. Or, he is paralyzed, immobile and terrified, trapped between "Despaire behind, and death before." Sin wastes his "feeble flesh," but acts like a dead weight plunging him to hell. Donne then counters the despair of the octave with the resolution of the sestet:

> Onely thou art above, and when towards thee
> By thy leave I can looke, I rise againe;
> But our old subtle foe so tempteth me,
> That not one houre my selfe I can sustaine;
> Thy Grace may wing me to prevent his art,
> And thou like Adamant draw mine iron heart.

The resolution does not find Donne any more capable of trusting in himself. His rising is temporary and only possible by God's "leave." But, we may suppose, God's grace is his mercy; and it will wing—wound? give wings to?—him so that Satan's testing will not prove effective. Like a magnet God will draw the poet's iron heart to himself and so keep what he has made from decay and death.

From another perspective Donne sees the art of dying not merely as God's work but as his own response to God's grace. In the Hymne to God My God, in My Sicknesse Donne thinks of heaven as the concert hall where the choir of saints will sing and make music forever. He will "be made thy Musique; As I come / I tune the Instrument here at the dore, / And what I must doe then, thinke here before." His thoughts are directed to the narrow strait of his death. He is like a map his doctors consult, and like maps where West and Each touch one another, "So death doth touch the Resurrection." Just as straits lead to the riches of the new world or of the Orient or to Jerusalem, so the strait of death will be for him the gate to the riches of heaven. The joy of this confidence, however, springs from his meditation on the cross, which stood in the very place where Adam's tree was:[93]

> Looke Lord, and finde both *Adams* met in me;
>   As the first *Adams* sweat surrounds my face,
>   May the last *Adams* blood my soule embrace.

The poem ends with the prayer that the Lord will receive him, wrapped in Christ's purple robe, and give him his crown because of Christ's crown of thorns.

Of course, Donne's best and fullest discussion of death is in his last sermon, Death's Duel. His text is Psalm 68:20—"And unto God the Lord belong the issues of death." The structure of the sermon, as is usually the case with Donne's sermons, is a good deal looser and harder to pin down than what he says would suggest. The fragility of the structure seems designed to ensnare the listeners, draw them into the sermon, and point them beyond it to the object of Donne's meditation. But with this qualification, he establishes a kind of structure toward the beginning of the sermon:[94]

> In all these three lines then, we shall look upon these words. First, as the God of power, the Almighty Father rescues his servants from the jaws of death. And then as the God of mercy, the glorious Son rescued us, by taking upon himself this issue of death. And then between these two, as the God of comfort, the Holy Ghost rescues us from all discomfort by his blessed impressions beforehand, that what manner of death soever be ordained for us, yet this *exitus mortis* shall be *introitus in vitam*, our issue in death shall be an entrance into everlasting life. And these three considerations, our deliverance *a morte, in morte, per mortem*, from death, in death, and by death, will abundantly do all the offices of the foundations. . . .

Donne does not immediately honor the hopeful implications of this introduction. The deliverance "from death" turns out to be no more than a deliverance "into death." We leave the death of our mother's womb only to enter "the manifold deaths of this world." And the last of these deaths is the one we normally call death; "we come to seek a grave."[95] The manifold deaths represented by the ages of man are not like phoenixes risen from their ashes, but like what carrion or dung breed. "Our youth is hungry and thirsty after those sins which our infancy knew not. And our age is sorry and angry that it cannot pursue those sins which our youth did."[96] Our sins are our deaths, and should be of more consequence to us even than death itself that is an entrance into the death of corruption.

Only at the very end of the first section of the sermon does Donne make his positive point:[97]

by recompacting this dust into the same body, and reanimating the same body with the same soul, he shall in a blessed and glorious resurrection give me such an issue from this death as shall never pass into any other death, but establish me into a life that shall last as long as the Lord of life himself.

Nevertheless, to think of the whole of human life as a movement from death to death is to imply that we need not only deliverance *from* death, but also deliverance *in* death. At any rate our "critical day" is not the day we die but the whole of our life. And Donne supposes that we are always surrounded by the mercies of God. The conclusion he draws is,[98]

God does not say, live well and you shall die well, that is, an easy, a quiet death; but live well here, and you shall live well forever. As the first part of a sentence pieces well with the last, and never respects, never hearkens after the parenthesis that comes between, so does a good life here flow into an eternal life, without any consideration what manner of death we die. But whether the gate of my prison be opened with an oiled key (by a gentle and preparing sickness), or the gate be hewn down by a violent death, or the gate be burned down by a raging and frantic fever, a gate into heaven I shall have, for from the Lord is the cause of my life, and with the Lord God are the issues of death.

We begin to see that God's deliverance of us *from* death depends on his deliverance of us *in* the deaths of this life. And Donne continues by making all this hinge on Christ's death, the death *through* which God delivers us.

The last part of the sermon Donne himself calls "a passion sermon."[99] It is really a meditation on Christ's suffering and death. He asks the congregation to examine themselves as to whether they have followed Christ in his passion. In great humility Christ washes the feet of the disciples at the Last Supper:[100]

In your preparation to the holy and blessed Sacrament, have you with a sincere humility sought a reconciliation with all the world, even with those that have been averse from it, and refused that reconciliation from you? If so, and not else, you have spent that first part of his last day in a conformity with him.

Questions like this follow as Donne describes the events that lead up to Christ's death. My impression is that it is not clear to him that anyone can answer the questions he asks in a fully satisfying way. At any rate, the sermon ends by turning attention away from our poor efforts to the one who through death redeemed us:[101]

> For though to this God our Lord, belonged these issues of death, so
> that considered in his own contract, he must necessarily die, yet at no
> breach or battery which they had made upon his sacred body issued
> his soul, but . . . "he gave up the Ghost," and as God breathed a soul
> into the first Adam, so this second Adam breathed his soul into God,
> into the hands of God. There we leave you in that blessed dependency,
> to hang upon him that hangs upon the cross, there bathe in his tears,
> there suck at his wounds, and lie down in peace in his grave, till he
> vouchsafe you a resurrection, and an ascension into the Kingdom,
> which he has purchased for you with the inestimable price of his
> incorruptible blood. *Amen.*

And so the deliverance from death assured to us through the death of
Christ is the mercy that enables God to deliver us in the deaths of this
life and, finally, to bring us to the resurrection of the next life. Or, we
could say that this deliverance through death is what has built the bridge
that we must cross to get to heaven and what has guaranteed to us that
God's mercy outweighs our sin.

Let me conclude this section by citing as Donne's considered judgment about death Holy Sonnet 6:[102]

> Death be not proud, though some have called thee
> Mighty and dreadfull, for, thou art not soe,
> For, those, whom thou think'st, thou dost overthrow,
> Die not, poore death, nor yet canst thou kill mee.
> From rest and sleepe, which but thy pictures bee,
> Much pleasure, then from thee, much more must flow,
> And soonest our best men with thee doe goe,
> Rest of their bones, and soules deliverie.
> Thou art slave to Fate, Chance, kings, and desperate men,
> And dost with poyson, warre, and sicknesse dwell,
> And poppie, or charmes can make us sleepe as well,
> And better then thy stroake; why swell'st thou then?
> One short sleepe past, wee wake eternally,
> And death shall be no more; death, thou shalt die.

Conclusion

If we were to assess Donne as a theologian, no more or less, then we
should have to examine him in the context of his own time and see him
in relation to the theological spectrum we strive to discern in the Church
of England early in the seventeenth century. There is no real difficulty in
concluding that Donne's stance is one that sees opponents on either
hand, and so we can think of him as treading the middle way between

Rome and Geneva. Up to a point, I think, this kind of assessment poses no serious problems, provided we understand that Donne is certainly willing to make use of what he regards as true and good in the party platforms of his opponents. To take an obvious example, he owes a great debt to Counter-Reformation conventions of meditation. As well, he would be unwilling to abandon the Puritan emphasis on scripture and its careful reading. At the same time, one difficult question remains. Is he influenced by the beginnings of what the Puritans called "Arminianism" and what certainly became the anti-Calvinism implied by the term. Donne knew Launcelot Andrewes and must certainly have been acquainted with the controversy over "Arminianism." By 1629, in Charles I's last Parliament before he was obliged to summon the Long Parliament in 1640, a committee of the House of Commons drew up a condemnation of Arminianism in the Church of England that included the teaching of any doctrine contrary to those of the Church of England (that is, any denial of predestination, of justification by faith, of the sole authority of scripture), the fostering of any Romanizing doctrines, and the re-establishment of Romish ceremonies. So far as I can tell Donne never addresses this controversy; indeed we might be able to read his disapproval of theological squabbles as his resolution to stay out of them. My guess is that he remained more or less loyal to the kind of interpretation given the Elizabethan Settlement by Richard Hooker.

If that guess has any merit, then we should expect Donne to combine a sincere commitment to the kind of Augustinian theology we find in Hooker together with Hooker's reluctance to draw narrow boundaries. And we can without difficulty suppose that Hooker seeks to remain true to the Articles of Religion. The structure of thought would look something like this. Because of Adam's fall humanity is in a state of original sin. As Article IX puts it,

> Original sin . . . is the fault and corruption of the Nature of every man, that naturally is engendered of the offspring of Adam, whereby man is very far gone from original righteousness, and is of his own nature inclined to evil, so that the flesh lusteth always contrary to the Spirit; and therefore in every person born into this world, it deserveth God's wrath and damnation. And this infection of nature doth remain, yea in them that are regenerated. . . . And although there is no condemnation for them that believe and are baptized; yet the Apostle doth confess, that concupiscence and lust hath of itself the nature of sin.

The Article is filled with ambiguities; but while it falls short of arguing for total depravity, it clearly takes a radical view of the human predicament not only before but after "regeneration." Moreover, regeneration takes place by faith and baptism, even though we do not learn how these two are supposed to be related. Clearly, then, Donne would have no difficulty subscribing to this view of original sin. It leaves room for his idea that faith can use natural reason as a place to begin regeneration, and it allows him to say what he does about baptism as one place we can find the "first grace."

Articles X and XI treat free will and justification. The first of these states that because of the fall

> Man [*sic*] . . . cannot turn and prepare himself, by his own natural strength and good works, to faith, and calling upon God. Wherefore we have no power to do good works pleasant and acceptable to God, without the grace of God by Christ preventing us, that we may have a good will, and working with us, when we have that good will.

Once again Donne honors the article. He distinguishes the first grace from "auxiliant" graces and supposes that all our good works depend on "the grace of God preventing us." Reading the Article this way enables him to think of all God's graces as prevenient. And, as I have argued, while he seldom speaks of justification by faith, he wants to think of the first grace as another way of speaking of the same thing. Article XVII sketches a view of predestination and election. The article speaks explicitly only of "Predestination to Life" as the

> everlasting purpose of God, whereby (before the foundations of the world were laid) he hath constantly decreed by his own power secret to us, to deliver from curse and damnation those whom he hath chosen in Christ out of mankind, and to bring them by Christ to everlasting salvation, as vessels made to honour.

The article continues by pointing out that election actualizes itself in a series of steps—calling, justification, adoption, conformity to Christ's image, walking in good works, and, finally, everlasting felicity. Moreover, the article points out that this doctrine is a dangerous one for "curious and carnal persons." Donne certainly speaks of election to salvation, but he takes advantage of the ambiguity of the article. He does not speak of God's eternal decrees of reprobation, and his attention is not so much directed to predestination itself as to the sanctification supposed to be its consequence. It is not impossible to think that Donne's view is the one adopted by the English delegates to the Synod of Dort and the one that seems to predominate in the Church of England. That view would oppose the High Calvinist conviction that God's eternal decrees of election and reprobation are the *cause* of salvation and damnation. Instead, his decrees of election do cause salvation; but his decrees of reprobation are based on his foreseeing sin. Thus, it is sin that

damns and not God. But Donne seldom speaks of election; and when he
does, it is as often as not to argue that we should never seek to restrict
God's elective purpose.

In these ways, then, we can argue that Donne's theological position,
at least in its main lines, is perfectly in accord with the views we find in
the Articles of Religion and in Hooker's writings. But, of course, this
conclusion does not really take us very far. Donne's emphasis is on the
sovereignty of God's grace, but also on the role of grace in sanctification,
in the Christian life once we presuppose regeneration whether by justification, by baptism, or by both. Because of this emphasis he is concerned to argue that we have our part to play, and much depends on our
use of God's grace. We can assume that this means we ought to obey
God's commands in spirit and in deed. But Donne is far too mistrustful
of the good works that should be engendered by faith to think that the
moral life as such is a sufficient response to grace. Instead, it is as though
he remembered the words from the Prayer Book confession—"we have
left undone those things which we ought to have done, and we have
done those things which we ought not to have done, and there is no
health in us." It seems significant to me that sins of omission take precedence over the sins we have committed. The implication is that we
inevitably fall short in our obedience. Does Donne have these words in
mind when he writes "A Hymn to God the Father," playing on his own
surname?[103]

> Wilt thou forgive that sinne where I begunne,
>   Which is my sin, though it were done before?
> Wilt thou forgive those sinnes through which I runne,
>   And do run still: though still I do deplore?
>   When thou hast done, thou hast not done,
>   For, I have more.
>
> Wilt thou forgive that sinne by which I' have wonne
>   Others to sinne? And, made my sinne their doore?
> Wilt thou forgive that sinne which I did shunne
>   A yeare, or two: but wallow'd in, a score?
>   When thou hast done, thou hast not done,
>   For, I have more.
>
> I have a sinne of feare, that when I have spunne
>   My last thread, I shall perish on the shore;
> But sweare by thyself, that at my death thy sonne
>   Shall shine as he shines now, and heretofore;
>   And, having done that, Thou hast done,
>   I have no more.

The true response, in one sense the only response we can make to God's grace is repentance. But, finally, the godly sorrow of repentance is, paradoxically a joy that fills the pilgrim's life and like a river flows to the boundless eternity of God's mercy.

If I am correct in seeing these attitudes as Donne's basic theology, a theology tied to the teaching of his church, then I should want to make one final point. The theology really represents no more than a glass of vision. He has shaped it from the tradition for which he speaks, and it has its roots in scripture. It touches on his experience and is shaped by that experience even though that is not, I think, where it originates. But as a glass of vision it acts as a way of looking at scripture and at his experience. He does not impose it on either, but it allows him to notice what would otherwise not be apparent. In this way he gives his own twist to the Augustinian theology of his day, and he articulates that theology in rhetorical and poetic modes that are carefully designed to move the hearts of those who read or listen to his words.

Notes

1. Izaak Walton, *The Life of Dr. John Donne*, in *John Donne: Devotions upon Emergent Occasions, Together with Death's Duel* (Ann Arbor: University of Michigan Press, 1959), xx.

2. Ibid., in *Devotions*, xvi–xvii. One other reference occurs toward the end of Walton's *Life*. He speaks of Donne's joy that his poem "An Hymn to God the Father" had been set to music and sung in St. Paul's. Speaking of his own sorrow that the Puritans had stopped such music, Walton says, "And the reader of St. Augustine's life may there find, that towards his dissolution he wept abundantly, that the enemies of Christianity had broken in upon them, and profaned and ruined their sanctuaries, and because their public hymns and lauds were lost out of their Churches" (*Devotions*, xxix).

3. Ibid., xxviii.

4. Ibid., xxii–xxiii.

5. Ibid., xxvii.

6. *John Donne: The Complete English Poems*, ed. A. J. Smith (Harmondsworth: Penguin Books, 1971/1973), 84–85.

7. Holy Sonnet 17; CWS, 84.

8. Walton, *Life*, in *Devotions*, vii.

9. *John Donne*, ed. A. J. Smith, 161–64.

10. Holy Sonnet 18; CWS, 84–85.

11. On John 10:10, Christmas Day: *The Sermons of John Donne,* ed. G. R. Potter and E. M. Simpson, sermon 5 (10 vols.; Berkeley and Los Angeles: University of California Press, 1953–62), 9:141.

12. On Ps 6:6-7: *The Sermons of John Donne,* sermon 8, 8:215; and On John 5:28-29, Easter Day, 1625: sermon 13, 6:268.

13. On John 10:10, Christmas Day: sermon 5, 9:153.

14. Ibid., 150.

15. Walton, *Life*, in *Devotions*, xli–xlii.

16. Ibid., xliii–xliv.

17. Ibid., xxi.

18. CWS, 171.

19. CWS, 172.

20. CWS, 173.

21. CWS, 175.

22. CWS, 177.

23. CWS, 179.

24. CWS, 179.

25. CWS, 180.

26. CWS, 180.

27. CWS, 182.

28. CWS, 183.

29. CWS, 184.

30. CWS, 184.

31. CWS, 185–86.

32. *Devotions*, Meditation 1; p. 8.

33. *Devotions*, Expostulation 1, p. 10.

34. Ibid.

35. *Devotions*, Prayer 1, p. 12. Cf. Expostulation 13, p. 85: "or hath thy Son himself no spots, who hath all our stains and deformities in him?"

36. Ibid., 11. Cf. Prayer 15, p. 102: "yet thou wilt consider me, as I was in thy purpose when thou wrotest my name in the book of life in my election. . . ."

37. On 1 Peter 1:17, Trinity Sunday: *The Sermons of John Donne*, sermon 13, 3:288.

38. CWS, 290.

39. On Ps 32:1-2: *The Sermons of John Donne*, sermon 11, 9:265.

40. Ibid., 263.

41. Holy Sonnet 3; CWS, 79.

42. Holy Sonnet 10; CWS, 81.

43. *Devotions*, Expostulation 21, p. 140.

44. *Devotions*, Prayer 21, p. 144.

45. On 1 Cor 15:26, March 8, 1621: *The Sermons of John Donne*, sermon 1, 4:56–57.

46. Ibid., 58.

47. Ibid., 60.

48. On John 5:28-29, Easter Day, 1625: *The Sermons of John Donne*, sermon 13, 6:264–65.

49. On Rev 20:6, Easter Day, 1624: *The Sermons of John Donne*, sermon 2, 6:71–72.

50. Ibid., 72–73.

51. On Acts 2:36, Easter Day, 1623: *The Sermons of John Donne*, sermon 14, 4:359.

52. CWS, 100.

53. On Matt 19:17, March 4, 1624: *The Sermons of John Donne*, sermon 11, 6:225.

54. On Ps 32:1-2: *The Sermons of John Donne*, sermon 11, 9:266.

55. On Ps 6:6-7, April 5, 1628: *The Sermons of John Donne*, sermon 8, 8:215.

56. CWS, 218.

57. CWS, 227–28.

58. CWS, 220.

59. CWS, 221.

60. CWS, 229.

61. CWS, 230.

62. CWS, 292–93.

63. On Ps 6:1: *The Sermons of John Donne*, sermon 16, 5:318.

64. On John 11:35, First Friday in Lent, 1622: *The Sermons of John Donne*, sermon 13, 4:338–39.

65. Ibid., 343.

66. CWS, 78.

67. CWS, 79.

68. *Devotions*, Expostulation 5, p. 33.

69. A Litanie IV; CWS, 87.

70. CWS, 119.

71. Ibid., 120.

72. Ibid., 122, 121.

73. Ibid., 123.

74. Ibid., 125.

75. Ibid., 125–26.

76. Ibid., 130.

77. Ibid., 132–33.

78. Ibid., 134–35.

79. Ibid., 127.

80. Ibid., 138.

81. Ibid., 145.

82. Ibid., 146.

83. Ibid., 150.

84. Ibid., 150–51.

85. Cf. Helen Gardner's judgment about his religious poetry in "The Religious Poetry of John Donne," in *John Donne: A Collection of Critical Essays*, ed. H. Gardner (Englewood Cliffs, NJ: Prentice-Hall, 1962), 135–36: "But although the Divine Poems are not the record of discoveries, but of struggles to appropriate a truth which has been revealed, that truth does not 'defeat all Poetry,' but gives us a poetry whose intensity is a moral intensity. Some religious poetry, Herbert's perhaps, can be regarded as a species of love-poetry; but Donne's is not of that kind. The image of Christ as Lover appears in only two of his poems—both written soon after the death of his wife. The image which

dominates his divine poetry is the image of Christ as Savior, the victor over sin and death."

86. CWS, 163.
87. CWS, 164.
88. CWS, 83.
89. CWS, 85.
90. CWS, 82.
91. CWS, 79.
92. CWS, 82–83.
93. CWS, 105.
94. CWS, 234.
95. CWS, 236.
96. CWS, 237.
97. CWS, 242.
98. CWS, 244.
99. CWS, 245.
100. CWS, 248.
101. CWS, 250.
102. CWS, 80.
103. CWS, 106.

5

Jeremy Taylor–
Holy and Heavenly Living

THERE IS MUCH WE DO NOT KNOW about Jeremy Taylor's life. Most of the evidence we might have used has been swept away, partly through the loss of family papers but partly through the chaos that resulted from the English Revolution.[1] Indeed, Taylor's reasonable hopes of a promising career were dashed by the outbreak of civil war and the defeat of the royalist cause. Charles I summoned the Long Parliament in 1640 and very quickly found the House of Commons disposed to make revolutionary changes in the church as well as the state. Within a year William Laud, the Archbishop of Canterbury and Jeremy Taylor's patron, was imprisoned. On August 22, 1642, the king raised the royal standard at Nottingham and the civil war began. By 1645 it was all over. Laud was executed, and Charles I imprisoned, destined for execution or martyrdom, depending on one's point of view, on January 30, 1649. Leadership of the revolution had passed into the hands of the army and Oliver Cromwell; episcopacy and the Book of Common Prayer had been abolished. Those who remained loyal to the Church of England found themselves no longer tolerated and were obliged to find employment in England as teachers or chaplains in country houses or to flee the country altogether. Jeremy Taylor had been staunch in his support of king and church. But in 1650 he found himself without a career, though freed from imprisonment and sheltered by Richard Vaughan, the Earl of Carbery, whose country house, Golden Grove, was in Wales. It was in that year that he published the first of his two best-known works, *The Rule and Exercises of Holy Living*. *The Rule and Exercises of Holy Dying* followed a year later.

Taylor's reaction to his own dashed hopes, which he equated with those of his cause, finds expression in *Holy Living*. In chapter three he is concerned with Christian justice, and among the prayers he adds at this point is one "to be said by subjects, when their land is invaded and overrun by barbarous or wicked people, enemies of the religion or the government":[2]

> O eternal God, Thou alone rulest in the kingdoms of men . . . now at last be pleased to let the light of Thy countenance, and the effects of a glorious mercy and a gracious pardon return to this land. Thou seest how great evils we suffer under the power and tyranny of war; and although we submit to and adore Thy justice in our sufferings, yet be pleased to pity our misery, to hear our complaints, and to provide us of remedy against our present calamities: let not the defenders of a righteous cause go away ashamed, nor our counsels be for ever confounded, nor our parties defeated, nor religion suppressed, nor learning discountenanced, and we be spoiled of all the exterior ornaments, instruments, and advantages of piety which thou hast been pleased formerly to minister to our infirmities, for the interests of learning and religion. Amen.

It would be easy to multiply examples of Taylor's counterrevolutionary attitude. In his dedication of *Holy Living* to Lord Carbery he complains that he has lived to see "religion painted upon banners" and God worshiped as "the Lord of hosts" rather than "the King of sufferings" and "the Prince of peace."[3] And it is easy to see what he means when he condemns a time when "the Christian charity ends in killing one another for conscience sake, so that faith is made to cut the throat of charity."[4]

Fifteen years earlier Taylor must have thought himself well on the way to a prosperous career in service to church and king. Though his family boasted of an ancestor who figured as a Protestant martyr in Foxe's book, it was by no means prosperous or influential. Jeremy's father was a barber surgeon in Cambridge, but was able to supply his son with an excellent education. In 1626, at the age of thirteen, Jeremy Taylor entered Caius College, Cambridge, as a sizar—what we should think of as a scholarship student obliged to earn his education by work in the college. Taylor took his bachelor's degree four years later and was ordained. In 1633 he spelled one of his friends by preaching at St. Paul's Cathedral in London. Perhaps in this way he came to the attention of William Laud, who had in that year received appointment as Archbishop of Canterbury. Whatever the details, Taylor soon was basking in Laud's patronage. Once more we cannot be sure of exactly how Laud managed it, but by the beginning of 1636 Taylor was a fellow of All Souls College, Oxford. He seems to have formed friendships with William Chillingworth and Francis à Sancta Clara. The first of these had become a Roman Catholic but was persuaded by Laud to return to the Church of England. The second, whose birth name was Christopher

Davenport, had become a Roman Catholic in 1615 at the age of seventeen, had fled to Douai, whence he returned to England as a missionary and was a chaplain to Queen Henrietta, who retained her faith and practiced it in her own chapel. These associations, together with the fact of Laud's patronage, apparently cast a degree of suspicion on Taylor as one who sympathized with Roman Catholicism. In the short run this could scarcely have mattered, and Taylor certainly had plenty of company. In the spring of 1638 he accepted the living of Uppingham and a year later married Phoebe Langsdale. We can know little with certainty about Taylor's personal life. It is clear that in 1642 he buried one of his three sons; and it is not impossible that Phoebe died the same year. It seems more likely, however, that Phoebe is the wife who died in 1651 and that she and Taylor had at that time two surviving sons and three surviving daughters.

Taylor's career, then, began in a usual but promising fashion. His university connections, his cure at Uppingham, and above all the patronage of Laud looked like guaranteeing him further preferment. All that changed, of course, once Laud was imprisoned and the civil war began. Two of Taylor's earliest works appeared at this time. In 1642 he dedicated *Episcopacy Asserted* to Christopher Hatton, a wealthy squire, who was his neighbor at Uppingham. And in 1647 he published *A Discourse on the Liberty of Prophesying*. It is almost certainly too simple to suppose that Taylor's views shifted in any substantial way. Nevertheless, it is tempting to suggest that in 1642 he still hoped for the triumph of king and church, while in 1647 he hoped only for a religious settlement that would allow the survival of the Church of England. *The Liberty of Prophesying* is, indeed, a plea for toleration; but the plea rests on the idea that no one group of Christians can claim infallibility rather than on the notion of toleration as an inalienable human right. I should think we are on the way to Locke's view but have not quite arrived. Taylor's movements and activities from 1642 till 1650 must remain quite obscure. He apparently saw King Charles during his imprisonment on the Isle of Wight, perhaps in 1647. He was a prisoner of the commonwealth authorities in Wales, and set up a school at Newton Hall after his release from prison. He was, therefore, in the neighborhood of Golden Grove and found support and help at the hands of Lord and Lady Carbery. For a few years, then, he found a quiet refuge where he was able to pursue his writings. *The Great Exemplar* appeared in 1649. This long work is really a meditation on the life of Jesus and follows the structure of a narrative followed by "considerations" and prayers, all of which are interspersed by "discourses" on various subjects. Much of the material is thought to be the reworking of sermons preached at Uppingham.

As I have noted, *Holy Dying* was published in 1651 and commemorated the deaths of both Lady Carbery and Taylor's wife. Probably about this time Taylor married Joanna Bridges, whose small estate at Mandinam was not far from Golden Grove.

Quiet retirement, however, seems not to have suited Taylor. He apparently went to London with some frequency and came to the attention of John Evelyn. In his diary for March 18, 1655, Evelyn says that he went to London to hear Taylor preach and then notes that "On the 31st I made a visit to Dr. Jer. Taylor, to confer with him about some spiritual matters, using him thenceforward as my ghostly father. I beseech God almighty to make me ever mindful of and thankful for his heavenly assistances."[5] It is clear from Evelyn's diary and what survives of their correspondence that Taylor for some time past had held clandestine services in London. We know from one of Evelyn's letters, dated February 9, 1654, that Taylor had then only recently been released from prison. But we do not know where, for how long, or why he was imprisoned. Taylor's enemies, however, quite soon included important members of his own party. In 1655 he published *Unum Necessarium*, a work that treated repentance as the necessary basis for moral theology and that he intended as an introduction to his very long and very detailed work in casuistry, *Ductor Dubitantium* [A Guide to the Perplexed], which saw print only in 1660. He dedicated *Unum Necessarium* to Brian Duppa, the deprived bishop of Salisbury, and John Warner, the deprived bishop of Rochester. Chapter six of the work treated original sin in such a way that Duppa, Warner, and many others regarded Taylor's opinions as heretical. Thus began a controversy that came to a halt but left Taylor with a good deal of suspicion attached to him. Taylor was a prisoner, probably in Chepstow Castle in Wales and probably from May till October of 1655. During his imprisonment he wrote what is now chapter 7 of *Unum Necessarium* and what was designed to clear himself of heresy and of denying the Articles of Religion. If we except the voluminous correspondence, Taylor's last word was *Deus Justificatus*, also published in 1655. I shall want to examine these materials in what follows.

By 1656 Taylor found himself with enemies on all sides. He continued his travels to London, and in 1657 secured an annual pension from Evelyn, enabling him to work and travel. But in 1658 his bookseller made the mistake of publishing a "popish" picture of Christ praying as a frontispiece to Taylor's *Collection of Offices*, a mistake that put Taylor in the Tower of London. What seemed a solution to Taylor's difficulties and what may well have seemed to the authorities a happy removal of Taylor from the center of affairs came about through the kind help of Edward, Earl of Conway. In June of 1658 Taylor left London for Lord Conway's estate at Portmore in Ireland. There Taylor preached at the nearby church in Lisburn and may well have found some peace at last. But the peace was not to last long. Cromwell's death in 1658 was the beginning of a movement toward the restoration of Charles II as king. When Charles II entered London on May 29, 1660, Taylor was there seeing to the publication of *Ductor Dubitantium*. The rest of the story is one of disappointment. Taylor obviously hoped that the Church of England would be restored and that he would be given a bishopric of some consequence. That was not to be. Instead, he returned to Ireland, where he was appointed vice-chancellor of Trinity College, Dublin. Then on January 27, 1661, in St. Patrick's Cathedral, Dublin, there were consecrated ten bishops and two archbishops for Ireland. Old Archbishop Bramhall presided, and Jeremy Taylor preached at his own consecration as Bishop of Down and Connor in Ulster. These consecrations, like others in England, jumped the gun on the religious settlement, which did not take place until 1662. And so Taylor returned to his diocese to discover strong Presbyterian opposition.

The rest of Taylor's life was not happy. In March of 1661 he buried his two-year-old son, who seems to have been the last of four sons by his second marriage. The two surviving sons of his first marriage also died before he did, one in a duel and the other at the age of twenty-four, little more than ten days before Taylor's own death. We do not know enough to be certain, but it surely looks as though Taylor's family life was marked by tragedy. What we do know more about is the efforts Taylor exerted to establish himself as bishop in his diocese. The struggles with the Presbyterian ministers and with the Roman Catholic population cannot have been easy or pleasant, especially if we suppose that Taylor sought to use persuasion rather than force. Perhaps more lasting was his work as vice-chancellor of Trinity College. At any rate, it looks to me as though Taylor's life was a valiant, uphill struggle. His life did not follow easy lines, and he was clearly caught up not only in the difficulties of his times but also in his determination to swim against the tide. We might expect that this would drive him to a bitter pessimism. But, on the contrary, it seems to me that his writings tend toward a sunny optimism and a confidence in the value of our efforts that are surprising. Perhaps we should not assume that what people think always mirrors what seems to us the character of their experience. And perhaps it may even be the case that opinions drive more in the direction of what should be rather than what is. However this may be, let me now turn to Taylor's thought with a view of examining how he sees the Christian life informed by Christian hope.

The Novelty of Antiquity

Chapter 6 of *Unum Necessarium* makes little direct use of the church fathers, and Taylor's appeal is to scripture and to considerations revolving around what he regards as a right understanding of God. He also seems to me preoccupied with the fate of unbaptized children. Nevertheless, I want to argue that his subsequent attempts to justify his opinions reflect his study of the ancient church. That study also betrays itself in his liturgical work. From the present perspective, however, what I want to suggest is that his view of original sin amounts to a repudiation of the usual Augustinian doctrine and to the adoption of a view not unlike the one we discovered in Gregory of Nyssa's thought. Taylor, who by no means rejects Augustine entirely, insists that his repudiation of the idea that Adam's penalty and our inheritance includes spiritual and eternal death does not mean that he has committed himself to Pelagius's views. Instead, his position involves arguing that God's grace must be persuasive in character and universal in its scope. In this way he echoes the conviction of the early church before Augustine that God's loving providence represents the larger and more mysterious context in which we exercise our freedom. God's love makes available to us the gifts of his grace, but we must seek and accept those gifts and use them properly for them to have their intended effect. Let me make a second preliminary point. If from one point of view Taylor's concern is to portray a loving and merciful God, from another point of view he wants to be sure that religion will not lead to despair or to antinomianism. That is, if we have no part whatsoever in the work of salvation, then we are robbed both of the hope that we can make any choices that matter and of the responsibility to make choices that constitute the moral life. In general terms it seems possible to me to argue that Taylor is not at all alone in stressing the importance of holy living. A reaction against what happened in the name of religion during the English Revolution includes a fear of antinomianism, of sinning that grace may abound. We find the same emphasis in the Cambridge Platonists and in people like Richard Baxter, who was clearly a committed Protestant.

These general considerations will become clearer, I hope, as my argument continues. But now let me turn to chapter 6 of *Unum Necessarium*. We may remember that Taylor's topic in the work as a whole is repentance as the one thing necessary for the Christian life. The problem to which he turns in chapter 6 is "Of concupiscence, and original sin, and whether or no, or how far we are bound to repent of it." This title may well imply a sharper question: why should we be blamed for some-one else's fault? In any case, Taylor's conclusion comes as no surprise:[6]

> I dare say every man is sufficiently displeased that he is liable to sick-ness, weariness, displeasure, melancholy, sorrow, folly, imperfection, and death, dying with groans and horrid spasms and convulsions. In what sense these are the effects of Adam's sin, and though of them-selves natural, yet also on his account made penal, I have already declared. . . . But our share of Adam's sin either being in us no sin at all, or else not to be avoided or amended, it cannot be the matter of repentance.

It is the reasons Taylor gives for this conclusion that are of interest. He begins the chapter by explaining the doctrine from scripture, arguing that the penalty God imposed on Adam for his sin was a "certainty of dying, together with the proper effects and affections of mortality, . . . and he was reduced to the condition of his own nature."[7] The important point to note is that Taylor believes humanity was created mortal. And we must add that this natural mortality means not only that we must die but also that we are liable to all the imperfections of our nature. In pass-ing, let me note that a view like this is the common one held by the church fathers before Augustine. The only thing we inherit from Adam is death, but that inheritance of mortality includes an unstable relation-ship between the soul and the bodily passions that expresses itself in an inclination to sin.

If what we inherit from Adam is mortality, in what sense can this inheritance be understood as sin? Taylor's answer is a considered one:[8]

> [Adam's] sin infected us with death, and this infection we derive in our birth, that is, we are born mortal. Adam's sin was imputed to us unto a natural death; in him we are sinners, as in him we die. But this sin is not real and inherent, but imputed only to such a degree. So S. Cyprian affirms most expressly. . . . An infant hath not sinned, save only that being carnally born of Adam, in his first birth he hath contracted the contagion of the old death. 20. This evil which is the condition of all our natures, viz., to die, was to some a punishment, but to others not so.

What he means is that our mortality is the precondition for our sinning, but it is only actual sin that renders our inheritance from Adam sinful. "But to those who sinned not at all, as infants and innocents, it [death] was merely a condition of their nature, and no more a punishment, than to be a child is." It does seem to me somewhat peculiar to say, as Taylor does, that "Adam's sin was imputed to us unto a natural death." Would it not make more sense to argue that what Adam's sin did was to deprive him and all his progeny of the supernatural graces that would have bestowed immortality on humanity? Perhaps Taylor has designed his language to reassure those he knows are bound to be surprised and offended by his theology.

If the fall of Adam reduced humanity to its natural state and if that natural state is one of mortality, then we need to press beyond the fact that we must die to consider the other aspects of mortality to which Taylor has alluded. We are born, he says, with natural ignorance, a state "we derive from Adam, as we do our nature, which is a state of ignorance and all manner of imperfection." We cannot know what Adam's condition before the fall was like, but we can make guesses on the basis of what happened:[9]

> for if he had not had a rebellious appetite, and an inclination to forbidden things, by what could he have been tempted, and how could it have come to pass that he should sin?

What Taylor must mean is that Adam before the fall had a natural inclination to sin, one that ought to have been blocked by supernatural grace. Thus, we are born with that same natural inclination but do not become guilty until we act on it:[10]

> For in original sin we are to consider the principle, and the effects. The principle is the actual sin of Adam; this being to certain purposes by God's absolute dominion imputed to us, hath brought upon us a necessity of dying, and all the affections of mortality; which although they were natural, yet would by grace have been hindered. Another evil there is upon us, and that is concupiscence; this also is natural, but it was actual before the fall, it was in Adam, and tempted him. This also from him is derived to us, and is by many causes made worse, by him and by ourselves.

It ought to follow that natural ignorance, concupiscence, and an inclination to sin are neither the same thing as sins nor conditions that in any way necessitate Adam's sin or ours. Nevertheless, Taylor speaks in such a way as to suggest that we sin, if not by necessity, at least inevitably. In a sense, our "natural" condition after the fall is not so very different from the predicament those holding an Augustinian view of original sin would suppose to obtain.

Taylor, however, protects his view by arguing that even in our natural state we have the possibility of choosing the good. "Nature makes us miserable and imperfect, but not criminal."[11] He puts the point more positively somewhat later in the argument. He rejects the supposition that our present nature determines us to sin "by an irresistible necessity" and asks why this would be our condition any more than it was Adam's:[12]

we can choose good, and as naturally love good as evil, and in some instances more. A man cannot naturally hate God, if he knows any thing of Him: a man naturally loves his parents: he naturally hates some sort of uncleanness: he naturally loves and preserves himself: and all those sins which are unnatural, are such which nature hates: and the law of nature commands all the great instances of virtue, and marks out all the great lines of justice.

Here Taylor is appealing to the Stoicizing idea that we have "common conceptions" which include some knowledge of God and an understanding of right and wrong. His conclusion sits rather uneasily in its context, since he admits "an universal impiety." We cannot blame Adam for this. Moreover, "the universal wickedness of man is no argument to prove our will servile, and the powers of election to be quite lost in us."[13] Taylor wants to deny that our natural state is necessarily sinful and one that deprives us of all possibility of electing the good, but at the same time he wants to portray that state as one that deprives us of the supernatural grace that alone can bring us salvation and immortality and one that is, consequently, without any real hope. His two convictions may not be contradictory, but there certainly seems to me to be a conflict of sensibility.

We can better understand what Taylor is trying to say by noting the ideas he opposes. Augustine had argued that the "death" inflicted on Adam and inherited by all humanity included spiritual and eternal death. Thus, we are born incapable of good. Either we have lost the power of free choice, or we retain only the power of choosing evil. And we are born damned and liable to the eternal death of everlasting punishment. It is these two ideas that Taylor rejects:[14]

> But concerning the sin of Adam, tragical things are spoken; "it destroyed his original righteousness, and lost it to us for ever; it corrupted his nature, and corrupted ours, and brought upon him, and not him only, but on us also who thought of no such thing, an inevitable necessity of sinning, making it as natural to us to sin as to be hungry, or to be sick and die; and the consequent of these things is saddest of all, we are born enemies of God, sons of wrath, and heirs of eternal damnation."

These "tragical" additions to the doctrine of original sin are the chaff that must be sifted from the wheat, and Taylor's appeal is to scripture, and specifically to Paul's comparison of Adam and Christ in Romans 5:12ff. The crucial consideration is the meaning of verse 12, which is "usually" interpreted to mean that we all sinned "in Adam." Taylor is correct, however, in rejecting the view of those who "think these words *eph' hō pantes hēmarton*, 'forasmuch as all men have sinned,' ought to be expounded thus, Death passed upon all men; 'in whom' all men have sinned: meaning that in Adam we really sinned."[15] Taylor, then, sees his view as a faithful exposition of the crucial passage in Romans 5. But, of course, he is left with Paul's conclusion that all Adam's progeny have sinned on their own account, a conclusion that drives against Taylor's conviction that we retain the capacity for good even in our natural state.

In Taylor's attempt to resolve the controversy precipitated by chapter 6 it is difficult to find anything in what he wrote that alters the main lines of his doctrine. Nevertheless, let me note several points he makes in his letter to Bishop Warner, in what is now chapter 7 of *Unum Necessarium*, and in *Deus Justificatus*. Taylor begins chapter 7 by saying, "Having therefore turned to all the ways of reason and scripture, I at last apply myself to examine how it [the doctrine of original sin] was affirmed by the first and best antiquity."[16] He summarizes his conclusions as follows:[17]

> *Sec. 5. The doctrine of antiquity in this whole matter.* The sum of all is this.
> a. Original sin is Adam's sin imputed to us to many evil effects.
> b. It brings death and the evils of this life.
> c. Our evils and necessity being brought upon us, bring in a flood of passions which are hard to be bridled, or mortified.
> d. It hath left us in pure naturals, disrobed of such aids extraordinary as Adam had.
> e. It deprives us of all title to heaven or supernatural happiness, that is, it neither hath in it strength to live a spiritual life, nor title to a heavenly.
> f. It leaves in us our natural concupiscence, and makes it much worse.
>   Thus far I admit and explicate this article.
> But all that I desire of the usual propositions which are variously taught now-a-days, is this.
> a. Original sin is not an inherent evil; not a sin properly, but metonymically; that is, it is the effect of one sin, and the cause of many; a stain, but no sin.
> b. It does not destroy our liberty which we had naturally.
> c. It does not introduce a natural necessity of sinning.
> d. It does not damn any infant to the eternal pains of hell.

The argument continues by supplying more citations from the church fathers. Taylor denies that his view is Pelagian: "if every thing which was said against S. Austin in these controversies be Pelagianism, then all antiquity were Pelagians and himself besides; for he before his disputes in these questions said much against what he said after, as every learned man knows."[18]

Taylor not only tries to show that his teaching accords with antiquity, he also argues that it does not deny Article IX of the Church of England. He tells Bishop Warner that he "would rather die than either willingly give occasion or countenance to a schism in the church of England."[19] And while he recognizes that his is not the only possible interpretation of the article on original sin, he denies that the article excludes his view:[20]

> I will not pretend to believe that those doctors who first framed the article did all of them mean as I mean; I am not sure they did or that they did not; but this I am sure, that they framed the words with much caution and prudence, and so as might abstain from grieving the contrary minds of differing men."

Phrases in Article IX do seem capable of being understood in Taylor's sense. Original sin "is the fault and corruption of the nature of every man." "And this infection of nature doth remain, yea in them that are regenerated." "And although there is no condemnation to them that believe and are baptized, yet the Apostle doth confess that concupiscence and lust hath of itself the nature of sin." Taylor's parsing of the article may sometimes seem slightly forced, but it is hard to see that he is wrong in supposing that it falls short of teaching total depravity. If Taylor presents his view as a possible and persuasive interpretation of Article IX, he also presents it as a repudiation of the Westminster Confession and the articles of the Synod of Dort—and of presbyterian views in general.[21]

It would be easy to elaborate an account of the controversy, but more to my purpose is to say something about what motivates Taylor's view of original sin. The first and most obvious motive has to do with theodicy in the narrow sense, with justifying God by giving a proper account of his goodness and justice. Taylor regards the "tragical" additions to the doctrine as unreasonable because they make "too bold reflections upon God's honour, and the reputation of His justice and His goodness."[22] God was just in depriving Adam and his progeny of supernatural grace, but Taylor appears to think that this does not suffice to "justify" God. His emphasis is on the means God has devised to overcome original sin, or, better, to grant us what we could not have from our nature alone. God does not leave his punishment without the remedy of forgiveness, and "original sin is remitted in baptism."[23] But Taylor goes further. What about infants that die unbaptized? If such children are damned through no fault of their own, "I do not understand how it can in any sense be true that Christ died for all, if at least the children of christian parents should not find the benefit of Christ's death, because that without the fault of any man they want the ceremony."[24] In principle, the atonement effected by Christ's death must be universal in scope:[25]

> But when Christ came into the world, He opened the fountains of mercy, and broke down all the banks of restraint, He preached repentance, offered health, gave life, called all wearied and burdened persons to come to Him for ease and remedy, He glorified His Father's mercies, and Himself became the great instrument and channel of its emanation.

Of course, Taylor does not mean that what appears to be a universal possibility will be universally actualized. But there can be no doubt of his insistence on the all-embracing mercy of God expressed in Christ.

In one of his sermons Taylor presses the idea one final step further. God's mercy expresses itself in the fact that he pardons us before we ask. Indeed, God's merciful will to pardon supplies the motive for the incarnation and Christ's death. "He came to satisfy Himself, to pay to Himself the price of His own creature." It was because God was already reconciled to us that he came to bring us pardon, and his love preceded all:[26]

> This was hasty love. But it went further yet. God pardoned us before we sinned; and when He foresaw our sin, even mine and yours, He sent His Son to die for us; our pardon was wrought and effected by Christ's death above sixteen hundred years ago. . . . And this is not only a favour to us who were born in the due time of the gospel, but to all mankind since Adam; for God, who is infinitely patient in His justice, was not at all patient in His mercy. . . . For, as if God could not stay from redeeming us, He promised the Redeemer to Adam in the beginning of the world's sin; and Christ was "the Lamb slain from the beginning of the world" (Rev 13:8); and the covenant of the gospel, though it was not made with man, yet it was from the beginning performed by God as to His part, as to the ministration of pardon; the seed of the woman was set up against the dragon as soon as ever the tempter had won his first battle. . . .

God's mercy is wide indeed, and much that Taylor says suggests that we must understand his doctrine of original sin in the context of his conviction that God's pardon, in principle, extends to all. Up to a point Taylor's view is a harbinger of John Wesley's belief that God extended prevenient grace to all humanity immediately after the fall of Adam. For Wesley it is the conscience that betrays this work of grace and establishes in us the possibility of repentance and conversion. That is not quite what Taylor is saying, but at the least we can conclude that he insists on the fact that original sin cannot be understood without recognizing that its remedy is somehow immediately and universally a possibility. Indeed, Taylor's references to predestination often seem to reflect his understanding that God wishes all to be saved.

There is, however, another motive lying behind Taylor's view. I need scarcely say that he has no wish to offer cheap grace, and in the next section I shall wish to say more about Taylor's understanding of grace. For the moment let me suggest that his second motive is tied to his belief that original sin does not deprive us altogether of a capacity for good. In chapter seven of *Unum Necessarium* Taylor before turning to the ideas he wishes to refute summarizes his own view as follows:[27]

> This is the whole sum of Original Sin, which now I have more fully explicated than formerly; it being then only fitting to speak so much of it as to represent it to be a state of evil, which yet left in us powers enough to do our duty, and to be without excuse . . . and that not God but ourselves are authors of our eternal death in case we do perish.

In some sense, to argue that we are able to do our duty and so are the causes of our own condemnation when we fail to do so is to say that God does not directly damn us. We are the causes of our own punishment and cannot blame God. But Taylor wants to say more than this:[28]

> we by his [Adam's] fall received evil enough to undo us, and ruin us all; but yet the evil did so descend upon us, that we were left in powers and capacities to serve and glorify God; God's service was made much harder, but not impossible; mankind was made miserable, but not desperate, we contracted an actual mortality, but we were redeemable from the power of death; sin was easy and ready at the door, but it was resistible; our will was abused, but yet not destroyed; our understanding was cozened, but yet still capable of the best instructions; and though the devil had wounded us, yet God sent His Son, who like the good Samaritan poured oil and wine into our wounds, and we were cured before we felt the hurt, that might have ruined us upon that occasion.

The first part of this passage reads as though even in the natural state resulting from God's withdrawal of grace after the fall we retain real capacity for good. But the passage ends by appealing to the cure effected by Christ. I am tempted to read Taylor's second motive for the doctrine of original sin he elaborates according to the way Augustine leaves matters in *On Free Will*. We find ourselves in a penal state of ignorance and difficulty, and it would be right to complain did not one capacity remain to us. The one thing we can do, according to the early Augustine, is to ask God for his help, a help that will not be withheld. It might be possible to understand Taylor this way. That is, his insistence on our moral capacities do seem tied to his understanding of the availability of grace. And yet it is hard to deny that he often sounds moralizing.

Indeed, we can argue that Taylor supposes we have capacities that go beyond asking for God's grace because of his understanding of justification by faith. In a letter to Bishop Warner Taylor summarizes his view as follows:[29]

> Christ's righteousness is not imputed to us for justification directly and immediately; neither can we be justified by our own righteousness: but our faith and sincere endeavours are, through Christ, accepted instead of legal righteousness: that is, we are justified through Christ, by imputation not of Christ's nor our own righteousness, but of our faith and endeavours of righteousness, as if they were perfect: and we are justified by a non-imputation, viz., of our past sins, and present unavoidable imperfections: that is, we are handled as if we were just persons and no sinners.

This covenant or federal theology, commonly held in Taylor's time, sought to avoid the perils of antinomianism by appealing to a covenant of grace whereby our insufficient righteousness was accounted righteous because of Christ. Thus, while we cannot merit salvation, neither can we expect it without some movement toward righteousness. In another mood Taylor repudiates a neoscholastic approach to justification by faith. "[N]o man should fool himself by disputing about the philosophy of justification."[30] His interest is in the religious convictions underlying the theological disputes. In sum, the two motives I wish to identify as informing Taylor's doctrine of original sin, together with his teaching about God's mercy in Christ, seem to me to reflect the basic structure of Taylor's theology. God's persuasive grace and the human capacity to make use of that grace belong together. In this way Taylor's fundamental convictions ally him more with Gregory of Nyssa than with Augustine. In what follows let me turn first to his understanding of grace and then to the way he construes our use of grace by faith, repentance, and love.

Grace

I have already suggested the way we should understand Taylor's view of God's grace. By defining the human predicament as one of nature deprived of supernatural grace he implies several points. First, we require that grace if we are to find the promise of eternal life, a promise that brings hope to our hopeless condition. Second, this means that grace by no means cancels our striving for the good; rather God assists and enables our efforts. Third, God's grace is always persuasive; it cannot compel. Finally, grace and freedom belong together. Grace is primarily the context in which we exercise our freedom. In sum, Taylor's view seems to me in broad lines the same as the view we encountered in examining Gregory of Nyssa's thought. It correlates with the usual patristic view before and apart from Augustine and represents a decisive departure from Augustine's idea of operative or sovereign grace. In his doctrine of original sin Taylor appeals explicitly to the church fathers. Of course, they have for him no independent authority and are primarily guides to the true meaning of scripture.[31] In turning, however, to the doctrine of grace Taylor makes little or no appeal to antiquity. Thus, the connection of his view to antiquity is admittedly implicit rather than explicit. With this qualification we can, I think, still argue that Taylor in this dimension of his theology also appeals to the novelty of antiquity. In what follows let me seek to elaborate his view.

Taylor's *Holy Living* might not seem the best place to look for his doctrine of grace, since it is obvious that his emphasis is on our part in holy living. But it seems clear to me that he regards our part as one made possible only by God's grace. The basic structure of the work is a simple one. The first chapter sets the stage by examining the use of time, purity of intention, and the practice of the presence of God. The other three chapters follow the structure of Titus 2:11: "for the grace of God bringing salvation hath appeared to all men, teaching us that denying ungodliness and worldly lusts, we should live *soberly, righteously, and godly*, in this present world, looking for that blessed hope and glorious appearing of the great God and our Saviour Jesus Christ."[32] Taylor treats in succession Christian sobriety, justice, and religion. Chapter 4 begins with the specifically Christian virtues of faith, hope, and charity; it continues by discussing fasting, prayer, alms, repentance, and preparation for the Lord's supper. It is in the context of his discussion of charity that we find his identification of God's grace with his love:[33]

> Love is the greatest thing that God can give us, for Himself is love; and it is the greatest thing we can give to God, for it will also give ourselves, and carry with it all that is ours. . . . [Love] does the work of all other graces, without any instrument but its own immediate virtue. For as the love to sin makes a man sin against all his own reason . . . so does the love of God; it makes a man chaste without the laborious arts of fasting and exterior discipline, temperate in the midst of feasts, and is active enough to choose it without any intermedial appetites, and reaches at glory through the very heart of grace, without any arms but those of love.

Taylor equates love with God but also with our own love, which is God's gift. "Grace," then, can refer both to the giver and to the one who receives the gift. God gives us the grace of his love, and our possession of that gift is a grace that is now our own and enables us to respond to God in love. In a sense, "grace" refers not so much to what God or we do as to the relationship of love that is established.

In the passage I have just cited Taylor continues by clarifying the reciprocal relationship between God's love for us and our love for him:[34]

> It is a grace that loves God for Himself, and our neighbours for God. The consideration of God's goodness and bounty, the experience of those profitable and excellent emanations from Him, may be, and most commonly are, the first motive of our love; but when we are once entered, and have tasted the goodness of God, we love the spring for its own excellency, passing from passion to reason, from thanking to adoring, from sense to spirit, from considering ourselves to an union with God: and this is the image and little representation of heaven; it is beatitude in picture, or rather the infancy and beginnings of glory.

Once the gift is ours it is also *our* grace. But it cannot be ours unless God gives it. Moreover, the gift is not so much an act of God as one tied to God as love. Perhaps we can understand what Taylor means by appealing to a personal analogy. The child receives the gift of his parents' love, but this gift is not limited by what the parents do. Instead, it is really the attitude of the parents toward their child. Once the child recognizes that attitude of love, he can respond in love and find a loving union with his parents. And just as the parents' love is not merely passive, however much they respect the autonomy of their child, so God's love has active "emanations" toward us, even though that love refuses to compel us in any way. Finally, the union of grace and love is "the image and little representation of heaven." I shall want to return to this point later in this section of my argument.

Taylor's discussion in chapter 1 of *Holy Living* of God's presence correlates with his description of God's love. God is present to us in many ways—by his essence and power because he sustains and guides his creation. He is present in a more restricted way "in some places by the several and more special manifestations of Himself to extraordinary purposes." Taylor thinks first of those who "die in the Lord." They "may be properly said to be 'gone to God'; with whom although they were before, yet now they enter into His courts, into the secret of His tabernacle, into the retinue and splendour of His glory." God is also "by grace and benediction specially present in holy places, and in the solemn assemblies of His servants."[35] In another sense the human heart is the temple of God, and that is where God is present by His Holy Spirit:[36]

> For God reigns in the hearts of His servants: there is His kingdom. The power of grace hath subdued all His enemies. . . . And God dwells in our hearts by faith, and Christ by His spirit, and the Spirit by His purities: so that we are also cabinets of the mysterious Trinity; and what is this short of heaven itself, but as infancy is short of manhood, and letters of words? The same state of life it is, but not the same age. It is heaven in a looking-glass, dark but yet true, representing the beauties of the soul, and the graces of God, and the images of His eternal glory, by the reality of a special presence.

Once again we find the theme of God's union with the believer and the idea that this union is one that brings heaven to earth and earth to heaven.

The last mode of God's presence Taylor considers underlines his insistence on holy living and our own moral responsibility. God is "present in the consciences of all persons, good and bad, by way of testimony and judgment":[37]

> And although this manner of presence is in this life after the manner of this life, that is, imperfect, and we forget many actions of our lives; yet the greatest changes of our state of grace or sin, our most considerable actions, are always present, like capital letters to an aged and dim eye; and at the day of judgment God shall draw aside the cloud, and manifest this manner of His presence more notoriously, and make it appear that He was an observer of our very thoughts; and that He only laid those things by, which, because we covered with dust and negligence, were not then discerned. But when we are risen from our dust and imperfection, they all appear plain and legible.

At first Taylor seems to have moved from God's presence as a promise to the idea of that presence as a threat. And in the passage immediately following the one I have cited he does speak of "the all-seeing eye of God." "He is to be feared in public, He is to be feared in private: if you go forth, He spies you; if you go in, He sees you: when you light the candle, He observes you; when you put it out, then also God marks you." In contrast to what he says here, Taylor's sermon on Matt 5:26, following Augustine, opposes "pharisaical and evangelical righteousness" on the basis of differing motives. "They served the God of their fathers in the spirit of fear, and we worship the Father of our Lord Jesus in the spirit of love, and by the spirit of adoption."[38] It may be impossible to reconcile these contrary statements. Nevertheless, we might be able to argue that Taylor is speaking of "fear" in two rather different ways. Fear of God's punishment would seem by no means an adequate motive for holy living. But love can itself give birth to a godly fear. That is, the fear is not so much one of punishment as one of displeasing the God we love.

It is certainly fair to say that Taylor tends to see God's grace in the context of sin and forgiveness. And it may be that he sometimes appeals to God's judgment. On the whole, however, his emphasis is on God's mercy and his readiness to pardon. He can, then, associate God's grace not only with his love and presence, but also with his mercy. In one of his sermons, "The Miracles of the Divine Mercy," Taylor supplies us with a fairly comprehensive description of his understanding:[39]

> But as a circle begins every where and ends no where, so do the mercies of God. . . . God is (1) "good and gracious," that is, desirous to give good gifts: and of this God made us receptive, first by giving us natural possibilities; that is, by giving those gifts He made us capable of more; and next by restoring us to His favour, that He might not by our provocations be hindered from raining down His mercies. But God is also (2) "ready to forgive": and of this kind of mercy we made ourselves capable even by not deserving it. Our sin made way for His grace, and our infirmities called upon His pity; and because we sinned we became miserable, and because we were miserable we became pitiable; and this opened the other treasure of His mercy, that because our "sin abounds," His "grace may superabound."

God's mercy, then, is in the first instance his gift of creation and of our nature. Our natural gifts are also gifts of grace. But Taylor's emphasis is on God's mercy in his disposition to pardon sin. In the last section we saw how that disposition preceded not only our own sins but also Christ's death on the cross. Indeed, Christ is the lamb slaughtered before the foundation of the world (Rev 13:8); and God gave the promise of his redeeming death immediately after the fall of Adam and Eve. God's curse on the serpent includes the "protoevangelium." His offspring will strike the heel of Eve's progeny; but hers will crush his head (Gen 3:15).[40]

In the last chapter of *Holy Living* Taylor considers motives to repentance. He begins by saying that a sinner ought to be moved to repent simply by the fact that "unless he does, he shall certainly perish." But he immediately goes beyond this consideration and asks us to remember:[41]

> 1. That to admit mankind to repentance and pardon was a favour greater than ever God gave to the angels and devils: for they were never admitted to the condition of second thoughts; Christ never groaned one groan for them; He never suffered one stripe nor one affront, nor shed one drop of blood, to restore them to hopes of blessedness after their first failings: but this He did for us; He paid

the score of our sins only that we might be admitted to repent, and
that this repentance might be effectual to the great purposes of felicity and salvation.

2. Consider that as it cost Christ many millions of prayers and groans
   and sighs, so He is now at this instant, and hath been for these sixteen hundred years, night and day incessantly praying for grace that
   we may repent, and for pardon when we do, and for degrees of pardon beyond the capacities of our infirmities and the merit of our sorrows and amendment. . . .

The next two points underline Christ's joy at our repentance and the
great rewards of heaven. But Taylor's emphasis is on the simple idea that
God's gracious establishment of the possibility of repentance is what
enables us to repent. He uses the same idea in examining the problem of
postbaptismal sin. In *Discourse IX* from *The Great Exemplar* he cites
1 John 3:9: "whoever is born of God doth not commit sin, for His seed
remaineth in him; and he cannot sin, because he is born of God." Scripture, then, might seem to exclude the possibility that sins after baptism
could be forgiven. And yet the same book of scripture promises that "if
we confess our sins, He is faithful and just to forgive us our sins, and to
cleanse us from all unrighteousness."[42] There can be no problem supposing that the repentance associated with baptism will prove effective
for pardon; what is more difficult is the question whether we can repent
of postbaptismal sin.

Taylor's argument is long and involuted. He sees the necessity of
preserving the demand of the Gospel without ignoring its message of
forgiveness. The apparently contradictory texts from 1 John reflect the
tension. The first of the texts[43]

is no otherwise to be understood than according to the design of the
thing itself and the purpose of God; that is, that it be a deep engage-
ment and an effectual consideration for the necessity of a holy life; but
at no hand let it be made an instrument of despair, nor an argument to
lessen the influences of the divine mercy.

There is, of course, but one baptism; "yet the mercy of God, besides this
great feast, hath fragments, which the apostles and ministers spiritual
are to gather up in baskets, and minister to the after-needs of indigent
and necessitous disciples." Later in his argument Taylor contrasts two
states. The first is one that "reconciles us to God, putting us into an
entire condition of pardon, favour, innocence, and acceptance." The
opposite one "is such a condition which, as it hath no holiness or rema-
nent affections to virtue, so it hath no hope or revelation of a mercy,
because all that benefit is lost which they received by the death of

Christ." Nevertheless, "between these two states stand all those imperfections and single delinquencies, those slips and falls, those parts of
recession and apostasy . . . and so long as any thing of the first state is
left, so long as we are within the covenant of grace, so long as we are
within the ordinary limits of mercy and the divine compassion; we are
in possibility of recovery. . . . "[44]

Taylor associates God's grace with his love, his presence, and his
mercy, and in particular with his merciful promise of pardon. We can
already see that grace is, in the first instance, the context in which we
exercise our freedom. Moreover, it is worth underlining the fact that
grace works persuasively. At several points Taylor suggests in more
detail how we can understand this. One of the "means and instruments
to obtain faith" is[45]

> A humble, willing, and docile mind, or desire to be instructed in the
> way of God: for persuasion enters like a sunbeam, gently and without
> violence; and open but the window, and draw the curtain, and the Sun
> of righteousness will enlighten your darkness.

The implication is that grace works persuasively on our motives. In
Unum Necessarium Taylor speaks of God's grace as "a supernatural
principle . . . [which] gives new aptnesses and inclinations, powers and
possibilities, it invites and teaches, it supplies us with arguments, and
answers objections. . . ."[46] To speak of grace is to speak of God's "assistances." Just as "we cannot do God's work without God's grace; so
God's grace does not do our work without us." In the context of repentance and forgiveness Taylor elsewhere says that "God is so ready to
forgive that Himself works our dispositions towards it."[47] The first
point I should want to make is that grace works persuasively on our
motives quite simply because this is the effect of discerning God's love,
presence, mercy, and pardon. In one of his sermons Taylor repeats the
story of the spies Moses sends ahead to the promised land and who
return with a remarkable cluster of grapes (Numbers 13). This entice-
ment to persevere is like God's grace which "represents to the new con-
verts and the weak ones in faith, the pleasures and first deliciousness of
religion." God, of course, does not always work the same way; but
"God to every man does minister excellent arguments of invitation, and
such that if a man will attend to them they will certainly move either his
affections or his will, his fancy or his reason, and most commonly
both."[48]

Taylor can also think of Christ's example in this way. We are asked
to imitate Christ, but at the same time his example is what enables us to

imitate him. *The Great Exemplar* begins with a long exhortation to the imitation of Christ. At one point in the argument Taylor says:[49]

> Every action of the life of Jesus, as it is imitable by us, is of so excellent merit, that by making up the treasure of grace, it becomes full of assistances to us. And obtains of God grace to enable us to its imitation, by way of influence and impetration. For as in the acquisition of habits, the very exercise of the action does produce a facility to the action, and in some proportion becomes the cause of itself; so does every exercise of the life of Christ kindle its own fires, inspires breath into itself, and makes an univocal production of itself in a different subject. And Jesus becomes the fountain of spiritual life to us, as the prophet Elisha to the dead child. . . .

Taylor explains what he means by telling the story of King Wenceslaus and his servant. Going "to his devotions in a remote church, barefooted in the snow and sharpness of unequal and pointed ice," the king found his servant beginning "to faint through the violence of the snow and cold." He commanded the servant to follow in his footsteps, and they both arrived safely at the church:[50]

> In the same manner does the blessed Jesus; for since our way is troublesome, obscure, full of objection and danger, apt to be mistaken and to affright our industry, He commands us to mark His footsteps, to tread where His feet have stood, and not only invites us forward by the argument of His example, but He hath trodden down much of the difficulty, and made the way easier and fit for our feet.

Christ's example is not so much a challenge as something that enables us to follow him, and the gracious enabling is one that persuades us without compulsion.

In many ways Taylor tends to channel God's grace toward Christ. It is in Christ that we chiefly see God's love, presence, mercy, and pardon. But, of course, there is a further question. How can we learn to see Christ that way? In *Discourse VII* of *The Great Exemplar* Taylor seems to me to raise this question. We come to faith the way we come to love:[51]

> For as God enkindles charity upon variety of means and instruments, by a thought, by a chance, by a text of scripture, by a natural tenderness, by the sight of a dying or a tormented beast; so also He may produce faith by arguments of a differing quality, and by issues of His providence He may engage us in such conditions in which, as our understanding is not great enough to choose the best, so neither is it furnished with powers to reject any proposition: and to believe well is an effect of a singular predestination, and it is a gift in order to a grace, as that grace is in order to salvation.

God's persuasive grace operates through our nature and through scripture. As we shall see, it works through the life, worship, and communion of the church. But these ways are mysterious parts of a larger mystery. The accidents of our lives may be providential incitements to faith in Christ. Taylor wants to be sure that what God does is not severed from what we do and experience. The Christian life is always one in which grace and freedom intersect. And perhaps we can say that grace is a way of talking about the more mysterious dimensions of our lives. We can understand our own choices better than God's grace, but we need to see those choices in the larger context of the mystery of grace. Grace builds upon and improves our nature.[52] And it works gradually; we grow in grace.[53]

As I have suggested, Taylor understands grace—or better, the effect of grace properly used—as bringing heaven to earth. In *Unum Necessarium* he considers the question of perfection and argues that we must think in terms of degrees:[54]

> what we cannot attain to, we must at least desire. In this world we cannot arrive thither, but in this life we must always be going thither. It is a *status viae*, grace is the way to glory. And as he that commands us to enter into a city from which we are hugely distant, means we should pass through all the ways that lead thither: so it is here. The precept must be given here, and begun, and set forward, and it will be finished hereafter. But as a man may be an adulterer, or a thief, with his heart and his eye, as well as with his hand; so it is also in good things: a man's heart and eye may be in heaven, that is, in the state of perfection, long before he sets his feet upon the golden threshold.

Similarly, Taylor exhorts us to "consider and contemplate the joys of heaven, that when they have filled thy desires, which are the sails of the soul, thou mayest steer only thither."[55] In one mood Taylor sees quite clearly that our journey to heaven is a long and arduous one:[56]

> Since we stay not here, being people but of a day's abode, and our age is like that of a fly and contemporary with a gourd, we must look somewhere else for an abiding city [Hebr 13:14], a place in another country to fix our house in, whose walls and foundation is God, where we must find rest, or else be restless for ever.

Taylor's allusion is to the beginning of Augustine's *Confessions*, and we can discern the theme of the long journey Christians must make to arrive at their destiny, a journey made possible by God's grace. But unlike Augustine and Donne this is not where Taylor places his emphasis.

Instead, what he can call a state of grace is a present union of God and the believer. To be sure that union requires growth and perfection, and Taylor does not neglect the idea of growth in holiness. Nevertheless, he sees it as, in principle, a binding of heaven to earth and earth to heaven by the reciprocity of God's grace and our response. One of his prayers in *Holy Living* makes the point clear:[57]

> O eternal Father, Thou that sittest in heaven invested with essential glories and divine perfections, fill my soul with so deep a sense of the excellencies of spiritual and heavenly things, that my affections being weaned from the pleasures of the world and the false allurements of sin, I may, with great severity and the prudence of a holy discipline and strict desires, with clear resolutions and a free spirit, have my conversation in heaven and heavenly employments; that being, in affections as in my condition, a pilgrim and a stranger here, I may covet after and labour for an abiding city, and at last may enter into, and for ever dwell in, the celestial Jerusalem which is the mother of us all, through Jesus Christ our Lord. Amen.

Grace enables us to have "our conversation in heaven" (cf. Phil 3:20), however much our entrance into the heavenly Jerusalem lies in the future.

The fact that Taylor's doctrine of grace departs from Augustine's notion of operative grace and so from the dominant conventions of his time by no means should be equated with a judgment that Taylor fails to take God's grace seriously. Grace for him is primarily God's love, a love made present to us largely in God's mercy and pardon. God's love, then, is the context in which we live our lives. And it is a context that never compels our response. At the same time, love can elicit love. And so grace in a persuasive way mysteriously draws from us our response. If we respond in an honest way, grace assists us. The use we make of God's grace is decisive. Put another way, grace is a gift; and the effect of the gift depends on our using it correctly. But if there were no gift, we should find it impossible to transcend our natural mortality and concupiscence. Taylor seems to me to press beyond the usual Western understanding of the relationship between grace and freedom, an understanding that tends to ask which of the two comes first. And, of course, when we look at the issue that way, whichever one we place first will cancel out the other. If grace is first, it is hard to see that freedom remains. If freedom is first, it is hard to see why we need grace. It is my suggestion that Taylor basically sees the relationship a different way. Grace and freedom operate simultaneously but at different levels. Grace has a kind of priority since it is the larger context in which we must place freedom. But in the long run grace and freedom work simultaneously. We can think of our lives in terms of the free choices we make. But there is a more mysterious dimension that has to do with the possibilities and gifts we discover. Though we cannot argue that Taylor is necessarily dependent on the church fathers for his doctrine of grace, it seems clear to me that his view is in broad terms the same as that of Gregory of Nyssa. His is a schema of grace and response. We must, then, turn from this discussion of Taylor's understanding of grace to the way he articulates the response we should make. Thus, in the next section of the argument we can turn to faith, repentance, and love.

Faith, Repentance, and Love

Before turning to each of these three responses to God's grace or, to put it another way, to these three graces, it is important to point out that they belong together and cannot finally be severed from one another. Faith and love obviously belong together. "For the faith of a Christian hath more in it of the will than of the understanding."[58] In this way Taylor introduces a discussion of the point in *Discourse VII* of *The Great Exemplar*. He cites Galatians 5:6 and 6:15 and points out that Christian faith is "faith working by love." Faith is not "a mere believing," which even devils have. Rather "the faith of a Christian, the faith that justifies and saves him, is 'faith working by charity,' or 'faith keeping the commandments of God.'"[59] True faith, then, is a "lively" faith, one that is productive of good works. Taylor in this way sees Paul and James as in agreement and approves of the fact that "St. James says that faith lives not but by charity."[60] Faith, then, "is a duty made up of the concurrence of the will and the understanding." He continues by including repentance in the picture:[61]

> Faith and repentance begin the Christian course; "repent and believe the gospel," was the sum of the apostle's sermons: and all the way after it is, "faith working by love." Repentance puts the first spirit and life into faith, and charity preserves it and gives it nourishment and increase; itself also growing by a mutual supply of spirits and nutriments from faith. . . . faith supplies charity with argument and maintenance, and charity supplies faith with life and motion; faith makes charity reasonable, and charity makes faith living and effectual.

Faith, since it is "the beginning grace," can include not only charity but also hope; the three Christian virtues are really "parts of faith." Faith "is not a single star, but a constellation, a chain of graces . . . by which God intends to bring us to heaven."[62]

Taylor speaks in a similar way in *Discourse IX Of Repentance* in

The Great Exemplar. His emphasis here is not on the relation of faith and charity but on that of faith and repentance. These two sum up the "whole doctrine of the gospel," and they are related to "the Will and the Understanding, that is, the whole man considered in his superior faculties." Faith correlates with the understanding; repentance, with the will. And both of them address our fallen condition:[63]

> [Faith] supposes us naturally ignorant, and comes to supply those defects which in our understandings were left after the spoils of innocence and wisdom made in paradise upon Adam's prevarication, and continued and increased by our neglect, evil customs, voluntary deceptions, and infinite prejudices. And as faith presupposes our ignorance, so repentance presupposes our malice and iniquity. The whole design of Christ's coming, and the doctrines of the gospel, being to recover us from a miserable condition, from ignorance to spiritual wisdom, by the conduct of faith; and from a vicious, habitually depraved life, and ungodly manners, to the purity of the sons of God, by the instrument of repentance.

Here Taylor does not speak of love, but it is easy enough to suppose that he thinks of love as the product of faith and repentance. As he spoke in *Discourse VII* of faith working through love, so elsewhere he can speak of love and obedience as "the twin-daughters of holy repentance."[64] We can argue not only that Taylor insists on the intersection of faith, repentance, and love but also that he refuses to sever moral from spiritual considerations. To be sure, he can treat repentance and love in the context of moral theology; but he never forgets that the moral life must be integrated with the spiritual orientation of Christians to heaven.

With these points in mind we can turn to some examination of each of the three virtues or graces. Faith, Taylor points out, as the word occurs in scripture, is "infinitely ambiguous." Robert Stephens's concordance to the Vulgate sets down these scriptural meanings under "no less than twenty-two several senses."[65] Taylor, of course, remains cautious with respect to such complications and does not depart very far from the meaning we have seen him give to faith in the two discourses from *The Great Exemplar*. Nevertheless, he does see the difference between the faith *that* is believed and the faith *by which* we believe. And it is in *The Liberty of Prophesying* that he addresses the question of Christian belief in the first sense. He begins by recognizing the impossibility of reconciling the diverse religious opinions of his day:[66]

> And therefore although variety of opinions was impossible to be cured, and they who attempted it did like him who claps his shoulder to the ground to stop an earthquake; yet the inconveniences arising from it

might possibly be cured, not by uniting their beliefs, that was to be despaired of, but by curing that which caused these mischiefs and accidental inconveniences of their disagreeings.

People can disagree without coming to blows. More importantly, the unity of Christian faith need not be equated with uniformity of belief at every level.

One faith need not mean that people cannot differ from one another in their opinions:[67]

> For if it be evinced that one heaven shall hold men of several opinions, if the unity of faith be not destroyed by that which men call differing religions, and if an unity of charity be the duty of us all, even towards persons that are not persuaded of every proposition we believe, then I would fain know to what purpose are all those stirs and great noises in christendom; those names of faction, the several names of churches . . . distinguished by names of sects and men; these are all become instruments of hatred; thence come schisms and parting of communions, and then persecutions, and then wars and rebellion, and then the dissolutions of all friendships and societies.

Taylor is obviously addressing the situation that obtained in the English Revolution, and in one sense the remedy he is suggesting is toleration. But he is not thinking of toleration in a secular way. Rather, what he argues is that there can be a Christian unity that ought to transcend the competing claims of the churches or sects of his time. He is not suggesting that unity can be preserved by allowing any or all opinions. Instead, his proposal rests on the characteristic Anglican distinction between beliefs necessary for salvation and matters that must be regarded as indifferent. On the one hand, his appeal is to the "comprehension" that characterized Elizabethan Anglicanism. On the other hand, he points toward the Latitudinarian views that became common at the end of the seventeenth century. In any case, what he opposes is making "every opinion . . . an article of faith, every article . . . a ground of a quarrel." To such a pass have we come that "we think we love not God except we hate our brother, and we have not the virtue of religion unless we persecute all religions but our own."[68]

Taylor ties the unity of Christian faith to what is necessary for salvation. We should not believe propositions as ends in themselves, but only for their true purpose:[69]

> Now God's great purpose being to bring us to Him by Jesus Christ, Christ is our medium to God, obedience is the medium to Christ, and faith the medium to obedience, and therefore is to have its estimate in

proportion to its proper end; and those things are necessary which necessarily promote the end.

At first it looks as though Taylor wants to regard what is necessary for salvation as no more than belief in Christ crucified or in Christ as our lawgiver and our savior. Extending what we must believe beyond that is really to constrict belief by multiplying articles of faith. "I see not how any man can justify making the way to heaven narrower than Jesus Christ hath made it, it being already so narrow that there are few that find it."[70] Nevertheless, what Taylor regards as necessary for Christian belief is the apostolic faith preserved in the creed and found in scripture. The creed includes the *prima credibilia*, and these prime beliefs are really promises rather than propositions. And they are quite general in character.[71]

Taylor's argument continues partly by repeating points that his patron, Laud, had made in his *Conference with Fisher*. There is no such thing as an infallible church on earth. The church cannot establish its own foundation. Once we move beyond the prime beliefs of the creed we are on shaky ground. Our deductions from scripture and tradition cannot be trusted, and even reason is by no means an infallible guide. The arguments against infallibility support the initial distinction between beliefs necessary for salvation and beliefs in matters that are indifferent. Taylor's conclusion reads in part:[72]

> The sum of all is this; there is no security in any thing or to any person but in the pious and hearty endeavours of a good life. . . . And indeed this is the intendment and design of faith. For (that we may join both ends of this discourse together) therefore certain articles are prescribed to us and propounded to our understanding, so that we might be supplied with instructions, with motives and engagements to incline and determine our wills to the obedience of Christ. So that obedience is just so consequent to faith, as the acts of will are to the dictates of the understanding. . . . It is evident that if obedience and a good life be secured upon the most reasonable and proper grounds of christianity, that it, upon the APOSTLES' CREED, then faith also is secured.

What seems remarkable to me about this conclusion is that faith has now become not so much what we believe as the lively faith that expresses itself in obedience. In *Discourse VII Of Faith* Taylor speaks of faith as "an act of the understanding" that represents "the gate of duty, and the entrance to felicity."[73] The conclusion to *The Liberty of Prophesying* runs the risk, I think, of losing the idea of faith as a commitment of the understanding and of forgetting that obedience itself should be tied to eternal felicity.

Let me turn now to the way Taylor understands faith as "an act of the understanding." In some sense, faith appears to be an assent of the mind. And yet it is not simply intellectual in character. "The faith of the devils hath more of the understanding in it; the faith of Christians more of the will."[74] The assent of faith clearly includes a moral and spiritual commitment. Arguments and demonstrations cannot produce faith. Indeed,

> if we examine and consider the account, upon what slight arguments we have taken up Christianity itself (as, that it is the religion of our country, or that our fathers before us were of the same faith, or because the priest bids us, and he is a good man, or for something else, but we know not what) we must needs conclude it the good providence of God, not our choice, that made us Christians.[75]

A mystery attaches to the assent of faith, but the important point is that it represents only a beginning. Taylor cites Romans 1:16-17. Saint Paul calls faith:[76]

> "the power of God unto salvation to every believer"; that is, faith is all that great instrument by which God intends to bring us to heaven: and he gives this reason, "in the gospel the righteousness of God is revealed from faith to faith"; for "it is written, The just shall live by faith." Which discourse makes faith to be a course of sanctity and holy habits, a continuation of a Christian's duty as not only gives the first breath, but by which a man lives the life of grace. . . . For as there are several degrees and parts of justification, so there are several degrees of faith answerable to it. . . . For if we proceed "from faith to faith," from believing to obeying, from faith in the understanding to faith in the will, from faith barely assenting to the revelations of God to faith obeying the commandments of God, from the body of faith to the soul of faith, that is, to faith formed and made alive by charity; then we shall proceed from justification to justification. . . .

Faith transforms itself from assent to "faith formed," and this is faith working through love. But Taylor also seems to mean that faith is less an event than a process of growth. It can be "a grain of mustard seed," or it can "grow up to a plant" or even have "the fulness of faith."[77]

The goal of this growth is heaven. Taylor thinks not so much of the long journey by which we attain the goal as of the way the goal informs faith in the present. One of the signs of true faith is[78]

> To be a stranger upon earth in our affections, and to have all our thoughts and principal desires fixed upon the matters of faith, the things of heaven. For if a man were adopted heir to Caesar, he would, if he believed it real and effective, despise the present, and wholly be at

court in his father's eye; and his desires would outrun his swiftest
speed, and all his thoughts would spend themselves in creating ideas
and little fantastic images of his future condition. Now God hath made
us heirs of His kingdom, and co-heirs with Jesus; if we believed this,
we would think, and affect, and study accordingly.

The present is not the same as the future, but faith bridges the gap in
such a way that heaven becomes in some sense our portion on earth.
Faith from this perspective is virtually the same as hope; and hope is,
paradoxically, a *present* possession. "Faith believes the revelations of
God, hope expects His promises . . . and gives up all the passions and
affections to heaven and heavenly things."[79] Taylor does not speak very
much of hope, but perhaps this is because he sees it primarily as a dimension of faith and as a present reality. But he can also treat hope as essential to the godly fear that begins our repentance. "Godly fear is ever
without despair; because christian fear is an instrument of duty, and that
duty without hope can never go forward."[80]

The hopeful dimension of faith not only enables us to escape despair
and to repent, it also means that we can understand faith as an absolute
trust in God. In *Discourse VII* Taylor speaks of Abraham's faith in his
willingness to sacrifice Isaac and argues that we must imitate that faith
by "an entire confident relying upon the divine goodness in all cases of
needs or danger." He ends the discourse by saying,[81]

> if you can be cheerful in a storm, smile when the world frowns, be con-
> tent in the midst of spiritual desertions and anguish of spirit, expecting
> all should work together for the best, according to the promise; if you
> can strengthen yourselves in God when you are weakest, believe when
> you see no hope, and entertain no jealousies or suspicions of God,
> though you see nothing to make you confident; then, and then only,
> you have faith, which, in conjunction with its other parts, is able to
> save your souls.

This dimension of faith dominates Taylor's discussion "Of the practice
of the grace of faith in the time of sickness" in *Holy Dying*. The prayer
at the end of the two relevant sections begins:[82]

> O holy and eternal Jesus, who didst die for me and for all mankind,
> abolishing our sins, reconciling us to God, adopting us into the portion
> of Thine heritage, and establishing with us a covenant of faith and obe-
> dience, making our souls to rely upon spiritual strengths, by the sup-
> ports of a holy belief, and the expectation of rare promises, and the
> infallible truths of God: O let me for ever dwell upon the rock, leaning
> upon Thy arm, believing Thy word, trusting in Thy promises, waiting
> for Thy mercies, and doing Thy commandments. . . .

If faith is a "chain of graces," then it represents what links the beginning of the Christian life to its goal. But it also binds heaven to earth and earth to heaven.

As we have seen, faith requires repentance to be effective and to be translated into love. Indeed, we can argue that repentance is the key to Taylor's theology and that this allies him with Donne, however different their views are from one another. Repentance, of course, is the one thing necessary; and it is God's gift in the covenant of grace, which Taylor can call the covenant of repentance. The covenant of works, which represented the conditions of Adam's creation, made no provision for repentance for the simple reason that Adam could easily have fulfilled the obligations of this covenant. After the fall, however, this covenant became difficult "not only because man's fortune was broken, and his spirit troubled, and his passions disordered and vexed by his calamity and his sin, but because man upon the birth of children and the increase of the world contracted new relations, and consequently had new duties and obligations, and men hindered one another."[83] The covenant of works continued in the covenants with Abraham, Noah, and Moses. And the law of Moses had some place for repentance, but only for small sins. This was no more than "a little image of repentance" resembling the promises of the law. The successive covenants, however, were pedagogical, designed to prepare for the gospel:[84]

> For it was this which made the world of the godly long for Christ, as having commission to open the *krypton apo tōn aiōnōn* [cf. 1 Cor 2:7; Eph 3:9; Col 1:26], "the hidden mystery" of justification by faith and repentance. For the law called for exact obedience, but ministered no grace but that of fear, which was not enough to the performance or the engagement of exact obedience.

The covenant of grace, as we have seen, enables God to account our imperfect righteousness as sufficient. And it bestows as a free gift the possibility of repentance. God introduced this second covenant immediately upon Adam's fall, but it remained secret and not universally effective until the coming of Christ. "This is the mercy of God in Jesus Christ, springing from the fountains of grace, purchased by the blood of the holy Lamb, the eternal sacrifice, promised from the beginning, always ministered to man's need in the secret economy of God, but proclaimed to all the world at the revelation of God incarnate, the first day of our Lord Jesus."[85]

Taylor is quick to argue that the demand of the new covenant is in fact greater than that found in the covenant of works. The puzzle is how we can say that God is just in not imposing an impossible law and at the same time does not exact of us absolute obedience. We might rather suppose that God knows his law is impossible and would, consequently, be content with our best but feeble efforts to obey it. Taylor seeks to solve the puzzle in several ways. First, the command that we love God "with all our hearts and all our strengths" prevents us from "either a direct lessening of our opinion of God, by tempting us to suppose no more love was due to Him than such a limited measure, or else a teaching us not to give Him what was His due."[86] Second, "commanding us to do all that we can . . . does invite our greatest endeavours."[87] Taylor's fourth point is that God's design in imposing "great holiness in unlimited and indefinite measures" is "to give excellent proportions of reward answerable to the greatness of our endeavour."[88] This idea is related to his third and, as it seems to me, most interesting point:

> by this means still we are contending and pressing forwards; and no man can say he does now comprehend [Phil 3:13], or that his work is done, till he die; and therefore for ever he must grow in grace, which could not be without the proposing of a commandment the performance of which would for ever sufficiently employ him.

Taylor does not put it this way, but it would be simpler to argue that the very inexhaustibility of the demand of the gospel elicits from us a perpetual response by which we press forward to the goal of our calling, to paraphrase Philippians 3. Taylor does, however, continue his discussion in *Unum Necessarium* by raising the question of what scripture means by perfection. He concludes that "the whole design of the gospel [is] rarely abbreviated in these two words of perfection and repentance."[89]

Taylor's idea is in large part informed by the same passage from Philippians that we saw played an important role for Gregory of Nyssa and Augustine. Christian perfection in this life need not be equated with the perfection of the age to come or with a perfection that can be understood as an achieved and completed state. Rather,[90]

> Every person that is in the state of grace, and designs to do his duty, must think of what is before him, not what is past; of the stages that are not yet run, not of those little portions of his course he hath already finished. . . . And from hence S. Paul gives the rule I have now described, "Brethren, I count not myself to have apprehended; but this one thing I do, forgetting those things which are behind, and reaching forth unto those things which are before, I press toward the mark for the prize of the high calling: let therefore as many as be perfect be thus minded." [Phil 3:13ff.] That is, no man can do the duty of a Christian, no man can in any sense be perfect, but he that adds virtue to virtue, and one degree of grace unto another.

This movement from virtue to virtue and grace to grace would be impossible without repentance. I should want to conclude that Taylor equates Christian perfection with perpetual repentance. This is basically his point in *Unum Necessarium* I.iii and iv. Repentance must be such "as includes in it perfection, and yet the perfection is such as needs repentance."[91] The interaction of the two is both a movement and an orientation. Repentance "will bring us to heaven."[92] But it also brings heaven to us. Though his language differs from that of John Wesley, it seems to me that Taylor's understanding of Christian perfection correlates with Wesley's. This should not surprise us, since Taylor's writings were formative of Wesley's thought.

Another way of thinking of repentance is to speak of conversion, but of a conversion that is not so much an event as a constant growth. In his discussion of post-baptismal sin in *Discourse IX* Taylor makes three final points. He allows for sins that are "past hopes of pardon in this life." But he goes on to say, second, that sins are "pardoned by parts, revocably and imperfectly during this life, not quickly nor yet manifestly." Finally, "Repentance contains in it many operations, parts, and employments, its terms and purpose being to redintegrate our lost condition."[93] These two last points suggest that repentance and pardon represent a dialectic that continues throughout our lives. Moreover, he contrasts the true repentance that is "a renewing us in the spirit of our mind" (cf. Rom 12:2) with the "mere sorrow" that made repentance ineffective for Judas and Esau. That true repentance, preached by John the Baptist and our savior and exemplified by the Ninevites to whom Jonah preached, "is called 'conversion,' or 'amendment of life,' a repentance productive of holy fruits."[94] Similarly, in *Unum Necessarium* Taylor argues that there are two parts of repentance, "leaving our sins" and "doing holy actions." For this reason "All the whole duty of repentance, and every of its parts, is sometimes called 'conversion.'"[95] He continues by grounding this conclusion in scripture.[96] His insistence on the possibility and necessity of repeated repentance finds a place in *Holy Living*. Although "a man can be regenerated but once," it is nonetheless true that, provided we are "not in the entire possession of the devil," we are "in a recoverable condition" and "may repent often." "We repent or rise from death but once, but from sickness many times; and by the grace of God we shall be pardoned, if so we repent."[97]

Taylor quite consciously elaborates his doctrine of repentance in opposition to Roman Catholic moral theology.[98] He devotes part I, chapter ii, of the *Dissuasive from Popery* to the topic and argues that "popery" teaches impiety and "gives warranty to a wicked life." Positively, he insists on grounding his doctrine in scripture and on binding moral issues to the spiritual life. Negatively, he faults Roman Catholic moral theology for what he regards as its legalism and its tendency to offer cheap grace—"they break in pieces the salutary doctrine of repentance, making it to be consistent with a wicked life, and little or no amendment."[99] Taylor argues against the view that it is unnecessary to repent immediately on sinning, and he denies that resorting to the sacrament of penance is necessary to repentance. Indeed, the confessional allows "attrition" or imperfect contrition to be sufficient for pardon; and this cannot be true repentance. Taylor is willing to accept the conventional understanding of repentance as contrition, confession, and satisfaction provided these three not be severed, provided confession be made to God and not necessarily in the context of private penance, and provided the satisfaction be understood as amendment of life. While he is willing to admit the distinction between greater and lesser sins, he rejects the Roman Catholic distinction between mortal and venial sins, on the grounds that it leads to treating venial sins as matters of no consequence and requiring no repentance.[100] Similarly, he seriously qualifies the Roman Catholic distinction between sinful acts and sinful habits, a view that treats acts rather than habits as culpable. "The secret intention of which proposition, and the malignity of it, consists in this, that it is not necessary for a man to repent speedily; and a man is not bound by repentance to interrupt the procedure of his impiety, or to repent of his habit, but of the single acts that went before it."[101]

Taylor has no wish to substitute one kind of legalism for another, nor should we suppose his rigorism one he wishes to impose on others. His aim is to provoke his readers to examine themselves and to look for the inner repentance that represents a conversion. In one of his sermons he points out that people weep for trifling causes—losing sixpence, breaking a glass. We can see that "a man cannot tell his own heart by his tears, or the truth of his repentance by those short gusts of sorrow." True repentance lodges itself in the heart and not in outward things, yet even here we must be cautious:[102]

> Nay, our heart is so deceitful in this matter of repentance, that the masters of the spiritual life are fain to invent suppletory arts and stratagems to secure the duty; and we are advised to mourn, because we do not mourn; to be sorrowful, because we are not sorrowful.

We can keep in mind Taylor's recognition of the mystery of the human heart when we assess what appears to be the most obvious sign of his rigorism, his repudiation of the efficacy of a deathbed repentance.[103] He easily disposes of the clearest argument against his view, the story of the penitent thief whom Christ on the cross promises paradise. Christ's pardon of the thief is analogous to baptism and not to the pardoning of post-baptismal sins. However much Taylor insists on his rigorous view in principle, he is reluctant to impose it in practice. The last part of *Holy Dying* consists of instructions for the priest in ministering to the sick and of offices for the visitation of the sick. Taylor says that it is "the minister's office to invite sick and dying persons to the holy sacrament." One of the offices that follows elaborates on the Prayer Book rubric providing for private confession and adds sacramental penance to giving communion to the person. These ministrations are, of course, often not at all problematic. But "if the persons be of ill report, and have lived wickedly, they are not to be invited." Thus Taylor establishes his principle that deathbed repentance is invalid. Yet he continues by saying "if they demand it, they are not to be denied." We must not allow our judgments to interfere with God's grace. "God hath mercies which we know not of."[104]

From repentance let me turn, finally and briefly, to love. As we have seen, repentance quickens faith and enables it to work through love. Christians ought to exercise charity or love throughout their lives:[105]

> He that would die well and happily must in his life-time according to all his capacities exercise charity; and because religion is the life of the soul, and charity is the life of religion, the same which gives life to the better part of man, which never dies, may obtain of God a mercy to the inferior part of man in the day of its dissolution. Charity is the great channel through which God passes all His mercy upon mankind.

We can remember that Taylor thinks of God's mercy as "giving" and "forgiving."[106] What God does is what we must also do. So the dying person must put his affairs in order, make a will, and think of giving alms; and he must also seek forgiveness and reconciliation with all whom he knows. "Charity with its twin-daughters, alms and forgiveness, is especially effectual for the procuring of God's mercies in the day and the manner of our death."[107]

Discourse XI in *The Great Exemplar* treats charity the same way, though Taylor adds to forgiving and giving alms the duty of not judging. He elaborates these ideas at some length and includes a consideration of topics such as dueling, going to law, and the problem that alms can sometimes run the risk of ministering to idleness. His prayer at the end of the discourse takes us behind the detailed questions and problems he addresses to the basic grace as he understands it:[108]

> Holy and merciful Jesus, who art the great principle and the instrument of conveying to us the charity and mercies of eternity, who didst love

us when we were enemies, forgive us when we were debtors, recover us when we were dead, ransom us when we were slaves, relieve us when we were poor, and naked, and wandering, and full of sadness and necessities; give us the grace of charity, that we may be pitiful and compassionate of the needs of our necessitous brethren, that we may be apt to relieve them, and that according to our duty and possibilities we may rescue them from their calamities. Give us courteous, affable, and liberal souls; let us, by Thy example, forgive our debtors, and love our enemies, and do to them offices of civility, and tenderness, and relief; always propounding Thee for our pattern, and Thy mercies for our precedent, and Thy precepts for our rule, and Thy Spirit for our guide: that we, shewing mercy here, may receive the mercies of eternity by Thy merits, and by Thy charities, and dispensation, O holy and merciful Jesus. Amen

Taylor's treatment of love takes us firmly into his understanding of the Christian life as corporate. In his preface to *The Great Exemplar* he points out that "the law of charity is a law of nature."[109] What he means is that the union of Adam and Eve in paradise underlines the corporate context in which love must be expressed. And he goes on to say that "Christ made a more perfect restitution of the law of nature than Moses did, and so it became the second Adam to consummate that which began to be less perfect from the prevarication of the first Adam."[110]

Love, then, is what binds human beings to one another. It is friendship, but in a special and extended sense:[111]

by "friendship" I suppose you mean, the greatest love and the greatest usefulness, and the most open communication, and the noblest sufferings, and the most exemplar faithfulness, and the severest truth, and the heartiest counsel, and the greatest union of minds, of which brave men and women are capable. But then I must tell you that christianity hath new christened it, and calls this "charity."

What Taylor means is that Christian charity is universal, a "friendship to all the world." It is "expanded like the face of the sun when it mounts above the eastern hills." In this way it is more than natural "friendships and societies, relations and endearments." The universality of Christian love, however, by no means excludes special relationships that are concrete signs of love. One of Taylor's sermons on marriage begins by saying that God's first blessing to humanity "was society, and that society was a marriage."[112] Taylor addresses the three reasons for marriage—the procreation of children, a remedy for fornication, and mutual support. But his emphasis is on the last reason. He places marriage above the single life:[113]

the state of marriage fills up the numbers of the elect, and hath in it the labour of love, and the delicacies of friendship, the blessing of society, and the union of hands and hearts; it hath in it less of beauty, but more of safety, than the single life; it hath more care, but less danger; it is more merry, and more sad; is fuller of sorrows, and fuller of joys; it lies under more burdens, but is supported by all the strengths of love and charity, and those burdens are delightful. Marriage is the mother of the world, and preserves kingdoms, and fills churches, and heaven itself. Celibate, like the fly in the heart of an apple, dwells in a perpetual sweetness, but sits alone, and is confined and dies in singularity; but marriage, like the useful bee, builds a house and gathers sweetness from every flower, and labours and unites into societies and republics . . . and is that state of good things to which God hath designed the present constitution of the world.

We need not understand Taylor's rhetoric to mean that all must be married. But what he says betrays his emphasis on the corporate character of humanity. If the Christian life must lead to community, it is also true for Taylor that the community is where the Christian life begins and where it finds its proper context. Thus, we must turn to some discussion of Taylor's understanding of the church and its sacraments.

Church and Sacraments

Taylor begins *Discourse VI Of Baptism* in *The Great Exemplar* with a succinct statement of his understanding of the church:[114]

When the holy Jesus was to begin His prophetical office, and to lay the foundation of His church on the corner-stone, He first tempered the cement with water, and then with blood, and afterwards built it up by the hands of the Spirit: Himself entered at that door by which His disciples for ever after were to follow Him; for therefore He went in at the door of baptism, that He might hallow the entrance which Himself made to the house He was now building.

By "prophetical office" Taylor must mean Jesus' public ministry which began with his baptism by John, but he must also include Christ's death and resurrection as the climax of that ministry. Christ is himself the stone rejected by the builders in his death but made by God the corner-stone (cf. Matt 21:42-44 and parallels; 1 Pet 2:4ff.). He is the foundation of the church, and the two sacraments of baptism and the eucharist are what establish the communion Christians have with him and with one another. Taylor not only gives the corporate character of the church pride of place, he also implies that it is the church that makes Christians and not Christians that make the church. That is, becoming a Christian and growing in faith ordinarily requires the nurturing of the church. The church is a society rather than merely a voluntary association. Like the family it precedes the individual members and shapes their lives. Thus, it is baptism rather than a conversion experience that normally marks the beginning of the Christian life.

By "church," of course, Taylor does not mean simply the Church of England. There can be various "churches" that represent parts of the larger church. But the major distinction Taylor makes is between the "invisible" and the "visible church." The second consists of all who have been called "out of the whole mass of mankind" and "are gathered together by the voice and call of God, to the worship of God through Jesus Christ, and the participation of eternal good things to follow." In other words, the visible church is "a company of men and women professing the saving doctrine of Jesus Christ":[115]

> but because "glorious things are spoken of the city of God"; the professors of Christ's doctrine are but imperfectly and inchoatively the church of God; but they who are indeed holy and obedient to Christ's laws of faith and manners, . . . these are truly and perfectly "the church," and they have this signature, "God knoweth who are His."

Only God can make this distinction, and we should not suppose there to be two societies. Rather, the invisible church is always within the visible one. Taylor is not making his distinction in the light of predestination, as though the elect were the invisible church and the visible church consisted of both elect and reprobate. Instead, his distinction is one tied to his understanding of the Christian life as a call to holy living. The more a person has responded to this call, the more likely it is that he is a member of the invisible church. At least that is how I understand what Taylor is saying. In any case, he does not pursue a theoretical discussion of the church very far for the simple reason that disputes amongst Christians must be decided primarily by the appeal to scripture.

Ideally, then, the church is the body of Christ. And Taylor's emphasis is on the implication that Christ in heaven and the church on earth are united. In *Discourse VIII Of the Religion of Holy Places* he argues for the importance of ornament for church buildings and bases his argument on the theme I have just mentioned:[116]

> But when I consider that saying of St. Gregory, that the church is heaven within the tabernacle, heaven dwelling among the sons of men, and remember that God hath studded all the firmament and paved it with stars, because He loves to have His house beauteous and highly

representative of His glory; I see no reason we should not do as Apollinaris says God does, "in earth do the works of heaven."

Of course, Taylor here is repudiating the Puritan tendency to iconoclasm and betraying his Laudian sympathies. But what he means is that God is present both in heaven and in holy places. The altar in heaven corresponds with the altar on earth:[117]

> We looke men in the face when we speake to them, and if we may any where pray to God, and adore him because he is every where present and heares us, then by the same reason we must specially adore him where he is specially present, . . . that is in Heaven, and in all Holy places; And therefore the generall addresse of our devotion is towards heaven. . . . But this generall addresse is limited by a more speciall, and that is in Holy places, places consecrate to the service of God by acts of publike, and religious solemnity, in them, and from them to Heaven.

Taylor continues by citing part of Solomon's prayer in dedicating the temple (1 Kings 8:35) and a passage from Irenaeus that speaks of an altar in heaven. The church, then, is not only a community united to Christ and in its members, it is also a heaven on earth.

These themes also find expression in Taylor's treatment of baptism, which we can find most fully expressed in *Discourse VI Of Baptism*. He begins the discourse with a discussion of the types of and precedents for Christian baptism, but quickly turns to "that which will be of greatest concernment in this affair," that is, the benefits of the sacrament:[118]

> The first fruit is, that "in baptism we are admitted to the kingdom of Christ," presented unto Him, consigned with His sacrament, enter into His militia, give up our understandings and our choice to the obedience of Christ, and, in all senses that we can, become His disciples, witnessing a good confession, and undertaking a holy life.

The second step is "'adoption into the covenant,' which is an immediate consequent of the first presentation; this being the first act of man, that the first act of God."[119] It may be difficult to understand what Taylor has said of the first step as entirely the act of God. Nevertheless, putting the two points together does require us to think of baptism as the coincidence of God's work and ours. Grace and freedom coincide. God gives the covenant, and those baptized enter it. The third benefit Taylor lists really combines the points. Baptism is the new birth "by which we enter into the new world, the new creation, the blessings and spiritualities of the kingdom." Taylor cites John 3:5 and Titus 3:5; and then he says that God becomes our Father, Christ our elder brother, the Spirit "the earnest of our inheritance," and the church our mother. "[O]ur food is the body and blood of our Lord, faith is our learning, religion our employment, and our whole life is spiritual, and heaven the object of our hopes, and the mighty price of our high calling."[120] These first three benefits are the important ones, and they treat baptism as a sacrament of union—grace with freedom, God with the baptized, the baptized with all the members of the church, and heaven with earth.

The benefits Taylor goes on to describe seem less attached to baptism itself than to the baptized life. They include the pardon of sins, admission to a state of pardon for postbaptismal sins, sanctification, occasional temporal blessings, and the assigning of a guardian angel. The second part of the discourse turns to the question of infant baptism.[121] There can be no doubt that infants in baptism enter the kingdom of Christ, become members of the covenant of the gospel, and are born again. But Taylor recognizes that infants are unable to understand this or to act on their understanding. He makes a number of points designed to remove these obstacles. Pardon is not the only benefit of baptism. "Christ did not cure all men's eyes, but them only that were blind." Children, on Taylor's view, have no need of repentance. Consequently, baptism should not be thought designed in any restricted way to pardon original sin. Next, "baptism and its effect may be separated."[122] Taylor makes the same point in *Discourse IX Of Repentance*:[123]

> although by the present custom of the church we are baptized in our infancy . . . yet we must remember that there is a baptism of the Spirit as well as of water: and whenever this happens, whether it be together with that baptism of water, as usually it was when only men and women of years of discretion were baptized; or whether it be ministered in the rite of confirmation, which is an admirable suppletory of an early baptism, and intended by the holy Ghost for a corroborative of baptismal grace, and a defensative against danger; or that, lastly, it be performed by an internal and merely spiritual ministry, when we by acts of our own election verify the promise made in baptism, and so bring back the rite by receiving the effect of baptism . . . then let us look to our standing.

The baptized life, then, does not always begin with baptism. Instead, it finds its actualization when we take our responsibilities upon ourselves, whether at the time of confirmation or at some other time.[124]

Taylor's understanding treats the baptism of infants as the planting of a seed that will sprout and grow only when the children have reached the age of discretion. The kingdom of God, which belongs to little children, is "within us":[125]

It is "the seed of God"; and it is no good argument to say, here is no seed in the bowels of the earth because there is nothing green upon the face of it. For the church gives the sacrament, God gives the grace of the sacrament. But because He does not always give it at the instant in which the church gives the sacrament, (as if there be a secret impediment in the suscipient,) and yet afterwards does give it when the impediment is removed . . . it follows that the church may administer rightly, even before God gives the real grace of the sacrament.

For this reason faith and repentance are necessary not for baptism as such, but only for the baptized life. These "dispositions," though ordinarily required of those baptized, are only required "accidentally."[126] They enter the picture later on:[127]

Baptism is not to be estimated as one act, transient and effective to single purposes, but it is an entrance to a conjugation and a state of blessings. All our life is to be transacted by the measures of the gospel covenant, and that covenant is consigned by baptism; there we have our title and adoption of it: and the grace that is then given to us is like a piece of leaven put into a lump of dough, and faith and repentance do in all the periods of our life out it into fermentation and activity.

Faith and repentance, then, "are necessary to the effect of baptism, not to its susception." And these twin graces produce the fruits of a holy life. Thus, all that we have learned of Taylor's understanding of our response to God's grace in faith, repentance, and love finds its ordinary locus in baptism.

We can draw much the same conclusion with respect to Taylor's understanding of the eucharist, even though it differs from baptism the way nourishment differs from birth. Taylor's first instinct is to underline the mysterious character of the eucharist, and he does so partly because quarrels over the meaning of the sacrament divided Roman Catholics from Protestants and Protestants from one another. Even the New Testament fails to unveil the meaning of the holy communion, and the doctors of the church have succeeded only in making it more mysterious:[128]

So we sometimes espy a bright cloud formed into an irregular figure; when it is observed by unskilful and fantastic travellers, looks like a centaur to some, and as a castle to others; some tell that they saw an army with banners, and it signifies war; but another wiser than his fellow says it looks for all the world like a flock of sheep, and foretells plenty; and all the while it is nothing but a shining cloud. . . . So it is in this great mystery of our religion; in which some espy strange things which God intended not, and others see not what God hath plainly told. . . .

Of course, what turned the eucharist into an apple of discord in Christianity was the Protestant rejection of transubstantiation and the sacrifice of the Mass. Taylor addresses these issues. But the positive aim of Protestantism was to restore the practice of communion. During the Middle Ages few people communicated with any frequency, and the reformers sought to revive what they rightly supposed to be the practice of the ancient church—receiving the bread and wine. Richard Hooker's discussion of the eucharist in book V of *The Laws of Ecclesiastical Polity*, for example, distinguishes two themes: the presence of Christ in the hearts of worthy receivers and the presence of Christ in the elements of bread and wine. He says we must look for that presence in the first rather than in the second, and by saying so he is insisting on an understanding of the eucharist that makes it the holy communion. Hooker is hard to pin down with respect to the presence of Christ in the elements. It might be best to argue that he rejects transubstantiation and the Lutheran doctrine of consubstantiation, but remains agnostic on the question. In his general discussion of sacraments, however, he does say that the sacraments "give what they promise and *are what they signify*." Like Hooker, Taylor can distinguish Christ's presence in the hearts of worthy receivers from his presence in the elements of bread and wine. Let me, then, organize my discussion around this distinction.

Taylor, I think, sees the eucharist primarily as a sacrament of union, binding Christian hearts to Christ and heaven, to grace, and to one another. He articulates this view in *Discourse XIX* in *The Great Exemplar*. The discourse begins with one of Taylor's more baroque exercises in rhetoric:[129]

> As the sun among the stars, and man among the sublunary creatures, is the most eminent and noble, the prince of the inferiors, and their measure, or their guide: so is this action among all the instances of religion; it is the most perfect and consummate, it is an union of mysteries, and a consolidation of duties; it joins God and man, and confederates all the societies of men in mutual complexions, and the entertainments of an excellent charity. . . .

Union is, first of all, with God. Christ's power "is manifest, in making the symbols to be instruments of conveying Himself to the spirit of the receiver: He nourishes the soul with bread, and feeds the body with a sacrament; He makes the body spiritual by His graces there ministered, and makes the spirit to be united to His body by a participation of the divine nature."[130]

Taylor's allusion to 2 Peter 1:4 ("partakers of the divine nature") suggests that he understands the saving effect of communion as *theōsis*, divinization—a theme we have seen dominant in patristic theology. Just as in his discussion of baptism Taylor first thinks of the entrance into Christ's kingdom as the completion and perfection of our nature without an immediate reference to sin and forgiveness, so here becoming partakers of the divine nature serves toward completing our destiny, which is to become as like God as possible. Taylor thinks of divinization primarily in spiritual terms, but he does not neglect its physical dimension. In *The Worthy Communicant* he argues that through the eucharist,[131]

> our bodies are made capable of the resurrection to life and eternal glory. For when we are externally and symbolically in the sacrament, and by faith and the Spirit of God internally united to Christ and made partakers of His body and His blood, we are joined and made one with Him who did rise again; and when the head is risen, the members shall not see corruption for ever, but rise again after the pattern of our Lord.

Taylor confirms the point by appealing to the teaching of the ancient church, citing Hilary, Irenaeus, Ignatius, Cyril, Clement of Alexandria, and Cyprian. The holy communion, then, makes us partakers of Christ, the dead and risen Lord, in body as well as in soul.

The union effected by the sacrament is also the fellowship we have with one another in the body of Christ. In *Discourse XIX* he turns immediately from our union with Christ to the corporate character of that union:[132]

> It [Christ as the food of our souls] also tells us that from hence we derive life and holy motion; "for in Him we live, and move, and have our being." [Acts 17:28] He is the staff of our life, and the light of our eyes, and the strength of our spirit; He is the viand for our journey, and the antepast of heaven. And because this holy mystery was intended to be a sacrament of union, that lesson is morally represented in the symbols; that as the salutary juice is expressed from many clusters running into one chalice, and the bread is a mass made of many grains of wheat; so we also (as the apostle infers from hence, himself observing the analogy) should be "one bread and one body, because we partake of that one bread." [1 Cor 10:17]

The fact that scripture calls both the sacramental bread and the church "the body of Christ" requires the interpretation Taylor gives. In *The Worthy Communicant* he repeats the idea by arguing that "by the communion of this bread all faithful people are confederated into one body, the body of our Lord." To be sure, the language is metaphorical, "tropical and figurative"; but its spiritual sense

> means the most real event in this world; we are really joined to one common divine principle, Jesus Christ our Lord, and from Him we do

communicate in all the blessings of His grace and the fruits of His passion; and we shall if we abide in this union be all one body of a spiritual church in heaven, there to reign with Christ for ever.[133]

While Taylor associates the eucharist with the double effect of our communion with Christ, that is with our becoming partakers of the divine nature and brought into fellowship with one another, he also links it with the Western doctrine of the atonement and with the idea of Christ's death as a sacrifice. As the passage cited last in the preceding paragraph of my discussion shows, the benefits of the eucharist are "the fruits of His passion." Obviously, Taylor disavows the sacrifice of the mass as in any sense a repetition of Christ's death. But he is concerned to give Christ's sacrifice an eternal meaning. He follows the Prayer Book in thinking of Christ's death on the cross as "his one oblation of himself once offered, a full, perfect, and sufficient sacrifice, oblation, and satisfaction, for the sins of the whole world." But he interprets this language as follows:[134]

This sacrifice, because it was perfect, could be but one, and that once: but because the needs of the world should last as long as the world itself, it was necessary that there should be a perpetual ministry established, whereby this one sufficient sacrifice should be made eternally, effectual to the several new arising needs of all the world, who should desire it or in any sense be capable of it.

Christ's sacrifice, of course, establishes the possibility of pardon for repented sins; and Taylor by no means neglects this meaning. At the same time, I should argue that he sees pardon as reconciliation and, consequently, as the means to our communion with the divine nature and with one another through Christ.

Christ's sacrifice is central to the liturgy Taylor composed as an alternative to the Prayer Book, which was proscribed during the Commonwealth period. And in two well-known passages he articulates the meaning of that liturgy. Let me begin by citing the first of these discussions:[135]

When the holy man stands at the table of blessing and ministers the rite of consecration, then do as the angels do, who behold, and love, and wonder that the Son of God should become food to the souls of His servants; that He who cannot suffer any change or lessening, should be broken into pieces, and enter into the body to support and nourish the spirit, and yet at the same time remain in heaven while He descends to thee upon earth; that He who hath eternal felicity should become miserable and die for thee, and then give Himself to thee for ever to redeem thee from sin and misery; that by His wounds He should procure health to thee, by His affronts He should entitle thee to glory, by His death He should bring thee to life, and by becoming a man He should make thee partaker of the divine nature.

A parallel passage in *The Worthy Communicant* exhorts the reader to place himself "by faith and meditation in heaven" at the time of the consecration, and so "see Christ doing in His glorious manner this very thing which thou seest ministered and imitated upon the table of the Lord."[136]

The eucharist, then, is "a commemoration and representment of Christ's death" and so "a commemorative sacrifice." Christ's eternal pleading of his sacrifice in heaven becomes effective on earth. Moreover, "all the effects of grace . . . are applied to us, and made effectual to single persons and communities of men, by Christ's intercession in heaven; so also they are promoted by acts of duty and religion here on earth."[137] The structure of Taylor's liturgy reflects the idea that our reception of the benefits of Christ's eternal sacrifice ought to bear fruit in our lives. Taylor places the intercessions after the communion itself. One of the "eucharistical prayers" following the intercessions reads:[138]

> Glory be to Thee, O God our Father, who hast vouchsafed to make us at this time partakers of the body and blood of Thy holy Son: we offer unto Thee, O God, ourselves, our souls and bodies, to be a reasonable, holy, and living sacrifice unto Thee: keep us under the shadow of Thy wings, and defend us from all evil, and conduct us by Thy holy spirit of grace into all good; for Thou who hast given Thy holy Son unto us, how shalt Thou not with Him give us all things else? Blessed be the name of our God for ever and ever. Amen.

It is not, I think, misleading to suggest that Taylor would be willing to think of the sacrificing of ourselves as the life of faith, repentance, and love. Indeed, in *The Worthy Communicant* Taylor sees this triad as the chief way to prepare for communion. Chapters 3, 4, and 5 treat faith, charity, and repentance. There is a kind of circle. The grace we receive from Christ's heavenly sacrifice enables our response of faith, love, and repentance; but these three virtues are also what make it possible for us to find union with Christ. Taylor's emphasis on the importance of preparation for communion might imply a good deal of caution. But he actually argues for frequent communion, a position that would seem to drive against over-scrupulosity.[139]

Taylor's emphasis on how the eucharist binds heaven and earth together also finds expression in the way he handles the second way Christ is present in the sacrament. That presence, as we have seen, is in our hearts; but it is also in the elements of bread and wine. Taylor understands these two forms of Christ's presence as mutually involving:[140]

> The bread, when it is consecrated and made sacramental, is the body of our Lord: and the fraction and distribution of it is the communication of that body which died for us upon the cross. He that doubts of either of the parts of this proposition must either think Christ was not able to verify His word, and to make "bread" by His benediction to become to us "His body"; or that St. Paul did not well interpret and understand this mystery, when he called it "bread."

While there can be no doubt that Taylor wants to insist on the real presence of Christ in the elements of bread and wine, it is by no means easy to pin his view down. It is easier to understand the views he opposes. He repudiates transubstantiation and any view that would treat Christ's body in the bread as identical with his *natural* body. He equally disavows any view that treats the bread as Christ's body as no more than a symbol.[141]

The middle ground Taylor seeks might at first appear to be a high "virtualism," that is, a doctrine that the bread and wine *are* the body and blood of Christ in virtue of their function as instruments conveying Christ's presence to us. One passage in *The Worthy Communicant* appears to drive in this direction:[142]

> The sacraments and symbols, if they be considered in their own nature, are just such as they seem, water, and bread, and wine; they retain the names proper to their own natures; but because they are made to be signs of a secret mystery . . . therefore the symbols and sacraments receive the names of what themselves do sign; they are the body and blood of Christ; they are metonymically such. But because yet further; they are instruments of grace in the hand of God, and by these His holy spirit changes our hearts and translates us into a divine nature; therefore the whole work is attributed to them by a synecdoche. . . .

Characteristically, however, Taylor says more than this. The passage I have just cited correlates with Hooker's statement that sacraments "are what they signify." But Taylor presses Hooker's view further than, I suspect, Hooker would have liked. The bread and wine are "metonymically" the body and blood of Christ, but Taylor means to say more than that they are simply metaphorically and symbolically the body and blood. In *Discourse XIX* he had already treated "real" and "spiritual" as capable of being understood as equivalent terms:[143]

> I suppose it to be a mistake to think whatsoever is real must be natural; and it is no less to think spiritual to be only figurative: that's too much, and this is too little.

Taylor implies that most Western treatments of the eucharist make the false assumption that what is real must be opposed to what is symbolic and spiritual. His view seeks to reunite the two terms, and in this way goes beyond a virtualist understanding.

We can see Taylor's view most clearly in *The Real Presence and Spiritual of Christ in the Blessed Sacrament*. The treatise is primarily a refutation of transubstantiation, but Taylor makes his positive view clear enough. Perhaps mistakenly, he identifies that view with the one held by all Protestants:[144]

> The doctrine of the church of England and generally of the protestants in this article, is, that after the minister of the holy mysteries hath ritely prayed, and blessed or consecrated the bread and the wine, the symbols become changed into the body and blood of Christ, after a SACRAMENTAL, that is, in a SPIRITUAL, REAL manner.

He does go on to say that "the wicked receive not Christ, but the bare symbols only; but yet to their hurt." But what he seems to mean is that the elements are *really* and *spiritually* the body and blood of Christ, but as such they are effective only for those who discern Christ's presence in the elements. Taylor's insistence is that what is a spiritual presence is also a real one.[145] Moreover, he identifies Christ's body in the sacrament as "that body, that flesh that was born of the Virgin Mary, that was crucified, dead and buried." He knows no other body. But he is quick to argue that, while it is the same body, it is "not after the same manner." Christ's risen body differs from his earthly body.[146] Moreover, his natural body is now located in heaven and nowhere else; but spiritually it is "in the sacrament as He can be in a sacrament, in the hearts of faithful receivers as He hath promised it to be there; that is, in the sacrament mystically, operatively, as in a moral and divine instrument."[147] In sum, Taylor's doctrine of the real presence may well go beyond the usual views held by Anglicans of his time. Nevertheless, it accords with one peculiarity of the 1662 Book of Common Prayer. The Black Rubric, which had been added to the 1552 book to deny that kneeling to receive communion implied any "real and essential presence" of Christ in the elements, was quietly omitted in the Elizabethan book. In 1662 it was restored, but with the wording changed to "any corporal presence of Christ's natural flesh and blood." The revised rubric opens the door to an understanding of Christ's real and spiritual presence in the elements. In any case, Taylor's doctrine of real and spiritual presence is bound together with his insistence that in the sacrament heaven binds itself to earth, drawing us to heaven by the holy life that responds to God's grace and uses that grace wisely.

Conclusion

It is arguable that the key to understanding Anglicanism, at least in the sixteenth and seventeenth centuries, is the doctrine of repentance. The Book of Common Prayer itself is penitential in tone and seems designed to put worshipers in a mood of contrition. It is not easy to explain the origins of this sensibility. To be sure, it correlates with the Protestant understanding of justification by faith; but I suspect it is rooted more deeply in Western understandings of Christianity. However that may be, we have seen that repentance plays a central role for both Donne and Taylor. Nevertheless, there are differences. For Donne repentance is tied to the pilgrim's journey toward what lies beyond this life of sin and misery. It reflects the constant stumbling of the pilgrim and the consequent necessity of getting up and continuing the journey. For Taylor, however, repentance is primarily a conversion, a turning around from earth toward heaven. It is, of course, a duty; but it is a duty that binds us to Christ and his eternal sacrifice. It may also be the case that Taylor ties repentance more firmly to an ecclesiastical and sacramental piety than is the case with Donne. Another point that occurs to me is to suggest that in Donne and Taylor we find a contrast between pessimism and optimism in their understanding of repentance. For Donne there seems always to be the possibility that his repentance is insufficient. He is a sorrowful penitent, and his joy comes only because his hope is that God's mercy will in the long run triumph over his sin. But Taylor thinks more of the effect of repentance. It is really the constant renewal of the relationship we have with God through Christ because of our baptism. Granted that we remain sinners after baptism, Taylor remains optimistic that pardon is available provided we genuinely seek it. And he surely has more optimism with respect to our own capacities for good.

To the extent that this conclusion makes sense, the problem of Taylor's rigorism emerges. Has he turned the gospel into a set of impossible demands? He is himself aware that some people will react to his teaching in this fashion. In his preface to *Unum Necessarium*, addressed to the clergy of the Church of England, he recognizes that some will be troubled by supposing "that upon pretence of great severity, as if I were exact or could be, I urge others to so great strictness which will rather produce despair than holiness."[148] He disavows any such intention and regards the objection as "a mere excuse which some men would make, lest they should believe it necessary to live well." Judas is the only example in scripture of someone who despaired. And, of course, he was unwilling to repent. Taylor's emphasis on repentance seems to me crucial in order to argue that he is not, finally, a rigorist. The necessity of repentance reflects the fact that we are never able to meet the demands of the gospel exactly. But repentance is a necessary part of our movement further and further toward the holy living the gospel demands. Moreover, the very possibility of repentance and pardon is God's gift and the sure reflection of his mercies. Godly sorrow remains, but the conversion of repentance is a constant turning toward heaven itself.

In some ways with Taylor we have come full circle. As I have argued, his view of original sin is far more like that of the early church before and apart from Augustine. Similarly, his understanding of grace and freedom is neither Augustinian nor Pelagian. Grace is really God's love and mercy, and like most writers in the early church Taylor insists that love cannot compel. God's love is the context in which we live our lives, and it is what elicits from us our best endeavors. Those endeavors always take place with the coincidence of grace and freedom. Faith, repentance, and love are God's gift; but they are also our response to God's gift, our proper use of the gift that makes it effective for us. Taylor clearly belongs with the Restoration Church of England with its emphasis on holy living and on the church and sacraments. But he also seems to me a kindred spirit of Gregory of Nyssa. If Augustine and Donne belong together, Gregory and Taylor make up an alternative pair.

Notes

1. See Bishop Heber's *Life* in *The Whole Works of the Rt. Revd. Jeremy Taylor*, ed. Reginald Heber, revised and corrected by C. P. Eden (10 vol; London, 1847–52), 1:ixff. He describes the loss of the family papers on p. x. On p. xi he says, "I have still to lament the scantiness and imperfection of my materials; and that in this as in most other instances, the biography of an author must consist in the account of his writings rather than his actions or adventures."

2. *Holy Living* III.iv, in *The Whole Works*, 3:140.

3. Ibid., Dedication, in *The Whole Works*, 3:1.

4. *The Great Exemplar, Discourse VII: Of Faith*; CWS, 286.

5. Cited in *The Whole Works*, 1:cclxxvi.

6. Ibid., VI.vi.79, in *The Whole Works*, 7:283.

7. Ibid., VI.i.1, in *The Whole Works*, 7:243.

8. Ibid., VI.i.19-20, in *The Whole Works*, 7:250.

9. Ibid., VI.i.22, in *The Whole Works*, 7:251.

10. Ibid.

11. Ibid., VI.i.45, in *The Whole Works*, 7:262.

12. Ibid., VI.iv.67, in *The Whole Works*, 7:275.

13. Ibid., VI.v.71, in *The Whole Works*, 7:279.

14. Ibid., VI.i.5, in *The Whole Works*, 7:244.

15. Ibid., VI.i.9, in *The Whole Works*, 7:245.

16. Ibid., VII.i.1, in *The Whole Works*, 7:303.

17. Ibid., VII.v.18, in *The Whole Works*, 7:319–20.

18. Ibid., VII.v.23, in *The Whole Works*, 7:328.

19. *Letter to Bishop Warner*, in *The Whole Works*, 7:301.

20. *Unum Necessarium* VII.vi.27, in *The Whole Works*, 7:331.

21. *Deus Justificatus*, in *The Whole Works*, 7:500ff.

22. *Unum Necessarium* VI.i.6, in *The Whole Works*, 7:244.

23. Ibid., VI.vi.80, in *The Whole Works*, 7:284.

24. Ibid., VII.iv.17, in *The Whole Works*, 7:318.

25. Ibid., IX.i.4, in *The Whole Works*, 7:391.

26. *Sermon XXVII, Part III*, in *The Whole Works*, 4:664–65. Cf. *Unum Necessarium* I.i.8, in *The Whole Works*, 7:23

27. *Unum Necessarium* VII.i.9, in *The Whole Works*, 7:309.

28. *Deus Justificatus*, in *The Whole Works*, 7:498.

29. *Letter to Bishop Warner*, in *The Whole Works*, 7:551–52.

30. *Sermon III: Fides Formata*, in *The Whole Works*, 8:287.

31. See H. R. McAdoo, *The Eucharistic Theology of Jeremy Taylor Today* (Norwich: The Canterbury Press, 1988), 16f. McAdoo points out that Taylor was undoubtedly influenced by Daillé's *Du Vrai Usage des Pères* (1632) and by his association with Chillingworth and the Great Tew circle.

32. Taylor cites the verse at the beginning of chapter 2. *Holy Living* II.i, in *The Whole Works*, 3:44.

33. *Holy Living* IV.iii, in *The Whole Works*, 3:156.

34. Ibid.

35. Ibid., I.iii, in *The Whole Works*, 3:23–24.

36. Ibid., I.iii, in *The Whole Works*, 3:24.

37. Ibid., I.iii, in *The Whole Works*, 3:24–25.

38. *Sermon I: The Righteousness Evangelical Described*, in *The Whole Works*, 8:251.

39. *Sermon XXV: The Miracles of the Divine Mercy*, in *The Whole Works*, 4:636.

40. See above, 211.

41. *Holy Living* IV.ix, in *The Whole Works*, 3:212.

42. *The Great Exemplar, Discourse IX*; CWS, 314–15.

43. Ibid.

44. Ibid., CWS, 320.

45. *Holy Living* IV.i, in *The Whole Works*, 3:148.

46. *Unum Necessarium* V.v.52, in *The Whole Works*, 7:189.

47. *Sermon XXVII: The Miracles of the Divine Mercy*, in *The Whole Works*, 4:667.

48. *Sermon XIV: Of Growth in Grace*, in *The Whole Works*, 4:499.

49. *The Great Exemplar: An exhortation to the imitation of the life of Christ*, in *The Whole Works*, 2:43.

50. Ibid.

51. *The Great Exemplar: Discourse VII Of Faith*; CWS, 279.

52. See, e.g., *The Great Exemplar: Part I, Section I* (Gabriel found in Mary "a capacity and excellent disposition to receive the greatest honour that was

ever done to the daughters of men."); CWS, 93. Also, ibid. *Section II* (Elizabeth met Mary and John leaped in her womb—"all the faculties of nature were turned into grace"); CWS, 97.

53. See, e.g., *Sermon XIV: Of Growth in Grace*, in *The Whole Works*, 4:500, 502.

54. *Unum Necessarium* I.iii.42, in *The Whole Works*, 7:37.

55. *Holy Living* I.i, in *The Whole Works*, 3:47.

56. *Holy Dying* I.ii, in *The Whole Works*, 3:276.

57. *Holy Living* II.vi, in *The Whole Works*, 3:111.

58. *The Great Exemplar: Discourse VII Of Faith*; CWS, 280.

59. Ibid.

60. Ibid.; CWS, 283. James 2:20–3:6. See also Taylor's argument against severing faith and charity in *Sermon XII: Of Lukewarmness and Zeal*, in *The Whole Works*, 4:150.

61. Ibid.; CWS, 281.

62. Ibid.; CWS, 282.

63. *The Great Exemplar: Discourse IX Of Repentance*; CWS, 304.

64. *Sermon XII: The Mercy of the Divine Judgments*, in *The Whole Works*, 4:475.

65. *Sermon III: Fides Formata; Or, Faith Working by Love*, in *The Whole Works*, 8:285.

66. *The Liberty of Prophesying*, in *The Whole Works*, 5:366.

67. Ibid., 367–68.

68. Ibid., 368.

69. Ibid., 1.5, in *The Whole Works*, 5:370.

70. Ibid., 1.6, in *The Whole Works*, 5:371.

71. Ibid., 1.7, 8, 11, in *The Whole Works*, 5:371–73.

72. Ibid., 22.2, in *The Whole Works*, 5:603–4.

73. *The Great Exemplar: Discourse VII Of Faith*; CWS, 279.

74. Ibid., 284.

75. Ibid., 278.

76. Ibid., 282–83.

77. *Holy Living* IV.i, in *The Whole Works*, 3:146.

78. Ibid., IV.i, in *The Whole Works*, 3:147.

79. Ibid., IV, in *The Whole Works*, 3:145. Cf. Chap. 4, sec. 2: "Of the hope of a Christian."

80. *Sermon VII: Of Godly Fear*, in *The Whole Works*, 4:90.

81. *The Great Exemplar: Discourse VII Of Faith*; CWS, 289–90. Cf. *Holy Living* IV.i, in *The Whole Works*, 3:148, # 7.

82. *Holy Dying* IV.iv, in *The Whole Works*, 3:370. See the whole of sections iii and iv.

83. *Unum Necessarium* I.i.2, in *The Whole Works*, 7:21.

84. Ibid., I.i.6, in *The Whole Works*, 7:22–23.

85. Ibid., I.i.13, in *The Whole Works*, 7:25.

86. Ibid., I.ii.35, in *The Whole Works*, 7:35.

87. Ibid., I.ii.36, in *The Whole Works*, 7:35.

88. Ibid., I.ii.38, in *The Whole Works*, 7:36.

89. Ibid., I.iii.54, in *The Whole Works*, 7:44.

90. Ibid., I.iv.14, in *The Whole Works*, 7:48–49.

91. Ibid., I.iii.40, in *The Whole Works*, 7:37.

92. *The Great Exemplar: Discourse IX Of Repentance*; CWS, 333.

93. Ibid.; CWS, 325.

94. Ibid.; CWS, 329.

95. *Unum Necessarium* II.i.9-10, in *The Whole Works*, 7:65.

96. Ibid., II.ii, in *The Whole Works*, 7:66–74.

97. *Holy Living* IV.ix, in *The Whole Works*, 3:206.

98. See H. R. McAdoo, *The Structure of Caroline Moral Theology* (London: Longmans, Green and Co., 1949).

99. *Dissuasive from Popery* I.ii.13, in *The Whole Works*, 6:272.

100. Ibid., I.ii.6, in *The Whole Works*, 6:244. See also *Unum Necessarium* III, in *The Whole Works*, 7:83ff.

101. Ibid., I.ii.6, in *The Whole Works*, 6:243. See also *Unum Necessarium* IV-V, in *The Whole Works*, 7:124ff.

102. *Sermon VII: The Deceitfulness of the Heart*, in *The Whole Works*, 4:414.

103. See, e.g., *Sermons V-VI: The Invalidity of a Late or Death-Bed Repentance*, in *The Whole Works*, 4:381ff. The theme occurs with considerable frequency in Taylor's writings.

104. *Holy Dying* V.iv.10, in *The Whole Works*, 3:422. For Taylor's liturgical work see H. Boone Porter, *Jeremy Taylor: Liturgist* (London: Alcuin Club/S.P.C.K, 1979).

105. *Holy Dying* II.iii, in *The Whole Works*, 3:302.

106. See above.

107. *Holy Dying* II.iii.2, in *The Whole Works*, 3:303. See also IV.ix-x.

108. *The Great Exemplar: Discourse XI Of Charity*, in *The Whole Works*, 2:463.

109. *The Great Exemplar: Preface*, in *The Whole Works*, 2:29.

110. Ibid., 31.

111. *A Discourse of the Nature and Offices of Friendship*, in *The Whole Works*, 1:72.

112. *Sermon XVII: The Marriage Ring*; CWS, 261.

113. Ibid.; CWS, 265–66.

114. *The Great Exemplar: Discourse VI Of Baptism*, in *The Whole Works*, 2:229.

115. *Dissuasive from Popery* Part II.I.i, in *The Whole Works*, 6:340.

116. *The Great Exemplar: Discourse VIII Of the Religion of Holy Places*, in *The Whole Works*, 2:325.

117. *The Reverence Due to the Altar*; CWS, 222.

118. *The Great Exemplar: Discourse VI Of Baptism*, in *The Whole Works*, 2:233–34.

119. Ibid., 234.

120. Ibid., 234–35.

121. Taylor also considers the question of infant baptism in his treatment of the Anabaptists in *The Liberty of Prophesying* 18, in *The Whole Works*, 5:540–89.

122. *The Great Exemplar: Discourse VI Of Baptism*, in *The Whole Works*, 2:248.

123. *The Great Exemplar: Discourse IX Of Repentance*; CWS, 319.

124. Taylor's *A Discourse of Confirmation* (in *The Whole Works*, 5:609ff.) was written after the Restoration and to address the particular situation in Ireland at that time. Porter points out that Taylor's views in this treatise are inconsistent with his earlier writings. H. Boone Porter, *Jeremy Taylor: Liturgist*, 155: "The principal inconsistency in Taylor's liturgical writings is in regard to Baptism and Confirmation, whether the gift of the Holy Ghost to the new Christian is to be seen primarily in the first rite or the second. Here Taylor certainly changed the thrust of his emphasis from Baptism to Confirmation." Porter points out, however, that the Prayer Book is more than somewhat ambiguous regarding the relationship of baptism and confirmation.

125. *The Great Exemplar: Discourse VI Of Baptism*, in *The Whole Works*, 2:253–54.

126. Ibid., 248.

127. Ibid., 252–53.

128. *The Worthy Communicant*, Introduction, in *The Whole Works*, 8:8.

129. *The Great Exemplar: Discourse XIX Of . . . the Lord's Supper*, in *The Whole Works*, 2:637.

130. Ibid., 640. The last phrase alludes to 2 Pet 1:4. See also 641 and 642. We discover the same allusion in *Holy Living* IV.x, in *The Whole Works*, 3:217.

131. *The Worthy Communicant* I.iv.5, in *The Whole Works*, 8:40.

132. *The Great Exemplar: Discourse XIX Of . . . the Lord's Supper*, in *The Whole Works*, 2:641.

133. *The Worthy Communicant* I.iv.2, in *The Whole Works*, 8:35.

134. *Holy Living* IV.x.2, in *The Whole Works*, 3:214.

135. Ibid., IV.x.8, in *The Whole Works*, 3:217.

136. *The Worthy Communicant* VII.i.8, in *The Whole Works*, 8:224. See Porter's discussion and the parallel he cites from Chrysostom's *On the Priesthood*, in *Jeremy Taylor: Liturgist*, 61ff.

137. *The Great Exemplar: Discourse XIX Of . . . the Lord's Supper*, in *The Whole Works*, 2:643.

138. *A Communion Office*; CWS, 219–20.

139. See, e.g., *The Great Exemplar: Discourse XIX Of . . . the Lord's Supper*, in *The Whole Works*, 2:654. Also *Holy Living* IV.x, in *The Whole Works*, 3:220. Taylor can also commend the practice of communicating infants, though he comes short of recommending it. See, e.g., *Discourse XIX*, in *The Whole Works*, 2:652. Also *The Worthy Communicant* III.ii, in *The Whole Works*, 8:89ff.

140. *The Great Exemplar: Discourse XIX Of . . . the Lord's Supper*, in *The Whole Works*, 2:637–38.

141. See, e.g., *Discourse XIX*, in *The Whole Works*, 2:638. Also *The Wor-

thy Communicant I.i, in *The Whole Works,* 8:12–13. Taylor also underlines the difficulty involved in controversies over the eucharist that springs from the equivocal use of words. See *The Real Presence* I.i.10, in *The Whole Works,* 6:18. For a full discussion of Taylor's doctrine of the eucharist see H. R. McAdoo, *The Eucharistic Theology of Jeremy Taylor Today* (Norwich: The Canterbury Press, 1988).

142. *The Worthy Communicant* I.iii, in *The Whole Works,* 8:32.

143. *The Great Exemplar: Discourse XIX Of . . . the Lord's Supper,* in *The Whole Works,* 2:640.

144. *The Real Presence* I.4, in *The Whole Works,* 6:13.

145. Ibid. I.6, in *The Whole Works,* 6:14.

146. Ibid. I.11, in *The Whole Works,* 6:19.

147. Ibid. VI.1, in *The Whole Works,* 6:59.

148. *Unum Necessarium,* preface, in *The Whole Works,* 7:19.

Epilogue

IT DOES NOT SEEM TO ME possible to draw together what I have tried to say in any single or easy conclusion. The writers I have examined sought to tie their understandings of Christian hope to views of the Christian life that are as complex as they are various. Nevertheless, there are ways of reflecting on what we have learned. Brian Daley, at the end of his study of the hope of the early church, makes a similar point:[1]

> To return to our starting question: can one legitimately speak of "the hope of the early Church"? If one seeks such a hope in the finished form of conciliar definitions, or of an articulated and widely shared theological system, the answer is clearly no; the eschatological consensus we have sketched out here was far less well formed, far less consciously enunciated, in the Patristic centuries, than was the orthodox Christian doctrine of God or of the person of Christ. Nevertheless, the expectations of early Christians for the future formed, on the whole, a remarkably consistent picture, despite serious areas of unresolved disagreement.

I think the same judgment would apply to Anglican views, or, indeed, to Christian views at any time. We can begin by recognizing the unfinished form of the way Christians have articulated their hope. Perhaps the first rule for theologians must be that they are obliged to recognize that they do not understand what they are talking about. And, of course, the attempt to imagine the hope that in large measure lies beyond the world of our experience is rather as though the child in the womb sought to imagine the life into which he was about to be born. It is for this reason that I have chosen a line from T.S. Eliot's *Four Quartets* as a subtitle for these studies:[2]

> So here I am, in the middle way . . .
> Trying to learn to use words, and every attempt
> Is a wholly new start, and a different kind of failure. . . .
> . . . And so each venture
> Is a new beginning, a raid on the inarticulate
> With shabby equipment always deteriorating
> In the general mess of imprecision of feeling,
> Undisciplined squads of emotion.

Attempting to describe the Christian hope, then, is to articulate what is inarticulate.

Nevertheless, Eliot clearly believes that his "raid on the inarticulate" is valuable. The passage I have just cited goes on to speak of "home" as "where one starts from" and of getting older as seeing the world become "stranger, the pattern more complicated/ Of dead and living." The old find "a lifetime burning in every moment":[3]

> Love is most nearly itself
> When here and now cease to matter.
> Old men ought to be explorers
> Here and there does not matter
> We must be still and still moving
> Into another intensity
> For a further union, a deeper communion
> Through the dark cold and the empty desolation,
> The wave cry, the wind cry, the vast waters
> Of the petrel and the porpoise. In the end is my beginning.

I am never sure that I have understood Eliot, but he appears to be looking for some perspective, some hope that will free him from the tyranny of meaningless time, from the Wasteland. Somehow that visionary point is outside "here and now," even outside "here and there." Yet as the poem continues it becomes clear that this timeless glass of vision must be more than the abstraction of "what might have been."[4] It must somehow touch and so transform time. "But to apprehend/ The point of intersection of the timeless/ With time, is an occupation for the saint—/ No occupation either, but something given/ And taken, in a lifetime's death in love,/ Ardour and selflessness and self-surrender."[5]

Eliot equates this point of intersection with the incarnation. Our raids on the inarticulate give us hints and allow us to make guesses, and "The hint half guessed, the gift half understood, is Incarnation."[6] In something of the same way all the writers we have examined make Christ, the incarnate Lord and the dead and risen savior, the point of departure for their guesses about the Christian hope. These raids on the inarticulate first focus on Christ's resurrection as the firstfruits of ours, and so one set of guesses revolves around the physical character of redemption. The New Testament, I think, is united in seeing the story of Christ's death and resurrection as central to its message. Even John, the "spiritual gospel," portrays the raising of Lazarus as the crucial event that leads to Christ's death and, consequently, to his resurrection, which brings life for all. And if the Word was made flesh, it seems reasonable that the flesh should not be excluded from final redemption. Gregory of

Nyssa, of course, expands the physical dimension of the Christian hope. The age to come will represent the transfiguration and divinization of the entire physical creation, drawn as it will be into union with God's eternity. Augustine, too, despite his introspective piety that calls attention to the soul's movement toward God, harps on the physical character of the Christian hope in the last books of the *City of God*. John Donne sees our final issue from death as one effected by Christ and as a final deliverance from the deaths of this life. And Jeremy Taylor understands the eucharist as preparing our bodies for their resurrection. This dimension of the Christian hope may not always be where our writers have placed their emphasis, and it is certainly never the only way they make their guesses. Nevertheless, the hope of the resurrection from the dead remains firmly in place.

The other aspect of the Christian hope, made possible for us by Christ's incarnation, death, and resurrection, is moral and spiritual in character. Moreover, it is easier to see how this dimension has invaded the present world of our experience. Both in the New Testament and in the writers we have examined we find various ways of expressing this aspect of hope. It is justification by faith, the free forgiveness that overcomes our fallen condition and reconciles us to God. But it is also the vision of God, the knowledge and love of God, becoming children or friends of God. All these terms, of course, spring from the way we understand human life and have to do with relationship. The moral and spiritual dimension of redemption, then, has to do with full fellowship with God through Christ. And we can add three further points. This relationship carries with it our fellowship with one another and, in principle, with all people. The corporate dimension of redemption is important for all the writers we have examined. Second, the promise of union with God and with one another is also a demand and a challenge. We are obliged to respond to what we have been given. Finally, the moral and spiritual dimension of the Christian hope waits for its perfection in what lies beyond this world. Needless to say, each of these three points lends itself to a range of understandings. Does God will that all should be brought into union with him? Supposing he does, will that desire be accomplished? How do we receive the promise? What are our capacities to respond to the demand implied by the promise? To what degree can we see this dimension of our hope as something present to us in this life? We can add two further questions that attach to both dimensions of hope. First, how are we to understand the relationship of the physical to the moral and spiritual aspects of redemption? Second, while it seems clear that the Christian destiny is located in a future beyond all futures, it is also the case that we can think of that future as eternal. Thus, we can ask whether it is better to locate that destiny in the future or to think of it as heavenly.

It is clear enough that our writers have given various answers to these questions and equally obvious that their answers are seldom complete or systematic. Let me turn now, however, to several functions those answers have. If, as I have implied, the Christian hope in its differing aspects is a glass of vision we are meant to apply to the world of our experience, what do we see? The first point I should make is that hope exposes what is tragic in human life. Indeed, in some measure the hope is itself articulated by way of opposition to what we should probably all regard as what is hopeless in our world—the inevitability of death and affliction, the ways in which we make war on one another and on ourselves, the sense of meaninglessness and lovelessness that often overwhelms us. Hope and evil in the broadest possible sense are opposed to one another. Consequently, hope actually enables us to see evil for what it is and gives us a sense of the tragic that those who live at random often lack. Augustine and John Donne are the two writers that seem to me to emphasize this aspect of the Christian hope. The gap between our present predicament and our destiny seems more apparent to them than any continuity. And so hope, while it is a present possession, conveys to us very little of what is hoped for. To be sure, it builds a bridge that links the present with the age to come. For Augustine, we can stretch forth toward the cleaving to God's eternity that will be ours. And Donne can regard his repeated penitence as a walking along that bridge because he is convinced that God's mercy is greater than his sin. Nevertheless, the Augustinian perspective seems to me a pessimistic one, however much hope brings an ultimate optimism. There are, of course, anticipations of our destiny; and it is crucial that we have been given the medicine that will ultimately cure us and have been put on the right road. And these anticipations do bring us joy, but they cannot bring us happiness itself, only the happiness that stems from the hope that we shall be happy.

Another function of hope is to expose those aspects of our lives in this world that will last and find their completion and perfection in the age to come. We find this emphasis, I think, in the writings of Gregory of Nyssa and Jeremy Taylor. Both of them have a clear eye for the beauty and order of the physical creation and take delight in it. Both believe that there is a sense in which we can experience fellowship with God and with one another in this life. For Gregory there is the real possibility of a movement into the mystery of God here and now, however much our enjoyment of God will be after a different manner when we attain our destiny. Moreover, he seems to me willing to say that we do experience ways in which we are bound together with one another in the fellowship

of the church. Jeremy Taylor, of course, has a lively sense of God's presence in his life and an equally clear understanding of the corporate character of the Christian life. Theirs is a more optimistic view. Hope tends
to open their eyes to what is good about our world rather than what is
evil in it. Two reasons for this emphasis seem possible to me. First, both
Gregory and Taylor tend to understand the relationship between our
present life and our destiny as one of earth to heaven. To be sure, they
both think in terms of an age to come. But since that age is eternal, it has
the possibility of some presence to us in the here and now. The temporal framework that dominates the thought of Augustine and Donne
tends, I think, to treat our present existence between what has already
been accomplished in Christ and the consummation of that work after
the end of this world. Thus, it is more difficult for them to insist on the
intersection and tension between our present lives and our destiny.
Thinking in terms of heaven and earth allows heaven to be in some sense
a present reality. The second reason for the emphasis I find in Gregory
and Taylor revolves around their understanding of redemption. Both of
them, of course, can think of Christ as reversing Adam's fall; and from
this perspective the fall is the problem and Christ the solution. But both
of them see Christ's overcoming of the fall not so much as an end in itself
as the means whereby God brings creation to completion and perfection. For Gregory, Christ ushers in the new creation. For Jeremy Taylor,
Christ supplies the supernatural graces lost by Adam, graces that will
now effect God's original purpose for Adam.

I am thinking here of William Temple's distinction between a theology of redemption that puts sin and the cross in central place and a
theology of the incarnation that sees Christ as the consummator of creation. The first of these theologies is, of course, Augustinian in character. Original sin is the predicament from which we must be redeemed,
and an Anselmian doctrine of the atonement supplies the solution. It is
Christ's death on the cross that provides the possibility of forgiveness for
our sins, original and actual. And justification by faith, sometimes
understood in the context of predestination and election, actualizes for
believers the possibility established by Christ. Temple points out that
this theology, since it places evil at center stage, may be more relevant to
a time in human history when evil seems to dominate. The other theology is more optimistic. If salvation means the completion of creation,
then evil can easily be regarded as no more than a temporary interruption of the process, shavings cast off from the carpenter's bench. Indeed,
we could even argue that this theology informs writers like Charles Gore
and the other writers of *Lux Mundi* because it appears to them to accord
with nineteenth-century thought forms as they can be found in ideas of

evolution and history. And, if this is so, they have found this theology in the ancient church and, particularly, in Irenaeus's writings. For Irenaeus, the fall is far from a disaster, and it need not even be thought an interruption of the process by which God completes creation. When Adam and Eve ate of the tree, they grew into the knowledge of good and evil. And even though that had unfortunate consequences in the short run, in the long run the fall becomes an inevitable if not a necessary part of humanity's growth to perfection. Perhaps we could conclude that a theology of redemption, like that found in Augustine and Donne, runs the risk of a pessimism that would deprive hope of its meaning, whereas a theology of the incarnation runs the opposite risk of an optimism that is too easy. It may prove impossible to find a true balance.

One final function of hope has to do with the moral life. That is, hope as a promise carries with it a demand. How are we to respond to hope. Here it seems to me that Gregory and Augustine have not very much to say. Both Donne and Taylor, however, are preoccupied with the moral life. Donne's attention is very much fixed on sanctification; and, of course, Taylor's emphasis is on holy living. Both are in a real sense moral theologians. Both are equally preoccupied with repentance, even though their views are by no means identical. If what I am suggesting is true, then I must ask myself the question why the figures line up in a different way from this point of view. I suggest that here we do find a real difference between ancient and modern Christianity. The church fathers, of course, can understand Christianity as a way of life. And they are concerned with teaching Christians how to live their lives. But I think that their emphasis is very much on Christianity as a way of salvation. Indeed, I am tempted to say that for those who wrote before Augustine and those in the East who wrote apart from him, the central human problem is death rather than sin. In the West, however, perhaps thanks largely to the impact of Augustine, sin becomes the dominant problem. To the degree this is so, it is possible to say that the moral life tends to gain central attention. The theological agenda in the early period revolved around issues related to finding a Christian doctrine of God and, consequently, a right understanding of Christ. This agenda seems to me designed to sharpen the church's understanding of the Christian story. With Augustine, however, the agenda shifts. The questions that engage the theologian are more anthropological in their orientation. What is the *effect* of the Christian story? How are we to understand God's grace and human capacities? Who will be saved? These are large generalizations, and I admit I may be pressing them too far. But some of these considerations help explain why I think John Donne and Jeremy

Taylor are more preoccupied with the moral life than either of the two ancient figures.

The first two functions of hope, however, seem to me the more important ones; and it is they that shape an understanding of the Christian life in this world. And while it is almost certainly an oversimplification, I suggest that there are two rather different paradigms that emerge. The first calls attention primarily to the discontinuities between our present life and our destiny and so thinks of the Christian life as an *anticipation* of the life to come. Augustine and Donne belong in this paradigm, and there is a poem by George Herbert that helps to bring it to focus. In *The Flower* Herbert begins on an optimistic note—"How fresh, O Lord, how sweet and clean/ Are thy returns!" He is describing spring and its flowers, but what really concerns him is the springtime of the soul. "Grief melts away/ Like snow in May. . . . " The flowers in spring come as a surprise, since each year after blossoming they depart "To see their mother-root . . . Where they together/ All the hard weather,/ Dead to the world, keep house unknown." Similarly, "Who would have thought my shrivel'd heart/ Could have recovered greennesse?" In the third stanza the mood of the poem begins to change:

> These are thy wonders, Lord of power,
> Killing and quickning, bringing down to hell
>   And up to heaven in an houre;
> Making a chiming of a passing-bell.
>   We say amisse,
>   This or that is:
> Thy word is all, if we could spell.

God's power brings new life, but it also kills. Moreover, we are poor at discerning the deaths and resurrections in our lives. We sometimes think that the church bell tolling for someone's death is instead ringing to summon us to the life and fellowship of the church. Herbert's flowerlike spiritual resurrection, then, is as short-lived as the flowers themselves.

Stanzas 4 through 6 are partly the poet's lament that each time he grows and blossoms God's "anger comes, and I decline." This happens despite his tears of repentance. "Nor doth my flower/ Want a spring-showre,/ My sinnes and I joining together." And it is in fact his sin, his pride, that explains God's anger, which comes upon him "while I grow in a straight line,/ Still upwards bent, as if heav'n were mine own." Nonetheless, these stanzas are also a prayer that the poet may bloom in God's garden. "O that I once past changing were,/ Fast in thy Paradise, where no flower can wither!" And stanza 6 returns to the optimism of the poem's beginning:

And now in age I bud again,
After so many deaths I live and write;
I once more smell the dew and rain,
And relish versing: O my onely light,
It cannot be
That I am he
On whom thy tempests fell all night.

Herbert's poem as a whole may be alluding to two passages from scripture that stand in tension with one another. "My beloved speaks and says to me: 'Arise, my love, my fair one, and come away; for now the winter is past, the rain is over and gone. The flowers appear on the earth, the time of singing has come, and the voice of the turtledove is heard in our land'" (Song of Songs 2:10-12). But, "All people are grass, their constancy is like the flower of the field. The grass withers, the flower fades, when the breath of the Lord blows upon it; surely the people are grass. The grass withers, the flower fades; but the word of our God will stand forever" (Isaiah 40:6-8).

There can be no resolution of this tension during our life in this world. All our resurrections and springtime blossomings are as short-lived as the flowers themselves. But these new births point beyond themselves to what lies beyond the grave:

These are thy wonders, Lord of love,
To make us see we are but flowers that glide:
Which when we once can finde and prove,
Thou hast a garden for us, where to bide.
Who would be more,
Swelling through store,
Forfeit their Paradise by their pride.

This seventh and final stanza firmly locates hope beyond the confines of this life. We have no possibility here and now of blossoming forever in God's garden. Nevertheless, our short and repeated bursts of new life are anticipations and hints of the destiny that awaits us.

The second paradigm of the Christian life as it is shaped by hope seems to me to stress the continuities between this life and the next, or between earth and heaven. Our lives are in a real sense capable of *participating* in our destiny. Another poet will supply me with an illustration. Thomas Traherne was a younger contemporary of Jeremy Taylor. In one way he belongs in the same visionary company as Blake and, later, Wordsworth. But like Taylor his thought emphasizes God's presence and goodness, and he supposes that a holy life is a heavenly one. Traherne is usually wholly optimistic. But there is one poem in which he fully recognizes the evils of this world: *Mankind is sick*. The first stanza speaks of "sins and miseries . . . a long corrupted train/ Of poison, drawn from Adam's vein. . . ." It concludes by saying "The world's one Bedlam, or a greater cave/ Of madmen, that do always rave." As the poem continues, however, it becomes apparent that Traherne and "the wise and good" do not belong to this fallen world. He explains what he means in his *Centuries of Meditation*:[7]

> Truly there are two worlds. One was made by God, the other by men. That made by God was great and beautiful. Before the Fall, it was Adam's joy, and the temple of His glory. That made by men is a Babel of confusions: invented riches, pomps, and vanities, brought in by sin. Give all (saith Thomas à Kempis) for all. Leave the one that you may enjoy the other.

Traherne wants to underline the fact that we are free agents and can choose not to belong to the world of Bedlam and Babel. To be sure, this is possible only for those who choose to live a holy life. God's world is his gift to us, but it is also "the theatre of virtues." He speaks of fidelity, wisdom, courage, prudence, temperance, and "the fruits of faith and repentance." If we can "delight in God's laws," we can be "in Heaven everywhere."[8]

Traherne puts the idea into his poem *Mankind is sick*. The wise and good need not belong to this sick world not only because they can choose to live lives that separate them from it but also because Christ has given them that possibility. Stanza 11 reads,

> O holy Jesus who didst for us die,
>   And on the altar bleeding lie,
> Bearing all torment, pain, reproach and shame,
>   That we by virtue of the same,
>   Though enemies to God, might be
>   Redeem'd, and set at liberty.
>   Thou didst us forgive,
> So meekly let us love to others show,
>   And live in Heaven on earth below!

Living in heaven on earth, then, is tied to a life of love. And Traherne's major point in the poem is the role those who dwell in heaven have toward the blind madmen of the fallen world. "The wise and good like kind physicians are,/ That strive to heal them by their care." Traherne and his kind actually participate in heaven, and the holy life is both what enables them to do so and is also the fruit of that participation. This paradigm is one that fits Gregory of Nyssa and Jeremy Taylor.

We come full circle. Raiding the inarticulate means pressing beyond what is here and now, leaving the world of our experience in order to discover hope. But the discovery, which for the Christian is made possible by Christ, is one that obliges us to return to that world. The return reshapes our world in differing ways. T.S. Eliot recognizes this. The rose-garden of *Burnt Norton* must be more than what might have been, an abstraction, a "perpetual possibility . . . in a world of speculation." To make it that we must cast a cold eye on the wasteland of this world; we must find the love that "is most nearly itself/ When here and now cease to matter." But finally we must return. *Little Gidding* concludes the *Four Quartets*. It is a place "Where prayer has been valid." It is, of course, the place where Nicholas Ferrar, George Herbert's friend, established his community in the early seventeenth century. Here, says Eliot, eternity and time meet:

> Here, the intersection of the timeless moment
> Is England and nowhere. Never and always.

Eliot returns to this idea in the concluding section of Little Gidding:

> . . . A people without history
> Is not redeemed from time, for history is a pattern
> Of timeless moments. So, while the light fails
> On a winter's afternoon, in a secluded chapel
> History is now and England.
>
> With the drawing of this Love and the voice of this Calling
>
> We shall not cease from exploration
> And the end of all our exploring
> Will be to arrive where we started
> And know the place for the first time. . . .
> Quick now, here, now, always –
> A condition of complete simplicity
> (Costing not less than everything)
> And all shall be well and
> All manner of thing shall be well
> When the tongues of flame are in-folded
> Into the crowned knot of fire
> And the fire and the rose are one.

Notes

1. Brian E. Daley, *The Hope of the Early Church: A Handbook of Patristic Eschatology* (Cambridge: Cambridge University Press, 1991), 223.

2. *Four Quartets: East Coker V.*

3. Ibid.

4. *Four Quartets: Burnt Norton I.*

5. *Four Quartets: The Dry Salvages V.*

6. Ibid.

7. *Centuries of Meditation: The First Century* 7, in *Thomas Traherne: Selected Poems and Prose*, ed. Alan Bradford (London: Penguin Books, 1991), 189.

8. Ibid., 38-39, in *Thomas Traherne*, 285.

Texts and Translations

Abbreviations

ACW	Ancient Christian Writers
CWS	Classics of Western Spirituality
LCC	Loeb Classical Library
LCL	Library of Christian Classics
NPNF	Nicene and Post-Nicene Fathers
SC	Sources chrétiennes

New Testament

I have used the United Bible Societies Greek text and the New Revised Standard Version of the Bible.

Gregory of Nyssa

Texts of the complete works are available only in Migne, *Patrologia Graeca*, vols. 44–46. W. Jaeger's edition, *Gregorii Nysseni Opera*, is essential but does not yet include the text of *De hominis opificio* or of *De anima et resurrectione*.

I have used the following English translations:

On Virginity, On the Making of Man, and *On the Soul and the Resurrection*. NPNF 2/5.

Gregory of Nyssa: The Life of Moses. Trans. A. J. Malherbe and E. Ferguson. CWS. New York: Paulist Press, 1978.

Catechetical Oration (Address on Religious Instruction). In *Christology of the Later Fathers*. Ed. E. R. Hardy. LCC 3. Philadelphia: Westminster, 1954.

The Easter Sermons of Gregory of Nyssa: Translation and Commentary. Ed. A. Spira and C. Klock. Cambridge, MA: Philadelphia Patristic Foundation, 1981.

Maximus the Confessor: Selected Writings. Trans. G. C. Berthold. CWS. New York, Mahwah, NJ, and Toronto: Paulist Press, 1985.

A. Louth. *Maximus the Confessor*. The Early Church Fathers. Ed. C. Harrison. London & New York: Routledge, 1996.

Augustine

Texts may be found in CSEL (Corpus Scriptorum Ecclesiasticorum Latinorum) and for *Confessions* and *City of God* in the Loeb Classical Library.
I have used the following English translations:

Confessions. Trans. R. S. Pine-Coffin. Harmondsworth: Penguin Books, 1961.
Confessions. Trans. H. Chadwick. Oxford: Oxford University Press, 1991.
City of God. Trans. H. Bettenson. Harmondsworth: Penguin Books, 1984.
Saint Augustine: The Trinity. Trans. E. Hill. Brooklyn, NY: New City Press, 1991.
On Christian Doctrine. Trans. D. W. Robertson, Jr. The Library of Liberal Arts. Upper Saddle River, NJ: Prentice Hall, 1958.
Soliloquies, Of True Religion, On Free Will, in *Augustine: Earlier Writings*. Ed. J. H. S. Burleigh. LCC 6. Philadelphia: Westminster, 1953.

John Donne

The Sermons of John Donne. 10 vols. Ed. G. R. Potter and E. M. Simpson. Berkeley and Los Angeles: University of California Press, 1953–62.
John Donne: The Complete English Poems. Ed. A. J. Smith. Harmondsworth: Penguin Books, 1971, 1973.
John Donne: Devotions upon Emergent Occasions, Together with Death's Duel. Ann Arbor Paperbacks. Ann Arbor: University of Michigan Press, 1959. [The book includes, with some omissions, Walton's *Life* of Donne.]
John Donne: Selections from Divine Poems, Sermons, Devotions, and Prayers. Ed. J. Booty. CWS. New York and Mahwah, NJ: Paulist Press, 1990.

Jeremy Taylor

The Whole Works of the Rt. Revd. Jeremy Taylor. 10 vols. Ed. Reginald Heber. Revised and corrected by C. P. Eden. London, 1847–52.
Jeremy Taylor: Selected Works. Ed. T. K. Carroll. CWS. New York and Mahwah, NJ: Paulist Press, 1990.

Suggestions for Further Reading

The New Testament

It would be relatively easy to suggest further readings by compiling a bibliography of books dealing with the New Testament, but I am doubtful doing so would prove in any way helpful. The secondary literature is impossibly vast and correspondingly unmanageable. There are, however, two excellent books that represent good places to start for those who are not familiar with New Testament scholarship but who wish to enter more deeply into the study of the New Testament:

Raymond E. Brown. *An Introduction to the New Testament*. New York: Doubleday, 1997.
Luke Timothy Johnson, *The Writings of the New Testament: An Interpretation*. Philadelphia: Fortress Press, 1986.

In broad terms both Johnson and Brown agree in understanding their task. They seek to give an account of the New Testament "not written for fellow scholars" (Brown, p. vii) but attentive to scholarly work, something "neither repellingly technical nor appallingly trivial" (Johnson, p. ix). Both deny that their approach is "idiosyncratic"—Brown because his view is "centrist" (p. xi), Johnson although he is "independent" (p. ix). While taking the historical questions and methods of New Testament scholarship seriously, both regard their task as one demanding full concentration on the writings of the New Testament canon, which they treat not merely as historical evidence for the origin and development of early Christianity. And both see this orientation as one designed to interpret the New Testament in its religious significance.

Johnson's book is somewhat more self-conscious than Brown's with respect to these assumptions. He argues that his aim is to interpret in order to introduce, recognizing that not "every introduction [is] an interpretation" (p. ix). He wishes to employ a historical method but seeks to place its results in "an experience-interpretation model" rather than in a historical model. It will probably be obvious to the attentive reader that I find Johnson's approach congenial. My own work has been informed by seeing the New Testament as supplying points of departure for the religious and theological development of the ancient church, a perspective that leaves room for historical considerations and conclusions but that focuses attention on theology and on the continuities between the New Testament writings and the patristic development. Brown would not, I think, fundamentally disagree. Both Johnson and Brown supply the reader with extensive bibliographies and a basis for further study.

Gregory of Nyssa

One obvious approach to further study of Gregory of Nyssa's thought is to consult the volume in the Routledge series edited by Carol Harrison and entitled The Early Church Fathers:

Anthony Meredith. *Gregory of Nyssa*. London & New York: Routledge, 1999.

Meredith has translated excerpts from Gregory's writings under three headings—doctrinal issues, philosophy, and spirituality. His general introduction and his epilogue, as well as the specific introductions to the works translated, orient the reader to scholarly work devoted to Gregory of Nyssa. (See his bibliography on pp. 162–64.) Let me list several books I have found particularly helpful, employing Meredith's three categories:

General works on the doctrinal and ecclesiastical controversies:
A. Grillmeier. *Christ in Christian Tradition*. New York: Sheed & Ward, 1965.
R. P. C. Hanson, *The Search for the Christian Doctrine of God: The Arian Controversy 318–381*. Edinburgh: T. & T. Clark, 1988.
J. N. D. Kelly. *Early Christian Doctrines*. New York: Harper & Row, 1958.
P. J. Fedwick. *The Church and the Charisma of Leadership in Basil of Caesarea*. Studies and Texts 45. Toronto: Pontifical Institute of Medieval Studies, 1979.
P. Rousseau. *Basil of Caesarea*. Berkeley, Los Angeles, and London: University of California Press, 1994.

Philosophy:
D. L. Balás. *Metousia Theou: Man's Participation in God's Perfections according to St. Gregory of Nyssa*. Rome: Studia Anselmiana, 1966.
R. M. Hübner. *Die Einheit des Leibes Christi bei Gregor von Nyssa: Untersuchungen zum Ursprung der "physischen" Erlösungslehre*. Leiden: Brill, 1974.
J. Pelikan. *Christianity and Classical Culture: The Metamorphosis of Natural Theology in the Christian Encounter with Hellenism*. New Haven & London: Yale University Press, 1993.
J. Zachhuber. *Human Nature in Gregory of Nyssa: Philosophical Background and Theological Significance*. Leiden: Brill, 2000.

Spirituality:
H. U. von Balthasar. *Présence et pensée: Essai sur la philosophie religieuse de Grégoire de Nysse*. Paris: G. Beauchesne, 1942. English translation by M. Sebanc. *Presence and Thought: An Essay on the Religious Philosophy of Gregory of Nyssa*. San Francisco: Ignatius Press, 1995.

J. Daniélou. *Platonisme et théologie mystique: Essai sur la doctrine spirituelle de saint Grégoire de Nysse*. Paris: Aubier, 1944.

J. Gaïth. *La conception de la liberté chez Grégoire de Nysse*. Paris: J. Vrin, 1953.

W. Jaeger. *Two Rediscovered Works of Ancient Christian Literature*. Leiden: Brill, 1954.

R. Leys. *L'image de Dieu chez Grégoire de Nysse: Esquisse d'une doctrine*. Brussels: Edition universelle, 1951.

V. Lossky. *The Mystical Theology of the Eastern Church*. Reprint, Crestwood, NY: St. Vladimir's Seminary Press, 1974.

W. Völker. *Gregor von Nyssa als Mystiker*. Wiesbaden: F. Steiner, 1955.

Lacking in the secondary literature is any single comprehensive study of Gregory's thought. Perhaps the obvious inconsistencies and contradictions in his writings have discouraged any such attempt. Let me add one final note. Brian E. Daley in *The Hope of the Early Church: A Handbook of Patristic Eschatology* (Cambridge: Cambridge University Press, 1991) has given us excellent accounts of the eschatological views of Gregory of Nyssa (pp. 85–89) and of Augustine (pp. 131–50). My aim has differed from his in that my concern has been not so much with these views as such but with the ways in which they intersect with understandings of the Christian life.

Augustine

It seems to me impossible to study Augustine's thought, particularly as it develops, without paying attention to his life. There are now two excellent biographies:

Peter Brown. *Augustine of Hippo: A Biography*. Berkeley and Los Angeles: University of California Press, 1999.

Garry Wills. *Saint Augustine*. Penguin Lives. Harmondsworth: Viking Penguin, 1999.

Brown's biography is a reprint without change of the 1967 book. But it includes an epilogue in two parts—new evidence and new directions. Here Brown not only supplies an extremely lucid and full account of new work accomplished in the last thirty or thirty-five years, but also reflects on ways in which his own attitudes and interpretations have shifted during that time. Wills's book, of course, is a briefer and more popular treatment. But it seems to me not only firmly based in a detailed study of the evidence but also persuasively sane in its judgments. Another short but extremely helpful book is Henry Chadwick's introduction to Augustine's theology in the "Past Masters" series. (H. Chadwick, *Augustine* [Oxford and New York: Oxford University Press, 1986]).

Needless to say, the secondary literature dealing with Augustine is almost as overwhelming as that concerned with the New Testament. There now exists, however, *Augustine through the Ages: An Encyclopedia*, ed. A. D. Fitzgerald (Grand Rapids and Cambridge: Eerdmans, 1999). This encyclopedia will not solve all problems, but in addition to its entries it includes a general bibliography and lists of Augustine's writings that supply information concerning editions, translations, and dates.

The following books have been especially helpful to me in my own attempts to understand Augustine's thought:

H. Arendt. *The Life of the Mind: Thinking and Willing.* 2 vols. New York: Harcourt Brace Jovanovich, 1978.

————. *Love and Saint Augustine.* Chicago and London: University of Chicago Press, 1996. J. V. Scott and J. C. Stark have edited Arendt's 1929 Heidelberg dissertation on the basis of annotations and revisions she made in the late 1950s and early 1960s.

J. Burnaby. *Amor Dei: A Study in the Religious Thought of St. Augustine.* London: Hodder and Stoughton, 1938, 1947.

J. P. Burns. *The Development of Augustine's Doctrine of Operative Grace.* Paris: Etudes Augustiniennes, 1980.

P. Courcelle. *Recherches sur les Confessions de saint Augustin.* Paris: de Boccard, 1950, 1968.

G. R. Evans. *Augustine on Evil.* Cambridge: Cambridge University Press, 1982.

W. H. C. Frend. *The Donatist Church.* 2d edition. Oxford: Clarendon Press, 1985.

R. A. Markus. *Saeculum: History and Society in the Theology of St. Augustine.* Cambridge: Cambridge University Press, 1970, 1989.

E. TeSelle. *Augustine the Theologian.* London: Burns and Oates, 1970.

F. Van der Meer. *Augustine the Bishop.* London: Sheed & Ward, 1961.

John Donne

John Booty's volume in the Classics of Western Spirituality series provides an excellent introduction to Donne's writings and particularly to his religious poetry and prose. It also includes a helpfully organized bibliography. Much of the secondary literature on Donne focuses on his metaphysical poetry, a strong interest of T.S. Eliot and the "new critics," such as Cleanth Brooks. Frank Kermode has edited a collection of essays that includes Eliot's "The Metaphysical Poets" (1921) and Brooks's discussion of "The Canonization," "The Language of Paradox" (first published in 1942 and included in *The Well Wrought Urn* in 1947). Kermode also includes essays by Dr. Johnson and by Coleridge. (F. Kermode, *Discussions of John Donne* [Boston: D. C. Heath and Co., 1962]). For Donne's poetry I have also found helpful Louis L. Martz, *The Poetry of Meditation: A Study in English Religious Literature of the 17th Century*, Yale Studies in English 125 (New Haven: Yale University Press, 1954). Stanley Fish's discussion of Donne's prose rhetoric and his analysis of "Death's Duel" provide useful insights (*Self-Consuming Artifacts: The Experience of 17th Century Literature* [Berkeley, Los Angeles, and London: University of California Press, 1972]).

Jeremy Taylor

T. K. Carroll's volume on Jeremy Taylor in the Classics of Western Spirituality is a good place to begin the study of Taylor. One disadvantage of the selections that are made stems from the character of Taylor's writings. Save for the sermons, they are for the most part quite lengthy. Consequently, Carroll is obliged to give us selections from the longer works, and we sometimes miss the character and structure of those works themselves. Another obstacle has to do with contrary assessments of Taylor's views and of his theology. For example, Bishop Allison sees Taylor as one of the figures whose view "rent the fabric of soteriology and split the elements of religion so radically that doctrine became almost irrelevant and ethics became so harsh as to be cruel" (C. F. Allison, *The Rise of Moralism* [Wilton, CT: Morehouse Barlow, 1966], 192). Needless to say, I side with those who take a more positive view. Nevertheless, Allison is clearly correct to see that many Anglicans in the seventeenth century moved away from any unqualified commitment to the central doctrines of the Reformation. The historical background seems to me important, and I recommend John Spurr's *The Restoration Church of England: 1646-1689* (New Haven & London: Yale University Press, 1991). For Taylor's theology I am deeply indebted to the work of Bishop (H. R.) McAdoo. His general work, *The Spirit of Anglicanism* (London: Adam and Charles Black, 1965), supplies an excellent account of the seventeenth-century development. *The Structure of Caroline Moral Theology* (London: Longmans, Green, and Co., 1949) is an impressive study of moral theology during Taylor's time as well as a succinct yet searching account of Taylor's own views. Finally, *The Eucharistic Theology of Jeremy Taylor Today* (Norwich: Canterbury Press, 1988) takes us beyond the issue primarily addressed to a broader understanding of Taylor's theology as a whole. Let me single out one other book I have found helpful: H. B. Porter, *Jeremy Taylor: Liturgist* (London: Alcuin Club/S.P.C.K., 1979). Porter studies the liturgy Taylor constructed during the interregnum from a theological as well as a narrowly liturgical perspective.

Index

Adeodatus (son of Augustine), 116
Ahlstrom, Sydney, 5
Alaric the Visigoth, 117
Alypius (friend of Augustine), 116
Ambrose, 115, 117
Andrewes, Launcelot, 142, 201
Anselm, 265
Antony (desert hermit), 115
Arianism, 67, 98
Aristotle, 89, 99
Arius, 66
Arminianism, Arminians, 5, 168, 201
Articles of Religion, 162, 166, 168, 201–3, 211, 218
Athanasius, 115
Augustine, 7–8, 32, 112–60, 161–62, 164, 169, 170, 171, 173, 213, 214, 216, 217, 220, 221, 222, 224, 229, 230, 238, 255, 264, 265, 266
  on Christ's death and resurrection, 141–47
  and the contemplative ideal, 119
  conversion of, 113–16
  on creation, 133–35, 137
  on free will, 121, 122, 123
  on the gift of healing, 140–41
  on God's grace, 125–27
  heaven of heavens in, 137, 138, 157
  on hope, 156–57
  introspective piety of, 156–57
  on knowledge, 149–52
  on love of God and neighbor, 153–55

  on memory, 112, 149–52
  on original sin, 120, 123–25, 132
  Ostia vision of, 127
  on the present/future question, 131–32
  on the problem of evil, 121, 122, 123, 125,
  on the soul, 140
  "stretching forth" in, 138, 139–48, 149–55
  theōsis in, 142–43
  time and eternity in, 133–39
  on the Trinity, 139–40
  on the victory over Satan, 143–44
  on the vision of God, 127–33

Basil (brother of Gregory of Nyssa), 65, 66, 67, 68, 69, 80
Bellarmine, Cardinal Robert, 166
Bridges, Joanna (wife of Jeremy Taylor), 211

Calvin, John, 32, 162
catacombs
  themes of frescoes in, 27–28
Chillingworth, William, 209
Christianity
  "here and now," 3–7, 93, 107, 155
  "there and then," 8–9, 93, 107, 120, 155
  and views of Jesus, 11–12
Cicero, 114

279